Administering and Securing the Apache Server

Administering and Securing the Apache Server

Ashok Appu

WITH

NIIT

Premier

Press

Acknowledgements

A book is the result of the combined efforts of many. This book is no exception. First of all, I want to thank my mom, dad, and brother, who stood by me regardless of the hectic schedules and odd working hours.

I want to thank Anita Sastry, my project manager, for all the timely advice to ensure smooth execution of the project and for assigning this book to me in the first place! I would also like to thank Shadab Siddiqui, Rashi Gupta, Ashish Wilfred, Nitin Pandey, Meeta Gupta, and Sripriya for providing timely support when I needed it the most.

A big thanks to the editor, Melba Hopper, whose reviews made the book more interesting and pleasurable to read. I would also like to thank Stacy Hiquet, Vineet Whig, and Shantanu Phadnis, without whom I would not have received the opportunity to write this book.

Thanks to Sandip Bhattacharya and Raj Mathur for technical advice and valuable reviews. I really appreciate your patience and effort to make the book better and attain its present form.

Last but not the least, I also want to take the opportunity to thank my friends who bucked me up all through this project. I want to thank Subramani A, Amit Soni, and Sonal Chawla for always being at my side, providing me with all the encouragement and support I needed.

About the Author

Ashok Appu is a holder of an advanced degree in computer applications and has received formal training on all RHCE 7.0 modules (RH033, RH133, and RH253). Ashok works at NIIT. He began his tenure with NIIT by writing instructor led training manuals and then went on to write textbooks.

Ashok is the author of *Making Use of PHP* and has coauthored *Microsoft Commerce Server 2000 Configuration and Administration* and contributed to *ASP.NET Weekend Crash Course*. In addition, he actively provides SME (Subject Matter Expert) support for technologies such as the Linux operating system, TCP/IP, PHP, and network and OS security.

When not writing, Ashok is an active member of the India Linux Users Group Delhi (ILUGD). His hobbies include working out, reading about health and nutrition, playing the guitar, white water rafting, and listening to heavy metal.

About NIIT

NIIT is a Global IT Solutions Corporation with a presence in 38 countries. With its unique business model and technology creation capabilities, NIIT delivers Software and Learning Solutions to more than 1000 clients across the world.

The success of NIIT's training solutions lies in its unique approach to education. NIIT's Knowledge Solutions Business conceives researches and develops all the course material. A rigorous instructional design methodology is followed to create engaging and compelling course content. NIIT has one of the largest learning material development facilities in the world with more than 5000 person years of experience.

NIIT trains over 200,000 executives and learners each year, in Information Technology areas, using Stand-up Training, video-aided instruction, computer-based training (CBT) and Internet-based training (IBT). NIIT has featured in the Guinness Book of World Records for the largest number of learners trained in one year!

NIIT has developed over 10,000 hours of instructor-led training (ILT) and over 3000 hours of Internet-based training and computer-based training. IDC ranked NIIT among the Top 15 IT Training providers globally for the year 2000. Through the innovative use of training methods and its commitment to research and development, NIIT has been in the forefront of computer education and training for the past 20 years.

Quality has been the prime focus at NIIT. Most of the processes are ISO-9001 certified. It was the 12th company in the world to be assessed at Level 5 of SEI-CMM. NIIT's Content (Learning Material) Development facility is the first in the world to be assessed at this highest maturity level. NIIT has strategic partnerships with companies such as Computer Associates, IBM, Microsoft, Oracle, and Sun Microsystems.

Contents at a Glance

Contents

Chapter 8   Working With Apache Modules. 205

Introduction

Goal of the Book

This book provides a comprehensive, hands-on approach to administering and securing the Apache Web server. It's written for people who are already familiar with the Linux operating system but who want to learn more about the Apache Web server, which is, by and far, the most popular Web server used on the Linux platform.

The book begins with basic concepts pertinent to the Apache Web server and then moves on to more advanced topics. As a result, both inexperienced and experienced administrators will benefit from reading and working through this book. I designed the book so that concepts related to administering and securing the Apache Web server are discussed simultaneously. The book contains graphics that complement and realistically illustrate the concepts being discussed.

You will find multiple-choice questions that you can use to check your understanding of the concepts discussed in the chapter. The answers are provided, of course!

Part I, "Introducing the Apache Web Server," provides an overview of the Apache Web server. This part begins with basic concepts related to Web servers in general and explains how information is exchanged on the Web. Later in this part you'll learn how to customize your installation of the Apache Web server. Finally, you find a detailed explanation of the Apache configuration file.

Part II, "Implementing Basic Features of Apache," explains the Apache Web server's most common features. In this part, you'll learn about access control, virtual hosts, and CGI scripts.

Part III, "Advanced Configuration," deals with, as the title indicates, advanced configuration features of Apache. This part covers important topics such as security and performance tuning, which might be an eye opener for Apache administrators. In addition, you'll find discussions on concepts related to modules, server side includes, URL mapping, and content negotiation.

Part IV includes three appendixes. Appendix A contains the most common, best practices for administering and securing the Apache Web server. Appendix B includes questions frequently asked about Apache. Appendix C discusses the new features of Apache 2.0, which was released on August 9th, 2002.

Conventions Used in This Book

I have tried to organize this book so that you can easily grasp its concepts. In addition, in a number of places, I highlighted some useful information by using these eye-catching icons:

- ◆ **Tips.** Provide special advice or helpful shortcuts.
- ◆ **Notes.** Give additional information that is likely to be of interest but that is not essential to performing the task at hand.
- ◆ **Cautions.** Warn users of possible disastrous results if they perform a task incorrectly.

PART I

Introducing the Apache Web Server

Chapter 1

Introduction to Web Servers

In the fast-paced world of e-commerce, every minute witnesses new technologies that help the world knit closer by way of the Internet. This chapter discusses an inseparable part of the Internet—Web servers. Simply put, a Web server is a dedicated repository for Web site files and is used to host Web sites on the Internet.

In more technical terms, a Web server accepts, processes, and responds to HyperText Transfer Protocol (HTTP) requests. These requests are sent by Web browsers, which are used by client computers to communicate, send, and receive information on the Internet. The relationship between a Web server and a Web client is called a *client/server relationship*.

In this chapter, I discuss the basics of networking software. Then I discuss the basic concept of Web servers and how they work. Finally, I touch upon the concepts of HTTP /1.1.

Basic Concepts of Networking Software

Before I begin discussing the more technical aspects of a Web server and how it operates, I will first discuss the underlying networking terms that you will come across time and again while reading this book. The following are the important networking terms that you should be familiar with while working with Web servers:

- ◆ IP addresses
- ◆ Name resolution
- ◆ Ports
- ◆ Sockets
- ◆ Protocol

IP Addresses

When working with Web servers and managing networks, the most important thing that system administrators manage and use are Internet Protocol (IP) addresses. An *IP address* is a unique numeric identifier that is set for each computer on the network. On a network, every computer is identified by its IP address. The IP address is 32 bits and is a combination of four numeric values separated by a period. For example, 172.17.68.130 is a valid IP address. However, each numeric value used for the IP address should be a number in the range of zero to 255, with both the lower and upper range values included. In an intranet, IP addresses can be set for computers at random, as long as they are unique. However, while connecting to the Internet, a computer requires a registered IP address. This helps distinguish one computer on the Internet from another.

NOTE

You need to know much more about IP addresses. The relevant concepts are discussed in the subsequent chapters.

Name Resolution

The main objective of name resolution is to map (that is, to associate) the *hostname* of a computer with its respective IP address. A hostname is an alias for the IP address of the machine and is used because remembering IP addresses is always difficult. The maximum length of a hostname is 255 characters. A hostname can be a combination of alphabetic and numeric characters. A hostname can also contain hyphens and periods.

Ports

All computers have an interface that acts as an end point to a logical connection. These interfaces are denoted by numbers and are called *ports*. The number identifies the type of port and the type of connection that the port expects. For example, the port number 80 is used for HTTP connections, and the port number 443 is used for SSL connections.

Sockets

A *socket* can be defined as a software object or a method used to establish connectivity between a client program and a server program on a network. Sockets are also known as the end point in a connection. They can be created and used with the help of *function calls*. Function calls are a set of programming requests.

Protocol

A *protocol* is a set of rules that forms an inseparable part of networks. All communications that take place between two computers on the same network or on different networks are made possible by using the appropriate protocols. Protocols follow a layered architecture with each layer performing a specific task. The most common example of a protocol is TCP/IP, which is used for communication between two computers on a network. From a Web perspective, the most important protocol is HyperText Transfer Protocol (HTTP), which runs over TCP/IP. HTTP is used for viewing Web pages. You can install a number of protocols on a computer, but in order to communicate with other computers on the network, the right set of protocols should be installed. Each protocol has its advantages and disadvantages. The protocol is responsible for the following:

◆ Deciding how the computer sending the data will indicate that it has finished sending the complete data.

◆ Deciding how the computer receiving the data will indicate to the sender that it has received the complete data.

Understanding How Web Servers Work

Before learning how to make Web servers work in a desirable way, it is really important to understand how Web servers work internally. Most Web servers follow the same logic while operating internally. The basic understanding of the networking terms that were discussed in the previous section will help you understand how Web servers work. The process can be divided into four basic steps, and the components involved in this process are a Web browser and a Web server. The steps are as follows:

1. The client computer uses a Web browser to connect to the Web server and requests a Web page.

2. Upon receiving the request, the Web server locates the corresponding file or program in the file system.

3. After locating the file, the Web server retrieves the file from the file system.

4. The Web server sends the retrieved file to the Web browser. The requested file is then rendered on the client computer. This request and response process takes place as shown in Figure 1.1.

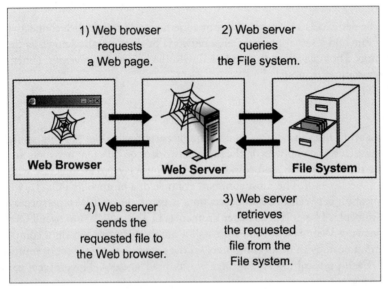

FIGURE 1.1 *The request–response process between a Web browser and a Web server*

The Uniform Resource Locater (URL)

You now have a basic idea about how communication takes place between a Web server and a Web browser. To connect to a Web server, you need to specify a valid URL. A Web browser installed on the client computer uses a Uniform Resource Locater (URL) to send a request to the server. This URL contains a unique domain name that distinguishes one site from another. For example, to access the FAQ posted on Apache's official Web site, you specify the URL, http://www.apache.org:80/faq.html. You can further split this URL into these four parts:

- ◆ **Protocol.** The URL begins with the protocol specification that will be used to communicate on the network. In the preceding URL, the HyperText Transfer Protocol (HTTP) is used. HTTP is the most commonly used protocol for communication on the Web.

- ◆ **Server name.** Followed by the protocol, the URL specifies the server name, which in this case is www.apache.org.

- ◆ **Port.** The port number is specified after the server name and is preceded by a colon. If not specified, the port number defaults to 80 for all HTTP requests that are sent to the Web server.

◆ **Filename.** After specifying the name of the server, you can also specify the name of the file that you want to view. In this case, the name of the file is faq.html. You can also specify the complete path name if the file that you want to view is in a different location.

Now that you have an idea of how a Web browser communicates with Web servers, peek into the internal workings of a Web server that facilitates the Web page to be viewed in the browser of the client computer. Here is the process:

1. While sending the requests, the browser converts the server name (http://www.apache.org) to an IP address. The browser connects to the server using this IP address.

2. After establishing a connection with the server using its IP address, the client computer sends requests to the server. The connection is established on port 80, which is, by convention, reserved for HTTP transactions taking place in a network.

3. The request that is sent by the client is typically a GET request. The GET request then asks for the file named faq.html.

4. After the Web server accepts the request for the file, the corresponding content of the file is sent to the client requesting the page. In this case, the content is HTML text.

5. The browser on the client computer interprets the HTML text and displays the Web page. The Web browser formats the page in accordance with the HTML tags present in the source of the HTML file.

Static versus Dynamic Web Pages

Content in a Web site can be either *static* or *dynamic*. When the Internet came into existence, all sites were created using HTML and predominantly contained *static content*. Web pages that are created using HTML are called *static Web pages* because after they are ready to be sent to the client the content of the page cannot be changed before being delivered. These resulted in Web pages being rigid, less interactive, and lacking in visual appeal. However, the evolution of the Internet gave birth to dynamic content, and today the popularity of a site depends on how interactive and visually appealing it is. Dynamic content helps a developer achieve this. Dynamic Web pages contain content that can be modified at runtime while the user is interacting with the Web server. In other words, dynamic Web pages are generated on the basis of user input.

CGI (Common Gateway Interface) scripts have been a powerful way to generate dynamic content on the Web. Here is how a CGI script works:

1. A user requests a CGI program located on the Web server.

2. The Web server invokes the CGI script.

3. The Web server retrieves the output from the CGI program and sends the output to the user's Web browser. Typically, CGI programs produce HTML output so that a browser can interpret it.

Figure 1.2 depicts how this process takes place.

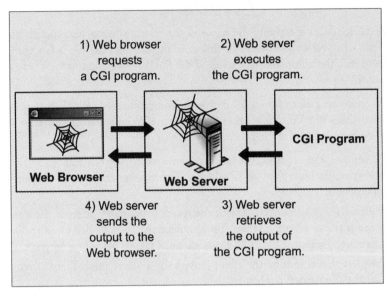

FIGURE 1.2 *How dynamic Web pages are generated*

Types of Web Servers Available

Software is either free (open source) or proprietary (closed source). Free software doesn't just mean that it is available free of cost, but also means that the source code of the same is available for redistribution, modification, or customization. On the other hand, proprietary software can be acquired free of cost (in some cases), but the source code is still not available for modification or customization. In most cases, you will need to make a payment to acquire a license before using proprietary software.

Web servers can be classified as free or proprietary. The first category is comprised of Web servers that can be acquired without paying for a license and whose source code is also available for modification and redistribution. The second category includes Web servers for which users must make a payment in order to acquire a license (in most cases) and whose source code is not available for modification or customization.

 TIP

At times, software that is available free of cost is closed source *and* proprietary. One example is Microsoft Internet Explorer, which is available free of cost and proprietary but is not open source.

Free (Open Source) Web Servers

The most popular among free servers is the Apache Web server. Though Apache is the most widely used Web server in this category, a few other Web servers are fast gaining popularity. Here are a few of the popular Web servers in this category:

♦ Apache

♦ Boa

♦ Red Hat Content Accelerator

♦ thttpd

♦ Mathopd

Apache

Apache is one of the most popular open source Web servers. Apache has become the obvious choice of many organizations due to its numerous useful features. The Apache Web server is packed with features such as speed, portability, stability, and security. You can download Apache for free at its official Web site at http://httpd.apache.org/.

 NOTE

Chapter 2, "Introduction to Apache," discusses the features of the Apache Web server in detail.

Boa

In 1991 Paul Phillips created the Boa Web server. However, Larry Doolittle, who now has taken on the responsibility of its maintenance, has made significant improvements. The Boa Web server is ideal for Web server administrators whose primary goals are speed and security. However, all this doesn't come easy, because in order to use the Boa Web server, administrators need to do away with some functionality. Unlike other Web servers, Boa is a single-tasking HTTP server. It neither makes multiple copies of itself to fork HTTP requests nor forks each connection that is requested. You can download Boa from its official site at http://www.boa.org.

Red Hat Content Accelerator

Red Hat Content Accelerator (RHCA) is an open source, kernel-based, powerful HTTP server that can be downloaded from the official Red Hat site. It is capable of serving static content and caching dynamic content. For more information about the RHCA server, visit http://www.redhat.com/docs/manuals/tux/TUX-2.2-Manual/intro.html.

thttpd

thttpd is another open source Web server that is quickly gaining popularity. thttpd, which stands for *tiny/turbo/throttling HTTP server,* was developed by Jef Poskanzer. The main features of thttpd are portability, speed, ability to handle extreme load, and security. The only drawback to thttpd is its feature-free nature. When I say *feature-free,* I mean that thttpd is built primarily for speed, and only the bare-minimum features essential for getting a Web server running are built in. For more information about thttpd, refer to http://www.acme.com/software/thttpd/.

Mathopd

Mathopd is an interesting Web server that was developed with an aim to incorporate the fewest features possible. Call it a drawback or call it restricted design, Mathopd is supported only by UNIX and Linux operating systems. If performance is your only criterion when choosing a Web server, you can consider Mathopd as a strong contender in comparison to its competition. The source code for this Web server is written so that it can handle numerous simultaneous connections. In addition, Mathopd occupies minimal memory on the computer. You can download this Web server free of cost at http://mathop.diva.nl/download.html.

Proprietary Web Servers

All Web servers that require the purchase of a license before you begin using them fall into the category of proprietary Web servers. Web server administrators who are more interested in using proprietary Web servers have a long list to choose from. IIS, IBM, Zeus, Roxen, iPlanet, and Stronghold are the most popular ones in this category. Organizations that are reluctant to use free software or are inclined to use proprietary software opt for Web servers that fall into this category. I will now discuss a few proprietary Web servers.

Microsoft IIS

Microsoft Internet Information Server is a popular Web server that has existed for several years. Microsoft IIS comes preinstalled with Windows NT, Windows 2000, and Windows XP. IIS is a powerful Web server and possesses many interesting features. The only drawback is that it is not portable and forces you to use Windows NT, Windows 2000, or Windows XP as the platform. IIS doesn't work with other operating systems such as Solaris, UNIX, and Linux. People deploying Web sites on a Windows platform should seriously consider IIS as a Web server to host the sites. You can obtain more information about this Web server from the official Microsoft site.

IBM

The IBM HTTP Server is IBM's version of the Apache Web server. Several years ago, IBM declared that it would support the Apache Web server for its Internet Commerce Solutions. As a result, the IBM HTTP Server comes bundled with solutions such as IBM Websphere Application Server. You can find more information about this Web server at http://www-3.ibm.com/software/webservers/httpservers/.

Zeus

The Zeus Web server is an ideal Web server for Linux and UNIX platforms. Though many users prefer to use free software, Zeus is not a bad option to consider. Its powerful features include support for Apache/NCSA httpd compatibility and ease of configuration. The only drawback is the cost associated with acquiring this Web server. You can obtain more details about this Web server at http://www.spec.org/osg/web96.

iPlanet

The iPlanet Web server is arguably one of the best Web servers guaranteeing high performance. This product is the result of Sun-Netscape Alliance. The iPlanet Web server is most often used with high-end multiprocessing hardware. Primarily developed for Java programmers, the maximum benefits of this Web server can be reaped if you choose to develop applications in Java. Portability is not a concern with iPlanet. The platforms that support iPlanet Web server include Solaris, Linux, Windows, and many more.

 NOTE

The iPlanet Web server is now called Sun ONE Web server. More information is available at http://wwws.sun.com/software/iplanet/products/iplanet_application/home_ias.html.

Stronghold

If security is the primary concern, an organization that wants to choose a Web server to deploy applications might not be entirely comfortable using free software. Although free software cannot be declared less secure, those organizations that can afford high costs with respect to deployment may be ready to pay any price to guarantee security for their applications. The ideal Web server for such organizations is Stronghold. The Stronghold Web server, which is designed along the lines of Apache, is implemented on Secure Socket Layer (SSL) to ensure maximum security. You can find more information about this Web server at http://www.redhat.com/software/apache/stronghold/.

Role of a Web Server

Web servers perform various functions apart from accepting HTTP requests. They can be summed up as follows:

◆ **Access control.** Users should be able to access only those resources on the Web server for which they have permissions. Each user should be able to access only those sets of files that belong to him. Web servers allow only authorized users to access files on the server if configured accordingly. This mechanism is called *access control.* Access control can be practiced in numerous ways, such as setting appropriate permissions on files and directories and implementing hostname/IP address restrictions. Access control can also be implemented using authentication in which the user is required to enter a valid username and password in order to access the resources on the server.

◆ **Server-side page processing/parsing.** Parsing is a process by which a Web server substitutes field names with appropriate values depending upon user input. After parsing the document, the Web server sends the document to the client computer.

◆ **Log maintenance.** To ensure that no pitfalls or shortcomings are in the performance and availability of Web servers, the Web server uses a mechanism to maintain logs on a regular basis. These logs help the Web server administrator keep a track of the functioning of the Web server, analyze the problems (if any), and take corrective actions to troubleshoot the problems. Typically, logs are maintained to monitor successful accesses, errors, and failures.

◆ **CGI script and custom API program execution.** Another important feature of Web servers is that they allow execution of CGI scripts and custom API programs. These CGI scripts and custom API programs are usually used to evaluate the information entered into a Web form.

All about the HTTP Protocol

By now you have a fair idea of what Web servers are and how they operate. However, for a better understanding of Web servers and how they function, you need to be familiar with how the HTTP protocol works. The concept is so detailed that a whole book could be written on its specification. This section covers important concepts pertaining to the HTTP protocol, but the scope is limited to what you need to understand for the functioning of Web servers.

A Brief History of HTTP

The first version of HTTP, HTTP/0.9 was released in 1991. However, this was not an official release. This protocol was simple and was used to transfer raw data over the Internet. The Web servers that accepted HTTP requests at that time responded to simple requests such as this one:

```
GET /index.html
```

In this scenario, if a file with the name index.html were in the document root (the directory that stores the Web site-related files) of the Web server, the contents would be displayed on a Web page. If such a file were not found, the Web server would respond with an error. It was not long before this version became obsolete, and in May 1996 Request For Comments (RFC) for HTTP 1.0 was released. A new feature was incorporated into this release. This version of HTTP used *headers*. Headers are pieces of text that are attached to data packets and that describe the data being transported. The most common header looks something like this:

```
Content-Type: text/html
```

This header indicates that the data being transported is text that is marked up using HTML. Before sending requests to the Web server, the browser attaches headers to the data packets. The latest version of HTTP is HTTP/1.1. This version was officially announced in June 1999 with the release of RFC 2616.

New Features of HTTP /1.1

HTTP/1.1 is the latest version of HTTP and has new features incorporated in its specification. Most of today's Web servers, including Apache and IIS, support HTTP/1.1. I describe the new features of HTTP/1.1 in the following sections.

Hostname Identification

Hostname identification was one of the most important features incorporated in HTTP/1.1. In earlier versions of HTTP, the Web server was never aware of the hostname used in the URL. However, in HTTP /1.1, each request should specify the hostname. For example, if the URL http://www.apache.org is requested, the hostname www.apache.org should be identifiable by the Web server. This enables the Web server administrator to avoid allocating unique IP addresses to each domain. This implies that more than one domain can share the same IP address. Consider a case where a user requests the page www.apache.org and another user requests the page www.php.net. In such a case, the respective pages will be retrieved and displayed on each user's browser even if both the sites are actually two different domains sharing the same IP address. This condition is made possible by hostname identification. Earlier versions of HTTP would have considered the IP address in order to extract content for each of the domains. Therefore, each domain had to be allocated a unique IP address to avoid conflict.

Now, you must be asking, "How does one specify the hostname while sending an HTTP request?" This can be done in two ways:

◆ Specify the complete URL that includes the hostname in the request line.

◆ Specify the hostname in the header information. To do so, specify the hostname next to the Host: header as shown here:

```
GET / HTTP/1.1
Host: www.apache.org
```

Content Negotiation

The term *content negotiation* refers to the availability of several versions of the same document on the same host machine. Consider a simple example in which the content of a site can be viewed in German and Chinese in addition to English—the same document will have a German as well as a Chinese version. Moreover, the same document might also be available in PDF as well as an HTML format. This implies that more than one version of the same document is on the host computer. The different versions of the same document are referred to as *variants* or *representations*. Content negotiation can be categorized in two categories, *server-driven negotiation* and *agent-driven negotiation*.

◆ **Server-driven negotiation.** In this type of content negotiation, the Web server decides which is the best way to render content to the Web browser. The decision that the Web server makes is entirely dependent on the information provided by the browser while sending a request.

◆ **Agent-driven negotiation.** In this type of content negotiation, the Web server does not decide or guess the best possible way to render the content to the Web browser. Instead, it presents a list of representations or variants. The browser then decides which one from the list will be used. The browser can be configured to automatically select a representation or present a choice that it wants to use.

 NOTE

Though both server-driven negotiation and agent-driven negotiation form a part of content negotiation, agent-driven negotiation hasn't been documented completely in the HTTP /1.1 specification. The specification includes a brief explanation on the headers that are used.

New Request Methods

With HTTP /1.1, four new request methods were introduced. The HTTP /1.1 protocol supports these request methods in addition to the conventional request methods such as GET, HEAD, and POST. These request methods are as follows:

◆ OPTIONS

◆ DELETE

◆ PUT

◆ TRACE

NOTE

Request methods are discussed in detail in the section "Request Methods," later in this chapter.

Persistent Connections

The highly useful mechanism of *persistent connection* was introduced with HTTP /1.1. The Web pages hosted on the Internet today consist of more than mere content. A Web page might contain several inline documents within a document. These inline documents can be image files, Shockwave presentations, sound files, and even video clippings. The Web pages that are loaded with such inline documents adversely affect the download speed—because each of these inline documents needs to be downloaded over a separate connection. In order to download these inline documents, the browser first connects to the Web server and retrieves the document before disconnecting, consequently hogging a lot of time. The concept of persistent connections helps the browser download several inline documents over a single connection, instead of having to establish a new connection for each inline document. Though the connection is just one, all inline documents are downloaded one after the other, persistently. By default, all connections that are established using the HTTP /1.1 protocol are persistent connections unless you otherwise configure your browser.

Chunked Transfer-Coding

Chunked transfer-coding is an ideal mechanism used by the HTTP /1.1 protocol for message transmission. Chunked transfers enable the message's sender to break the message body into smaller arbitrary chunks. After the message body is broken into smaller chunks, each chunk is transferred individually to the receiver. The length of each chunk is pre-appended, and the end of the message is marked with zero length to depict the end of the message. In order to signify that chunking is being used for transferring the message, the sender uses the `Transfer-Encoding` header. Consider the following example:

```
Transfer-Encoding: chunked
```

In the preceding example, the value `chunked` signifies that the sender will use chunking while transmitting the message.

In addition to chunking the message, this mechanism helps the sender buffer the chunked pieces of message, instead of having to buffer the entire message as a whole. Therefore, the whole message need not be buffered before being transmitted to the receiver. As soon as a chunk of the message is buffered, it is sent to the user. This saves a lot of time, and the receiver doesn't have to wait long before receiving a part of the message.

Byte Ranges

HTTP /1.1 protocol allows the browser to request parts of a document. Specifying a byte range allows the browser to request a part of a document. In addition to requesting parts of a document, byte ranges can be specified to continue an interrupted transfer. You can specify the byte range in the Range header, as shown here:

```
Range: bytes=400-600
```

When you specify the byte range as 400–600, the portion of the document that occupies the last 200 bytes of the entire document is requested.

Caching

Caching is a very useful mechanism that involves retaining pages that are already downloaded on a user's computer. When a user tries to view a downloaded Web page, the Web page is retrieved from the cache. This mechanism saves considerable download time and bandwidth by eliminating the need for transmitting already downloaded network data. Another advantage of caching is that it reduces the load on the Web server. Most Web browsers, proxies, and Web servers support client-side caching.

TIP

Caching is often managed on a separate, dedicated computer.

The HTTP /1.1 protocol has taken caching to a new dimension. While retaining the original caching support features that were also a part of HTTP /1.0, HTTP /1.1 promises loads of new features. Not only does the new HTTP /1.1 protocol specification contain new caching features, but also it contains a more improvised version of caching features that were a part of HTTP /1.0.

According to HTTP /1.1 specification, a cache entry is declared *fresh* until its date of expiration. After the date of expiration, the cache entry is declared *stale*. All stale entries need to be revalidated with the origin Web server before being returned in response to the request of the client.

HTTP /1.1 has overruled the way HTTP /1.0 used to revalidate a cache entry; in HTTP /1.0, the cache used the If-Modified-Since header to revalidate an entry. This header used absolute time stamps with one-second resolution that resulted in errors due to failure in clock synchronization and lack of resolution. HTTP /1.1 deals with caching problems using the concept of *entity tag*. An entity tag is an opaque cache validator string that can be customized by the origin server. If two responses with similar entity tags exist, according to the specification, it can be concluded that they are identical. The Web servers that incorporate HTTP /1.1 use the ETag header. The HTTP /1.1 protocol includes headers such as If-None-Match, If-Unmodified-Since, and If-match. Clients can present one or more entity tags for a resource using the If-None-Match header.

Upgrading to Other Protocols

The HTTP /1.1 protocol includes a new request-header named Upgrade. The purpose of this header is to avoid protocol incompatibility issues. With the rapid growth in technology, it is likely that the near future will witness yet another new protocol. The Upgrade request-header ensures ease of deployment even if a new protocol is introduced. When a client sends a request to the Web server, it can specify the alternate protocols that it supports using the Upgrade header. This way the server will have an option to switch to an alternate protocol in case the client doesn't support the protocol originally used by the Web server.

Security Features

Security is a major area of concern for anyone who has a relationship with the Web in one or more ways. Security is an ongoing, essential process. Therefore, several features have been incorporated in HTTP /1.1 protocol to ensure integrity of content while in transit. The following features make HTTP /1.1 a more secure protocol than all earlier versions:

◆ **Digest authentication.** HTTP /1.1 uses digest access authentication rather than basic authentication used by HTTP /1.0. A major problem with using basic authentication is that the username and password that are transmitted as the credentials of the user are transmitted as plain text. In other words, these credentials are vulnerable to snooping because they are transmitted in an unencrypted format. However, in the case of digest access authentication, the credentials of a user are transmitted in a scrambled format making it difficult for intruders to decipher the credentials.

◆ **Proxy authentication.** HTTP /1.1 protocol supports proxy authentication. It uses Proxy-Authenticate and Proxy-Authorization headers to achieve this. Proxy Authentication helps ensure that only properly authenticated clients are provided the services.

Request Methods

The HTTP protocol uses different methods for sending requests to the Web server. These methods are called *request methods*. It is essential to understand how request methods work. Every HTTP request that is sent over the network contains a header that specifies the request method used. The most common request method used to send requests to the Web server is the GET method. The GET method uses the specified URL to connect to the Web server and extract the resource located on the server. In addition to the GET method, there are several other types of HTTP request methods. As discussed earlier, a few new request methods have been incorporated in the HTTP /1.1 specification. I will now discuss each of these HTTP request methods in a bit more detail.

The GET *Method*

As just mentioned, the GET method is the most common HTTP request method used to send HTTP requests. The main function of this method involves requesting resources on the Web server. The request is sent to the Web server through a valid URL.

The HEAD *Method*

The HEAD method is somewhat similar to the GET method, as this request method also involves sending requests to the Web server. The only difference between the GET request method and the HEAD request method is that, unlike the GET request, the HEAD request method doesn't return a message body to the client. The purpose of this request method is only to return HTTP headers.

The POST *Method*

The POST request method is the one most commonly used to retrieve information entered in Web forms. The POST request method tells the server to receive requests sent by the client and transfers data from the client to the server.

The PUT *Method*

The PUT method requires the client to send a request to a server. In this type of request, after the client sends the request, the server either accepts or rejects the request. If the server accepts the request, it saves the information received from the client in a file.

The OPTIONS *Method*

The Web server provides certain communications options that are used by clients to communicate with the server. You use the OPTIONS request method to request the communication options offered by the server. After requesting the connection options, the client computer can negotiate an appropriate set of communication parameters with the server.

The TRACE *Method*

The TRACE method is ideally used for testing purposes. This method helps simulate how a server sees a request on the client's computer.

The DELETE *Method*

When the client computer sends a request, the URL points to a resource on the server. The DELETE method, as its name suggests, is used to delete the resource identified in the request URL.

The CONNECT *Method*

The CONNECT method allows a Web proxy to tunnel the connection between the client and the server, which means that this method is not actually proxying the request.

Using Telnet to View How HTTP Works

Now that you understand HTTP, it's time to use telnet to view how HTTP works. However, this time I will not use a conventional Web browser. Instead, I will use telnet and a set of HTTP commands. Telnet is a handy tool that you can use to connect to a specific Transmission Control Protocol (TCP) port on a remote system. All you do is connect to a remote server running a Web server using the following command:

```
telnet host.com 80
```

In the preceding example, the host can be replaced by any server name that is running a Web server. The number 80 indicates the port that is being used by the remote computer. By convention, port 80 is used for all HTTP transactions. If you don't have access to a host on the Internet, it is a good idea to telnet to the local Linux machine. By default, the hostname for Linux systems is localhost. I will now use telnet to connect to localhost at port 80. Consider the following example, where I am logged in as a user named steve.

```
[steve@localhost steve]$ telnet localhost 80
Trying 127.0.0.1...
Connected to localhost.localdomain (127.0.0.1).
Escape character is '^]'.
```

The command indicates that a TCP connection is established. However, unless you send requests to the HTTP server after connecting, the server will not respond. This is what is documented in the HTTP specification. As a result, you will need to send a request to the Web server. The simplest request that you can send is GET /. Here is the output you will receive after you send this request:

```
[steve@localhost steve]$ telnet localhost 80
Trying 127.0.0.1...
Connected to localhost.localdomain (127.0.0.1).
Escape character is '^]'.
GET / <Press Enter>
<HTML>
<HEAD>
<TITLE>This is the default Web page</TITLE>
</HEAD>
```

```
<BODY>
<H1>Hi! Welcome to the world of Apache Web server!
</H1>
</BODY>
</HTML>
Connection closed by foreign host.
```

In the preceding example, after establishing a connection with the server, the client used the GET / request. This request retrieves the default Web page of the server. By convention, the default Web page is located in the document root of the Web server under the name index.htm or index.html. This request retrieves the content of the home page from the server. Also, notice that after the content of the home page is retrieved, the connection is closed automatically. The request specified in the preceding example doesn't specify the version of HTTP used. Therefore, the version HTTP /0.9 is assumed. Now examine what happens when I specify a later version of the HTTP protocol:

```
[steve@localhost steve]$ telnet localhost 80
Trying 127.0.0.1...
Connected to localhost.localdomain (127.0.0.1).
Escape character is '^]'.
GET / HTTP/1.0 <Press Enter>
<Press Enter>
HTTP/1.1 200 OK
Date: Tue, 19 Mar 2002 18:20:45 GMT
Server: Apache/1.3.24 (Unix)  (Red-Hat/Linux) mod_python/2.7.6 Python/1.5.2 mod_ssl/2.8.4
OpenSSL/0.9.6b DAV/1.0.2 PHP/4.0.6 mod_perl/1.24_01 mod_throttle/3.1.2
Last-Modified: Wed, 13 Mar 2002 23:14:15 GMT
ETag: "24b8f-91-3c8fdd47"
Accept-Ranges: bytes
Content-Length: 145
Connection: close
Content-Type: text/html

<HTML>
<HEAD>
<TITLE>This is the default Web page</TITLE>
</HEAD>
```

```
<BODY>
<H1>Hi! Welcome to the world of Apache Web server </H1>
</BODY>
</HTML>
Connection closed by foreign host.
```

In the preceding example, when you specify the protocol version as HTTP /1.0, the HTTP server responds with information pertaining to the Web server. However, when you send the request, you need to follow the request with two consecutive new lines by pressing Enter twice; otherwise, the Web server will not reply. Notice that even when you specify the protocol version as HTTP /1.0, the server responds using the HTTP /1.1 protocol. Also notice that a list of installed packages is sent with the reply. This is an Apache-specific feature.

Finally, I will now use the latest version of HTTP, HTTP /1.1, to send a request to the server. This is the output that I received:

```
[steve@localhost steve]$ telnet localhost 80
Trying 127.0.0.1...
Connected to localhost.localdomain (127.0.0.1).
Escape character is '^]'.
GET / HTTP/1.1 <Press Enter>
<Press Enter>
HTTP/1.1 400 Bad Request
Date: Fri, 15 Mar 2002 22:08:09 GMT
Server: Apache/1.3.24 (Unix)  (Red-Hat/Linux) mod_python/2.7.6 Python/1.5.2 mod_ssl/2.8.4
OpenSSL/0.9.6b DAV/1.0.2 PHP/4.0.6 mod_perl/1.24_01 mod_throttle/3.1.2
Connection: close
Transfer-Encoding: chunked
Content-Type: text/html; charset=iso-8859-1

175
<!DOCTYPE HTML PUBLIC "-//IETF//DTD HTML 2.0//EN">
<HTML><HEAD>
<TITLE>400 Bad Request</TITLE>
</HEAD><BODY>
<H1>Bad Request</H1>
Your browser sent a request that this server could not
understand.<P>
client sent HTTP/1.1 request without host name (see
RFC2616 section
```

```
14.23): /<P>
<HR>
<ADDRESS>Apache/1.3.20 Server at localhost.localdomain
Port
80</ADDRESS>
</BODY></HTML>

0

Connection closed by foreign host.
```

As you can see, the result of the request is completely different because the request was labeled as a Bad Request. The error occurs because when you choose to use HTTP /1.1, the client must furnish a hostname. This hostname should be similar to that of the Web server.

Examining HTTP Headers

Headers are an integral part of HTTP requests. While transmitting HTTP requests, several headers are added to the data packets. I will now take up each of the important headers and explain them categorically. I have divided the headers into four main categories:

◆ Request headers
◆ Response headers
◆ Entity headers
◆ General headers

Request Headers

Request headers contain information that is sent by the client to the HTTP server. You use request headers to further qualify a request. In other words, request headers allow the client to specify additional information indicating what comprises an acceptable response.

Response Headers

To specify additional information with its response to the client computer, the server uses response headers. Response headers contain information about the response message and sometimes about the resource being sent as a response.

Entity Headers

The server uses entity headers to specify information about the resource that it transmits to the client as a response to a request sent by the client. This means that entity headers contain information about the content or the message body that a server sends to the client. The information specified in the entity headers helps the client determine what application to invoke in order to handle the resource. For example, if the requested resource is a video clip, the entity header will help the client invoke the application that is used to view the video clip.

General Headers

When a client interacts with a Web server over the Internet or vice versa, a variety of headers carry information about the messages being transmitted. All such headers fall into the category of general headers. The information that these headers carry is limited to details related to the entire session. These headers don't contain information related to the content included in the message.

Summary

In this chapter, you learned about the basic concepts that you need to be familiar with before considering working with Web servers. The first section provided an overview of the general networking terminology such as IP addresses, name resolution, ports, sockets, and protocols. The next section presented a detailed explanation on how the Web server works. In this section, you learned how a Web server accepts and processes requests and then sends responses to the client computer. The next section discussed the difference between dynamic and static content. Next, you learned about the types of Web servers, including commercial and non-commercial Web servers, and about the most commonly used commercial and non-commercial Web servers. The chapter then moved on to discuss the role of Web servers, including a brief discussion about the main tasks a Web server performs. Finally, you read about the HTTP protocol, including the history and features of the HTTP protocol, followed by the concept of request methods. The section also explained the use of telnet to view how the HTTP protocol works, followed by an explanation on the type of HTTP headers used by the HTTP protocol.

Check Your Understanding

Multiple Choice Questions

1. Which of the following are not valid IP addresses for a host? (Choose all that apply.)

    a. 172.17.68.222

    b. 134.147.10

    c. 172.17.10.258

    d. 127.0.0.1

2. Which of the following Web servers is an open source, kernel-based, multithreaded, powerful HTTP server and is also a product of Red Hat?

    a. Internet Information Server

    b. Apache

    c. TUX

    d. iPlanet

3. Which of the following roles is not performed by Web servers?

    a. Maintaining logs

    b. Page processing/parsing

    c. Accessing Web site-related files

    d. Requesting documents from the browser

4. Which of the following request methods were introduced with HTTP /1.1?

    a. HEAD

    b. POST

    c. TRACE

    d. GET

5. Which of the following request methods is most commonly used to send information entered in Web forms?

    a. HEAD

    b. PUT

    c. DELETE

    d. POST

6. Which of the following types of HTTP headers sent by the Web server contain information about the content or the message body that a server sends to the client?

    a. General

    b. Response

    c. Entity

    d. Request

Answers

Multiple Choice Answers

1. b, c. 134.147.10 is not a valid IP address because an IP address should be a combination of four numbers separated by a period. 172.17.10.258 is also not valid because the maximum limit of any number specified in an IP address is 255. In this case, the fourth number exceeds the predefined limit.

2. c. TUX is an open source, kernel-based, multithreaded, powerful HTTP server and is also a product of Red Hat.

3. d. A browser requests documents/resources from the Web server. Other roles, such as maintaining logs, storing Web site-related files and parsing are performed by a Web server.

4. c. The TRACE request method was introduced with HTTP /1.1. Request methods, such as GET, POST, and HEAD were also a part of HTTP /1.0.

5. d. The POST method is most commonly used to retrieve information entered in Web forms. It is preferred over the GET method for security reasons.

6. c. The Entity headers contain information about the resource that is sent in response to a client request.

Chapter 2

Introduction to Apache

Technology is rapidly evolving, and the result is a plethora of software solutions, which means a plethora of options. Therefore, software developers have a tough time keeping up with competition and are perpetually working to improve the quality of software.

In such a fast-paced technical environment, the ability of a Web server to occupy 61 percent of the market share is commendable. I am talking about none other than the Apache Web server. Over the years, there has been a surge in the use of Apache as a Web server on various platforms. This chapter covers the features of the Apache Web server in detail. It also sheds light on how the Apache Web server works and the architecture that makes it an obvious choice for millions of worldwide organizations.

Features of the Apache Web Server

The design of Apache is robust, secure, and stable, and by the time you finish this section, you may well agree with this claim! The fact is that Apache has numerous features that make it so popular. I discuss the main features of this powerful Web server in the following sections. For a brief history of the Apache Web server, check out the upcoming sidebar "History of Apache."

HISTORY OF APACHE

Apache is an HTTP Web server developed by a group of volunteers. The base of the Apache Web server was a public domain HTTP server developed by Rob McCool at the National Center for Supercomputing Applications (NCSA), University of Illinois, Urbana-Champaign. Soon after its development, many Web masters were creating their own extensions of this server—after applying much-needed bug fixes. At that point, only a common distribution was required. In February 1994, Brian Behlendorf and Cliff Skolnick started inviting ideas about improvising Apache from people all over the world through a mailing list. Several volunteers collaborated and wrote the source code for Apache. The name of the Apache Web server originated from the phrase "A patchy" (the developers who wrote the source code for Apache made improvisations to the code in the form of patches). Later, the *Apache Group,* was formed. This group consisted of eight core members of the original development team: Brian Behlendorf, Roy T. Fielding, Rob Hartill, David Robinson, Cliff Skolnick, Randy Terbush, Robert S. Thau, and Andrew Wilson. The outcome of this disciplined, collaborative effort was the first release of the Apache Web server, 0.6.2, in April 1995.

Though this server was successful, the quest for perfection was enough incentive to drive the developers to redesign the Web server. After a lot of overhauling and the addition of many new features, Apache 1.0 was released in December 1995. Because it went through a series of beta tests before being officially released, it was a more stable than its predecessor.

In 1999, the members of the Apache Group formed the *Apache Software Foundation.* This foundation was created to provide legal and financial support for the development of the Apache Web server.

The Apache Web server, which is now a benchmark for Web server developers, attained its position because of the hard work put in by developers all over the world. The fact that the Apache source code was freely available allowed developers to examine the source code and suggest valuable ideas to improve its design. The movement is still going on and is called the *Apache HTTP Server Project.* The Apache Server Project is an improvement initiative that allows people, irrespective of their location, to contribute code, ideas, and documentation.

Freely Distributable

You can obtain Apache free of cost from its official Web site (http://httpd.apache.org). All you need is an Internet connection to download the software. Several mirror sites allow you to download the software from a Web server that is closer to your location. The links to these mirror sites are listed on the Apache Web site. You can choose the appropriate mirror site for downloading Apache depending on your location.

Ease of Installation

If you are familiar with the Linux console and have a fair amount of knowledge of a few commands, installing Apache will not be a problem. The Apache software is available in two forms:

◆ **Precompiled form.** The precompiled form (binaries) of the software is available as an RPM (RedHat Package Manager) file for Red Hat Linux distribution. In addition, various other formats are available for distributing binary or precompiled software. The formats differ from operating system to operating system. Binaries are also available for different distributions for the same operating system. For example, separate binaries are available for Mandrake, Debian, and Red Hat distributions of Linux. This type of installation is ideal for people who have basic knowledge of the Linux operating system. To install Apache using the RPM file, just type a command and you are ready to use Apache. Though this is an easy way to install Apache, expert users don't prefer it because they cannot customize the installation.

◆ **Source form.** You can install the source form of the software by issuing a series of commands at the Linux console. This type of installation requires you to compile from the source file. Expert users prefer this installation type because they can specify several install options and customize the installation accordingly.

 NOTE

For a more detailed explanation on how to install Apache, see Chapter 3, "Installing Apache," which discusses both previously mentioned installation methods.

Ease of Configuration

Apache is very easy to configure, provided you are familiar with using a text editor in Linux. Though the installation options are numerous, the basic configuration is simple. You need to configure just one configuration file to get Apache up and running. All you need to do in order to configure Apache is to specify a few file locations, name your server, and specify the document root for your Web site files.

An easier option is to use a GUI to configure Apache. Several third-party graphical tools are available for configuring Apache. One popular tool is Webmin, which you can obtain at http://www.webmin.com/webmin/index2.html.

High Performance and Low Resource Consumption

The Apache server works on a *preforking model*. A preforking model is one in which forking (launching a process) occurs even before a request is sent to the server. As a result, server processes wait to answer requests. Other Web servers operate on a different model. They start a process only when a request is sent to them. After the request is answered, the process dies. When a user sends another request, the process starts all over again. This results in stopping and restarting processes each time a request is received. Launching a process repeatedly can be an expensive proposition, particularly in a UNIX-based environment. Apache is a solution to this problem. While using Apache, servers can be pre-allocated to wait for requests. In such a case, Apache can respond more quickly than Web servers that are not preforked.

Open Source

Often people misinterpret the term *open source*. The term open source means that the source code of a particular software program is available free of cost. However, the aspect that this term doesn't explain is whether this code can be modified or reused. Consider the example of Java programming language. Its source code is available; however, Java source code cannot be modified per user requirements. Even a slight modification to the source code requires necessary permissions. This is not the case with the Apache Web server. A user can get, use, modify, alter, or rewrite Apache source code per his needs. As a result, developers can modify the code and design a Web server tailored to their requirements.

Customizable Design

As discussed earlier, the source code of Apache can be modified. This attribute helps customize the design of Apache. In addition to this, you can program your own modules to customize Apache and extend its functionality. The next question that comes to mind is how to go about doing this. You can customize Apache using the Apache Module API. You can use the Apache Module API to write modules using C or Perl. These modules can then be added to Apache to attain additional functionality.

Security

Apache has a set of security features that makes it less vulnerable to threats. Its security features include authentication mechanisms and Secure Sockets Layer (SSL). Apache supports a wide range of database servers, including Oracle and MySQL. These database servers are capable of storing large lists of authorized users and are an effective mechanism for user authentication.

You can add SSL support to Apache as required, by adding a module named mod_ssl. SSL is a time-tested and universally accepted mechanism used by Internet Web servers to ensure security. SSL uses digital certificates and encryption to secure data while in transit over the Internet.

Also, there are no widespread viruses that cause a threat to Apache. Despite its popularity, there are only a few reported vulnerabilities compared to other Web servers.

Support for HTTP /1.1

Apache is an HTTP /1.1-compliant Web server, which means that it uses all the new features of HTTP /1.1, such as support for virtual hosts, persistent connections, resource caching, client-file uploading, enhanced error reporting, and content negotiation. The support for HTTP /1.1 makes Apache a flexible and desired Web server.

Language Support

Apache supports a large list of server-side scripting languages that can be used for Web development. The languages supported by Apache are PHP: Hypertext Preprocessor, Active Server Pages (ASP), Java Server Pages (JSP), Perl, Common Gateway Interface (CGI), Server Side Includes (SSI), and many more.

Proxy Caching

Over the years, Apache has also been used as a general-purpose proxy server. However, with the introduction of a module named mod_proxy, you can use it as an effective and efficient proxy-caching mechanism. When used as a proxy-caching mechanism, Apache can cache the content downloaded from remote servers. This is particularly useful for client computers on an intranet because it saves a considerable amount of bandwidth and download time. After the Web content is cached, the origin server doesn't have to be contacted when a client computer sends a request. Instead, the content in the cache can be used.

Dynamic Shared Objects

Apache supports a mechanism called *dynamic shared objects* that enables the loading of extension modules at runtime. This means that you don't have to recompile the server engine every time you add or remove Apache-specific features.

Support for Windows

Apache supports most Windows-based platforms, such as Windows NT, Windows 2000, Windows 98, and Windows 95. Though the support is built in and Apache runs on these platforms, they are not considered ideal for production environments.

TIP

The latest release of Apache, Apache 2.0, is designed to work well on Windows platforms, so you can use Apache 2.0 with Windows for production environments.

Scalability

You can configure Apache so that multiple Web sites can be hosted on a single server. You achieve this by creating multiple virtual hosts. Implementing virtual hosts is an ideal way to run multiple Web services on a single computer. Though the URLs and hostnames of sites are different, they can reside on the same computer. This feature is useful for Internet Service Providers (ISPs) that want to host multiple sites with the least possible cost.

Portability

Portability is another important feature of the Apache Web server. As a result of its portability, you can install Apache on almost any platform—for example, Linux, UNIX, Windows, Solaris, BeOs, and mainframes.

Architecture of Apache

In order to understand how Apache functions, it is essential to understand how it works internally. This section, which discusses the architecture of the Apache Web server, will help you understand what happens internally while client computers send HTTP requests to Apache. Apache has a modular design (a design that allows you to extend functionality, if needed, by using add-on modules) that makes it more powerful than Web servers with a monolithic design (a rigid design that doesn't allow you to add functionality easily).

Because many Web servers are definitely faster than Apache, I was initially surprised to discover that Apache is the most widely used Web server. However, after closer examination, I understood the reason for the high speed of those Web servers. Those Web servers stripped out a lot of functionality to achieve high speed. This is not the case with Apache. The Apache Web server has a full-fledged list of functions and features.

How Apache Functions

In Chapter 1, "Introduction to Web Servers," I discussed the function of Web servers in general. Now I go into the specifics of the function of the Apache Web server. Superficially, Apache handles HTTP requests the same way other Web servers do. However, it is advisable to have a better understanding of how Apache works internally. This is because Apache follows a different way of handling requests than other servers do. To understand how Apache functions, you need to be familiar with multithreaded and multiprocessed Web servers.

Multithreaded and Multiprocessed Web Servers

When an HTTP request arrives, the Web server starts fetching the resource as requested by the client. While the Web server is busy fetching resources, client computers might send more requests. These requests are either ignored or handled simultaneously by the Web server.

Web servers that ignore other requests or even queue them while they are busy are called *single-threaded* Web servers. This means that they are incapable of handling high Web server traffic. However, these types of Web servers are ideal for Web sites that encounter low or moderate traffic. A few good examples of single-threaded Web servers are thttpd, Medusa, and Zeus.

Web servers that can handle simultaneous requests, manage the requests in two ways. Either they start a new process or they start a new thread within a process. Web servers that start a new process on each request are called *multiprocessed* Web servers, while those that start a new thread within the main process are called *multithreaded* Web servers.

IIS on the Windows platform is an example of a multithreaded Web server. On the other hand, Apache on the Unix platform is a multiprocessed Web server. However, due to limitations of the Windows platform (namely, the lack of support for *forking*—a standard way of starting a new process in Unix), Apache follows a multithreaded mode of functioning for Windows platforms.

 NOTE

> Starting off a new process on every Web request is typically an expensive task in terms of server resources. Therefore, in order to improve its performance, the Apache Web server follows a preforking model. As a result, it starts several new processes before a new request arrives. As soon as a request arrives, it simply hands the request over to one of these idle processes.

Security Perspective

You now know what multiprocessed Web servers are and how Apache qualifies to be one. Another important aspect that is worth discussing is how processes work. I previously said that several processes are invoked when the Apache Web server is started. Two types of processes are invoked, *parent* and *child*. The parent process is the main process from which several child processes are invoked. Whenever a request is sent to the Apache Web server, the parent process receives the request. Then the parent process forwards the request to one of the child processes. The child process then handles the request by responding to it. This behavior is supported for a valid reason: security.

The root user initiates the parent process of the Web server in UNIX systems. The root user, as you know, is the most powerful user on the UNIX system. Therefore, the parent process doesn't directly process the requests sent by the clients. Consider a situation in which a client sends a request with malicious intentions and the parent process handles the request. The parent process being run as a root user will have all necessary rights to perform any operation on the computer, thereby making the system vulnerable. However, if the request is forwarded to a process that has restricted permissions on the computer, no harm can be done. This is because child processes are run as users with restricted privileges.

Request Handling in Apache

The process of handling requests can be divided generally into these consecutive phases:

1. Check Uniform Resource Identifier (URI). In this phase, the Apache Web server first analyzes the request sent by the client and determines the information that the client requires. After doing so, the Apache Web server locates the place where the requested information is stored.

2. Check authentication ID (Auth ID). This phase involves validating the credentials of the user. In other words, in this phase, the Apache Web server verifies whether the user is an authenticated user.

3. Check Auth access. This phase involves checking whether the user is authorized to view or access the requested resources.

4. Check other access. In this phase, the Web server uses other mechanisms for checking the access permissions of the user.

5. Determine the MIME type. After checking the access permissions of the user, the Web server determines the MIME type of the requested resource.

6. Send a response to the client. Finally, in this phase, the Web server sends a response to the client. The action taken by the server depends on the method specified in the request.

7. Log the request. The request is then logged for future reference.

The Apache Web server manages these phases using *modules*. Modules are an integral part of the Apache Web server and impart the so-called modular design to it. I briefly discuss modules in the next section.

Conceptual Architecture of Apache

Theoretically, the architecture of Apache consists of two main parts, the *core* and the *modules*. These parts of the server help Apache attain its modular design. The core uses modules when the Web server receives a request. In return, the modules provide the core with control and data. Figure 2.1 shows how the core and modules interact.

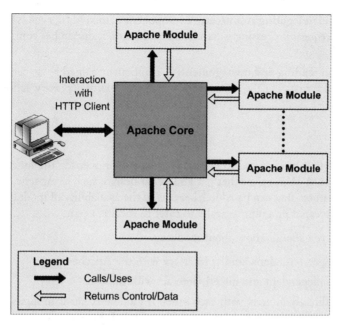

FIGURE 2.1 *Interaction of the core and modules with an HTTP client*

The Core

The core, as the name suggests, is the heart of the Apache Web server, and represents its basic functionality. In addition, the core is responsible for implementing utility functions. One utility is provision of the number of resources allocated per request pool. The core contains components that are used for the following purposes:

- ◆ **Resource allocation.** A component named alloc.c is responsible for allocating resource pools. After appropriately allocating resource pools, this component also keeps track of the allocated resources.

- ◆ **Core functionality.** A component named http_core.c helps Apache implement the bare minimum functionality. This means that it is functional enough to serve documents (that is, to help the Web server send the requested documents), but not in a significantly helpful way.

- ◆ **Managing the parent process.** A component named http_main.c manages the startup of the Apache Web server. In addition to this, it manages the behavior of the server. This component's main tasks are to make the server wait and accept connections, which is made possible by the server loop that is part of this component. Finally, this component is responsible for managing server timeouts.

- ◆ **Managing the protocol handler.** A component named http_protocol.c is responsible for data transfers that take place while a client is interacting with the Web server. This component contains routines that make direct communication with the client possible.

◆ **Processing and delegating resources.** A component named `http_request.c` manages the way request processing is handled. In addition, it dispatches control to modules.

◆ **Configuration reading and management.** A component named `http_config.c` is primarily used for parsing the configuration files and taking necessary actions based on the result.

Modules

A module is an entity that can be used to implement, extend, or override the functionality of the Apache Web server. A Web server that has a modular design, such as Apache, is not limited in terms of the features that can be added, because of the availability of modules. In addition, modules can be created programmatically to cater to specific needs.

Here are some points you should know about modules:

◆ All modules operate under a similar interface with the Apache core.

◆ Modules are independent and directly interact with the core.

◆ They cannot directly interact with each other. If module A needs to interact with module B, then module A must interact with module B through the Apache core.

 NOTE

I cover modules in detail in Chapter 8, "Apache Modules."

The next section sheds light on the interoperability of TCP/IP with Apache.

TCP/IP and Apache

Another important concept is the relationship between TCP/IP and Apache. Consider a situation in which you are administering a live server and the Web site hosted on your server has several thousand hits every day. There is a limit to how many connections a Web server can handle at a given point. Have you ever wondered what happens when the number of requests at a given time crosses the permissible limit?

This is a point worth thinking about. The first possible thought is that the requests exceeding the permissible limit will be rejected. However, doing so will adversely affect the rapport of the site. The solution is to configure Apache in such a way that the requests are not rejected. You can maintain a queue for requests that cannot be processed immediately. These requests can be processed later when the Web server is ready to handle the queued requests.

You can modify TCP/IP parameters on the host computer to achieve this functionality (which I cover in Chapter 9, "Improving Apache's Performance"). For now, remember that configuring TCP/IP is an integral part of configuring Apache for optimized performance.

Summary

In this chapter, I first focused on the salient features of Apache that make it a strong and secure Web server. Next, I discussed the architecture of the Apache Web server to spell out how it works internally. Finally, I discussed the relationship between TCP/IP and Apache.

Check Your Understanding

Multiple Choice Questions

1. Which one of the following phrases best defines the Apache distribution?
    a. Software can be obtained free of cost.
    b. Software and source code can be obtained free of cost.
    c. Software and source code are free, but the source code cannot be modified.
    d. Software and source code are free, and the source code can be modified.

2. Why don't expert users like to install Apache using the RPM file?
    a. It is easy to install.
    b. It has several configuration options that are confusing.
    c. Only a few configuration options can be specified at the time of installation.
    d. No configuration options can be specified because it contains precompiled options.

3. Which of the following best define the nature of the Apache Web server? (Choose all that apply.)
    a. Multiprocessed Web server
    b. Multithreaded Web server
    c. Single-threaded Web server
    d. Preforked Web server

4. Why is Apache Web server's request handling considered secure? (Choose all that apply.)

   a. All the server processes are run as root user.

   b. Only the parent process, which doesn't accept requests, is run as the root user.

   c. Child processes that accept requests are run as root user.

   d. Child processes that accept requests are run as a user with restricted access permissions.

5. Which of the following components of the Apache core is responsible for allocating resource pools?

   a. `http_core.c`

   b. `alloc.c`

   c. `http_config.c`

   d. `http_main.c`

Answers

Multiple Choice Answers

1. d. Apache software and source code can be obtained free of cost. In addition, the Apache source code can be modified to build a customized version of Apache.

2. d. Expert users don't like to install Apache using an RPM file because an RPM contains precompiled options. As a result, the installation cannot be customized.

3. a, d. Apache is a multiprocessed Web server. It is also a preforked Web server.

4. b, d. The root user invokes the parent process in Apache. However, the parent process doesn't handle requests. Child processes are run with the privileges of users with restricted access permissions and are responsible for handling requests. This helps to secure the Web server.

5. b. The component of the Apache core named `alloc.c` is responsible for allocating resource pools.

Chapter 3

The previous chapter covered the salient features of the Apache Web server. It also discussed the working and architecture of Apache. Now you need to install Apache.

There are several install options that you may want to omit and a few that you can't afford to do away with. The installation of Apache is flexible and can be a cakewalk or as intricate as open-heart surgery. You need to know how you will use Apache so that you can customize its installation based on your requirements. This chapter focuses on the installation of the Apache Web server on both Linux and Windows platforms in a stepwise, systematic manner.

Types of Installation

In general, you can install the Apache Web server in two ways: by using a binary distribution or by compiling from the source code. These types of installation apply to Linux and Windows systems.

Binary Installation

Installing Apache by using binaries is the most common and easiest method. Binaries are pre-compiled and can be installed without compiling the source code. For Red Hat Linux, binaries are available in the form of RPM files. To install an RPM file, just execute the rpm command, and you are ready to use Apache. Although RPM files are easy to install, a few constraints prevent them from becoming popular with Web server administrators. The precompiled options make it impossible for Web server administrators to customize the installation. An RPM installation is like a typical or default installation in which the standard Apache packages are installed.

TIP

In the recent past, binaries that were available for Apache were statically precompiled. This means that the binaries installed could not be extended. Fortunately, most distributions today offer Apache with shared object support. As a result, the functionality of Apache can be extended after compilation or after being installed as a binary file. Most distributions offer Apache add-on binaries. For example, Red Hat Linux comes with modules such as mod_php and mod_perl, among others.

As for Windows, Apache can be installed as a binary as well! The installer file is available from Apache's official site. The installer file has a .msi *(Microsoft System Installer)* extension and is 3.23MB in size. The Microsoft System Installer is incorporated into the design of Windows 2000. However, if you want to install Apache on Windows NT or Windows 98, you will need to download the installation file that is available as an .exe *(executable)* file. You will also need to download and install the Microsoft System Installer separately. After downloading the required files, you can double-click the installer file and follow the instructions to perform the installation.

Apache developers are also trying to improve support for other operating systems, such as Windows 95, Windows 98, Windows ME, and Windows XP. Although Apache can be installed on these operating systems, the support for these operating systems is still not considered production quality.

You can download Apache binary distributions at http://www.apache.org/dist/httpd/binaries/. Figure 3.1 displays the Web page on the official site from where the binaries can be downloaded. Apache binaries are available for several operating systems.

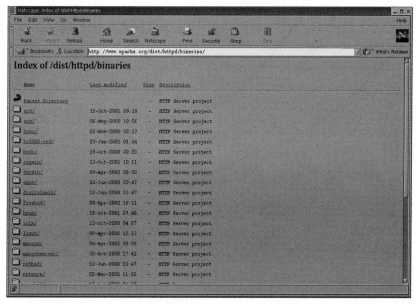

FIGURE 3.1 *The Web page displaying the binary distributions*

Compiling from Source Code

If you are a Web server administrator who wants to customize Apache installation or a person who is adventurous, compiling Apache from the source code will be an attractive idea. You can use several installation options while compiling Apache from the source code. I discuss the most important options later in this chapter. However, before you begin, allow me to reiterate that this installation type is ideal if you want Apache installation to be flexible and dynamic. In other words, this installation type helps you extend the functionality of Apache at any given time. Unlike binary installation, this type of installation allows you to compile additional modules at install time. This means that several add-on features can be included with Apache at the time of installation.

If you choose to install Apache 1.3 or a later version on Linux, you can use Autoconf-style Interface (APACI) to configure your Apache build. APACI is a configuration module that you can use to configure Apache at install time. This utility is similar to the GNU (which stands for "GNU is Not UNIX") Autoconf package, which is a popular GNU utility. It is important to understand that APACI does not compile Apache. Instead, you use it to configure Apache source before compilation.

The main task performed by APACI is to create *makefiles*. Makefiles are files that are used by the `make` utility. The options specified in makefiles are used to direct the C compiler on how to perform the compilation. These files also include exact locations for the compiled programs after installation is completed. The `make` utility at the time of installation uses these locations to place the compiled programs appropriately. In addition to specifying compiler options, you can specify the modules that you want to include while compiling Apache.

APACI performs numerous tests on your computer. These tests ascertain all necessary details related to the hardware and operating system that are essential for Apache compilation.

 NOTE

In this chapter, I also provide details on the installation for both Linux and Windows.

Binary Installation versus Source Compilation

Choosing the ideal installation type might appear to be a perplexing task. To help you decide which type of installation to use, I will compare of the two types based on the following features:

- ◆ Ease of installation
- ◆ Customization options
- ◆ Support for third-party modules
- ◆ Ability to apply patches
- ◆ Compiler optimization

Ease of Installation

If you are a novice user or a Linux newbie, you will probably look for ease of installation. In that case, go for binary installation. Installing Apache by compiling the source code can appear to be complex to novice users.

Customization Options

As discussed earlier, compiling Apache from source provides several customization options at the time of installation. Compiling by using source code keeps your Apache installation open to extensions and alterations, which appeals to system administrators who are abreast of technological enhancements and want the ability to compile the source code in a way that allows flexibility during installation. Installing from a binary file makes installation rigid to a degree, and you can't customize the installation.

Support for Third-Party Modules

There are several tried and true third-party modules that don't come with the standard distribution of the Apache Web server. These are add-on modules that you can download and add to Apache.

Binaries have a standard yet limited set of preexisting modules. Advanced expertise is required to create binaries. Typically, vendors such as Red Hat distribute binaries with their software packages. Add-on modules are not built into the binaries that are distributed by a specific vendor. Therefore, it becomes very frustrating for people to look for module binaries that are compatible with the binary version of Apache that they have installed. As a result, adding more modules depends on the availability of their binaries. So it is advisable to dynamically compile Apache from source code if you need to use third-party modules.

Ability to Apply Patches

As you know, Apache source code goes through tremendous research, and several developers work continuously to improvise its design. In addition, they work on reported bugs so that these bugs don't show up in future releases. As a result, new patches that can be used to upgrade the system keep appearing. However, these patches cannot be applied if you have installed Apache by using a binary file. Binaries may not always contain the latest patches, and once a binary is installed, it is not possible to apply the new patches.

This is not the case if you installed Apache by using the source code. You can feel free to apply as many patches as you want and then recompile the Apache source code to incorporate new patches.

Compiler Optimization

In the past, it was thought that for hardware-specific and system-specific compiler optimization, you should install Apache by compiling the source code. In today's scenario this is a debatable, because binaries are available for almost any hardware or operating system. However, certain distributions, such as Red Hat, don't include Apache RPMs that are optimized for various CPU types. You can optimize Apache for your CPU type by compiling Apache using source code.

Installing Apache on Linux

You can install Apache on Linux by using the RPM file or by compiling the source code. This section focuses on both these installation types and helps you install Apache.

RPM Installation

You can handle RPM installation with a single command. However, you should follow a few guidelines within the context of RPMs. Before you begin downloading the RPM, ensure the following:

◆ The RPM is for the latest version and is specific to the operating system that you are using.

◆ The RPM is built with the precompiled options that will be most beneficial to you.

You can obtain RPMs from http://www.rpmfind.net, the official Web site of Apache, or from a Red Hat mirror site. Follow these steps to install Apache from an RPM file:

1. Download the RPM file from the site.

2. Type the following command while logged on as the root user.

   `#rpm -ivh apache-1.3.xx-y.i386.rpm`

This command will install the version of RPM that you specify. However, you may already have an older version of Apache running. In this case, you might encounter an error while executing the command. Follow these steps to upgrade the installation:

1. Stop the older version of Apache that is currently running.

   `#/etc/rc.d/init.d/httpd stop`

2. Use the `rpm` command to upgrade to the new version.

   `#rpm -Uvh apache-1.3.xx-y.i386.rpm`

 NOTE

If you still encounter errors, it is probably because other packages depend on the older version of Apache. You will need to remove these packages or applications before proceeding with the installation. You can use the command, `rpm -e application_name` to remove these packages or applications. Another option is to use the `--nodeps` option while uninstalling Apache. Using this option will uninstall Apache regardless of the dependencies. You can also use the `--force` option to forcibly uninstall the older version of Apache. You will have to install the dependent packages again if you choose to uninstall each of them before you proceed with the installation. Therefore, you might prefer to use the `--nodeps` or the `--force` options.

Compiling Apache from Source

Compiling Apache from source is not as easy as installing from the RPM file. You need to take into account certain preinstallation requirements before beginning to compile Apache. The requirements are different for different operating systems. I will focus only on the preinstall requirements for Linux because later in this section I discuss the steps for compiling Apache on Linux.

Before Commencing

Before you begin installing Apache on a Linux computer, note these minimum requirements:

◆ 12MB of temporary disk space is a minimum requirement. After installation, Apache will occupy approximately 3MB of disk space. However, disk occupancy can vary depending on the number of modules that are installed.

◆ An ANSI-C compiler should be installed before you begin the installation. The Red Hat distribution contains the GNU C Compiler (GCC) that is recommended.

◆ The Perl 5 interpreter is another prerequisite. Apache uses certain support scripts, such as apxs and dbmmanage, which are written in Perl. Apache can be compiled irrespective of whether the Perl 5 interpreter is installed. However, you will not be able to use these scripts after installation.

◆ Support for Dynamic Shared Object (DSO) is another optional requirement. The DSO mechanism in Apache is used to load modules at runtime.

Download the Source Code

After you ensure that all preinstall requirements have been met, you download the Apache source code. The Apache source code is available from the official Apache Web site. The file, which is in UNIX tar format and is compressed using GNU Zip, is available with a .tar.gz or a .tgz extension. You can download the Apache source code by going to http://www.apache.org/dist/httpd/. Be sure to download the latest version of Apache. Figure 3.2 shows the Web page from which you can download the source code.

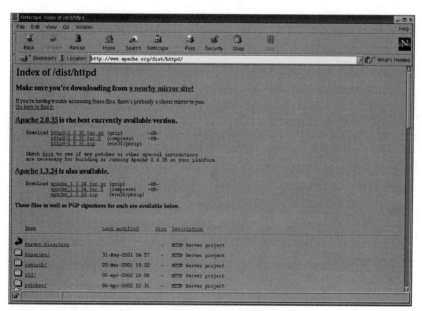

FIGURE 3.2 *The Web page that displays source code distributions*

Unpack the Apache Source Code

After you download the source code, you unpack it. On a Linux system, the source code is commonly kept in the /usr/local/src directory. Therefore, it is preferable to unpack the source code to this directory. After moving to this directory, type the following command:

```
#tar zxvf apache_1.3.24.tar.gz
apache_1.3.24/
apache_1.3.24/cgi-bin/
apache_1.3.24/cgi-bin/printenv
apache_1.3.24/cgi-bin/test-cgi
apache_1.3.24/ABOUT_APACHE
apache_1.3.24/Announcement
apache_1.3.24/INSTALL
apache_1.3.24/LICENSE
apache_1.3.24/Makefile.tmpl
apache_1.3.24/README
apache_1.3.24/README-WIN.TXT
apache_1.3.24/README.configure
apache_1.3.24/WARNING-WIN.TXT
apache_1.3.24/config.layout
apache_1.3.24/configure
apache_1.3.24/conf/
apache_1.3.24/conf/access.conf-dist
...many more files extracted
```

After you type this command, all the compressed files are extracted. The main, top-level directory for the Apache source code is /usr/local/src/apache_1.3.24. You need to access this directory every time you make changes in the source code to customize the Apache installation.

 NOTE

Keep in mind that this directory consists of the Apache source code and is not the installation directory. The installation directory is where Apache is installed. This is the directory from which you run Apache.

Adding a Default Group and a User

By default, in Linux (Red Hat Linux 7.2), the Apache server is run by a user named apache. However, you can configure Apache so that a user other than apache is used. I prefer the user www, though choosing the username depends on the discretion of the Web server administrator. For versions of Red Hat earlier than 7.0, the default user for the Apache service was nobody. However, the user nobody was the default user for many other services. Therefore, it was advisable to create a separate user exclusively for Apache. Follow these steps to add a default group and a user for Apache:

```
#groupadd www
//This command will add a group named www.
#useradd -g www www
//This command will add a user named www to the group named www.
```

TIP

After creating the user account, use the passwd command with the -1 option to lock the www user account. This will ensure maximum security because this user account will then be available only to the root user.

Use the configure Script

Before you begin compiling Apache, you should be familiar with a file/script named *configure*. This file resides in the top-level Apache source directory. You do not use this file to compile Apache. However, this file is important because it identifies the system capability and locates required supporting files. The configure script is very useful for the following reasons:

◆ It doesn't allow you to install Apache if a problem exists.

◆ It provides instructions on how to solve the problems that are encountered.

◆ It identifies the best combination of options for the system on which you want to install Apache. The combination of options can differ from one operating system to another.

◆ It stores relevant information, such as the best possible install options in a file named Configuration.apaci. This file is located in the /usr/local/src/apache_1.3.24/src/ directory.

◆ It uses the make utility to create files that are necessary for compiling and installing Apache.

Several configuration options can be specified while using the configure script. If you choose to install Apache with the default options, you don't need to specify additional options. Web administrators prefer customizing the installation by specifying all possible options that will install Apache based on their requirements. Options can be specified to extend the functionality of Apache or even to override the default settings of Apache. Consider the following command that configures Apache:

```
#./configure --with-layout=RedHat
```

This is the basic way of compiling Apache. The `--with-layout=RedHat` argument can be used to specify that the files should be installed in the same locations that Red Hat Linux uses by default. This option is ideal for system administrators who want the files to be located in the default locations or for inexperienced users who have no idea what options should be specified while installing Apache. If you are into experimenting or if you have a clear understanding about what functionality you want from Apache, you may find the following command quite interesting:

```
#./configure --prefix=/usr/local/apache \
>--enable-module=most \
>--disable-module=auth_dbm \
>--enable-shared=max
```

This command looks complex, doesn't it? Believe me, when you are comfortable using Apache, you will prefer this command to the previous one. I will now consider each option specified in the preceding command in isolation.

The *--prefix=/usr/local/apache* Argument

You use this argument to specify the path where Apache should be installed on the file system. In this case, the path is specified as /usr/local/apache. This is the default directory where Apache is installed. However, you can specify an alternate path in this argument.

You might have several reasons for installing Apache in a directory other than the default directory. One reason might be your intention to preserve the default locations used by a specific Linux distribution. In addition, some people install several versions of Apache for testing purposes and, as a result, install different versions of Apache in different locations.

The *--enable-module=most* Argument

This argument specifies that all modules included in the standard distribution of Apache and supported by all platforms should be enabled. However, using this argument omits certain modules that are not supported by all platforms. It is advisable to use the `--enable-module=most` argument and exclusively specify the additional modules that you want to install.

TIP

Rather than specifying `--enable-module=most.`, you can specify the `--enable-module=all` argument. You can use this argument to enable all modules included in the standard distribution.

The *--enable-shared=max* Argument

You use this argument to specify that Dynamic Shared Objects (DSO) are to be used while compiling the modules. All modules except the `http_core` module and the `mod_so` module are compiled using DSO. These modules should be statically linked to Apache, exclusively. This is important because the function of the `http_core` module is to provide core directives for managing the Apache server. The `mod_so` module is used to enable the server to use DSO modules.

DSO support was built into Apache with version 1.3. DSO allows modules to be enabled or disabled during runtime without the need to relink the Apache kernel. This is particularly useful because disabling the modules results in reducing the size of the Apache executable file. You can, therefore, easily run multiple instances of Apache at a given time using limited memory.

Observing the configure *Options*

There are so many configure options that it is practically impossible to remember all of them by heart. The best practice is to always view the help file for the configure script. This helps you choose your favorite options while compiling. After you extract the necessary files, you can move to the /usr/local/src/apache_1.3.24/ directory and type the following command:

```
#./configure --help
```

This command will display all the available options with a brief description of each option. The output of this command appears as shown here:

```
[hang on a moment, generating help]

Usage: configure [options]
Options: [defaults in brackets after descriptions]
General options:
  --quiet, --silent      do not print messages
  --verbose, -v          print even more messages
  --shadow[=DIR]         switch to a shadow tree (under DIR) for building
```

```
Stand-alone options:
  --help, -h             print this message
  --show-layout          print installation path layout (check and debug)

Installation layout options:
  --with-layout=[F:]ID   use installation path layout ID (from file F)
  --target=TARGET        install name-associated files using basename
TARGET
  --prefix=PREFIX        install architecture-independent files in PREFIX
  --exec-prefix=EPREFIX  install architecture-dependent files in EPREFIX
  --bindir=DIR           install user     executables in DIR
  --sbindir=DIR          install sysadmin executables in DIR
  --libexecdir=DIR       install program  executables in DIR
  --mandir=DIR           install manual pages in DIR
  --sysconfdir=DIR       install configuration files in DIR
  --datadir=DIR          install read-only data files in DIR
  --iconsdir=DIR         install read-only icon files in DIR
  --htdocsdir=DIR        install read-only welcome pages in DIR
  --manualdir=DIR        install read-only on-line documentation in DIR
  --cgidir=DIR           install read-only cgi files in DIR
  --includedir=DIR       install includes files in DIR
  --localstatedir=DIR    install modifiable data files in DIR
  --runtimedir=DIR       install runtime data in DIR
  --logfiledir=DIR       install logfile data in DIR
  --proxycachedir=DIR    install proxy cache data in DIR

Configuration options:
  --enable-rule=NAME     enable  a particular Rule named 'NAME'
  --disable-rule=NAME    disable a particular Rule named 'NAME'
                         [CYGWIN_WINSOCK=no DEV_RANDOM=default EXPAT=defa]
                         [IRIXN32=yes     IRIXNIS=no       PARANOID=no    ]
                         [SHARED_CHAIN=default SHARED_CORE=default SOCKS4]
                         [SOCKS5=no        WANTHSREGEX=default            ]
  --add-module=FILE      on-the-fly copy & activate a 3rd-party Module
  --activate-module=FILE on-the-fly activate existing 3rd-party Module
  --permute-module=N1:N2 on-the-fly permute module 'N1' with module 'N2'
  --enable-module=NAME   enable  a particular Module named 'NAME'
```

```
  --disable-module=NAME   disable a particular Module named 'NAME'
                          [access=yes      actions=yes     alias=yes       ]
                          [asis=yes        auth_anon=no    auth_dbm=no     ]
                          [auth_db=no      auth_digest=no  auth=yes        ]
                          [autoindex=yes   cern_meta=no    cgi=yes         ]
                          [digest=no       dir=yes         env=yes         ]
                          [example=no      expires=no      headers=no      ]
                          [imap=yes        include=yes     info=no         ]
                          [log_agent=no    log_config=yes  log_referer=no  ]
                          [mime_magic=no   mime=yes        mmap_static=no  ]
                          [negotiation=yes proxy=no        rewrite=no      ]
                          [setenvif=yes    so=no           speling=no      ]
                          [status=yes      unique_id=no    userdir=yes     ]
                          [usertrack=no    vhost_alias=no                  ]
  --enable-shared=NAME    enable  build of Module named 'NAME' as a DSO
  --disable-shared=NAME   disable build of Module named 'NAME' as a DSO
  --with-perl=FILE        path to the optional Perl interpreter
  --with-port=PORT        set the port number for httpd.conf
  --without-support       disable the build and installation of support tools
  --without-confadjust    disable the user/situation adjustments in config
  --without-execstrip     disable the stripping of executables on installation
  --server-uid=UID        set the user ID the web server should run as [nobody]
  --server-gid=GID        set the group ID the web server UID is a memeber of [#-1]


suEXEC options:
  --enable-suexec         enable the suEXEC feature
  --suexec-caller=NAME    set the suEXEC username of the allowed caller [www]
  --suexec-docroot=DIR    set the suEXEC root directory [PREFIX/share/htdocs]
  --suexec-logfile=FILE   set the suEXEC logfile [PREFIX/var/log/suexec_log]
  --suexec-userdir=DIR    set the suEXEC user subdirectory [public_html]
  --suexec-uidmin=UID     set the suEXEC minimal allowed UID [100]
  --suexec-gidmin=GID     set the suEXEC minimal allowed GID [100]
  --suexec-safepath=PATH  set the suEXEC safe PATH [/usr/local/bin:/usr/bin:/bin]
  --suexec-umask=UMASK    set the umask for the suEXEC'd script [server's umask]


Deprecated options:
  --layout                backward compat only: use --show-layout
  --compat                backward compat only: use --with-layout=Apache
```

As you can see, the help file categorizes the compile options into six categories, namely General options, Stand-alone options, Installation layout options, Configuration options, suEXEC options, and Deprecated options.

Sample Use of the configure Script

By now you must be familiar with a lot of configure options. However, each Web server administrator operates under different circumstances and is influenced by different perceptions. To me, the following command has proven to be the most helpful:

```
#./configure --prefix=/usr/local/apache \
>--server-uid=www \
>--server-gid=www \
>--htdocsdir=/opt/web/html \
>--cgidir=/opt/web/cgi-bin \
>--enable-module=most \
>--enable-shared=max
```

Now, review the additional options that I specified:

◆ The `--server-uid=www` option indicates that the Apache server will run as the user ID `www`. Remember that you created a user named `www`.

◆ The `--server-gid=www` option indicates that the Apache server will run with the group ID `www`.

◆ The `--htdocsdir` option indicates that the default Web site files will be located in the /opt/web/html directory. This is an optional argument.

◆ The `--cgidir=/opt/web/cgi-bin` option indicates that the default CGI files will be located in the /opt/web/cgi-bin directory.

The output of the preceding command appears as shown here:

```
Configuring for Apache, Version 1.3.24
 + using installation path layout: Apache (config.layout)
Creating Makefile
Creating Configuration.apaci in src
 + enabling mod_so for DSO support
Creating Makefile in src
 + configured for Linux platform
 + setting C compiler to gcc
 + setting C pre-processor to gcc -E
 + checking for system header files
```

```
+ adding selected modules
    o rewrite_module uses ConfigStart/End
+ using -lndbm for DBM support
        enabling DBM support for mod_rewrite
    o dbm_auth_module uses ConfigStart/End
+ using system Expat
+ using -ldl for vendor DSO support
+ checking sizeof various data types
+ doing sanity check on compiler and options
Creating Makefile in src/support
Creating Makefile in src/regex
Creating Makefile in src/os/unix
Creating Makefile in src/ap
Creating Makefile in src/main
Creating Makefile in src/modules/standard
Creating Makefile in src/modules/proxy
```

Now you are ready to compile the Apache source. The configure script has laid down the instructions for the compiler. The compiler will use these instructions to compile the source code. After running the configure script, a set of makefiles is generated. These makefiles are used by the make utility to do the following:

◆ Compile the source files.

◆ Link the source files to function libraries.

◆ Install the source files in appropriate locations.

You should be familiar with two more important files, config.status and config.layout. These files contain certain essential information that assists in the compilation process. Now examine each of these files in detail before compiling the source.

The config.status *File*

After you use the configure script, Apache is ready to be compiled. A set of files assists Apache during the compilation process. One such file is the config.status file. This file is created automatically when you run the configure script. However, if this file exists, it is overwritten when you specify the ./configure command.

The config.status file is an executable file that contains the last command that you used to run the configure script. The contents may vary based on how you used the configure script. This script can be executed for restoring your configuration. If you used a ./configure command similar to the one I used, the contents of this file will be somewhat like what's shown on the next page.

```
#!/bin/sh
##
##   config.status -- APACI auto-generated configuration restore script
##
##   Use this shell script to re-run the APACI configure script for
##   restoring your configuration. Additional parameters can be supplied.
##

./configure \
"--with-layout=Apache" \
"--prefix=/usr/local/apache" \
"--server-uid=www" \
"--server-gid=www" \
"--htdocsdir=/opt/web/html" \
"--cgidir=/opt/web/cgi-bin" \
"--enable-module=most" \
"--enable-shared=max" \
"$@"
```

As you can see, all the options specified with `./configure` appear in this file.

The config.layout *File*

The config.layout file is another important configuration file. This file contains information that Apache uses to locate final installation paths for files at the time of compilation. During compilation, several files need to be installed in several distinct locations. The information regarding these locations is also contained in this file in the form of *named layouts*. Named layouts are the default directory path specifications that are used by Apache during compilation to copy necessary files. The directory specifications are called named layouts because each entry is identified by a system name. The files are copied to certain default locations at the time of installation. These locations can be distinct for different systems.

When you run the configure script, Apache attempts to determine the operating system that you are using. A script named /src/helpers/GuessOS helps Apache determine the operating system. If Apache successfully determines the operating system, it uses the corresponding layout in the config.layout file to determine the correct path information. However, if Apache is unable to determine the operating system, the default layout is used. This is the Classical Apache path layout. The default paths specified in this layout are as follows:

```
#   Classical Apache path layout.
<Layout Apache>
    prefix:         /usr/local/apache
    exec_prefix:    $prefix
```

```
  bindir:         $exec_prefix/bin
  sbindir:        $exec_prefix/bin
  libexecdir:     $exec_prefix/libexec
  mandir:         $prefix/man
  sysconfdir:     $prefix/conf
  datadir:        $prefix
  iconsdir:       $datadir/icons
  htdocsdir:      $datadir/htdocs
  manualdir:      $htdocsdir/manual
  cgidir:         $datadir/cgi-bin
  includedir:     $prefix/include
  localstatedir:  $prefix
  runtimedir:     $localstatedir/logs
  logfiledir:     $localstatedir/logs
  proxycachedir:  $localstatedir/proxy
</Layout>
```

As is evident from the contents of the config.layout file, all the entries in this file are directory paths. Certain path names are defined based on path names defined earlier in this file. Notice that all the listed paths are derived from the one defined as prefix. Therefore, you can use the --prefix option to change the default paths for the Apache installation. Always look at the layout that will be used by the configure script while compiling Apache. You can view the layout by typing the following command:

```
#./configure --show-layout
```

The output of the command appears as shown here:

```
Configuring for Apache, Version 1.3.24
 + using installation path layout: Apache (config.layout)


Installation paths:
            prefix: /usr/local/apache
       exec_prefix: /usr/local/apache
            bindir: /usr/local/apache/bin
           sbindir: /usr/local/apache/bin
        libexecdir: /usr/local/apache/libexec
            mandir: /usr/local/apache/man
        sysconfdir: /usr/local/apache/conf
           datadir: /usr/local/apache
          iconsdir: /usr/local/apache/icons
```

```
       htdocsdir: /opt/web/html
      manualdir: /opt/web/html/manual
        cgidir: /opt/web/cgi-bin
     includedir: /usr/local/apache/include
   localstatedir: /usr/local/apache
      runtimedir: /usr/local/apache/logs
      logfiledir: /usr/local/apache/logs
    proxycachedir: /usr/local/apache/proxy


Compilation paths:
         HTTPD_ROOT: /usr/local/apache
     SHARED_CORE_DIR: /usr/local/apache/libexec
      DEFAULT_PIDLOG: logs/httpd.pid
   DEFAULT_SCOREBOARD: logs/httpd.scoreboard
    DEFAULT_LOCKFILE: logs/httpd.lock
     DEFAULT_XFERLOG: logs/access_log
    DEFAULT_ERRORLOG: logs/error_log
    TYPES_CONFIG_FILE: conf/mime.types
   SERVER_CONFIG_FILE: conf/httpd.conf
   ACCESS_CONFIG_FILE: conf/access.conf
  RESOURCE_CONFIG_FILE: conf/srm.conf
```

As you can see, this command displays all the locations that will be used to store Apache-related files after compilation. This command is a convenient way to have a quick look at the locations where necessary files will be copied.

Using the make Utility

You use the make utility to determine pieces of a large program that need to be recompiled. After locating these pieces of program, the make utility issues the essential commands required to recompile the chunks of code. The make utility is a launch pad to the actual compilation phase of Apache installation. Simply type **make** at the console to begin as shown:

```
#make
===> src
make[1]: Entering directory `/usr/local/src/apache_1.3.24'
make[2]: Entering directory `/usr/local/src/apache_1.3.24/src'
===> src/regex
sh ./mkh  -p regcomp.c >regcomp.ih
gcc -I.  -I../os/unix -I../include   -DLINUX=22 -I/usr/include/db1 -
```

```
DUSE_HSREGEX `../apaci` -DPOSIX_MISTAKE   -c -o regcomp.o regcomp.c
sh ./mkh  -p engine.c >engine.ih
gcc -I.  -I../os/unix -I../include  -DLINUX=22 -I/usr/include/db1 -DUSE_
HSREGEX `../apaci` -DPOSIX_MISTAKE  -c -o regexec.o regexec.c
gcc -I.  -I../os/unix -I../include  -DLINUX=22 -I/usr/include/db1 -DUSE_
HSREGEX `../apaci` -DPOSIX_MISTAKE  -c -o regerror.o regerror.c
gcc -I.  -I../os/unix -I../include  -DLINUX=22 -I/usr/include/db1 -DUSE_
HSREGEX `../apaci` -DPOSIX_MISTAKE  -c -o regfree.o regfree.c
…..numerous deleted lines
```

Taking Preinstall Precautions

After you use the `make` command to compile, you will need to call it again to complete the installation. However, you need to do a few things before you finally install the new version of Apache. If you have been using an older version of Apache, you must immediately get rid of it. Before you do so, though, take the following precautions so that uninstalling the earlier version of Apache doesn't harm the prevailing system configuration:

1. Stop the `httpd` service. First, check whether the `httpd` service is running. This service is required for Apache to function. If the service is running, type the following command to stop this service:

    ```
    #service httpd stop
    Stopping httpd:                                        [ OK ]
    ```

2. Uninstall the preexisting version. After you stop the `httpd` service, you are in a safer position to uninstall the earlier version of Apache. You can do this using the following command:

    ```
    #rpm -e apache
    ```

 NOTE

> This command will uninstall the already existing version only if you had installed Apache using the binary RPM file. If you installed the earlier version of Apache using the source, this command will not work.

While executing this command, you may encounter an error message. This error message suggests that uninstalling Apache will break dependencies, which means that certain packages (modules) that the earlier installation was using will become unusable after you uninstall Apache. It is best to list each of these packages and uninstall each of them before uninstalling the earlier version of Apache or use the `--force` or `--nodeps` option while uninstalling.

Using the make install *Command*

Finally, now you can install Apache by using the make install command. This command will install Apache by moving the support files and binaries to the appropriate locations on the file system. These locations are default locations unless you have specified an alternate location. Most of the files are copied to the Apache root directory that you specified with the --prefix argument. I used the directory /usr/local/apache with the --prefix argument.

Type the following command to complete the installation:

```
#make install
make[1]: Entering directory `/usr/local/src/apache_1.3.24'
===> [mktree: Creating Apache installation tree]
./src/helpers/mkdir.sh /usr/local/apache/bin
mkdir /usr/local/apache
mkdir /usr/local/apache/bin
./src/helpers/mkdir.sh /usr/local/apache/bin
./src/helpers/mkdir.sh /usr/local/apache/libexec
mkdir /usr/local/apache/libexec
./src/helpers/mkdir.sh /usr/local/apache/man/man1


…..numerous deleted lines
+-----------------------------------------------------+
| You now have successfully built and installed the   |
| Apache 1.3 HTTP server. To verify that Apache actually |
| works correctly you now should first check the      |
| (initially created or preserved) configuration files |
|                                                     |
|    /usr/local/apache/conf/httpd.conf                |
|                                                     |
| and then you should be able to immediately fire up  |
| Apache the first time by running:                   |
|                                                     |
|    /usr/local/apache/bin/apachectl start            |
|                                                     |
| Thanks for using Apache.       The Apache Group     |
|                                http://www.apache.org/ |
```

After you execute the command, the screen is filled with numerous lines indicating that the installation is in progress. After the installation is complete, you will see a message like the preceding one. This message indicates that Apache was successfully built and installed.

Creating Symbolic Links

This section helps you create useful *symbolic links*. This part of the installation is purely optional. However, I like to create certain symbolic links that make it easier to work with Apache. Creating a symbolic link for the contents of /usr/local/apache/bin directory to /usr/local/bin does wonders. The /usr/local/apache/bin directory contains certain commands. You can use these commands after you create a symbolic link of this directory to the /usr/local/bin directory that contains other executable commands. To create a symbolic link, type the following command:

```
#ln -s /usr/local/apache/bin/* /usr/local/bin
```

TIP

If you don't create the symbolic link, you can still use the commands in the /usr/local/apache/bin directory by specifying the complete path for the command. For example, to execute the `apachectl` command to start the Apache server, you need to specify the complete path, `/usr/local/apache/bin/apachectl start`. Your work becomes easier when you create the symbolic link because then you can use the `apachectl` command without specifying the complete path. After creating the symbolic link, you can start Apache directly by specifying the command `apachectl start`. I discuss this command in the next section.

Using the apachectl *Command*

The `apachectl` command is an important command that you can use to administer the Apache Web server. However, to use this command, you may want to create the symbolic link that I created in the previous section. To view the options that can be used with this command, type the following command at the console:

```
#apachectl --help
usage: /usr/local/bin/apachectl (start|stop|restart|fullstatus|status|
graceful|configtest|help)


start      - start httpd
stop       - stop httpd
restart    - restart httpd if running by sending a SIGHUP or start if not running
fullstatus - dump a full status screen; requires lynx and mod_status enabled
status     - dump a short status screen; requires lynx and mod_status enabled
graceful   - do a graceful restart by sending a SIGUSR1 or start if not running
configtest - do a configuration syntax test
help       - this screen
```

You can perform a syntax check for the Apache configuration using the `configtest` option with the `apachectl` command. The `configtest` option helps an Apache administrator check the syntax of the configuration file every time it is edited. The use of this option is as follows:

```
#apachectl configtest
Syntax OK
```

If you see the message `Syntax OK` after typing the preceding command, you can be assured that you have done everything correctly.

Now you are ready to start Apache. To do so, type the following command at the console:

```
#apachectl start
/usr/local/bin/apachectl start: httpd started
```

When executed, the preceding command starts the `httpd` service.

TIP

If the `httpd` service is already running, using the `restart` option with the `apachectl` command will restart the `httpd` service.

Testing the Installation

Installation is not complete until you test it. You can test your Apache installation in a variety of ways. I test the installation in two ways. First, I check the installation by using the lynx text browser. Second, I test the installation by connecting from a remote client computer.

Connecting Using *lynx*

To test the installation by using `lynx`, type the following command:

```
#lynx hostname/IP_address
```

This is the output that I received when I tested the installation using `lynx`:

```
  Test Page for Apache Installation


  If you can see this, it means that the installation of the Apache web
server software on this system was successful.
  You may now add content to this directory and replace this page.
```

```
              Seeing this instead of the website you expected?

    This  page  is  here because the site administrator has changed the
configuration of this web server. Please contact
    the  person  responsible for maintaining this server with questions.
The Apache Software Foundation, which wrote the
    web  server  software this site administrator is using, has nothing to
do with maintaining this site and cannot help
    resolve configuration issues.
```

```
    The Apache documentation has been included with this distribution.

    You are free to use the image below on an Apache-powered web server.
Thanks for using Apache!
```

Connecting from a Remote Client

It is ideal to check the installation from a remote client on the same network to be doubly sure of the installation. Type the following URL on the Address bar of the browser window:

```
http://ip_adress_of_remote_host
```

 NOTE

In addition to checking the installation on Linux, in this case I used a Windows client to test the installation of Apache.

Figure 3.3 illustrates the page that appeared when I connected to the Linux computer with the IP address 172.17.68.130.

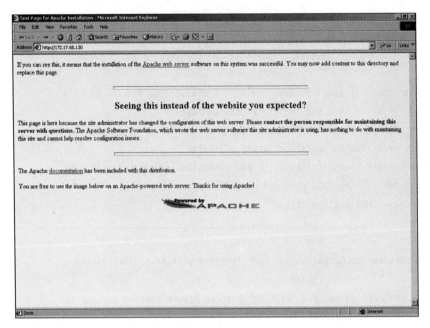

FIGURE 3.3 *Testing Apache installation from a remote Windows client*

Installing Apache on Windows

In the previous sections, I discussed the installation of Apache on Red Hat Linux systems. This section focuses on installing Apache on Windows 2000. I am using the binary distribution of Apache for Windows to install Apache. As discussed earlier, the Apache distribution for Windows is available as a .msi file. This file can be obtained from the official Web site of Apache. The steps for installing Apache on Windows 2000 are as follows:

1. Obtain Apache for Windows. The Apache binary file, apache_1.3.24-win32-x86-src.msi for Windows, can be downloaded from http://www.apache.org/dist/httpd/binaries/win32/. Just double-click the installation file to begin the installation.

2. Double-click the installation file. The HTTP Server – Installation Wizard is initiated, and a Welcome screen appears. Figure 3.4 shows the Welcome screen.

3. Click Next to proceed. The License Agreement screen appears. In this screen, select the "I accept the terms in the license agreement" option. Figure 3.5 shows the License Agreement screen.

4. Click Next to proceed. A screen appears containing help regarding the things you need to remember while installing Apache on Windows. Be sure to read this information before proceeding. Figure 3.6 shows the Read This First screen.

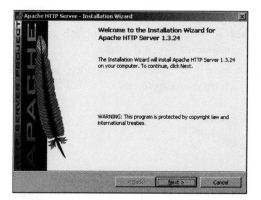

FIGURE 3.4 *The Welcome screen*

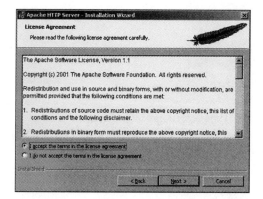

FIGURE 3.5 *The License Agreement screen*

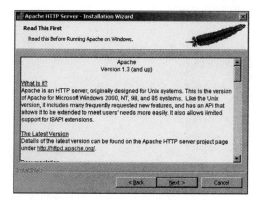

FIGURE 3.6 *The Read This First screen*

5. Click Next after you read the information on the Read This First screen. The Server Information screen appears. In this screen, you specify details such as the Network Domain, Server Name, and Administrator's Email Address.

6. Ensure that the "Run as a service for All Users -- Recommended" option is selected. Figure 3.7 illustrates the Server Information screen.

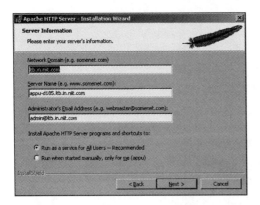

FIGURE 3.7 *The Server Information screen*

7. Click Next to proceed. The Setup Type screen appears. Select the Complete option to install all the default components of Apache. To undergo customized installation, you need to use the Custom option. This option allows you to install only the packages that you require. Figure 3.8 illustrates the Setup Type screen.

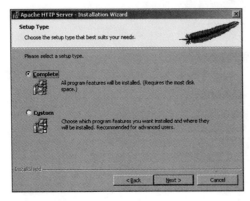

FIGURE 3.8 *The Setup Type screen*

8. Click Next to proceed. The Destination Folder screen appears. By default, Apache is installed in the C:\Program Files\Apache Group directory. However, you can click the Change button to specify an alternative location. Figure 3.9 shows the Destination Folder screen.

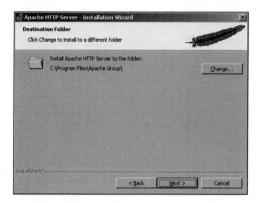

FIGURE 3.9 *The Destination Folder screen*

9. Click Next to proceed with the installation. The Ready to Install the Program screen appears. This screen prompts you to click the Install button to begin the installation. You cannot change any settings after clicking the Install button. Click the Back button if you want to change any of the installation settings specified earlier. Figure 3.10 illustrates the Ready to Install the Program screen.

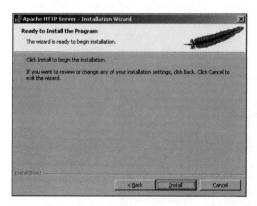

FIGURE 3.10 *The Ready to Install the Program screen*

10. Click the Install button to begin the installation. A progress bar appears indicating that the Apache installation has begun. Figure 3.11 displays the installation in progress.

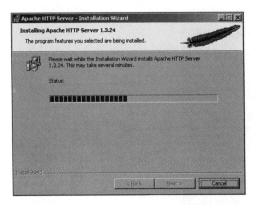

FIGURE 3.11 *The installation in progress screen*

11. After Apache is installed successfully, the Installation Wizard Completed screen appears. Click Finish to close this screen.

Starting Apache on Windows

You can start the Apache server on Windows 2000 by choosing Start, Apache HTTP Server, Control Apache Server, Start. This opens a command prompt window and starts the Apache server. After the Apache server starts, the window exits on its own. Figure 3.12 illustrates the window that appears when you start the Apache Web server.

FIGURE 3.12 *Starting Apache on Windows 2000*

NOTE

You can install the Apache Web server using the source code on Windows as well. However, explaining this is beyond the scope of this book because I am discussing the Apache Web server in relation to the Linux operating system.

Testing Apache on Windows

After you install and start the Apache Web server, you need to check whether the Apache Web server is working. You can do so by using Internet Explorer, the default Web browser of Windows 2000. To test whether Apache is working, type the following URL in the Internet Explorer Address box:

```
http://localhost
```

If you have installed Apache properly, you should see a window similar to the one that appears when you install Apache on Linux.

Summary

This chapter focused on the installation of the Apache Web server. First, I discussed the steps for installing the Apache RPM file on Red Hat Linux systems. Next, I talked about the steps for installing Apache on Linux by compiling the source code. Finally, I provided step-by-step directions for installing Apache on Windows 2000 Server.

Check Your Understanding

Multiple Choice Questions

1. For which of the following reasons will an experienced Apache administrator prefer to install Apache by using the source code rather than the RPM file? (Choose all that apply.)

   a. Ease of installation

   b. Ability to apply patches after installation

   c. Ability to customize the installation using install-time options

   d. Ability to install third-party modules using DSO support

2. Which of the following options is used with the configure script while installing Apache to specify the inclusion of all modules in the standard distribution of Apache that are supported by all platforms?

   a. `--enable-module=all`

   b. `--enable-module=most`

   c. `--enable-module=max`

   d. `--enable-module=NAME`

3. Which of the following `rpm` commands is used to install a new version of Apache when an older version is already running?

   a. `rpm -vh package_name`

   b. `rpm -Uvh package_name`

   c. `rpm -e package_name`

   d. `rpm -i package_name`

4. Which of the following scripts contains information that Apache uses to locate the final installation paths of files during compilation?

   a. configure

   b. GuessOS

   c. config.status

   d. config.layout

5. While installing Apache on Windows, which of the following screens is used to specify details such as the network domain, server name, and administrator's e-mail address?

   a. The Server Information screen

   b. The Setup Type screen

   c. The Destination Folder screen

   d. The Ready to Install the Program screen

Answers

Multiple Choice Answers

1. b, c, d. You can perform a customized installation, add third-party modules, and apply patches only when you install Apache using the source code.

2. b. Use the `--enable-module=most` option with the configure script while installing Apache to specify that all modules in the standard distribution of Apache that are supported by all platforms are to be enabled.

3. b. The `rpm -Uvh` command is used to install a newer version of Apache when an older version is already running.

4. d. The config.layout file contains information that Apache uses to locate files during compilation.

5. a. The Server Information screen is used to specify details such as the network domain, server name, and administrator's e-mail address.

Chapter 4

In the previous chapter, I discussed the steps for installing Apache Web server and helped you perform the installation on Linux and Windows platforms. I also discussed the steps to start Apache and test whether Apache is working.

After you install and test your Apache installation, you need to configure Apache in a customized way that best suits your requirements. Believe me, you can configure Apache numerous ways, and you can alter the Apache configuration to a great extent to ensure maximum performance and security. However, in this chapter, I merely acquaint you with the configurable options, because it is practically impossible to suggest the best solution for configuring Apache server. The way you choose to configure Apache is based entirely on the use and benefits you want to derive. I have tried to explain each configuration option so that it will be easy for you to decide which options should be configured and how.

First, I cover the Apache configuration that is specific to Red Hat Linux 7.2. You can configure the Apache server two ways. You can edit the Apache configuration file or use the GUI utility, Apacheconf, available with Red Hat Linux 7.2.

The Apache Configuration File

The Apache configuration file is httpd.conf. If you performed a Custom-Everything installation of Red Hat Linux 7.2, the Apache Web server is installed automatically. In this case, you can find the Apache configuration file in the /etc/httpd/conf/ directory. However, the location of this file can differ if you compile the source code of Apache and specify a separate location in the --prefix argument while installing.

TIP

If you followed the installation steps specified in the previous chapter, you will find the httpd.conf file in the /usr/local/apache/conf directory.

The httpd.conf file is a text file and has numerous options that can be configured by adding, commenting, uncommenting, and deleting the options in it. This file is based on the configuration files of the NCSA server that were originally developed by Rob McCool. It contains plenty of options and, at first sight, might appear complex to novice Web server administrators.

Editing the Apache configuration file is the most common method of configuring Apache server. However, this method is more popular among Web server administrators who have prior experience in UNIX/Linux Web server administration. If you are a novice user, you might initially find it difficult to understand the options specified in this file.

NOTE

If you are an inexperienced user, always make a backup of the original httpd.conf file before you begin making changes to it. When a configuration blunder occurs, you can always revert to the original file and use it. Doing so will help you avoid the hassle of reinstalling Apache if something goes wrong with the configuration and you are unable to set it correctly.

Directives

Before examining the options in this file, you need to be familiar with the concept of *directives*. The httpd.conf file uses directives to configure Apache. Directives follow a specific syntax that is similar to any programming language. However, directives can't be called commands and don't operate like programming languages. They can be referred to as *instructions* to the Apache server that help Apache behave in a particular manner and help it locate the resources to be used. It is important, though, to understand that directives don't directly control the actions of Apache. The purpose and use of Apache directives should be clear to every individual who takes up Apache Web server administration. As a matter of fact, only with experience do Apache administrators gain expertise in using these directives. The more hands-on experience you have with Apache, the better are your chances for "sharpening your saw" with it.

Directives can be broadly classified as *core directives* and *configuration directives supplied by add-on modules*. Before you begin examining the sections and options of the httpd.conf file, turn your attention to a brief discussion of these types of directives.

Core Directives

As the name suggests, core directives are the most important directives that Apache uses. These directives are always compiled in the Apache executable and are available by default. No special configuration is required for them. The core directives are essential for the proper functioning of Apache Web server.

Directives Supplied by Add-On Modules

Earlier, I said that you could use numerous add-on modules with Apache. When you install these add-on modules, they make directives available to the Apache server. In other words, the Web server administrator can use these directives only when the corresponding add-on module is added. These directives are of no use until the add-on modules are enabled for use.

Layout of the httpd.conf File

Before beginning, you need to understand the layout of the httpd.conf file. The configuration directives in the httpd.conf file are grouped under three main sections. Each section contains directives that help you configure Apache. You will also see many comments that help you understand the configuration options in the httpd.conf file.

The sections make it convenient for the user to locate the configuration options while editing the httpd.conf file. Sometimes, experienced Web server administrators prefer maintaining different configuration files for each of these sections for their convenience. The three main sections are:

- ◆ The Global Environment section
- ◆ The Main server configuration section
- ◆ The Virtual Hosts section

The Global Environment Section

This section contains those directives that globally affect the functioning of the Apache Web server. These directives are essential for the overall operation of Apache. The directives in this section determine how the Apache server processes will be controlled.

The Main Server Configuration Section

The Main server is the default Apache Web server. The Main server configuration section consists of all directives that are used to define the parameters used by the main server. It is always more convenient to have a separate section for the main server configuration and the virtual host configuration. Therefore, the third section in the httpd.conf file is exclusively for configuring virtual hosts in Apache.

The Virtual Hosts Section

This section is dedicated to configuration pertaining to virtual hosts. All other hosts that you configure on your Apache server apart from the main server are virtual hosts. There are various advantages to using virtual hosts. One major benefit is the ability to host more than one Web site with separate domain names on a single Apache server.

Examining the Configuration Options

By now, you know how to examine the options of the httpd.conf file. In this section, I include extracts of the httpd.conf file and discuss the relevance and use of each option. By uncommenting or commenting on existing lines, you can handle most of the Apache configuration. However, most options work best if they are not altered.

TIP

I suggest that you open the httpd.conf file using the `vim` text editor. The `vim` text editor applies different colors to the lines in the httpd.conf file, depending on the nature of the lines. For example, the commented entries will have a different color than the uncommented configurable options. This way, you can easily identify the configuration options in the midst of hundreds of lines of text. To open the file using `vim`, specify the command `vim /usr/local/apache/conf/httpd.conf` at the console.

I divided the configurable options into three different sections, as shown in the following subsections.

Global Environment Configuration Options

As the name suggests, the Global Environment configuration options help you perform settings that will be used globally by Apache. I discuss the configuration options included in this section in the following subsections.

The *ServerType* Directive

You can configure the ServerType option with two modes, inetd or standalone. The inetd mode is used only when you install Apache on UNIX platforms. The following example illustrates the use of the ServerType directive:

```
# ServerType is either inetd, or standalone.  Inetd mode is only supported on
# Unix platforms.
#
ServerType standalone
```

Do not tamper with the ServerType option. The default value for this option is standalone. Notice that the fourth line of the extract, which is not commented, is the actual configurable option for which a value can be specified.

The *ServerRoot* Directive

You use the ServerRoot directive to specify the location where the following important files will be located:

- ◆ Configuration files
- ◆ Error files
- ◆ Log files

The location that you specify in the ServerRoot directive to store the configuration, error, or log files can be the local file system or a network file system (NFS). If you use a location on the local file system, you can simply specify the directory path in this directive:

```
# ServerRoot: The top of the directory tree under which the server's
# configuration, error, and log files are kept.
#
# NOTE!  If you intend to place this on an NFS (or otherwise network)
# mounted filesystem then please read the LockFile documentation
# (available at <URL:http://www.apache.org/docs/mod/core.html#lockfile>);
# you will save yourself a lot of trouble.
#
ServerRoot "/usr/local/apache"
```

Notice that the directory path specified is /usr/local/apache. This is because you performed a custom install of Apache in the previous chapter. If you are using the standard Apache install, the ServerRoot will be /etc/httpd. You should avoid tampering with the path specified in the ServerRoot directive unless you are very sure about what you want to do.

The *LockFile* Directive

You use the LockFile directive to specify the path for the *lockfile*. A LockFile directive is used when Apache is compiled using USE_FCNTL_SERIALIZED_ACCEPT or USE_FLOCK_SERIALIZED_ ACCEPT. You should leave the value of this directive as default. However, if the lockfile is located on an NFS mounted file system, the default path of the lockfile should be changed accordingly. The following example shows the use of the LockFile directive:

```
# The LockFile directive sets the path to the lockfile used when Apache
# is compiled with either USE_FCNTL_SERIALIZED_ACCEPT or
# USE_FLOCK_SERIALIZED_ACCEPT. This directive should normally be left at
# its default value. The main reason for changing it is if the logs
# directory is NFS mounted, since the lockfile MUST BE STORED ON A LOCAL
# DISK. The PID of the main server process is automatically appended to
# the filename.
#
#LockFile /usr/local/apache/logs/httpd.lock
```

As you can see, the path for the lockfile is set as /usr/local/apache/logs/httpd.lock. If you are using the standard installation of Apache, the path will ideally be /var/run/httpd.lock.

The *PidFile* Directive

Pid stands for *process identification number*. Whenever Apache starts, it is allocated a process ID. This Pid is stored in a file. The PidFile directive is used to specify the path for the file that stores the Pid of the Apache Web server.

 NOTE

Use this file only if you configured the value of the ServerType directive as standalone.

The following example shows the use of the PidFile directive:

```
# PidFile: The file in which the server should record its process
# identification number when it starts.
#
PidFile /usr/local/apache/logs/httpd.pid
```

As you can see, the path set for the Pid file is /usr/local/apache/logs/httpd.pid. If you are using the standard installation of Apache, the path should be /var/run/httpd.pid.

The *ScoreBoardFile* Directive

You use the ScoreBoardFile directive to specify the location for a file named httpd.scoreboard. You use this file to store information related to internal server processes. In other words, this file determines how the parent and child processes invoked by Apache will communicate with each other.

You do not need to configure the ScoreBoardFile directive for all architectures. To find out whether the architecture you are using requires the ScoreBoardFile directive to be configured, just start the Apache server and look for the file named httpd.scoreboard. If you find this file, your architecture requires that you configure the ScoreBoardFile directive by specifying the path for the httpd.scoreboard file. If you are using the ScoreBoardFile directive you should also ensure that no more than one instance of Apache is using this file at a given time. The following example illustrates the use of the ScoreBoardFile directive:

```
# ScoreBoardFile: File used to store internal server process information.
# Not all architectures require this.  But if yours does (you'll know because
# this file will be  created when you run Apache) then you *must* ensure that
# no two invocations of Apache share the same scoreboard file.
#
ScoreBoardFile /usr/local/apache/logs/httpd.scoreboard
```

As you can see, the path specified for the ScoreBoardFile directive is /usr/local/apache/logs/httpd.scoreboard. I installed Apache on Intel i386 architecture, and I couldn't find this file. Therefore, it is better not to alter the value specified for this directive.

The *ResourceConfig* and *AccessConfig* Directives

You use the ResourceConfig directive to store the path for the file srm.conf and the AccessConfig directive to store the path for the file access.conf. The files srm.conf and access.conf were used with versions of Apache prior to 1.3.4. Later, it was recommended to store all directives in a single file. So, for later versions of Apache, all the directives are stored in the file httpd.conf.

Although srm.conf and access.conf files are not required anymore, they are still a part of the Apache distribution. These files contain mere comments, and you can safely get rid of them. The best way to get rid of them is to replace these filenames with /dev/null in the respective directives. In Linux, the /dev/null directory is considered a black hole. Administrators generally get rid of temporary files by pointing them to the /dev/null directory. You can specify the value /dev/null for both ResourceConfig and AccessConfig directives.

Consider the following extract that shows the use of the ResourceConfig and AccessConfig directives:

```
# In the standard configuration, the server will process httpd.conf (this
# file, specified by the -f command line option), srm.conf, and access.conf
# in that order.  The latter two files are now distributed empty, as it is
# recommended that all directives be kept in a single file for simplicity.
# The commented-out values below are the built-in defaults.  You can have the
# server ignore these files altogether by using "/dev/null" (for Unix) or
# "nul" (for Win32) for the arguments to the directives.
#
#ResourceConfig conf/srm.conf
#AccessConfig conf/access.conf
```

As you can see, these directives are commented by default, so you don't want to tamper with the configuration. However, if you really want to specify a value in these directives, you can specify /dev/null.

NOTE

If you specify a directory as a value for these directives, the Apache Web server will parse all the files in the specified directory as if they are configuration files. To avoid loading all the stray files in the specified directory as configuration files, keep the specified directory empty.

The *Timeout* Directive

You use the Timeout directive to specify the time that Apache will wait before it sends a time-out message. The value specified in this directive holds good for three things:

◆ Time taken to receive a GET request
◆ Time taken to receive a POST or PUT request
◆ Time taken to send TCP packets as responses to a request

The following example shows the use of the Timeout directive:

```
# Timeout: The number of seconds before receives and sends time out.
#
Timeout 300
```

In versions of Apache earlier than 1.2, the default value set for this directive was 1200 seconds. That value is now 300 seconds, for reasons of security and performance.

The *KeepAlive* Directive

In Chapter 1, "Introduction to Web Servers," I wrote that HTTP /1.1 uses a mechanism called *persistent connections*. Persistent connections allow the client to establish multiple connections at a given time, resulting in faster download. You use the KeepAlive directive to specify whether Apache should use the persistent connections feature.

The following example shows the use of the KeepAlive directive:

```
# KeepAlive: Whether or not to allow persistent connections (more than
# one request per connection). Set to "Off" to deactivate.
#
KeepAlive On
```

By default, the value for the KeepAlive directive is set to On, which means that Apache will allow the use of persistent connections. However, if you don't want to use persistent connections, you can set the value to Off.

The *MaxKeepAliveRequests* Directive

If you enabled support for the KeepAlive directive, you might want to specify the maximum number of requests that should be allowed for each connection. You use the MaxKeepAlive-Requests directive to specify the number of maximum requests that can be sent to the server for each connection if persistent connections are enabled. You can assign a numeric value to this directive to specify the maximum number of allowed requests in a persistent connection. If the number 0 is specified, unlimited requests are allowed. If you are using persistent connections, you should set the value of this directive to a large number. The following example shows the use of the MaxKeepAliveRequests directive:

```
# MaxKeepAliveRequests: The maximum number of requests to allow
# during a persistent connection. Set to 0 to allow an unlimited amount.
# We recommend you leave this number high, for maximum performance.
#
MaxKeepAliveRequests 100
```

The default value for this directive is 100, which means that 100 requests will be allowed per connection. You can set this value to a higher number to improve performance.

Allowing keepalive connections uses up machine resources. Every operating system has a limit on the maximum number of simultaneous Transmission Control Protocol (TCP) connections it can allow. For high-traffic production servers, allowing keepalives means using these TCP connections. I recommend that you set the MaxKeepAliveRequests to a number that neither adversely affects the performance nor overloads the server. Consequently, the default value of 100 is recommended.

The *KeepAliveTimeout* Directive

You use the KeepAliveTimeout directive to specify the time at which Apache will close a keepalive connection if the client has not sent any more requests. The following example shows the use of the KeepAliveTimeout directive:

```
# KeepAliveTimeout: Number of seconds to wait for the next request from the
# same client on the same connection.
#
KeepAliveTimeout 15
```

By default, the value specified for this directive is 15 seconds, which means that after 15 seconds, Apache will close a keepalive connection if the client has not sent any more requests.

The *MinSpareServers* and *MaxSpareServers* Directives

You use the MinSpareServers and MaxSpareServers directives to specify the number of minimum servers and the number of maximum processes that are idle and waiting for requests at a given time. It is important to remember that the number specified in these directives does not determine the maximum number of clients that can connect to an Apache server at a given time. The spare servers parameter should be left unaltered unless the network traffic on your site is considerably high.

If less than the specified minimum number of servers is idle, the Apache server automatically creates child processes until it reaches the specified minimum limit.

On the other hand, the maximum limit is specified to keep a check on the number of child processes invoked. If the number of child processes exceeds the limit specified in the MaxSpareServers directive, the parent process automatically kills the excess processes. The following example shows the use of the MinSpareServers and the MaxSpareServers directives:

```
# Server-pool size regulation.  Rather than making you guess how many
# server processes you need, Apache dynamically adapts to the load it
# sees --- that is, it tries to maintain enough server processes to
# handle the current load, plus a few spare servers to handle transient
# load spikes (e.g., multiple simultaneous requests from a single
# Netscape browser).
#
# It does this by periodically checking how many servers are waiting
# for a request.  If there are fewer than MinSpareServers, it creates
# a new spare.  If there are more than MaxSpareServers, some of the
# spares die off.  The default values are probably OK for most sites.
#
MinSpareServers 5
MaxSpareServers 10
```

The default values for these directives are 5 for the MinSpareServers directive and 10 for the MaxSpareServers directive.

The *StartServers* Directive

The StartServers directive allows you to specify the number of child processes that should be created during startup. However, being an intelligent Web server, Apache takes into account the server load before deciding how many child processes should be running at a given time. So you might not need to edit the value specified in this directive, and may be able to safely leave the default option for this directive unaltered. The following example shows the use of the StartServers directive:

```
# Number of servers to start initially --- should be a reasonable ballpark
# figure.
#
StartServers 5
```

As you can see in the preceding extract, the default value assigned to the StartServers directive is 5, which means that five child processes will be automatically created at the start time. This directive has no effect on Windows platforms; therefore, you will not find it in the Apache configuration file if you installed Apache on Windows.

The *MaxClients* Directive

Consider an example of a busy site that expects a large number of simultaneous connections. Shouldn't there be a limit that specifies the maximum number of clients who can simultaneously connect to Apache so that the server is not overloaded? The MaxClients directive helps you specify the maximum number of clients that can connect simultaneously at a given time:

```
# Limit on total number of servers running, i.e., limit on the number
# of clients who can simultaneously connect --- if this limit is ever
# reached, clients will be LOCKED OUT, so it should NOT BE SET TOO LOW.
# It is intended mainly as a brake to keep a runaway server from taking
# the system with it as it spirals down...
#
MaxClients 150
```

Note that the default value set for this directive is 150. This implies that at any given time Apache will not handle more than 150 simultaneous connections. Whenever this limit is exceeded, no more connections from clients are entertained, and the clients are locked out. Be sure that you don't set a low value for this directive.

The *MaxRequestsPerChild* Directive

You use the MaxRequestsPerChild directive to specify the maximum number of requests that a child process handles before Apache terminates it and starts another process to take its place:

```
# MaxRequestsPerChild: the number of requests each child process is
# allowed to process before the child dies.  The child will exit so
# as to avoid problems after prolonged use when Apache (and maybe the
# libraries it uses) leak memory or other resources.  On most systems, this
# isn't really needed, but a few (such as Solaris) do have notable leaks
# in the libraries. For these platforms, set to something like 10000
# or so; a setting of 0 means unlimited.
#
# NOTE: This value does not include keepalive requests after the initial
#       request per connection. For example, if a child process handles
#       an initial request and 10 subsequent "keptalive" requests, it
#       would only count as 1 request towards this limit.
#
MaxRequestsPerChild 0
```

The default value set for this directive is 0, which means that a child process will never die.

The *Listen* Directive

The Listen directive is an important directive that can be configured for performance and security. You can configure it so that Apache listens to IP addresses and ports other than the default ones. You can specify the IP interface or a combination of the IP interface and port number.

If you specify only the port number, Apache will listen to all IP interfaces on the specified port number. On the other hand, if you specify a combination of the IP interface and the port number, Apache will listen to the IP interfaces only on the specified port number.

You can use the Listen directive to specify more than one IP interface and port. In this case, the server will respond to all the specified IP interfaces and ports:

```
# Listen: Allows you to bind Apache to specific IP addresses and/or
# ports, in addition to the default. See also the <VirtualHost>
# directive.
#
#Listen 3000
#Listen 12.34.56.78:80
```

The preceding extract shows that the Listen directive is commented. To use the Listen directive, you first need to uncomment the entries. You can use the Listen directive as an alternative to the BindAddress and Port directives that I discuss later in the chapter. However, it is still advisable to use the Port directive because Apache generates certain URLs that point to your server. These URLs work only when the Port directive is used.

Consider the following example in which the Listen directive uses just the port numbers. Notice that more than one port number is used:

```
Listen 80
Listen 8000
```

Consider another example in which multiple IP interfaces as well as port numbers are specified with the Listen directive:

```
Listen 172.17.68.131:80
Listen 172.17.68.181:8000
```

CAUTION

Be careful when specifying IP addresses in the Listen directive. The IP addresses you specify should be available on the server. If the specified IP address is not a valid IP address, Apache will not start and will abort with an error.

The *BindAddress* Directive

You use the BindAddress directive to specify the IP address on which Apache will listen. The BindAddress directive can contain any of these three values:

◆ *. This value directs Apache to listen to all IP addresses configured on the server machine. If you want to specify only one IP address, you must specify the IP address exclusively.

◆ **IP address.** An IP address that is used by the server can be specified. However, only one IP address can be specified if you want to specify an IP address.

◆ **Domain name.** A fully qualified domain name can be specified in the BindAddress directive. Doing so directs Apache to listen only to the Internet domain name specified. Unlike the Listen directive, only one BindAddress directive can be specified in the configuration file.

The following example shows the use of the BindAddress directive:

```
# BindAddress: You can support virtual hosts with this option. This directive
# is used to tell the server which IP address to listen to. It can either
```

```
# contain "*", an IP address, or a fully qualified Internet domain name.
# See also the <VirtualHost> and Listen directives.
#
#BindAddress *
```

By default, the value of BindAddress directive is set to *****. However, this directive is commented by default. The BindAddress directive is deprecated and will not be included in the forthcoming versions of Apache.

The *LoadModule* Directive

You use the LoadModule directive for each DSO that you use in your server. If you often add new modules to your Apache installation, the LoadModule is an important directive to check for. This directive consists of the module and the filename. The syntax for using this directive is as follows:

```
LoadModule sample_module modules/mod_sample.so
#sample is the name of a module
```

The LoadModule directive occupies a huge amount of space in the Apache configuration file. All the modules used by Apache must be specified with this directive.

When you build a module with DSO support, you must specify the module using the Load-Module directive. This indicates that the newly added modules are available for use. The following is a sample extract of the httpd.conf file that shows a few entries made to the LoadModule directive:

```
# Dynamic Shared Object (DSO) Support
#
# To be able to use the functionality of a module which was built as a DSO you
# have to place corresponding `LoadModule' lines at this location so the
# directives contained in it are actually available _before_ they are used.
# Please read the file http://httpd.apache.org/docs/dso.html for more
# details about the DSO mechanism and run `httpd -l' for the list of already
# built-in (statically linked and thus always available) modules in your httpd
# binary.
#
# Note: The order in which modules are loaded is important.  Don't change
# the order below without expert advice.
#
# Example:
# LoadModule foo_module libexec/mod_foo.so
```

```
LoadModule vhost_alias_module libexec/mod_vhost_alias.so
LoadModule env_module         libexec/mod_env.so
LoadModule config_log_module  libexec/mod_log_config.so
LoadModule mime_magic_module  libexec/mod_mime_magic.so
LoadModule mime_module        libexec/mod_mime.so
LoadModule negotiation_module libexec/mod_negotiation.so
LoadModule status_module      libexec/mod_status.so
LoadModule info_module        libexec/mod_info.so
LoadModule includes_module    libexec/mod_include.so
LoadModule autoindex_module   libexec/mod_autoindex.so
LoadModule dir_module         libexec/mod_dir.so
LoadModule cgi_module         libexec/mod_cgi.so
LoadModule asis_module        libexec/mod_asis.so
LoadModule imap_module        libexec/mod_imap.so
LoadModule action_module      libexec/mod_actions.so
LoadModule speling_module     libexec/mod_speling.so
......numerous deleted lines.......
```

The preceding extract shows that the LoadModule directive is used to specify the modules that need to be loaded.

Sometimes, you might even come across the <IfDefine> and </IfDefine> directives in this part of the httpd.conf file. The IfDefine directive is a conditional directive that checks for a condition. If the result of the condition is true, the IfDefine section is processed. If the result of the condition is false, the text within <IfDefine> and </IfDefine> is simply ignored.

 NOTE

The main purpose of the IfDefine directive is to check whether a particular module is compiled with Apache. If the module has been compiled, an attempt is made to load these modules. It is a safe configuration practice to use the IfDefine directive. However, if you are sure about the modules that are compiled, you can do away with these directives.

The *ClearModuleList* Directive

Apache is installed with a built-in list of active modules. The ClearModuleList directive is used to clear this list. This directive acts like a precursor to the AddModule directive, which repopulates the list of modules.

The *AddModule* Directive

As just mentioned, you use the AddModule directive to repopulate the list of modules. Any module specified in the LoadModule section should also have a corresponding AddModule entry. The following example shows the use of the AddModule directive:

```
#  Reconstruction of the complete module list from all available modules
#  (static and shared ones) to achieve correct module execution order.
#  [WHENEVER YOU CHANGE THE LOADMODULE SECTION ABOVE UPDATE THIS, TOO]
ClearModuleList
AddModule mod_vhost_alias.c
AddModule mod_env.c
AddModule mod_log_config.c
AddModule mod_mime_magic.c
AddModule mod_mime.c
AddModule mod_negotiation.c
AddModule mod_status.c
AddModule mod_info.c
AddModule mod_include.c
AddModule mod_autoindex.c
AddModule mod_dir.c
AddModule mod_cgi.c
AddModule mod_asis.c
AddModule mod_imap.c
AddModule mod_actions.c
AddModule mod_speling.c
…..numerous deleted lines…..
```

The preceding is a small extract of AddModule entries. Though not specified in this extract, the IfDefine directive can also be used with the AddModule directives.

 NOTE

For Apache Web server administration, it is important to know that the order of specifying the modules is significant. You cannot make an AddModule entry just anywhere. Apache follows a sequence while loading the modules. If the sequence is not correct, the modules might not be loaded properly. In addition, you need to ensure that the order of modules specified in the LoadModule section is similar to the order of modules specified in the AddModule section.

The *ExtendedStatus* Directive

You use this directive to specify whether the extended status information for each request should be tracked. Configuring this directive is useful if you have already enabled the status module in the server. The following example shows the use of the ExtendedStatus directive:

```
# ExtendedStatus controls whether Apache will generate "full" status
# information (ExtendedStatus On) or just basic information (ExtendedStatus
# Off) when the "server-status" handler is called. The default is Off.
#
#ExtendedStatus On
```

Notice in the preceding extract that the default value for this directive is On. However, by default, the entry is commented. Another thing worth mentioning about this directive is that it is applicable to the entire Web server. In other words, this setting will affect the Web server as a whole and cannot be configured exclusively for each virtual host.

Main Server Configuration Options

As discussed earlier, the main server configuration section contains directives that are used to handle all requests except the ones handled by virtual hosts. The main server configuration section contains several configurable options.

The *Port* Directive

You use the Port directive to specify the port number on which Apache will listen to requests. By default, the port used by HTTP is 80. Therefore, the default value assigned to the Port directive is 80. The following example shows the use of the Port directive:

```
# Port: The port to which the standalone server listens. For
# ports < 1023, you will need httpd to be run as root initially.
#
Port 80
```

Though the default port used by Apache is 80, there is no hard and fast rule that the port number assigned to the Port directive can only be 80. The administrator has the option of choosing any port number from 0 to 65535. However, if you don't want to use 80 as the port number, don't specify a port number lower than 1024 because port numbers below 1024 are reserved for certain specific protocols. You can view the port allocation in the /etc/services file in a Red Hat Linux system. Keep the following points in mind while configuring the Port directive:

◆ The server listens to the port number specified in the Port directive (in Main server configuration) only when a port number is not specified in the Listen or BindAddress directives.

◆ You use the Port directive to set the environment variable named SERVER_PORT. This environment variable is used for Common Gateway Interface (CGI) and Server Side Includes (SSI).

◆ Only the root account can start the port 80. However, running Apache as a root service can make the system vulnerable to security threats. Therefore, after binding to the port, Apache service is run by a low-privileged user before accepting any requests from the client.

◆ If you decide not to use the port number 80, the port number should be greater than 1024 for non-root users. The port number generally assigned for non-root users is 8000.

◆ Sometimes, you might want to use SSL for secure transmission of data. To do so, you need to explicitly specify the port number that will be used by Secure HyperText Transfer Protocol (HTTPS). This port number is ideally 443 and is specified with the Listen directive as shown here:

```
##  When we also provide SSL we have to listen to the
##  standard HTTP port (see above) and to the HTTPS port
##
<IfDefine HAVE_SSL>
Listen 80
Listen 443
</IfDefine>
```

Notice that the <IfDefine> and </IfDefine> directives check whether SSL support is required.

 TIP

Port 80 is an Internet Assigned Numbers Authority (IANA) specified port that is reserved for the Web. By default, all Web servers and browsers try to connect to this port, so use port 80 for HTTP transactions.

The *User* and *Group* Directives

These are important directives whose purposes should be clear to a Web server administrator. In the previous chapter when you installed Apache, you created a group (www) and a new user (www) as part of this group. Then you compiled Apache utilizing user www and group www. You use the User and Group directives to store the default user information that runs Apache. Initially, the root user starts Apache. Later, it is run by a user with low privileges. This is particularly useful for security because running a service with root privileges might create a threat to the system.

The following example shows the use of the User and Group directives:

```
# If you wish httpd to run as a different user or group, you must run
# httpd as root initially and it will switch.
#
# User/Group: The name (or #number) of the user/group to run httpd as.
#   . On SCO (ODT 3) use "User nouser" and "Group nogroup".
#   . On HPUX you may not be able to use shared memory as nobody, and the
#     suggested workaround is to create a user www and use that user.
#   NOTE that some kernels refuse to setgid(Group) or semctl(IPC_SET)
#   when the value of (unsigned)Group is above 60000;
#   don't use Group www on these systems!
#
User www
Group www
```

In the preceding extract, the user and group is www , because while installing Apache, you specified the user and group for Apache as www. By default, the user and group for Apache is apache (in Red Hat Linux 7.2).

The *ServerAdmin* Directive

You use the ServerAdmin directive to specify an e-mail address. This e-mail address appears in certain Web pages that are generated by the server. For example, the error documents that appear contain this e-mail address.

This e-mail address is the server administrator's e-mail address, which can be used to contact the server administrator in case the client is facing a problem. The following example shows the use of the ServerAdmin directive:

```
# ServerAdmin: Your address, where problems with the server should be
# e-mailed.  This address appears on some server-generated pages, such
# as error documents.
#
ServerAdmin root@localhost.localdomain
```

By default, the e-mail address specified in this directive is root@localhost.localdomain. You should specify a dedicated e-mail address that can be associated with the server administrator. For example, admin@someserver.com is a valid e-mail address that belongs to the administrator of the Web server.

The *ServerName* Directive

As its name suggests, you use the ServerName directive to specify the name by which the server is identified. You use this name at the time you create redirection URLs. If you don't specify a server name at the time of installation, the value localhost is used by default. The value localhost implies that the Apache server is using the TCP/IP local loopback address, 127.0.0.1. You can use the value localhost if you are using Apache for testing or development purposes. The following example shows the use of the ServerName directive:

```
# ServerName allows you to set a host name which is sent back to clients for
# your server if it's different than the one the program would get (i.e., use
# "www" instead of the host's real name).
#
# Note: You cannot just invent host names and hope they work. The name you
# define here must be a valid DNS name for your host. If you don't understand
# this, ask your network administrator.
# If your host doesn't have a registered DNS name, enter its IP address here.
# You will have to access it by its address (e.g., http://123.45.67.89/)
# anyway, and this will make redirections work in a sensible way.
#
# 127.0.0.1 is the TCP/IP local loop-back address, often named localhost. Your
# machine always knows itself by this address. If you use Apache strictly for
# local testing and development, you may use 127.0.0.1 as the server name.
#
#ServerName localhost.localdomain
```

When specifying a domain name other than localhost, be careful which name you decide to specify. The domain name specified in the ServerName directive must be a valid, registered DNS name. Preferably, the domain name should have the following format:

```
servername.domainname
```

 NOTE

A valid DNS name is one that is registered on a local network (intranet) or on the Internet. If your local intranet is running a DNS server, you can specify the hostnames that are valid in the domain. However, the hosts on the intranet will not be accessible by hosts that are not a part of your intranet.

The *DocumentRoot* Directive

You use the DocumentRoot directive to specify the document root of a Web server. The document root is the location where all Web site-related content files are stored. For example, if you want to host an HTML site, you need to copy all site-related files in the document root directory. The example on the next page shows the use of the DocumentRoot directive.

```
# DocumentRoot: The directory out of which you will serve your
# documents. By default, all requests are taken from this directory, but
# symbolic links and aliases may be used to point to other locations.
#
DocumentRoot "/opt/web/html"
```

The default value assigned to the DocumentRoot directory is /var/www/html. However, you can specify an alternate location when you compile Apache as in the previous chapter. If you followed the installation steps presented in the previous chapter, the value assigned to the DocumentRoot directive is /opt/web/html. This is the directory in which all HTML files will be stored.

The *<Directory>* and *</Directory>* Directives: Configuration for the / (Root) Directory

The <Directory> and </Directory> directives are used to enclose other directives. These directives are applicable only to the directory specified in the <Directory> directive. The following example shows the use of the <Directory> and </Directory> directives:

```
# Each directory to which Apache has access, can be configured with respect
# to which services and features are allowed and/or disabled in that
# directory (and its subdirectories).
#
# First, we configure the "default" to be a very restrictive set of
# permissions.
#
<Directory />
    Options FollowSymLinks
    AllowOverride None
</Directory>
```

In this extract, notice that within the opening <Directory> tag, the directory / (root) is specified. The / directory is the topmost directory in the Linux file system. All directives specified in the <Directory> and </Directory> directives apply only to the /directory.

Within the <Directory> and </Directory> directives, two more directives named Options and AllowOverride are specified. You use the Options directive to specify the server features that will be available for the specified directory. When the Option directive is set using the FollowSymlinks value, it directs the server to follow the symbolic links in the specified directory.

You use the AllowOverride directive to specify which options specified in the .htaccess file can be overridden. You use the .htaccess file for specifying access rights and authentication services to users. Setting the value for the AllowOverride directive to None directs Apache to ignore all the .htaccess files.

TIP

For security reasons, be sure to have a `Directory` directive for the / (root) file system. Consider a situation in which a hacker with malicious intent causes the Web server to access the files located outside the document root directory. In such a situation, the permissions specified in the `Directory` directive for / (root) will apply. As a result, the hacker will be denied access to the files outside the document root directory.

The *<Directory>* and *</Directory>* Directives: Configuration for the Document Root Directory

You use the next portion of the httpd.conf file to configure the `<Directory>` directive for the document root directory:

```
# Note that from this point forward you must specifically allow
# particular features to be enabled - so if something's not working as
# you might expect, make sure that you have specifically enabled it
# below.
#

#
# This should be changed to whatever you set DocumentRoot to.
#
<Directory "/opt/web/html">

#
# This may also be "None", "All", or any combination of "Indexes",
# "Includes", "FollowSymLinks", "ExecCGI", or "MultiViews".
#
# Note that "MultiViews" must be named *explicitly* --- "Options All"
# doesn't give it to you.
#
    Options Indexes FollowSymLinks MultiViews

#
# This controls which options the .htaccess files in directories can
# override. Can also be "All", or any combination of "Options", "FileInfo",
```

```
# "AuthConfig", and "Limit"
#
    AllowOverride None


#
# Controls who can get stuff from this server.
#
    Order allow,deny
    Allow from all
</Directory>
```

In the preceding extract, notice the following:

◆ Three values are specified for the Options directive. The first value, Indexes, signifies that if the document root doesn't have a default Web page (index.html), a directory listing of the contents of the document root directory will be displayed. The value FollowSymlinks directs the server to follow symbolic links with respect to the document root directory. The value MultiViews tells Apache that content-negotiated MultiViews are allowed.

◆ The AllowOverride None option indicates that .htaccess file will be ignored.

◆ You use the Order directive to specify the default access state for the specified directory. The Order directive is also used to specify the order in which the Allow and Deny directives will be used. The Allow directive is used to specify the hosts that can access a particular part of the file system of the server. Hostnames, IP addresses, and IP address ranges can be specified with the Allow directive. The Deny directive is just the opposite of the Allow directive. You use the Deny directive to restrict access to particular areas of the file system of the server.

◆ Specifying the value of the Order directive as allow,deny implies that the Allow directive will be considered before the Deny directive. This means that the hostnames or IP addresses specified in the Allow directive will be checked first.

 NOTE

All options specified with the <Directory> and </Directory> directives are applicable to the directory in question and also the respective sub-directories, unless configuration for a sub-directory overrides them.

The *UserDir* Directive

When a user accessing the Web server from a client machine tries to connect, a directory is appended to a user's home directory. You use the UserDir directory to specify the name of the directory, as shown here:

```
# UserDir: The name of the directory which is appended onto a user's home
# directory if a ~user request is received.
#
<IfModule mod_userdir.c>
    UserDir public_html
</IfModule>
```

As you can see in the preceding extract, the UserDir directive is assigned the value public_html. Also notice that the IfModule directive is used. The IfModule directive is a separate conditional directive (not a feature of UserDir directive). In other words, conditional directives can be included in the IfModule directive. The conditional directives specified in the IfModule directive are processed only if the result is true.

Controlling Access to *UserDir* Directories

The configuration lines from the following extract need to be uncommented if you want to implement user control on UserDir directories.

 NOTE

The concept of access control is discussed in Chapter 5, "Implementing Access Control in Apache."

The following example shows how to control access to UserDir directories:

```
# Control access to UserDir directories.  The following is an example
# for a site where these directories are restricted to read-only.
#
#<Directory /home/*/public_html>
#    AllowOverride FileInfo AuthConfig Limit
#    Options MultiViews Indexes SymLinksIfOwnerMatch IncludesNoExec
#    <Limit GET POST OPTIONS PROPFIND>
#        Order allow,deny
#        Allow from all
#    </Limit>
```

```
#       <LimitExcept GET POST OPTIONS PROPFIND>
#            Order deny,allow
#            Deny from all
#       </LimitExcept>
#</Directory>
```

The *DirectoryIndex* Directive

You use the DirectoryIndex directive to specify the resources that should be searched in the Web server when the client specifies a / at the end of the directory name. Every directory on the server has a local URL that points to a file in the requested directory. As a result, the file in the directory is called.

You have the option of specifying one or more filenames with the DirectoryIndex directive. If only one filename is specified, the local URL will point to this file, and its contents will be displayed. However, if several files are specified, the server will return the first file that it finds in the directory. If you haven't specified resources or files and the Indexed option is set, the server returns its own directory listing of the requested directory. The following example shows the use of the DirectoryIndex directive:

```
# DirectoryIndex: Name of the file or files to use as a pre-written HTML
# directory index.  Separate multiple entries with spaces.
#
<IfModule mod_dir.c>
    DirectoryIndex index.html
</IfModule>
```

As you can see in the preceding extract, the index.html file has been specified as a part of the DirectoryIndex directive.

The *AccessFileName* Directive

This is one of the most important directives used for access control and ensuring security. You use the AccessFileName directive to specify a name of the file that will be checked in each directory before allowing access to the resources of the directory. However, you will need to enable access control files for the directory before using them. Consider the following example:

```
AccessFileName .somefile
```

This example indicates that the AccessFileName directive has been specified a file named .somefile. Now, consider a situation in which a user requests a file named index.html located in the directory /opt/web/html. In such a situation, before the server returns the requested document to the user, it will check the .somefile file in each directory to confirm that the user is allowed to access the resource. As a result, the .somefile file will be checked in /, /opt, /web, and /html directories. The server will also check /opt/web/html/.somefile for directives before it sends the requested document to the client. The following example shows the use of the `AccessFileName` directive:

```
# AccessFileName: The name of the file to look for in each directory
# for access control information.
#
AccessFileName .htaccess
```

This extract from the httpd.conf file indicates that the `AccessFileName` directive has been assigned the value `.htaccess`. You use the .htaccess file for access control.

NOTE

I discuss access control in more detail in Chapter 5, "Implementing Access Control in Apache."

The *CacheNegotiatedDocs* Directive

If uncommented, this directive allows the proxy to cache content-negotiated documents. This helps clients behind the firewall extract the cached documents and, as a result, save time and bandwidth.

NOTE

The concept of how Apache uses content negotiation is discussed in Chapter 13, "Metainformation and Content Negotiation."

The following example shows the use of the `CacheNegotiatedDocs` directive:

```
# CacheNegotiatedDocs: By default, Apache sends "Pragma: no-cache" with each
# document that was negotiated on the basis of content. This asks proxy
# servers not to cache the document. Uncommenting the following line disables
# this behavior, and proxies will be allowed to cache the documents.
#
#CacheNegotiatedDocs
```

As you can see, the `CacheNegotiatedDocs` directive is commented by default.

The *UseCanonicalName* Directive

The *canonical name* is the primary name used by the Web server. However, there can be situations in which you want to specify more than one hostname for your Web server. You can achieve this by creating aliases to the existing canonical name. You can use the UseCanonical-Name directive to specify whether you want to use the canonical name for your server. The following example shows the use of the UseCanonicalName directive:

```
# UseCanonicalName:  (new for 1.3)  With this setting turned on, whenever
# Apache needs to construct a self-referencing URL (a URL that refers back
# to the server the response is coming from) it will use ServerName and
# Port to form a "canonical" name.  With this setting off, Apache will
# use the hostname:port that the client supplied, when possible.  This
# also affects SERVER_NAME and SERVER_PORT in CGI scripts.
#
UseCanonicalName On
```

Using the CanonicalName directive if assigned the value On directs Apache to use the canonical name.

The *TypeConfig* Directive

You use the TypesConfig directive to set a location for the configuration file that contains details about the MIME types. The MIME type configuration file contains details about the mapping of file extensions to the associated content type. You should not change the MIME type configuration file. The following example shows the use of the TypeConfig directive:

```
# TypesConfig describes where the mime.types file (or equivalent) is
# to be found.
#
<IfModule mod_mime.c>
    TypesConfig /usr/local/apache/conf/mime.types
</IfModule>
```

The path /usr/local/apache/conf/mime.types signifies the path for the MIME types configuration file. You can also specify a path relative to the path specified in the ServerRoot directive to specify the location of the mime.types file. In this case, you specify the path as conf/mime.types (without a "/" before conf).

The *DefaultType* Directive

At times, a client might request a document that has a MIME type the server does not recognize. In such cases, the server responds to the request using a default MIME type. You use the `DefaultType` directive to specify the default MIME type that will be used by the Web server:

```
# DefaultType is the default MIME type the server will use for a document
# if it cannot otherwise determine one, such as from filename extensions.
# If your server contains mostly text or HTML documents, "text/plain" is
# a good value.  If most of your content is binary, such as applications
# or images, you may want to use "application/octet-stream" instead to
# keep browsers from trying to display binary files as though they are
# text.
#
DefaultType text/plain
```

The extract from the httpd.conf file indicates that the `DefaultType` directive is assigned the value `text/plain`. This means that the default MIME type used by the server is plain text.

The *MIMEMagicFile* Directive

The Apache Web server uses a module called `mod_mime_magic`. This module enables Apache to examine the contents of a file, look for hints, and determine the type of the file. You use the `MIMEMagicFile` directive to specify the location where the `module_mime_magic` module can look for hints that help determine the file type:

```
# The mod_mime_magic module allows the server to use various hints from the
# contents of the file itself to determine its type.  The MIMEMagicFile
# directive tells the module where the hint definitions are located.
# mod_mime_magic is not part of the default server (you have to add
# it yourself with a LoadModule [see the DSO paragraph in the 'Global
# Environment' section], or recompile the server and include mod_mime_magic
# as part of the configuration), so it's enclosed in an <IfModule> container.
# This means that the MIMEMagicFile directive will only be processed if the
# module is part of the server.
#
<IfModule mod_mime_magic.c>
    MIMEMagicFile /usr/local/apache/conf/magic
</IfModule>
```

In the preceding extract, the location specified for the `MIMEMagicFile` directive is /usr/local/apache/conf/magic. You can also specify the path as conf/magic. Specifying the path as conf/magic (without a "/" before conf) would mean that path is relative to the directory specified in the `ServerRoot` directive.

The *HostnameLookups* Directive

This directive is responsible for specifying whether *DNS lookups* should be enabled. DNS lookups are used to log the names of the clients. However, enabling this option can slow down the server considerably because every client request initiates a lookup request to the DNS server. As a result, HostNameLookups is disabled by default. The following example shows the use of the HostNameLookups directive:

```
# HostnameLookups: Log the names of clients or just their IP addresses
# e.g., www.apache.org (on) or 204.62.129.132 (off).
# The default is off because it'd be overall better for the net if people
# had to knowingly turn this feature on, since enabling it means that
# each client request will result in AT LEAST one lookup request to the
# nameserver.
#
HostnameLookups Off
```

As evident from the preceding extract, specifying the value Off disables the HostnameLookups directive.

The *ErrorLog* Directive

As the name suggests, you use the ErrorLog Directive to specify the location where the error logs will be stored:

```
# ErrorLog: The location of the error log file.
# If you do not specify an ErrorLog directive within a <VirtualHost>
# container, error messages relating to that virtual host will be
# logged here.  If you *do* define an error logfile for a <VirtualHost>
# container, that host's errors will be logged there and not here.
#
ErrorLog /usr/local/apache/logs/error_log
```

By default, the ErrorLogs directive is uncommented, and the value assigned to it is /usr/local/apache/logs/error_log. If the path is specified without a forward slash at the beginning, the path name is relative to the path specified in the ServerRoot directive.

The *LogLevel* Directive

You use the LogLevel directive to specify the type of messages that are recorded in the error logs:

```
# LogLevel: Control the number of messages logged to the error_log.
# Possible values include: debug, info, notice, warn, error, crit,
```

```
# alert, emerg.
#
LogLevel warn
```

Several options can be specified with the `LogLevel` directive. The value `Warn` indicates messages that generate a warning.

The *LogFormat* Directive

As the name suggests, you use the `LogFormat` directive to specify the names of log formats for the log file:

```
# The following directives define some format nicknames for use with
# a CustomLog directive (see below).
#
LogFormat "%h %l %u %t \"%r\" %>s %b \"%{Referer}i\" \"%{User-Agent}i\""
combined
LogFormat "%h %l %u %t \"%r\" %>s %b" common
LogFormat "%{Referer}i -> %U" referer
LogFormat "%{User-agent}i" agent
```

The preceding extract suggests different values for the `LogFormat` directive. Don't alter these entries.

> **NOTE**
>
> Log file analyzers such as Webalyzer use the log formats specified in the `LogFormat` directive.

The *CustomLog* Directive

The `CustomLog` directive uses three arguments to log requests to the server. The arguments specified are used do the following:

- ◆ Specify the location where the logs will be stored.
- ◆ Specify what will be written to the log file.
- ◆ Specify whether a particular request should be logged. This is an optional argument.

The following example shows the use of the `CustomLog` directive:

```
# The location and format of the access logfile (Common Logfile Format).
# If you do not define any access logfiles within a <VirtualHost>
# container, they will be logged here.  Contrariwise, if you *do*
```

```
# define per-<VirtualHost> access logfiles, transactions will be
# logged therein and *not* in this file.
#
CustomLog /usr/local/apache/logs/access_log common


#
# If you would like to have agent and referer logfiles, uncomment the
# following directives.
#
#CustomLog /usr/local/apache/logs/referer_log referer
#CustomLog /usr/local/apache/logs/agent_log agent


#
# If you prefer a single logfile with access, agent, and referer information
# (Combined Logfile Format) you can use the following directive.
#
#CustomLog /usr/local/apache/logs/access_log combined
```

The preceding extract indicates that all CustomLog entries except one are commented by default.

 NOTE

I discuss the directives used for logging in detail, in Chapter 9, "Improving Apache's Performance."

The *ServerSignature* Directive

Specifying the value On for the ServerSignature directive implies that a server signature will be included at the end of the document when error messages are generated. If you set the value Off for this directive, the server signature will not be generated in the footer of the document. The following example shows the use of the ServerSignature directive:

```
# Optionally add a line containing the server version and virtual host
# name to server-generated pages (error documents, FTP directory listings,
# mod_status and mod_info output etc., but not CGI generated documents).
# Set to "EMail" to also include a mailto: link to the ServerAdmin.
# Set to one of:  On | Off | EMail
#
ServerSignature On
```

The preceding extract indicates that the value assigned to the ServerSignature directive is On, which means that the server signature will appear in the footer of the document. Another option that can be specified with the ServerSignature directive is the EMail option. This option adds a mailto: link to the ServerAdmin directive.

The *EBCDICConvert* and *EBCDICConvertByType* Directives

You use the EBCDICConvert and EBCDICConvertByType directives to configure Extended Binary-Coded Decimal Interchange Code (EBCDIC). EBCDIC is a code used to represent characters as numbers. It is most widely used with IBM architectures. The corresponding entries for EBCDIC in the httpd.conf file are as follows:

```
# EBCDIC configuration:
# (only for mainframes using the EBCDIC codeset, currently one of:
# Fujitsu-Siemens' BS2000/OSD, IBM's OS/390 and IBM's TPF)!!
# The following default configuration assumes that "text files"
# are stored in EBCDIC (so that you can operate on them using the
# normal POSIX tools like grep and sort) while "binary files" are
# stored with identical octets as on an ASCII machine.
#
# The directives are evaluated in configuration file order, with
# the EBCDICConvert directives applied before EBCDICConvertByType.
#
# If you want to have ASCII HTML documents and EBCDIC HTML documents
# at the same time, you can use the file extension to force
# conversion off for the ASCII documents:
# > AddType        text/html .ahtml
# > EBCDICConvert Off=InOut .ahtml
#
# EBCDICConvertByType  On=InOut text/* message/* multipart/*
# EBCDICConvertByType  On=In     application/x-www-form-urlencoded
# EBCDICConvertByType  On=InOut application/postscript model/vrml
# EBCDICConvertByType Off=InOut */*
```

Notice that all the lines are commented, which means that the default configuration doesn't use EBCDIC.

The *Alias* Directive

The main use of the Alias directive is to enable Apache store documents on a location other than the directory specified in the DocumentRoot directive. This section can have any number of aliases.

The format for specifying an alias is as follows:

```
Alias fakename realname
```

The fake name represents the fake path for the file and the real name represents the actual location of the file. Consider the following example to understand how aliases are created and how they operate:

```
Alias /graphics /ftp/pub/graphics
```

When a client requests a graphic named `graphicone.jpg`, the following URL is specified:

```
http://localhost/graphics/graphicone.jpg.
```

However, because of the alias you created, `graphicone.jpg` will be extracted from `/ftp/pub/graphics`. The following excerpt displays the corresponding entries related to the `Alias` directive in the httpd.conf file.

```
# Aliases: Add here as many aliases as you need (with no limit). The
#format is
# Alias fakename realname
#
<IfModule mod_alias.c>

    #
    # Note that if you include a trailing / on fakename then the server
    #will
    # require it to be present in the URL.  So "/icons" isn't aliased in this
    # example, only "/icons/".  If the fakename is slash-terminated, then the
    # realname must also be slash terminated, and if the fakename omits the
    # trailing slash, the realname must also omit it.
    #
    Alias /icons/ "/usr/local/apache/icons/"

    <Directory "/usr/local/apache/icons">
        Options Indexes MultiViews
        AllowOverride None
        Order allow,deny
        Allow from all
    </Directory>

    # This Alias will project the on-line documentation tree under /manual/
    # even if you change the DocumentRoot. Comment it if you don't want to
    # provide access to the on-line documentation.
```

```
#
Alias /manual/ "/opt/web/html/manual/"

<Directory "/opt/web/html/manual">
    Options Indexes FollowSymlinks MultiViews
    AllowOverride None
    Order allow,deny
    Allow from all
</Directory>

#
# ScriptAlias: This controls which directories contain server scripts.
# ScriptAliases are essentially the same as Aliases, except that
# documents in the realname directory are treated as applications and
# run by the server when requested rather than as documents sent to the client.
# The same rules about trailing "/" apply to ScriptAlias directives as to
# Alias.
#
ScriptAlias /cgi-bin/ "/opt/web/cgi-bin/"

#
# "/opt/web/cgi-bin" should be changed to whatever your ScriptAliased
# CGI directory exists, if you have that configured.
#
<Directory "/opt/web/cgi-bin">
    AllowOverride None
    Options None
    Order allow,deny
    Allow from all
</Directory>

</IfModule>
# End of aliases.
```

Notice that another directive named ScriptAlias is specified at various locations. The role of the ScriptAlias directive is similar to the Alias directive. The only difference between the two is that the ScriptAlias directive is used to treat the files in the specified directory as CGI scripts so that they can be executed.

The *Redirect* Directive

From time to time, you may want to remove certain documents from the site. In such situations, the URLs that point to these documents cease to work. You use the `Redirect` directive to redirect the client to an alternate location instead of the old location. To redirect the user to an alternate location, you need to use the old URL as well as the new URL with the `Redirect` directive. The following example shows the use of the `Redirect` directive:

```
# Redirect allows you to tell clients about documents which used to exist
#in
# your server's namespace, but do not anymore. This allows you to tell the
# clients where to look for the relocated document.
# Format: Redirect old-URI new-URL
Redirect /images http://server2.images.com/graphics
```

The preceding extract indicates that the `Redirect` directive has been used. Requests for files in the images directory will now be redirected to the new URL, http://server2.images.com/graphics.

NOTE

I discuss the concepts of redirection in Chapter 12, "URL Mapping."

Directives Used for Directory Listing

The directives that are used for directory listing occupy a considerable amount of space in the httpd.conf file. You can use several directives to customize the directory listing on your server. The following directives are used:

- ◆ **FancyIndexing.** Use this directive to set fancy indexing for a directory.

- ◆ **IndexOptions.** This directive is responsible for specifying how directory indexing should behave. Several options that determine the behavior of directory indexing can be specified with the `IndexOptions` directive.

- ◆ **AddIconByEncoding.** Use this directive to display an icon next to files that are MIME encoded.

- ◆ **AddIconByType.** Use this directive to display an icon next to files that are of MIME-type.

- ◆ **AddIcon.** Use this directive to display an icon next to different files depending on the type of file. For example, different icons will be displayed for text files and executable files.

◆ **DefaultIcon.** As the name suggests, you use the DefaultIcon directive to specify the default icon that will be used for files whose file type is not recognized.

◆ **AddDescription.** Use the AddDescription directive to specify that a description will be displayed for each file that is displayed as a part of the indexed directory.

◆ **ReadmeName.** Use this directive if you want a file to be appended to the end of the index listing.

◆ **HeaderName.** Use this directive to specify that a file will be added to the header of the indexing list.

◆ **IndexIgnore.** Use this directive to specify a list of files that you don't want to display with all other files in the indexed directory.

Consider the following extract of the httpd.conf file that is responsible for generating server-generated directory listings:

```
# Directives controlling the display of server-generated directory
#listings.
#
<IfModule mod_autoindex.c>

    #
    # FancyIndexing is whether you want fancy directory indexing or
    #standard
    #
    IndexOptions FancyIndexing

    #
    # AddIcon* directives tell the server which icon to show for different
    # files or filename extensions.  These are only displayed for
    # FancyIndexed directories.
    #
    AddIconByEncoding (CMP,/icons/compressed.gif) x-compress x-gzip

    AddIconByType (TXT,/icons/text.gif) text/*
    AddIconByType (IMG,/icons/image2.gif) image/*
    AddIconByType (SND,/icons/sound2.gif) audio/*
    AddIconByType (VID,/icons/movie.gif) video/*

    AddIcon /icons/binary.gif .bin .exe
    AddIcon /icons/binhex.gif .hqx
```

```
AddIcon /icons/tar.gif .tar
AddIcon /icons/world2.gif .wrl .wrl.gz .vrml .vrm .iv
AddIcon /icons/compressed.gif .Z .z .tgz .gz .zip
AddIcon /icons/a.gif .ps .ai .eps
AddIcon /icons/layout.gif .html .shtml .htm .pdf
```
.....Many lines deleted.....

Directives Used for Document Types

Several directives are used in the portion of httpd.conf that allows you to configure certain options for document types. The main directives in this section are as follows:

- **AddEncoding.** This directive is solely used for mapping filename extensions to a corresponding encoding type.
- **AddLanguage.** Use this directive to map the extension of a file to the specified content language.
- **LanguagePriority.** Use this directive to specify which languages will have primacy over other languages.
- **AddHandler.** Use this directive to map the extension of a file with the handler name.

The following extract from the httpd.conf file shows the configurable options for document types:

```
# Document types.
#
<IfModule mod_mime.c>

    #
    # AddEncoding allows you to have certain browsers (Mosaic/X 2.1+)
    #uncompress
    # information on the fly. Note: Not all browsers support this.
    # Despite the name similarity, the following Add* directives have
    #nothing
    # to do with the FancyIndexing customization directives above.
    #
    AddEncoding x-compress Z
    AddEncoding x-gzip gz tgz

    #
    # AddLanguage allows you to specify the language of a document. You
    #can
```

```
# then use content negotiation to give a browser a file in a language
# it can understand.
#
# Note 1: The suffix does not have to be the same as the language
# keyword --- those with documents in Polish (whose net-standard
# language code is pl) may wish to use "AddLanguage pl .po" to
# avoid the ambiguity with the common suffix for perl scripts.
#
# Note 2: The example entries below illustrate that in quite
# some cases the two character 'Language' abbreviation is not
# identical to the two character 'Country' code for its country,
# E.g. 'Danmark/dk' versus 'Danish/da'.
#
# Note 3: In the case of 'ltz' we violate the RFC by using a three
#char
# specifier. But there is 'work in progress' to fix this and get
# the reference data for rfc1766 cleaned up.
#
# Danish (da) - Dutch (nl) - English (en) - Estonian (ee)
# French (fr) - German (de) - Greek-Modern (el)
# Italian (it) - Korean (kr) - Norwegian (no) - Norwegian Nynorsk (nn)
# Portugese (pt) - Luxembourgeois* (ltz)
# Spanish (es) - Swedish (sv) - Catalan (ca) - Czech(cz)
# Polish (pl) - Brazilian Portuguese (pt-br) - Japanese (ja)
# Russian (ru)
#
AddLanguage da .dk
AddLanguage nl .nl
AddLanguage en .en
AddLanguage et .ee
…..Many deleted lines…..

</IfModule>
# End of document types.
```

The *Action* Directive

You use the Action directive to specify an action. This action activates a *cgi-script* when a request from the client triggers an action-type. The cgi-script is a URL path. This path points to a resource that is configured as a CGI script. On the other hand, the action-type is either a handler or a MIME content type. The corresponding contents of the httpd.conf file that contain the Action directive are as follows:

```
# Action lets you define media types that will execute a script whenever
# a matching file is called. This eliminates the need for repeated URL
# pathnames for oft-used CGI file processors.
# Format: Action media/type /cgi-script/location
# Format: Action handler-name /cgi-script/location
```

The content indicates that the Action directive is not used by default because all the lines are commented.

The *MetaDir* Directive

You use the MetaDir directive to specify the location for *meta information files*. Meta information files are used to store information that is hidden from the user. In the Apache context, meta information files store additional HTTP headers that are included in the document before it is sent to the client. The following part of the httpd.conf file contains the MetaDir directive:

```
# MetaDir: specifies the name of the directory in which Apache can find
# meta information files. These files contain additional HTTP headers
# to include when sending the document
#
#MetaDir .web
```

As you can see, all the lines are commented, which means that you will need to enable the MetaDir directive exclusively for use.

The *MetaSuffix* Directive

You use this directive to specify the suffix for the meta information files. The following is an extract from the httpd.conf file that contains the MetaSuffix directive:

```
# MetaSuffix: specifies the file name suffix for the file containing the
# meta information.
#
#MetaSuffix .meta
```

The value .meta is assigned to the MetaSuffix directive. This indicates that the suffix for the meta information file will be .meta.

The *ErrorDocument* Directive

You use the ErrorDocument directive to specify an action the Web server will take if a problem or error is encountered. This directive can be configured so that the following occurs:

◆ A hard-coded message appears when an error is encountered.

◆ A customized message appears in the event of an error.

◆ The URL specified by the client is redirected to a local URL, which in turn solves the problem or error.

◆ The URL specified by the client is redirected to an external URL, which in turn solves the problem or error.

The following extract from the httpd.conf file shows the default options that are set for this directive:

```
# Customizable error response (Apache style)
#  these come in three flavors
#
#    1) plain text
#ErrorDocument 500 "The server made a boo boo.
#  n.b.  the single leading (") marks it as text, it does not get output
#
#    2) local redirects
#ErrorDocument 404 /missing.html
#  to redirect to local URL /missing.html
#ErrorDocument 404 /cgi-bin/missing_handler.pl
#  N.B.: You can redirect to a script or a document using
#server-side-includes.
#
#    3) external redirects
#ErrorDocument 402 http://some.other-server.com/subscription_info.html
#  N.B.: Many of the environment variables associated with the original
#  request will *not* be available to such a script.
```

By default, the ErrorDocument directive is commented and not used. However, for professional Web sites, it is recommended that suitable values for the ErrorDocument directive be specified so that the user is provided with a suitable explanation if there is a server error. This improves the browsing experience of users accessing the Web site.

The *BrowserMatch* Directive

You use the BrowserMatch directive to define environment variables. These environment variables are based on the HTTP request header field named User-Agent. The following code shows the use of the BrowserMatch directive:

```
# Customize behaviour based on the browser
#
<IfModule mod_setenvif.c>

    #
    # The following directives modify normal HTTP response behavior.
    # The first directive disables keepalive for Netscape 2.x and browsers
    # that
    # spoof it. There are known problems with these browser
    #implementations.
    # The second directive is for Microsoft Internet Explorer 4.0b2
    # which has a broken HTTP/1.1 implementation and does not properly
    # support keepalive when it is used on 301 or 302 (redirect)
    #responses.
    #
    BrowserMatch "Mozilla/2" nokeepalive
    BrowserMatch "MSIE 4\.0b2;" nokeepalive downgrade-1.0
    #force-response-1.0

    #
    # The following directive disables HTTP/1.1 responses to browsers
    #which
    # are in violation of the HTTP/1.0 spec by not being able to grok a
    # basic 1.1 response.
    #
    BrowserMatch "RealPlayer 4\.0" force-response-1.0
    BrowserMatch "Java/1\.0" force-response-1.0
    BrowserMatch "JDK/1\.0" force-response-1.0

</IfModule>
# End of browser customization directives
```

The preceding extract shows the use of the BrowserMatch directive to customize the behavior of the browser based on the type of the browser. The BrowserMatch directive helps trigger special responses from the server when accessed by a certain kind of browser.

Allow Server Status Reports

To allow server status reports, you uncomment the following lines:

```
# Allow server status reports, with the URL of http://servername/
#server-status
# Change the ".your-domain.com" to match your domain to enable.
#
#<Location /server-status>
#    SetHandler server-status
#    Order deny,allow
#    Deny from all
#    Allow from .your-domain.com
#</Location>
```

As you can see, the preceding lines are commented. By default, these lines are commented for security reasons.

Allow Remote Server Configuration

The configurable lines from the following extract need to be uncommented in order to allow the generation of remote server configuration reports:

```
# Allow remote server configuration reports, with the URL of
# http://servername/server-info (requires that mod_info.c be loaded).
# Change the ".your-domain.com" to match your domain to enable.
#
#<Location /server-info>
#    SetHandler server-info
#    Order deny,allow
#    Deny from all
#    Allow from .your-domain.com
#</Location>
```

Proxy Server Directives

The configurable lines from the following extract need to be uncommented if you want to configure Apache as a proxy server:

```
# Proxy Server directives. Uncomment the following lines to
# enable the proxy server:
#
#<IfModule mod_proxy.c>
#    ProxyRequests On

#    <Directory proxy:*>
#        Order deny,allow
#        Deny from all
#        Allow from .your-domain.com
#    </Directory>

    #
    # Enable/disable the handling of HTTP/1.1 "Via:" headers.
    # ("Full" adds the server version; "Block" removes all outgoing Via:
    #headers)
    # Set to one of: Off | On | Full | Block
    #
#    ProxyVia On

    #
    # To enable the cache as well, edit and uncomment the following lines:
    # (no cacheing without CacheRoot)
    #
#    CacheRoot "/usr/local/apache/proxy"
#    CacheSize 5
#    CacheGcInterval 4
#    CacheMaxExpire 24
#    CacheLastModifiedFactor 0.1
#    CacheDefaultExpire 1
#    NoCache a-domain.com another-domain.edu joes.garage-sale.com

#</IfModule>
# End of proxy directives.
```

NOTE

I discuss the concepts for configuring Apache for proxying and caching in Chapter 9, "Improving Apache's Performance."

Virtual Host Configuration Options

The third section of the httpd.conf file contains options that you can configure for virtual host support. I discuss the directives related to virtual hosts in the Chapter 6, "Configuring Virtual Hosts."

Using Apacheconf

By now, you have some idea about the directives and configurable options in the httpd.conf file. However, this is not the only way you can configure Apache Web server. Besides editing the httpd.conf file, you can use a GUI tool named Apacheconf to configure Apache. This tool is available with standard Red Hat 7.2 distribution.

You can invoke Apacheconf from the GNOME or KDE desktop environments by typing the command apacheconf on the Terminal Emulation Program window. Though you can't use this utility to the extent that you can the httpd.conf file, Apacheconf is a good GUI tool for novice administrators.

NOTE

Leave the httpd.conf file untouched if you want to use Apacheconf to configure your Apache Web server.

The Apache Configuration window contains four tabs: Main, Virtual Hosts, Server, and Performance Tuning.

The Main Tab

You use the Main tab to specify the general server settings, such as the Server Name and the Webmaster email address. Figure 4.1 displays the Main tab of the Apache Configuration dialog box.

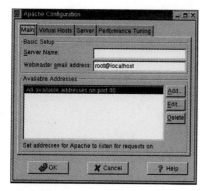

FIGURE 4.1 *The Main tab*

The Virtual Hosts Tab

You use the Virtual Hosts tab to specify the settings for Virtual Hosts. You can add, delete, and edit Virtual Hosts in the Virtual Hosts tab. Figure 4.2 displays the Virtual Hosts tab.

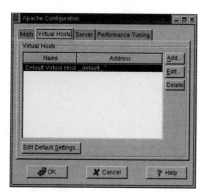

FIGURE 4.2 *The Virtual Hosts tab*

The Server Tab

You use the Server tab to configure basic server settings. However, keeping the default settings in this tab is recommended. Figure 4.3 displays the Server tab.

The Performance Tuning Tab

As the name suggests, you use the Performance Tuning tab to specify settings to improve the performance of the Apache Web server. Figure 4.4 displays the Performance Tuning tab.

FIGURE 4.3 *The Server tab*

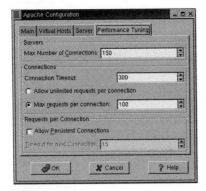

FIGURE 4.4 *The Performance Tuning tab*

Summary

In this chapter, I focused on the different ways you can configure the Apache Web server. I discussed the httpd.conf file, which is the conventional way of configuring Apache. Finally, I discussed the GUI utility named Apacheconf, which you can also use to configure Apache.

Check Your Understanding

Multiple Choice Questions

1. Considering that you have performed a standard installation of Apache, in which directory is the httpd.conf file located?

    a. /root

    b. /etc/httpd/conf

    c. /home/www

    d. /usr/local/apache/conf

2. Which of the following directives do you use to specify the default location for all Web site files hosted by Apache Web server?

    a. ServerRoot

    b. ResourceConfig

    c. DocumentRoot

    d. AccessConfig

3. Which of the following directives do you use to specify the location for error logs?

    a. ErrorLog

    b. LogLevel

    c. LogFormat

    d. CustomLog

4. Which of the following directives do you use to check whether a particular module is installed?

    a. LoadModule

    b. AddModule

    c. Directory

    d. IfModule

5. Which of the following commands do you use to invoke Apacheconf?

    a. apacheconf

    b. apachectl

    c. service httpd start

    d. /etc/rc.d/init.d/httpd restart

Answers

Multiple Choice Answers

1. b. If you used the standard installation for Apache, the httpd.conf file will be located in the /etc/httpd/conf directory. You can specify a different directory for the httpd.conf file only when you perform a custom install.

2. c. You use the `DocumentRoot` directive to specify the default location for all Web site files hosted by Apache Web server.

3. b. You use the `ErrorLog` directive to specify the location for the error logs.

4. d. The `IfModule` directive is a conditional directive that checks whether a particular module exists before loading or adding it.

5. a. To invoke Apacheconf, you need to type the command `apacheconf`.

Chapter 5

Implementing Access Control in Apache

The Internet is a huge repository of information that is accessible to millions of users across the world. Numerous Web servers host a wide range of information on the Internet. In such a scenario, it is important to keep a check on who is allowed to access resources of a Web site on a Web server.

When you request a resource from a site, chances are that your request is either accepted or rejected outright. The latter might happen because you are not entitled to access the document you requested. It is quite possible that the Web server you are accessing contains certain sensitive information that is meant only for a few specific people and excludes you. From the perspective of a Web server administrator, it is extremely important to protect this information from anybody who is not entitled to access it. Now, the question that arises is how all this is managed in Apache. Restricting or allowing access to resources in Apache can be managed on the host computer by using host-based access control, authentication-based access control, and .htaccess files.

In this chapter, I discuss the most important aspects of controlling and restricting access to resources. First, I take up using host-based access control to ensure that only people who are allowed to access the resources are able to. Second, I discuss the concept of authentication-based access control and how to implement it. Finally, I take up the concept of .htaccess files.

Introducing Access Control

An integral part of any Web server is its capability to implement access control on the resources in it. Access control is the basic method for ensuring that the resources on the Web server are safe. I define access control as a regular check performed by the Web server on the basis of predefined criteria that determine whether a request should be accepted or rejected. This definition can be split into three parts:

- **A regular check performed by the Web server.** The first part of the definition suggests that access control is initiated when Apache performs a check on the request. This helps Apache determine the nature of the request.

- **Check on the basis of predefined criteria.** The next part of the definition suggests that Apache checks the requests on the basis of predefined criteria. This means that, as an Apache administrator, you can specify the condition or criteria that should be satisfied before the request is sent a positive response. A wide variety of criteria can be specified to restrict access to resources, such as hostname, IP address, and a combination of username and password.

- **Determine whether the request should be accepted or rejected.** The final part of the definition suggests that after Apache checks whether the request satisfies the predefined condition, it decides what action should be performed. If the request satisfies the specified criteria, the request is accepted. Specifying other conditions can customize the response of Apache when a particular request is accepted.

Types of Access Control

There are various ways of implementing access control to restrict access to files and directories on the host computer. The three most common methods are as follows:

- Using host-based access control
- Using authentication-based access control
- Using .htaccess files

Host-Based Access Control

Host-based access control signifies that the access control is dependent on the computer from which a user is sending a request. In other words, a request sent from a user will be accepted only if the computer sending the request is allowed to access the resource on the server computer. Host-based access control can be implemented by specifying IP addresses or domain names in the configuration file. If any portion of the specified IP address or domain name is restricted, the server will deny access to the requested resource. You can implement host-based access control using the following:

- Domain names
- IP addresses

Domain Names

Hostnames can be used to restrict or allow access to the resources on the Web server. However, there is a way in which you should specify the hostnames in the configuration file. You specify domain names either as *fully qualified domain names* or as *sub-domain names*.

Fully Qualified Domain Names

Fully qualified domain names are complete domain names that distinguish one host from another, as this example shows:

```
steve.niit.com
linda.niit.com
```

The preceding examples are fully qualified or complete domain names that can be specified in the configuration file to allow or deny access to resources.

Sub-Domain Names

Sub-domain names are incomplete names, but are applicable for all computers that are part of the specified domain. Consider the following example:

```
.niit.com
.org
```

The preceding names are sub-domain names. Notice that they are preceded by periods. This means that all hostnames that match the pattern (last part of the domain name) .niit.com or .org will be allowed or denied access.

If you have denied access to the preceding domain names, the following domain names will be restricted access:

```
steve.niit.com
netsity.in.niit.com
somename.us.org
```

As a result the preceding, domain names such as steve.niit.com and somename.us.org will be denied access.

IP Addresses

All DNS names have an associated IP address. IP addresses can also be used to implement host-based access control. However, there are a number of ways you can specify IP addresses to allow or deny access. The following are two methods you can use to specify the IP addresses:

- ◆ Absolute IP addresses
- ◆ Partial IP addresses

Absolute IP Addresses

Absolute IP addresses require the administrator to specify the complete IP address of a host-name. IP addresses within a network are distinct, and any request from a restricted IP address will be denied access. Consider the following example of an absolute IP address:

```
172.17.68.222
194.33.68.333
```

These IP addresses are complete and represent one host each. Both of the specified IP addresses are absolute IP addresses.

Partial IP Addresses

As the name suggests, partial IP addresses are not complete IP addresses. The primary reason for using partial IP addresses is to specify a range of IP addresses that should be allowed or denied access on the Web server. For example, you want to deny the following partial IP address:

```
172.17.68.
```

This IP address indicates that all IP addresses that begin with 172.17.68. will be denied access to the resources of the server. As a result, if there are 100 computers in the network whose IP addresses start from the specified partial IP address, all 100 computers will be denied access.

Sample Configuration

I will now discuss a sample configuration to help you understand how access control is implemented. The following is an extract from the httpd.conf file:

```
<Directory /opt/web/html>

        order allow, deny

        allow from .niit.com

</Directory>
```

In the preceding extract, note the following:

- ◆ The <Directory> and </Directory> directives are used to specify the directory on which access control will be implemented. In this case, the directory name is /opt/web/html, which is the document root.
- ◆ The Order directive is used to specify the sequence in which the Allow and Deny directives will be referred when the Web server receives a request.

◆ The `Allow` directive is used to specify the details about the hostnames, IP addresses, or domain names that will be allowed to access the document root.

◆ The `Deny` directive is used to specify the details about the hostnames, IP addresses, or domain names that will be denied access to the document root.

◆ The sub-domain name `.niit.com` is specified as a value to the `Allow` directive. This indicates that all hosts that are a part of this domain will be allowed access to the `/opt/web/html` directory.

 NOTE

I discuss the `Order`, `Allow`, and `Deny` directives in detail later in this chapter.

Authentication-Based Access Control

To *authenticate* means to validate or to verify whether the credentials provided by an individual prove that the individual is genuine. Authentication is used to validate the identity of users. Consider the example of an ATM counter. In order to withdraw money, you are first required to enter your secret pin (personal identification number). The secret pin is verified, and you are allowed to withdraw money only if you enter the correct pin. This is a basic example, which everyone can relate to. In the Internet terminology, the basic form of authentication is a unique combination of a username and a password. A username and a password are credentials that are used to validate the authenticity of a user.

A Web site might have certain protected areas that are reserved for only a specific user or a group of users. Consider the example of a mailbox. How would you feel if anybody and everybody could read your personal mail? Of course, you wouldn't like it! Several Web sites today are successfully providing e-mail capabilities that satisfy millions of users across the world, because each individual with an e-mail account uses a unique combination of username and password to access mail. As a result, others who don't know the username and password cannot access information that is specific to another user.

Authentication has evolved and newer mechanisms for ensuring authenticity, such as digital signatures, fingerprints, and public and private keys, are being used. However, the most widely used mechanism for authentication is still a combination of username and password. Authentication-based access control is implemented to validate the credentials of a user before the user gains access to resources on the Web server. This section discusses how authentication-based access control is implemented in Apache.

Types of Authentication

According to RFC 2616, there are two types of authentication, *basic* and *digest*. Both basic and digest authentication can be used for authenticating users before their requests can be processed by the Apache Web server.

Basic Authentication

Basic authentication is the simplest form of authentication available. When you protect the content on your Web server using basic authentication, the request-response process between the client and the server takes place as follows:

1. The client sends a request to the Apache Web server.

2. The Apache Web server determines that the request can be accepted only when the user specifies a valid username and a password.

3. The Web server sends a response to the client indicating that the user needs to specify a valid username and password. It sends a *401 Request header* to the client to ask for the credentials of the user.

4. Upon receiving the request header, the browser on the client computer prompts for the username and password.

5. The user on the client computer specifies the username and password that are sent by the browser to the Web server.

6. The username and password are verified at the server end. If the credentials supplied by the user are correct, the Web server responds with the requested document.

 NOTE

HTTP is a stateless protocol. This means that every HTTP request sent to the server is treated as a new connection even if the request is sent from the same client. If the server uses authentication to validate the integrity of the connection, the user will need to specify a username and password with each request. This could be a pain in the neck. Fortunately, the browser on the client computer handles this situation intelligently. Whenever a user specifies the username and password, they are cached in the browser. This means that the user doesn't need to specify the credentials with each request. Instead, the username and password are picked up from the cache maintained by the browser and sent to the server with each request.

The feature of caching is available only while the browser session is active. As soon as the session is closed, the user needs to specify the username and password the next time a connection is established. A few Web browsers also allow this information to be cached permanently, though it is not advisable to do so. In addition to using the caching feature, user credentials can be stored as cookies on the client or the server. Cookies are a mechanism that is used to maintain state of an HTTP connection.

The 401 Request Header

When you implement basic authentication on the Apache Web server, all requests received by the server are sent a 401 request header. A 401 request header causes the browser to prompt the user to enter a username and password. The server's 401 response consists of an authentication challenge that is sent to the client in the following format:

```
WWW-Authenticate: Basic realm="SecuredArea"
```

In the preceding example, note the following:

◆ The value, `Basic`, is assigned to the `WWW-Authenticate` header. This indicates that basic authentication is used.

◆ `realm` is the name associated with the area on the Web site that is protected using this specific basic authentication. The realm is also called the *authentication name.* Several different directories on the server can be a part of the same realm, provided the same authentication rules apply for the directories. When the user supplies the username and password to the server, these credentials are stored in the browser cache along with the authentication realm. Therefore, the user doesn't need to specify a username and password if the requested resource is a part of the same realm as the specified one. For example, say the marketing department of your company needs to access the /marketing directory and at the same time wants to access the /advertising directory. They can achieve this by putting both directories in the same realm. This way, the marketing department can access both these directories without entering the password exclusively for accessing each directory.

◆ `"SecuredArea"` is a string specified in the configuration for the protected area on the site to denote the realm name.

Basic Authentication: The Security Perspective

Authentication information specified by the user, such as the username and password, are sent using the `Authorization` header in the following format:

```
username:password
```

You use the *base64-encoding* technique (a method used to convert binary data to ASCII text) to convert a password to an unreadable format. This format is sent to the Apache Web server where it is decoded and converted to its original state. Then the username and password are compared with those present in the password file or database. If a match is found, the user is allowed to access the appropriate resource on the Web server.

```
Authorization: Basic some_encoded_string
```

The base64-encoding technique is not an encryption utility and can be easily decoded. Anybody who intercepts the `Authorization` header can extract the encoded value and decode it.

Therefore, using basic authentication is not safe as far as securing sensitive information on the Web is concerned. However, basic authentication is more commonly used because most Web browsers support it.

Digest Authentication

Digest authentication is an alternative method for protecting content on your Web server. It was proposed as an alternative to basic authentication. Digest authentication is considered to be more secure than basic authentication.

The main feature of digest authentication is that passwords specified by the users are not sent across the network. Instead a *digest* is sent to the server. A digest is a value derived by combining the following:

- **Username.** The identity of the user sending the request.
- **Password.** The secret pass phrase specified by the user.
- **Requested resource.** The resource on the server requested by the user.
- **Server.** The identity of the server that contains the requested resource.
- **Nonce.** A special key that is generated by the server and sent to the client.

 NOTE

A *nonce* is a special key generated afresh every time a new connection is established with Apache. This helps in securing the data being transmitted. If a user intercepts the connection and records the request headers, the captured data cannot be used at a later date. This is because a new nonce is generated when a new connection is established.

Digest Authentication: The Security Perspective

The mechanism of validation of credentials in case of digest authentication is very different than basic authentication. In the case of digest authentication, the Apache Web server maintains a copy of usernames and passwords. Whenever a client specifies a username and password, the server performs a few calculations. These calculations are performed using MD5 hash algorithm and are used to generate a *one-way hash* utilizing the username, password, and other information.

A one-way hash is a value that is impossible to reverse engineer; that is, the value generated by using a one-way hash cannot be cracked to derive the original value. However, the hash values can be compared. Therefore, the server compares the hash value calculated using the copy of the username and password that it maintains with the username and password specified by the user. If the values match, the requested resource is sent to the client. The only drawback to using digest authentication is that not all browsers support it.

CAUTION

No matter which authentication method you use, basic or digest, the body of the request sent by the client and body of the response sent by the Web server are clear text. This means that snoopers on the network can view the text of the request and response. Therefore, these authentication mechanisms don't ensure security of the actual data sent or received over the network.

Database-Driven Authentication

Both basic and digest authentication are effective ways of implementing authentication for your Web site. These authentication types use password files and database files for authentication. Better performance is one reason you might prefer database files for authentication. Using text files is preferred only if the number of users that you want to authenticate is limited. If you require authenticating hundreds of users, password files are not effective.

Every time a request is sent to Apache, the password file is checked, which could become cumbersome if the password file contains hundreds of entries. When there are numerous users listed in the password file, all the entries have to be checked before allowing or denying access to a particular user. This can take a lot of time. In such situations, it is also possible that an authorized user is denied access because the time taken to check the password file exceeds the time specified for server timeout. This can be highly irritating.

The only solution to this problem is to store passwords in databases. Databases are designed to store huge amounts of information. They are optimized to search for a piece of information within a large data set within less than a second. Most databases also use *query languages* (language used to extract, add, delete, and modify data in a database) that allow you to extract records that match a specified criteria. Therefore, if you must implement authentication on a Web server that has to serve hundreds of users, your best proposition is to use databases.

The Database Authentication Modules

Database authentication can be implemented in Apache using database authentication modules such as mod_auth_db and mod_auth_dbm. The utility of both these modules is the same as far as operating systems such as Linux and Free BSD are concerned. Before you start using these modules, you need to ensure that you have DB support on your platform.

Berkeley DB Files

Berkeley database files (known as Berkeley DB files) are ideal for storing authentication-related information. They are simple files that store key and value pairs. The key and value pairs include the name of the variable and the value of that variable. Unlike conventional databases, which have the capability of storing information in a number of fields, the Berkeley DB files store information in two fields in the form of a key and a value. Berkeley DB files are used for authentication because only the username and password are required to be validated.

Installing the Database Authentication Modules

Before you use the mod_auth_db or mod_auth_dbm modules, you need to install them. These modules are not included in the default installation of Apache. Therefore, you will need to rebuild Apache.

To build Apache with mod_auth_db or mod_auth_dbm built in, go to the directory where you stored the Apache source code and execute the following command:

```
#./configure -enable-module=auth_db
```

TIP

If you installed Apache using shared object support (DSO), you can build the modules separately from the Apache build and load them into Apache.

If you want to use mod_auth_dbm, you can replace auth_db with auth_dbm in the command. It is possible that you used several other options while compiling Apache. In such a situation, you can add either of the options (--enable-module=auth_db or --enable-module=auth_dbm) with the other configure options.

Directives Used for Configuring Authentication

You can use numerous directives to configure authentication on Apache. I will now focus on the most important directives that are used for configuring authentication.

The *AuthType* Directive

You use this directive to specify the authentication type that you choose to use. You have the choice of using either basic authentication or digest authentication. Whichever authentication method you choose to use should be specified in this directive. If you choose to use digest authentication, the syntax for this directive is as follows:

```
AuthType Digest
```

To use basic authentication, replace the word Digest with Basic in the AuthType directive.

The *AuthName* Directive

You use the AuthName directive to specify the realm of the protected resource. As discussed earlier, a realm is a collection of documents or resources on the Web server that are subject to the same set of authentication requirements. The realm symbolizes these resources and helps the client determine which username and password pair should be used. The string specified as the realm appears when the user is prompted to enter a username and password.

Consider the syntax of the AuthName directive:

```
AuthName InviteesOnly
```

In the preceding syntax, InviteesOnly is a string that represents the realm. If you want to use a realm name that consists of more than one word, you need to specify the name within double quotes.

The *AuthUserFile* Directive

You use this directive to specify the name of the password file. This password file contains the usernames and passwords. The passwords are stored in an encrypted form. Apache compares the usernames and passwords entered by the user with the values present in this file to authenticate the user.

TIP

Store the password file in a location other than the document root of the Web server. This is important from a security point of view—so that a user with malicious intentions doesn't download this file. Although cracking the encrypted password can be a pain, it is not impossible.

The usernames and passwords are stored in the password file in the following format:

```
username: encrypted_password
```

The syntax for using the AuthUserFile is as follows:

```
AuthUserFile /dirone/dirtwo/password_file_name
```

If the location of the file is specified using a leading slash as shown here, it is assumed that the path that is specified is an absolute path. On the contrary, if the leading slash is not specified, the path is considered to be a relative path. This path is relative to the server root. For example, if you specify the path as security/passwords/password_file and your server root is /usr/local/apache, it will be assumed that the file password_file is located in the /usr/local/apache/security/passwords directory.

NOTE

Typically, the password file is called the .htpasswd file. I discuss the .htpasswd file later in this chapter in the section "Access Control: Configuration."

The *AuthGroupFile* Directive

You use the AuthGroupFile directive to specify the location of the file that contains information about the user groups and the details of the members of the groups. Typically, this file is referred to as .htgroup.

Creating user groups makes the administrator's job easy because the administrator can specify a larger number of people to have access to a particular resource on the Web server. The information in this file is stored in the following format:

```
Team: user1 user2 user3
```

For security purposes, it is advisable to store this file in a location other than the document root. This is because a user with malicious intentions can possibly download this file and gather information about user groups that are allowed to access protected areas. The syntax for specifying the AuthGroupFile is as follows:

```
AuthGroupFile security/passwords/group_info
```

In the preceding syntax, the file named group_info contains the information about the user groups. The file is located in the security/passwords/ directory. Notice that the leading slash is not used in the path. This indicates that the path is relative to the server root of the Web server.

TIP

You might want to use only the password file and not the group file. In that case, you can specify the value /dev/null for the AuthGroupFile directive.

The *<Limit>* Directive

By default, the authentication directives that you configure are applicable for all the request methods that are used to access the resources on the Web server. However, it is possible to exclusively specify the methods on which the authentication directives will be applied. This can be achieved by using the <Limit> directive. You should be careful while using the <Limit> directive because the authentication directives will apply to only those request methods that are specified in the <Limit> directive. As a result, if a user is using an alternative method to access resources on the server, the authentication directives will cease to have an effect. This, in turn, will make the server prone to threats. The syntax of the <Limit> directive is as follows:

```
<Limit GET POST>
place authentication directives here
</Limit>
```

In the preceding syntax, notice that only the GET and POST methods are specified. This indicates that the authentication directives will apply only to these methods, leaving the rest of the methods unprotected.

The *<LimitExcept>* Directive

The use of ⟨LimitExcept⟩ directive is exactly the opposite of the use of the ⟨Limit⟩ directive. The authentication directives specified within this directive are applicable for methods that are not specified in this directive. The syntax for this directive is similar to that of the ⟨Limit⟩ directive. Consider the following example:

```
<LimitExcept POST>
place authentication directives here
</LimitExcept>
```

In the preceding example, the POST method is specified. This indicates that the authentication directives specified with the ⟨LimitExcept⟩ directive will be applicable for all the methods except POST. As a result, the authentication directives will not be applicable for requests sent using the POST request method.

The *Require* Directive

You use the Require directive to specify the identity of the users that will be allowed to access a set of specified resources on the Apache Web server. In order for the Require directive to work, though, you need to use the following directives with it:

- ◆ AuthName
- ◆ AuthType
- ◆ AuthUserFile
- ◆ AuthGroupFile

There are three ways in which you can use the Require directive to specify which users are allowed to access the server resources:

- ◆ Use the user ID
- ◆ Use the group ID
- ◆ Allow all valid users

Using the User ID

You can use the following syntax to specify one or more users who are permitted to access a specified directory:

```
require user user1 user2 user3
```

The preceding syntax indicates that three users, *user1*, *user2*, and *user3* are specified with the Require directive.

NOTE

Remember that you need to specify the users in accordance with the list of users listed in the AuthUserFile directive. In other words, you can specify only those users in the Require directive that appear in the referenced AuthUserFile directive.

Using the Group ID

You can use the following syntax to specify one or more groups that are permitted access:

```
require group groupone grouptwo
```

In the preceding syntax, the Require directive is used to specify that the groups named *groupone* and *grouptwo* are allowed access to the specified directories.

NOTE

Remember that you need to specify the groups in accordance with the AuthGroup-File directive. Only those users that are a part of the group listed in this directive will be allowed access.

Allowing All Valid Users

Finally, you can use the Require directive to specify that all valid users should be allowed to access a specified directory. Use the following syntax to achieve this functionality:

```
require valid-user
```

The preceding syntax means that all valid users that are listed in the AuthUserFile will be allowed to access the resources present in the specified directory.

The *Order, Allow* and *Deny* Directives

As discussed earlier, you use Allow and Deny directives to specify which hosts can access a particular directory. You use the Order directive to specify the order in which the Allow and Deny directives will be referenced when the Apache Web server receives a request. I will now discuss the use of these directives.

The Allow *Directive*

You can use the Allow directive in two ways. The first way enables you to specify a hostname that will be allowed access. The second way is to specify an environment variable. To allow a particular host with the Allow directive, use the following syntax:

```
allow from hostspecification
```

In the preceding syntax, hostspecification can be any of the following:

- **All.** Will allow all the hosts to access the specified resource on the Web server.
- **Domain name.** Will allow the specified domain name to access the resource on the Web server.
- **Partial domain name.** Will allow all hosts that end with the string (partial domain name) specified with the Allow directive.
- **A full IP address.** Will allow the host whose IP address is specified.
- **Partial IP address.** Will allow all hosts that are a part of the specified subnet. To specify a subnet, you need to specify the first three octets of the IP address. For example, allow from 193.101.203.
- **Network/netmask pair.** Will allow the specified range of IP addresses. The netmask can be specified using the format, a.b.c.d. It can also be specified using the *high-order bits* (bits that contribute the greatest value in a given string of bits). Consider the following example:

```
allow from 192.168.0.0/255.255.0.0
#netmask is specified using the format, a.b.c.d.
allow from 192.168.0.0/16
#netmask is specified using the high-order bits
```

In addition to using the host specification with the Allow directive, you can use environment variables to allow or disallow access to resources on the Web server. The syntax for specifying environment variables with the Allow directive is as follows:

```
Allow from env=variable
```

You can use this method with directives such as BrowserMatch, SetEnvIf, and other related directives. Consider the following example, in which access to a resource is allowed when the client agent name is Metal:

```
BrowserMatch Metal Permitted
Allow from env=Permitted
```

The Deny *Directive*

The Deny directive is the opposite of the Allow directive. You use this directive to disallow requests that match criteria specified in the Deny directive. The syntax for using the Deny directive is similar to that of the Allow directive. The syntax is as follows:

```
deny from host_specification
```

In the preceding syntax, host_specification can be replaced with any of the following values:

- All (if specified, this value denies access to every host)
- A full domain name
- A partial domain name
- A full IP address
- A partial IP address
- A network and netmask combination

As in the case of the Allow directive, you can use the Deny directive to allow or disallow access based on environment variables. The syntax for the Deny directive is as follows:

```
deny from env=variable
```

In the preceding syntax, variable is the name of the environment variable.

The Order *Directive*

The Order directive is responsible for controlling the default access state for a directory. You use this directive to specify the sequence in which the Allow and Deny directives will be referred. The Order directive can be specified as three different arguments:

- **Deny, Allow.** Indicates that the hostnames, domain names, and IP addresses specified in the Deny directive are explicitly denied access. The rest of the values that are specified in the Allow directive are allowed access.
- **Allow, Deny.** Indicates that the hostnames, domain names, and IP addresses specified in the Allow directive are explicitly allowed access. The rest of the values specified in the Deny directive are denied access.
- **Mutual-Failure.** This argument indicates that only those hosts that are explicitly allowed in the Allow directive and that are not forbidden in the Deny directive will be allowed access. This argument is deprecated because it has the same effect as the Allow, Deny option.

Using the Allow *and* Deny *Directives with the* Order *Directive*

You can use the Allow and Deny directives with or without the Order directive. However, when you use these directives with the Order directive, don't leave a security loop. There might be situations in which the IP address of a host appears in both the Allow directive and the Deny directive. Such situations might appear confusing. I will now examine what happens when an IP address appears in both Allow and Deny lists. The following example explains which of the statements take precedence in those situations. Consider a situation in which IP addresses 172.17.68.0 to 172.17.68.22 are specified in the Allow directive and the IP address 172.17.68.3 is specified in the Deny directive. In this case, the sequence of the Allow and Deny directives will have the following impact:

◆ **Order allow, deny.** All hosts whose IP addresses are in the range 172.17.68.0/22 will be allowed access. The only exception will be the host with the IP address 172.17.68.3. This host will be denied access because it is listed in the Deny directive. In this case, the Deny directive takes precedence because it is specified later in the sequence.

◆ **Order deny, allow.** Although the IP address 172.17.68.3 is listed in the Deny directive, it will be allowed access. This is because this IP address is also a part of the Allow directive. The host with this IP address is allowed access because the Allow directive is specified after the Deny directive and, as a result, gains precedence over the Deny directive.

◆ **Order mutual-failure.** This argument will deny access to 172.17.68.3 because it is used in both Allow and Deny directives. This suggests that if the specified IP address is a part of both Allow and Deny directives, it will be denied access to the resources on the Web server.

The Satisfy Directive

The Satisfy directive proves to be useful when you have used Require as well as Allow or Deny directives. You use the Satisfy directive to specify whether to use Require or Allow and Deny directives. You can use two arguments with the Satisfy directive:

◆ **All.** Indicates that both conditions must be fulfilled before a user can access resources on the Web server.

◆ **Any.** Indicates that if either of the conditions is fulfilled, the user will be allowed to access the resources on the Web server. This argument can be set in such a way that some hosts need to specify a valid username and password to gain access, whereas the others can directly gain access to server resources.

Managing Password Files

No matter what type of authentication you choose to use, managing passwords is something you cannot do without. Passwords are typically stored in either text files or DB files. The steps for maintaining passwords are different for each type of authentication. Therefore, I will discuss how password files are created and maintained when I get into actual configuration in the upcoming section "Access Control: Configuration." However, there are certain guidelines related to managing password files and passwords that you can follow to prevent them from being hacked.

Guidelines for Managing Password Files

It is important that the server administrator follow these guidelines to ensure security for the password files:

◆ Store the password file at a secure location on the file system. Store the password file where users other than the root user do not have access permissions. Avoid keeping the password file under the document root directory.

◆ The password file should be a hidden file. When creating the password, preceding the name of the file with a period ensures that the file is hidden. Hidden files are visible only when you use the -a option with the ls command.

◆ Give the password file a name other than .htpasswd. The most commonly used name for password file is .htpasswd. Administrators find it convenient to use this name because this filename is universally propagated in several Apache documentations. However, it is advisable to use an alternative name for the password file so that it is difficult to guess in which file the passwords are stored.

Guidelines for Selecting the Appropriate Password

In order to ensure security, it is important that users who are allowed access by way of password files follow the following guidelines. Although passwords are not secure while being transmitted over the Internet, you need to take these precautions to prevent your password from being hacked:

◆ Always use passwords that are difficult to guess or crack. Using passwords such as "password" and "qwerty" (the first six letters on the keyboard) are easy to figure out. Also, do not use your name or your spouse's name as the password.

◆ Passwords should always be a combination of letters in the alphabet and numbers and should not be based on words found in a dictionary.

◆ Never use your desktop or network password for the password file that is used by Apache Web server. Whether you are using basic or digest authentication, passwords are not transmitted safely over the Internet. Therefore, do not use the same password that you use for your bank account or your desktop.

Using .htaccess Files

One of the most common requirements of any Web server administrator is to enable the Web server to behave in a way that all documents in a particular directory or a directory tree are treated the same way. One such configuration is to prompt a user for a password before accessing the contents of a particular directory. Another possible configuration is to allow or disallow directory listing for a particular directory. However, even users other than Apache server administrators need to be able to customize their space on the Web server.

This is made possible by using .htaccess files. The .htaccess file is a configuration file that allows you to specify exclusive configuration options for a particular directory. This helps the server administrator to customize the behavior of the Apache Web server or to allow the users to customize the space allocated to them. Using .htaccess files is fairly easy. All you have to do is include the required configuration directives in the .htaccess file. Of course, the file should be located in the directory for which the configuration is intended.

 NOTE

Using the name .htaccess for this file is not mandatory. You can choose the name you want for this configuration file. However, if you choose to use a filename other than .htaccess, you will need to specify the name in the `AccessFileName` directive.

Purpose of Using .htaccess Files

Any configuration that you choose to put in the .htaccess file can also be specified under the `<Directory>` section in the main Apache configuration file. This imparts the necessary characteristics to the directory in question. Moreover, using the `<Directory>` section is considered ideal because the options specified in this section are directly loaded into memory when the server is started.

You might be wondering about the utility of .htaccess files if directives and options can be specified in the main configuration file. A Web server administrator might be prompted to use .htaccess files for several reasons. I will now discuss a few situations that might require the use of .htaccess files.

There are situations in which several site developers need to work together to create content for the site. In such situations, developers might want to make configuration changes to the server as the need arises. However, these developers do not have access to the main configuration file. Also, contacting the administrator for every small configuration can be cumbersome and can waste a great deal of time. By using .htaccess files, you can give developers the ability to make required configuration changes to the server without involving the site administrator.

Another important benefit of using .htaccess files is the ability to make local configuration changes to affect the behavior of directories without having to involve the entire server. Also, by using .htaccess files, the numerous restarts that are required after making configuration changes can be eliminated. Consider an example in which one of the virtual sites hosted on your Web server requires a redirect from an old URL to a new URL.

You can manage this in a couple of minutes by using the .htaccess file and specifying the Redirect directive. This .htaccess file can then be placed at the base of the directory tree. Although the task is simple, asking the site administrator to fix this problem is not a good idea. First, the administrator will need to take time to fix the problem, make changes to the main configuration file, and then restart the server when there is minimum network traffic. In such cases, the better approach is to use .htaccess files to allow the individual handling the virtual host to make the required change without having to restart the server.

When to Avoid Using .htaccess Files

I discussed the benefits of using the .htaccess file in the previous section. However, doing so might not always be the best option. Here are some situations in which you will not want to use .htaccess files:

◆ If a single administrator is administering the entire Web server, it is advisable to maintain only one configuration file. All configuration changes should be made to the maintained file. Scattering .htaccess files all over the file system might prove to be confusing for the Web server administrator. In such cases, use the following option:

```
AllowOverride None
```

This option indicates that the .htaccess files cannot be used to override the configuration options specified in the main configuration file.

◆ Whenever a client requests a document from the Web server, the server checks whether the user is eligible to access the requested resource. When you use .htaccess files, each directory that is a part of the path to the file is checked for the presence of .htaccess files. If the server encounters .htaccess files, these files are parsed to check whether the user has adequate permissions on the directory. In situations where the requested file is located further down the directory structure, processing the .htaccess files for each directory before sending a response to the client might take a long time. You can avoid this situation by using directives in the main configuration file. Directives specified in the main configuration file are loaded in the memory at server startup and, as a result, are faster than .htaccess files.

Uses for .htaccess Files

There are several uses for the .htaccess file. The most important feature is that all of the directives can be specified in the .htaccess file except the ones that are used for server-wide settings such as ServerRoot, MaxClients, HostNameLookup, and ServerType. However, this is not a rule of thumb.

The directives most commonly used in .htaccess files are as follows:

◆ **AuthConfig.** Used for implementing authentication.
◆ **Indexes.** Used for specifying how the automatic directory listing should appear.
◆ **Limit.** Used to control which hosts will be allowed to access a resource on the Web server.
◆ **Options.** Used to specify various other configuration options.

One important thing to understand is that all the .htaccess files and the directives specified within them will be used only if the value of AllowOverride directive is not None. If the value of this directive is None, the .htaccess files cannot overrule the configuration of the main server.

Another important point to remember is that quite a few directives cannot be used in .htaccess files. If you use any of the directives that are not permitted, you will encounter a server error.

Now that you know the directives that are most commonly used with the .htaccess file, I will discuss the main configurations for which .htaccess files are used.

Authentication

The .htaccess file is most commonly used for authentication. To implement authentication, just specify the authentication-related directives in the .htacess file. The authentication-related directives, as discussed earlier, are `AuthType`, `AuthName`, `AuthUserFile`, and `AuthGroupFile`. These directives are specified in the .htaccess file, and, in turn, the file is placed in the directory on which the authentication should apply.

Permitting CGI Scripts

You can also use the .htaccess files to permit CGI *(Common Gateway Interface)* scripts for low-privileged users. Consider a situation in which a few users on a site want to execute CGI files from their home directories. This generally will not be possible because low-privileged users are not allowed to access the cgi-bin directory that contains CGI scripts. Using the .htaccess file and using the ExecCGI option with the Options directive as shown here can counter this problem:

```
Options ExecCGI
```

After specifying this option in the .htaccess file, you can place the file in the directory from which the execution of CGI scripts should be allowed.

Access Control: Configuration

Up to this point, I have discussed the concepts related to access control and the various methods for implementing it. In this section, I discuss the steps that you need to follow in order to implement access control on your server. Practice them to gain confidence.

Configuring Host-Based Access Control

I have already discussed the main concepts related to host-based authentication. I will now provide certain examples that will help you understand how host-based security is implemented.

Permitting Access from a Particular Domain

Consider a situation in which your company wants to deny access to a particular directory to everybody except hosts that are a part of the domain named `trustdomain.com`. The following example allows access only from the specified domain:

```
Order deny, allow
Deny from all
Allow from trustdomain.com
```

In the preceding example, note the following:

◆ The Order directive is used to specify the sequence in which the server will check Allow and Deny directives. In this case, the Allow directive will be checked after the Deny directive.

◆ The Deny directive is used to specify that the access will be blocked for all hosts.

◆ The Allow directive is used to specify that only the hosts that are a part of the domain named trustdomain.com will be able to access resources on the server.

Denying Access from a Particular Domain

Consider a situation in which your company wants to deny access to a specific domain named maliciousintent.com. However, the administrator wants the rest of the domains to be able to access the resources. The following example denies access only from the specified domain:

```
Order allow, deny
Allow from all
Deny from maliciousintent.com
```

In the preceding example, note the following:

◆ The Order directive is used to specify the sequence in which the server will check Allow and Deny directives. In this case, the Allow directive will be checked before the Deny directive.

◆ The Allow directive is used to specify that the access will be allowed for all hosts.

◆ The Deny directive is used to specify that only the hosts that are a part of the domain named maliciousintent.com will be denied access to resources on the server.

Configuring Basic Authentication

As far as configuring authentication is concerned, the steps are more or less the same for each type of authentication. However, I will discuss the steps for configuring each authentication type in detail. I will first take up the most common form of authentication used all over the world, basic authentication. The procedure for implementing basic authentication can be divided into three steps:

1. Create the password file.
2. Configure the authentication directives.
3. Create the group file.

Creating the Password File

The first step in using basic authentication is to have a password file in place. You use this file to store the usernames and passwords of the users who are to receive access to the resources on the Web server. In Linux, you can use the htpasswd utility to create the password file and later append the contents of this password file. Store this file on the server and be sure to preserve it at a location other than the document root.

The .htpasswd file is located in the bin directory of your Apache installation directory. If you performed a custom install similar to the one explained in Chapter 3, "Installing Apache," you will find this utility in the /usr/local/apache/bin directory. You can check this by moving to this directory and using the ls command to display the directory listing as shown here:

```
[root@localhost bin]# cd /usr/local/apache/bin/
[root@localhost bin]# ls -1
total 520
-rwxr-xr-x    1 root    root        33540 Apr 29 23:48 ab
-rwxr-xr-x    1 root    root         7103 Apr 29 23:48 apachectl
-rwxr-xr-x    1 root    root        21981 Apr 29 23:48 apxs
-rwxr-xr-x    1 root    root         4172 Apr 29 23:48 checkgid
-rwxr-xr-x    1 root    root        10938 Apr 29 23:48 dbmmanage
-rwxr-xr-x    1 root    root        13644 Apr 29 23:48 htdigest
-rwxr-xr-x    1 root    root        36224 Apr 29 23:48 htpasswd
-rwxr-xr-x    1 root    root       365129 Apr 29 23:48 httpd
-rwxr-xr-x    1 root    root         7944 Apr 29 23:48 logresolve
-rwxr-xr-x    1 root    root         6332 Apr 29 23:48 rotatelogs
```

The preceding output shows that the htpasswd utility is located in the /usr/local/apache/bin directory.

The syntax for using this utility is as follows:

```
#htpasswd -someoption passwordfile username
```

In the preceding syntax, note the following:

- ◆ someoption is used to specify an option.
- ◆ passwordfile is the location of the file in which you will store the passwords.
- ◆ username is the name of the user that you will add to your password file.

You can use several options with the htpasswd utility. To view the options that can be used with htpasswd, execute the following command:

```
[root@localhost bin]# htpasswd --help
Usage:
        htpasswd [-cmdps] passwordfile username
        htpasswd -b[cmdps] passwordfile username password
```

```
htpasswd -n[mdps] username
htpasswd -nb[mdps] username password
```

-c Create a new file.

-n Don't update file; display results on stdout.

-m Force MD5 encryption of the password.

-d Force CRYPT encryption of the password (default).

-p Do not encrypt the password (plaintext).

-s Force SHA encryption of the password.

-b Use the password from the command line rather than prompting for it.

On Windows, TPF and NetWare systems the '-m' flag is used by default.

On all other systems, the '-p' flag will probably not work.

The preceding output shows the options that can be used with the htpasswd utility. Notice that a brief description of each option is also displayed. In order to create a new password file, you need to specify the -c option with the htpasswd utility. However, you need to use this option only the first time you create the password file. After that, you can add entries to this file without specifying the -c option.

Configuring the Authentication Directives

After you create the password file, the next step is to configure the authentication directives. These authentication directives can be placed in the main configuration file within the <Directory> </Directory> section or in the .htaccess file. If you choose to use the .htaccess file, you need to place this file in the directory for which you want to grant or deny access. Consider the following example in which each authentication directive is configured:

```
AuthType Basic
AuthName "Restricted Entry"
AuthUserFile /usr/local/apache/passwd/.passwords
Require valid-user
```

In the preceding configuration, note the following:

◆ The value of AuthType directive is Basic. This indicates that basic authentication is used.

◆ The value for AuthName directive is "Restricted Entry". This indicates the realm name specified for the resource on the server. The realm name is in the dialog box that appears when a user tries to access the resource on the Web server using a graphical browser such as Netscape Navigator or Microsoft Internet Explorer.

◆ The AuthUserFile directive specifies that the password file named .passwords is located in the /usr/local/apache/passwd directory.

◆ The `Require` directive specifies which users listed in the password file should be able to access the resource. The value `valid-user` signifies that all the users listed in the password file will be able to access if they specify the correct password.

Creating the Group File

Creating a group file adds another layer of security to the protected content on the Apache Web server. The group file maintains a list of valid groups and users that are a part of the group. Maintaining a group file is particularly useful when you need to authenticate dozens of users. In such a situation, you can simply create a group file and define the users that can be a part of the group. Creating a group file is optional. Consider the following example:

```
AuthType Basic
AuthName "Core Development Team"
AuthUserFile /usr/local/apache/passwd/.passwords
AuthGroupFile /usr/local/apache/passwd/.groups
Require group devteam
```

In the preceding example, note the following:

◆ The value for `AuthName` directive is `"Core Development Team"`. This indicates the realm name specified for the resource on the server.

◆ The `AuthUserFile` directive specifies that the password file named `.passwords` is located in the `/usr/local/apache/passwd` directory.

◆ The `AuthGroupFile` directive specifies that the group file named `.groups` is located in the `/usr/local/apache/passwd` directory.

◆ The `Require` directive specifies that the authenticated users that are part of the group named `devteam` should be able to access the resource.

Configuring Digest Authentication

The configuration steps for digest authentication are almost the same as basic authentication. However, you should remember that the `mod_auth_digest` module is required before you can use digest authentication. The much-discussed benefit of using digest authentication is that the passwords are not sent as clear text. The following is an overview of the procedure for configuring digest authentication:

1. Create the password file.
2. Configure the authentication directives.
3. Create the group file.

Creating the Password File

The logic for creating a password file to be used for digest authentication is the same as that of creating a password file for basic authentication, but the steps for creating a password file for digest authentication are slightly different. Unlike basic authentication, for digest authentication, the password file is created using the htdigest utility. This utility is located in the /usr/local/apache/bin directory. The syntax of the htdigest utility is as follows:

```
#htdigest -option passwordfile realm username
```

In the preceding syntax, note the following:

- ◆ option is the command-line option that is specified with the htdigest utility.
- ◆ passwordfile depicts the location of the password file.
- ◆ realm depicts the name for the resources on the server for which digest authentication is implemented.
- ◆ username is the name of the user that will be added to the password file.

For more help on the htdigest utility, type the following command at the command prompt:

```
[root@localhost bin]# htdigest --help
Usage: htdigest [-c] passwordfile realm username
The -c flag creates a new file.
```

The output indicates that the -c option can be used to create a new password file. You need to use this option the first time you create the password file. After you create the password file, you can add the entries to the file without specifying this option.

Configuring the Authentication Directives

After you create the password file, the next step is to configure the authentication directives so that the Apache Web server knows where to find the source of authenticated user information. You can specify the authentication directives in the .htaccess file or within the <Directory> </Directory> section of the main configuration file. In either case, you first need to specify valid values for each of the authentication directives, as shown here:

```
AuthType Digest
AuthName "Secure Authentication"
AuthDigestFile /usr/local/apache/passwd/.digestpasswords
Require user steve lisa
```

In the preceding example, note the following:

- ◆ The value of AuthType directive is Digest. This indicates that digest authentication is used.
- ◆ The value for AuthName directive is "Secure Authentication". This denotes the realm name specified for the resource on the server.

◆ The `AuthDigestFile` directive specifies that the password file named `.digestpass-words` is located in the `/usr/local/apache/passwd` directory.

◆ The `Require` directive specifies which users listed in the password file should be able to access the resource. In this example, `steve` and `lisa` are the only users who will be allowed to access resources on the Web server.

Creating the Group File

The purpose of the group file used for digest authentication is the same as that of the group file used for basic authentication. The group file used for digest authentication also contains the name of the group and the users that are part of the group. Maintaining this file is purely optional. When a group file is used, this file is checked before the password file at the time of authentication.

Consider the following example:

```
AuthType Digest
AuthName "Secure Authentication"
AuthDigestFile /usr/local/apache/passwd/.digestpasswords
AuthDigestGroupFile /usr/local/apache/passwd/.digestgroup
Require group administrators
```

In the preceding example, note the following:

◆ The `AuthDigestFile` directive specifies that the password file named `.digestpass-words` is located in the `/usr/local/apache/passwd` directory.

◆ The `Require` directive specifies the group that will be allowed access. In this example, a user who is a part of the administrators group will be allowed access.

Configuring Apache to Use DB Files for Authentication

As discussed earlier, in order to use database authentication, you need to compile the `mod_auth_db` module in the Apache Web server. The general steps for configuring database authentication are the same as those for basic and digest authentication.

1. Create the user file.
2. Configure the authentication directives.
3. Create the group file.

Creating the User File

To implement database authentication, the first step is to create a user file that contains authentication details for the user. This file is similar to a password file. However, keep in mind that this is a DB file, not a text file. You create the user file by using the `dbmmanage` utility. This utility is available with Apache in the /usr/local/apache/bin directory (when you use custom installation).

The syntax for using the dbmmanage utility is as follows:

```
#dbmmanage passwordfile.db adduser steve
```

In the preceding syntax, note the following:

◆ passwordfile.db is the DB file that will be used to store the password of the user steve.

◆ adduser is a command-line option used with the dbmmanage utility to add a user.

When you use this command, you are prompted to set a password for the user steve. A number of options can be used with the dbmmanage utility. Type the following command to display these options:

```
[root@localhost bin]# dbmmanage --help
Usage: dbmmanage [enc] dbname command [username [pw [group[,group]
[comment]]]]

        where enc is  -d for crypt encryption (default except on Win32, Netware)
                      -m for MD5 encryption (default on Win32, Netware)
                      -s for SHA1 encryption
                      -p for plaintext

        command is one of: add|adduser|check|delete|import|update|view

        pw of . for update command retains the old password
        pw of - (or blank) for update command prompts for the password

        groups or comment of . (or blank) for update command retains old values
        groups or comment of - for update command clears the existing value
        groups or comment of - for add and adduser commands is the empty value
```

Configuring the Authentication Directives

After you create the user file, the next step is to configure the authentication directives. After specifying a value for the directives, place them in the .htaccess file or the <Directory> </Directory> section in the main configuration file.

Consider the following example:

```
AuthType Basic
AuthName "Restricted Access"
AuthDBUserFile /usr/local/apache/passwd/passwords.dat
require valid-user
```

In the preceding example, the `AuthDBUserFile` directive specifies the location of the user file that stores the authentication credentials of a user, such as the username and the password.

Creating the Group File

You create a group file using the `dbmmanage` utility. However, creating a group file is optional and can be avoided. To add a group file, use the following command:

```
#dbmmanage add groupfile steve admin development marketing
```

In the preceding command, note the following:

◆ The `add` command is used with the `dbmmanage` utility to create a group file.

◆ The name of the group file is `groupfile`.

◆ The user `steve` is added to the groups `admin`, `development`, and `marketing`.

After you create the group file, configure the authentication directives as shown here:

```
AuthType Basic
AuthName "Restricted Access"
AuthDBUserFile /usr/local/apache/passwd/passwords.dat
AuthDBGroupFile /usr/local/apache/passwd/groupfile
require valid-user
```

Notice that the `AuthDBGroupFile` directive is used to specify the location for the group file.

Putting Your Knowledge into Practice

In this section, I discuss a scenario for protecting content on your Web site. Imagine that you are a system administrator responsible for administering the Apache Web server. As a system administrator, you are responsible for the security of your site. You have been assigned the task of setting up password protection for the site in such a way that only valid users can access its resources. To accomplish this task, and assuming that you want to use basic authentication, you perform the steps in the following sections.

Create the .htaccess File

To create the .htaccess file, follow these steps:

1. Use the vi editor to create a file named .htaccess in the document root directory.

   ```
   #vi /opt/web/html/.htaccess
   ```

2. Add the following directives in the .htaccess file.

   ```
   AuthName "Please Enter Credentials"
   AuthType Basic
   AuthUserFile /usr/local/apache/passwd/.htpasswd
   Require valid-user
   ```

Create the Password File

To create the password file, follow these steps:

1. If the directory passwd in which you plan to place the password file doesn't exist, create it.

   ```
   #mkdir /usr/local/apache/passwd
   ```

2. Use the htpasswd utility to create the password file. As soon as you type the command to create a password file and specify a username, you will be prompted to specify a password for the user steve. Specify the password as password. After you specify the password, you will be prompted to retype the password for confirmation, as shown here:

   ```
   [root@localhost root]#htpasswd -c /usr/local/apache/passwd/.htpasswd steve
   New password:
   Re-type new password:
   Adding password for user steve
   ```

3. Open the .htpasswd file to see whether the user steve was added successfully. The following information should appear:

   ```
   steve:2yaRBjJqCJHKI
   ```

 NOTE

If a new user sets the same password as set by an existing user, the encrypted value of both passwords will be different, even though the text is the same.

Edit the httpd.conf File

After creating the password file, you need to make certain changes in the main configuration file of Apache, as shown here:

1. Open the Apache configuration file.

   ```
   #vim /usr/local/apache/conf/httpd.conf
   ```

2. Edit the configuration file and change the value of the AllowOverride directive to AuthConfig:

   ```
   # This controls which options the .htaccess files in directories can
   # override. Can also be "All", or any combination of "Options", "FileInfo"
   # "AuthConfig", and "Limit"
   #
        AllowOverride AuthConfig
   ```

3. Add the following lines to the httpd.conf file:

   ```
   #This is for implementing authentication for users!
   <Directory /opt/web/html>
   Order allow,deny
   Allow from all
   </Directory>
   #End of authentication configuration
   ```

This completes the configuration for using basic authentication to allow only valid users. As you can see in the preceding sets of steps, only steve was given access to the document root.

Test the Configuration

Now, it is time to test the configuration. Doing so is fairly simple; you just connect to the Web server and access the home page. In the following sections, you check whether the configuration is working when connecting from a Linux client and a Windows client.

From a Windows Client

1. Open Internet Explorer and type the IP address of the Linux server on which you configured Apache. The Enter Network Password dialog box appears.
2. You are prompted to enter your credentials, as shown in Figure 5.1.
3. In the User Name and Password text boxes, type **steve** and **password**, respectively. You should see the home page, as shown in Figure 5.2.

FIGURE 5.1 *The Enter Network Password dialog box*

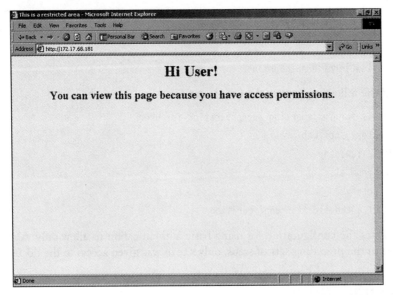

FIGURE 5.2 *The Web page that appears after you enter the correct username and password.*

Note that if you click Cancel in the Enter Network Password dialog box without entering valid credentials, the message shown in Figure 5.3 appears.

From a Linux Client

To access the Web page from a Linux client, you can use Netscape Navigator. Just specify the IP address of the Linux computer on which Apache is configured, and you will see the dialog box shown in Figure 5.4.

After you specify the correct username and password, you will gain access to the site.

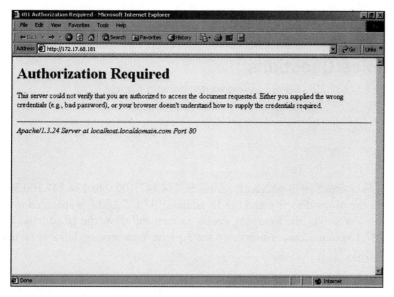

FIGURE 5.3 *This message appears if you refuse to specify the credentials.*

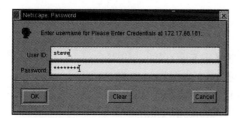

FIGURE 5.4 *The Netscape: Password dialog box*

Summary

In this chapter, you learned how to configure Apache so that you can implement access control. You learned how host-based and authentication-based access control work and how to use the .htaccess file.

Check Your Understanding

Multiple Choice Questions

1. Which of the following are fully qualified domain names?

    a. `.com`

    b. `.org`

    c. `.welcome.com`

    d. `colors.rednblue.com`

2. Consider a situation in which IP addresses 134.147.100.0 to 134.147.100.50 are specified in the `Allow` directive and the IP address 137.147.100.6 is specified in the `Deny` directive. Which of the following configurations will allow the IP address 134.147.100.6 to access resources on the Apache Web server? (Choose all that apply.)

    a. `Order deny, allow`

    b. `Order allow, deny`

    c. `Order mutual-failure`

    d. `Order allow, deny`
        `Allow from all`

3. Which of the following is not a feature of digest authentication?

    a. Credentials of the user are sent in encrypted format.

    b. The Web server sends resources to the client in encrypted form.

    c. A few browsers don't support digest authentication.

    d. A nonce is generated in digest authentication.

4. Which of the following is not used to derive a digest that is sent to the Web server when digest authentication is used?

    a. Username

    b. Password

    c. Name of the Web server

    d. Requested resource

5. Which of the following directives contain the location of the password file that is checked before authenticating a user? (Choose all that apply.)

    a. `AuthUserFile`

    b. `AuthDigestFile`

    c. `AuthName`

    d. `AuthType`

Answers

Multiple Choice Answers

1. d. Only `colors.rednblue.com` is a fully qualified domain name because it is not preceded by a period.

2. a, d. In the first option, the `Deny` directive will deny the IP address 134.147.100.6. However, this will be overridden by the `Allow` directive that includes 134.147.100.6 because the `Allow` directive appears later in the sequence of the `Order` directive. In the fourth option, the `Deny` directive denies access to the Web server for 134.147.100.6. However, later, the `Allow` directive specifies that all hosts should be allowed. As a result, 134.147.100.6 is allowed access even after it is specified in the `Deny` directive.

3. b. The resources sent by the Web server are unencrypted even if digest authentication is used.

4. c. The name of the server is not a part of the digest that is sent to the Web server when digest authentication is used.

5. a, b. `AuthUserfile` is used to specify the location for the password file when basic authentication is used. On the other hand, `AuthDigestFile` is used to specify the location for the password file when digest authentication is used.

PART II

Implementing Basic Features of Apache

Chapter 6

Configuring Virtual Hosts

Virtual hosting enables a Web server to host more than one Web site at a time. The Apache Web server was one of the first Web server to incorporate this functionality. Many Web-hosting companies today use the Apache Web server to host several Web sites for each of their customers.

The Web site that you plan to host on Apache could be a part of the same domain or of different domains. With the ever-increasing number of Web sites on the Internet, virtual hosting has become a necessity in order for a Web server to qualify as a good Web server.

In this chapter, I discuss the concepts related to virtual hosting in Apache and the types of virtual hosting options that are available. Finally, I discuss how virtual host support can be added to Apache.

The Virtual Hosts Section in httpd.conf

Before delving into a discussion on virtual hosts, you need to become familiar with the Virtual Hosts section in the httpd.conf file. The following section (Section 3) contains a few directives that you should be familiar with before you begin:

```
# Section 3: Virtual Hosts
#
# VirtualHost: If you want to maintain multiple domains/hostnames on your
# machine you can setup VirtualHost containers for them. Most configurations
# use only name-based virtual hosts so the server doesn't need to worry about
# IP addresses. This is indicated by the asterisks in the directives below.
#
# Please see the documentation at <URL:http://www.apache.org/docs/vhosts/>
# for further details before you try to setup virtual hosts.
#
# You may use the command line option '-S' to verify your virtual host
# configuration.

#
# Use name-based virtual hosting.
#
#NameVirtualHost *

#
# VirtualHost example:
# Almost any Apache directive may go into a VirtualHost container.
# The first VirtualHost section is used for requests without a known
# server name.
#
#<VirtualHost *>
#    ServerAdmin webmaster@dummy-host.example.com
#    DocumentRoot /www/docs/dummy-host.example.com
#    ServerName dummy-host.example.com
#    ErrorLog logs/dummy-host.example.com-error_log
#    CustomLog logs/dummy-host.example.com-access_log common
#</VirtualHost>
```

In the preceding section, note the following:

◆ You use the `NameVirtualHost` directive to specify that you will use name-based virtual hosts. The syntax of this directive is

```
NameVirtualHost address [:port]
```

where `address` is the IP address of the virtual host and `port` is the port number that the virtual host will listen to. This directive should be configured only for name-based virtual hosts.

 NOTE

I discuss name-based virtual hosts later in this chapter, in the section "Name-Based Virtual Hosts."

◆ You use the `<VirtualHost>` and `</VirtualHost>` directives to specify a list of configuration directives for a virtual host. These directives are referred when a document is requested from the virtual host. The syntax for using this directive is

```
<VirtualHost address[:port]>
...add configuration directives
</VirtualHost>
```

where `address` is either the IP address of the virtual host or a fully qualified domain name.

◆ Several directives are specified within the `<VirtualHost>` and `</VirtualHost>` section. These directives include, `ServerAdmin`, `DocumentRoot`, `ServerName`, `ErrorLog`, and `CustomLog`.

◆ You use the `ErrorLog` and `CustomLog` directives to maintain necessary logs for the virtual host configured on the Apache Web server.

Types of Virtual Hosts

Broadly speaking, there are three types of virtual hosts: name-based virtual hosts, IP-based virtual hosts, and dynamic virtual hosts. However, the most common methods of configuring Apache to use virtual hosts involve using name-based and IP-based virtual hosts. The `mod_virtual` module is the standard Apache module used for virtual hosting. Both IP-based and name-based virtual hosts can be implemented using the `mod_virtual` module.

IP-Based Virtual Hosts

IP-based virtual hosts are virtual hosts that are identified by using unique IP addresses. These virtual hosts receive client requests on an assigned IP address. All responses sent to the client are also sent using the same IP address assigned to the IP-based virtual host.

 NOTE

IP addresses are configured on the network interface card that the server is using. However, when you want to configure several virtual hosts, it might not be feasible to have that many network interface cards. To counter this, you can use *interface aliasing*. Interface aliasing allows you to configure multiple IP addresses on the same network interface card. Interface aliasing is also known as *IP aliasing*. I discuss interface aliasing later in this chapter in the section "Configuring Multiple IP Addresses on a Single NIC."

IP-based virtual hosting is particularly useful for Web sites that implement *secure sockets layer (SSL)*. SSL requires each SSL Web server to compulsorily have a unique IP address associated with its hostname. Therefore, Web-hosting companies and ISPs that provide site-hosting services for SSL Web sites use IP-based virtual hosting. This can be counted as one of the reasons why IP-based virtual hosts are still used.

Another important feature from an administration point of view is that IP-based virtual hosts can be set up with ease. All you need to do is use the `<VirtualHost>` and `</VirtualHost>` directives to include the configuration directives for the virtual host. You can specify the unique IP address in the `<VirtualHost>` container directive as follows:

```
<VirtualHost 172.17.68.222>
    include configuration directives here
</VirtualHost>
```

The IP address specified should be unique and valid. Consider another example in which I also included a few configuration directives within the `<VirtualHost>` directive:

```
<VirtualHost 172.17.68.222>
ServerName steve.mailserver.com
DocumentRoot /opt/web/html/steve
</VirtualHost>
```

In the preceding example, note the following:

◆ An IP-based virtual host is configured.
◆ The unique IP address assigned to the virtual host is 172.17.68.222.

◆ The ServerName directive is used to specify the hostname of the virtual host.

◆ The DocumentRoot directive is used to specify the document root directory for the virtual host.

This is the simplest example of configuring an IP-based virtual host using the most basic directives. However, a number of directives can be specified in this section to customize the behavior of virtual hosts. A few of these directives are global directives that are specified in the main server configuration section. You should take extra care not to include these directives in the virtual hosts section to avoid problems in the server configuration.

After creating a virtual host as specified in the preceding example, you can access the site by specifying the IP address of the virtual host in the URL. This will help you request resources from the Web site hosted on the virtual host. As soon as you specify the IP address of the virtual host in the browser, the index page of the site will be displayed. You can use the following URL to access the document root directory of the virtual host configured on the IP 172.17.68.222:

http://172.17.68.222

However, users will not always find it convenient to type the entire IP address. To avoid this situation, you associate the IP address with a domain name. Configuring the Linux machine as a DNS server can do this. After the appropriate settings are made to the DNS by associating a domain name with the IP address, the users can access the site using the domain name. Consider an example in which the IP address of the virtual host is associated with the domain name my.webserver.com. In this case, the user can access the document root of the virtual host by specifying the following URL:

http://my.webserver.com

 NOTE

In IP-based virtual hosts, configuring the IP address to use a domain name is purely for the convenience of the users. Doing so has no impact on the functioning of the virtual host. While using IP-based virtual hosts, the Apache Web server distributes the request to the respective virtual host only on the basis of the unique IP address.

Figure 6.1 depicts how IP-based virtual hosting functions.

Default Virtual Hosts

Default virtual hosts are virtual hosts that are contacted in case no <VirtualHost IP_address> is matched. Consider a situation in which a client sends a request and the server can be contacted on more than one IP address for which a virtual host is not defined. In such a case, the

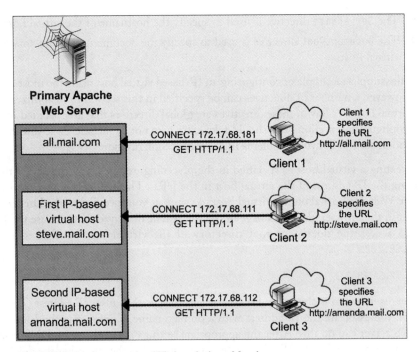

Primary Apache Web Server

all.mail.com

CONNECT 172.17.68.181
GET HTTP/1.1

Client 1 specifies the URL http://all.mail.com

Client 1

First IP-based virtual host steve.mail.com

CONNECT 172.17.68.111
GET HTTP/1.1

Client 2 specifies the URL http://steve.mail.com

Client 2

Second IP-based virtual host amanda.mail.com

CONNECT 172.17.68.112
GET HTTP/1.1

Client 3 specifies the URL http://amanda.mail.com

Client 3

FIGURE 6.1 *An example of IP-based virtual hosting*

main server configuration takes precedence, and the primary server is used to respond to the client. When this happens, all the directives that are applicable to the main server configuration are used by each request (these directives also include those directives that can't be used in the Virtual Hosts section).

Therefore, while using IP-based virtual hosts, you should configure a default server. Doing so will prevent the primary server configuration from being used to respond to requests.

You can define default virtual hosts in your server configuration by using the _default_ option in the Virtual Hosts section. The main server configuration contains several directives that are globally used for each of the defined virtual hosts. It is advisable to retain the default values for all directives that are universally applicable for all virtual hosts.

You can configure default virtual hosts to perform the following tasks:

◆ Answer requests addressed to unrecognized virtual hosts.

◆ Return error messages to the client computer.

◆ Redirect requests sent by the client to a recognized IP-based virtual host.

In summary, the default virtual hosts are used as a mechanism to handle misdirected queries received from the client. This helps to prevent the primary server from handling a request. You define default virtual hosts using the _default_ option. Consider the example on the next page.

```
<VirtualHost _default_: *>
    DocumentRoot /opt/web/html/defaultvhost
</VirtualHost>
```

In the preceding example, note the following:

◆ The `<VirtualHost>` directive contains the value `_default_:` *, which indicates that the directives specified within this section will be applicable to the default virtual host.

◆ * signifies that the default virtual host will handle all the requests sent to all ports and valid IP addresses that are not already assigned to an existing virtual host.

◆ It is also possible to specify a single port number for the default virtual host. In this case, the default virtual host will be responsible for listening to only those requests that are directed to the specified port number. Because you can specify exclusive port numbers while defining default virtual hosts, you can specify more than one default virtual host.

Consider an example in which you want one default virtual host to handle all misdirected requests that are sent using an SSL connection. You also want another default virtual host to handle all requests sent not using an SSL connection. In this case, the following configuration in which two default virtual hosts are defined is the best solution:

```
#Default virtual host used to handle misdirected requests on an SSL
#connection
<VirtualHost _default_:443>
DocumentRoot /home/www/html/ssl
</VirtualHost>
#Default virtual host used to handle misdirected requests on a non-SSL
#connections
<VirtualHost _default_:*>
DocumentRoot /home/www/html/nonssl
</VirtualHost>
```

In the preceding example, note the following:

◆ The port 443 is used for SSL connections. Therefore, specifying 443 as the port number will handle all misdirected requests on an SSL connection.

◆ The document root specified for the first virtual host is /home/www/html/ssl.

◆ The * specified in the second example represents all other ports that the virtual host will check for misdirected requests.

◆ The document root for the second virtual host is /home/www/html/nonssl.

◆ The _default_ option specified in the second virtual host setting ignores all connections made to the port number 443 because it is already assigned to another virtual host.

Configuring Multiple IP Addresses on a Single NIC

Configuring multiple IP addresses on a single network interface card (NIC) proves to be very useful while you are working with IP-based virtual hosts. This way, you can configure multiple virtual hosts using different IP addresses without having to use multiple network interface cards. However, you need to create separate DNS entries for each virtual host. Configuring multiple IP addresses on a single network card is referred to as *network interface aliasing* or *IP multiplexing/IP aliasing*.

In this section, I discuss how IP multiplexing can be achieved on a Linux computer. In Linux, allocating multiple IP addresses to the same network card is fairly easy and can be handled by using commands at the console. You use the ifconfig command to assign multiple IP addresses to the same network card. Consider the following example for configuring two additional IP addresses on the same network card.

 TIP

In order to execute the following command, you will need to log in as the root user. Only the root user can use the ifconfig command.

```
#/sbin/ifconfig eth0:0 172.17.68.111
#/sbin/ifconfig eth0:1 172.17.68.112
```

In the preceding example, note the following:

- ◆ /sbin/ifconfig is the path for the ifconfig command on the Linux system.
- ◆ eth0 is the is name used to denote the first network interface card of a Linux system.
- ◆ eth0:0 is used to specify the first additional IP address assigned to the network interface card. The first IP address that you specify is 178.17.68.111.
- ◆ eth0:1 is used to specify the second additional IP address assigned to the network interface card. The second IP address that you specify is 178.17.68.112.

This completes the task of assigning two additional IP addresses on a single network card. To confirm that the IP addresses were configured successfully, type the ifconfig command. The following output should appear:

```
[root@localhost root]# ifconfig
eth0      Link encap:Ethernet  HWaddr 00:D0:B7:40:EA:41
          inet addr:172.17.68.181  Bcast:172.17.69.255  Mask:255.255.254.0
          UP BROADCAST NOTRAILERS RUNNING  MTU:1500  Metric:1
          RX packets:4187059 errors:0 dropped:0 overruns:0 frame:1
```

```
           TX packets:19454690 errors:0 dropped:0 overruns:0 carrier:11
           collisions:248511
           RX bytes:315605284 (300.9 Mb)  TX bytes:1007704173 (961.0 Mb)


eth0:0     Link encap:Ethernet  HWaddr 00:D0:B7:40:EA:41
           inet addr:172.17.68.111  Bcast:172.17.255.255  Mask:255.255.0.0
           UP BROADCAST NOTRAILERS RUNNING  MTU:1500  Metric:1


eth0:1     Link encap:Ethernet  HWaddr 00:D0:B7:40:EA:41
           inet addr:172.17.68.112  Bcast:172.17.255.255  Mask:255.255.0.0
           UP BROADCAST NOTRAILERS RUNNING  MTU:1500  Metric:1


lo         Link encap:Local Loopback
           inet addr:127.0.0.1  Mask:255.0.0.0
           UP LOOPBACK RUNNING  MTU:16436  Metric:1
           RX packets:1027 errors:0 dropped:0 overruns:0 frame:0
           TX packets:1027 errors:0 dropped:0 overruns:0 carrier:0
           collisions:0
           RX bytes:80723 (78.8 Kb)  TX bytes:80723 (78.8 Kb)
```

The preceding output indicates that the network card is configured to use these three IP addresses:

```
172.17.68.181
172.17.68.111
172.17.68.112
```

An alternate method for checking that the IP addresses are functional is to ping to the newly assigned IP addresses using the ping command as shown here:

```
#ping 172.17.68.111
PING 172.17.68.111 (172.17.68.111) from 172.17.68.111 : 56(84) bytes of data.
Warning: time of day goes back, taking countermeasures.
64 bytes from 172.17.68.111: icmp_seq=0 ttl=255 time=170 usec
64 bytes from 172.17.68.111: icmp_seq=1 ttl=255 time=37 usec
64 bytes from 172.17.68.111: icmp_seq=2 ttl=255 time=68 usec
64 bytes from 172.17.68.111: icmp_seq=3 ttl=255 time=58 usec

--- 172.17.68.111 ping statistics ---
4 packets transmitted, 4 packets received, 0% packet loss
round-trip min/avg/max/mdev = 0.037/0.083/0.170/0.051 ms
```

This output suggests that the IP address 172.17.68.111 was successfully assigned to the network interface card. You can use the ping command to perform a similar test for other assigned IP addresses to confirm that they are working. But before you can configure virtual hosts that use these IP addresses, you need to configure the Linux server as a DNS server and the clients that want to access this server as DNS clients.

 NOTE

Later in this chapter, in the section "Configure Linux as a DNS Server," I discuss how to configure a Linux computer as a DNS server so that you can configure IP-based virtual hosts.

Configuring IP-Based Virtual Hosts

Now that you've covered the basic concepts related to IP-based virtual hosting, you are ready for a step-by-step tour to configuring IP-based virtual hosts on your Linux server. The topics in this section focus on what you need to do to configure IP-based virtual hosts.

Use IP Multiplexing to Assign Additional IP Addresses

Before you begin configuring an IP-based virtual host, you need a valid IP address. However, if you don't have an additional network interface card, the best possible way is to assign an additional IP address to the existing network card using IP multiplexing. In the previous section, you added two IP addresses using IP multiplexing. Now, you will use the IP address 172.17.68.111 to configure an IP-based virtual host.

 NOTE

Before assigning an IP address, you need to ensure that the IP address you want to allocate is not already assigned to another computer on the LAN. If you are not sure about which IP address to use, always contact your system administrator for unused IP addresses.

Edit the httpd.conf File

The next step is to make the required changes in the httpd.conf file. I added the following lines in the Virtual Hosts section in the httpd.conf file to specify the configuration directives for the virtual host:

```
<VirtualHost 172.17.68.111>
    ServerAdmin admin@steve.com
    DocumentRoot /opt/web/html/steve.com
    ServerName www.steve.com
</VirtualHost>
```

In the preceding extract, note the following:

- ◆ The IP address specified for the virtual host is 172.17.68.111.
- ◆ The ServerAdmin directive contains the value admin@steve.com. This is the e-mail address of the site administrator who can be contacted when users face any problem.
- ◆ The DocumentRoot directive is assigned the location /opt/web/html/steve.com. This is the document root of the virtual host.
- ◆ The ServerName directive contains the value www.steve.com.

Configure Linux as a DNS Server

After you add the necessary lines in the httpd.conf file for the virtual host, you need to configure DNS. Configuring DNS is essential if you want to connect to the virtual host using the server name www.steve.com.

The /etc/named.conf File

To configure DNS, the first file that you need to edit is the named.conf file that resides in the /etc directory. This is the configuration file for named, which is a daemon used for name resolution in Linux. Enter the following lines in this file:

```
zone "steve.com" IN {
      type master;
      file "steve.com";
};
```

In the preceding extract, note the following:

- ◆ zone defines a zone, which, in this case, is the site steve.com.
- ◆ type master indicates that the zone specified is a master zone. Specifying master zones is important because they play a major role in DNS configuration.
- ◆ file represents the text file that contains a particular zone's database. In this case, the file is steve.com.

The /var/named/steve.com File

The next step is to create a file in the /var/named/ directory. For this site, I created a file named steve.com in this directory. A series of entries must be made in this file so that the DNS server is configured. This file is not created by default, so you need to create it manually. I added the following lines in this file:

```
$TTL    86400
@       IN    SOA     steve.com. root.steve.com. (
                                 1997022700 ; Serial
                                 28800      ; Refresh
                                 14400      ; Retry
                                 3600000    ; Expire
                                 86400 )    ; Minimum
                IN    NS      steve.com.


www     A       172.17.68.111
```

In the preceding extract, note the following:

◆ @ signifies the domain, which, in this case, is steve.com.

◆ IN is an Internet class.

◆ SOA is used to designate the beginning of the zone data.

◆ NS is used to specify a nameserver (domain name server that will be used for translating domain names to IP addresses).

◆ A is used to associate a name with the specified IP address.

◆ The number 1997022700 is a serial number that is used to implement version control on DNS database files.

◆ The number 28800 denotes the time after which the master nameserver's serial number is refreshed to detect any changes.

◆ The number 14400 denotes the time after which the refresh operation should be performed again if the refresh operation fails once.

◆ The number 3600000 is the time after which the nameserver will stop serving DNS information for a lack of refresh from the DNS nameserver.

◆ The number 86400 is the minimum time limit that is applicable for all DNS records listed in the database file.

The /etc/resolv.conf File

You need to edit this file before you can use the virtual host. For my configuration, I used the IP address 172.17.68.181 as the DNS server. Therefore, I made the following entries in the resolv.conf file:

```
domain 172.17.68.181
nameserver 172.17.68.181
search 172.17.68.181
```

In the preceding contents of the `resolv.conf` file, notice that the IP address specified for domain, nameserver, and search is 172.17.68.181. You can also specify the domain name in place of the IP address for domain and search.

An Alternative Method to Configure DNS

An alternative method for configuring DNS is to use the /etc/hosts file. When you use the hosts file, you can avoid the preceding steps. However, for more complicated DNS configurations, I advise using the steps specified in the previous sections. This is because configuring the /etc/hosts file works only on the local computer. For remote computers to use the DNS server, you will need to use the preceding method for configuring DNS.

Using the /etc/hosts file to configure DNS is easy. All you need to do is open the file and specify the IP address and the hostname for the respective virtual hosts, and you are done. Consider the following contents of the hosts file:

```
# Do not remove the following line, or various programs
# that require network functionality will fail.
127.0.0.1        localhost.localdomain   localhost
172.17.68.181    linux.server.com
172.17.68.111    steve.com
```

The preceding contents indicate that the IP address 172.17.68.111 has been added to the hosts file. This will enable you to access the site steve.com.

Restart Necessary Services

After you make the required changes in the respective configuration file, you need to restart the named service and the httpd service. The named service should be restarted because you made changes in the DNS configuration file. Similarly, the httpd service should be restarted because you edited the httpd.conf file.

To restart the named service, execute the following command:

```
[root@linux root]# service named restart
Stopping named:                              [  OK  ]
Starting named:                              [  OK  ]
```

After restarting the named service, restart the httpd service using the following command:

```
[root@linux root]# apachectl restart
/usr/local/bin/apachectl restart: httpd restarted
```

Now you are ready to access the default Web site for the virtual host www.steve.com.

Testing the Configuration

Finally, it is always necessary to test the configuration so that you can determine whether the desired changes have taken place. To ensure this, on the console, type the following command:

```
#lynx www.steve.com
```
```
                    This is the home page for steve.com


      Hi Everybody!
```

This output indicates that the default Web page for the site `www.steve.com` is now accessible. However, this site will be accessible only from the local computer. To access this site from other client computers on the network, you need to configure them as DNS clients.

> ### NOTE
>
> The steps for configuring DNS clients are explained in the section "Configuring Windows and Linux as DNS Clients," later in this chapter.

Name-Based Virtual Hosts

Name-based virtual hosts are implemented with browsers and Web servers that are HTTP /1.1 compliant. Unlike HTTP /1.0, HTTP /1.1 uses a special request header, `Host`, which is sent by the client browser to the Web server to identify the hostname of the Web server. This feature was not present in HTTP /1.0, and the Web server could be recognized only on the basis of its IP address. As a result, in order to configure virtual hosts, the Web server administrator needed to use multiple IP addresses that were also unique.

The capability of the HTTP /1.1 protocol to recognize DNS names allows you to configure multiple virtual hosts on a single IP address. This is the concept of name-based virtual hosts. To configure name-based virtual hosts, you can allocate different hostnames on the same IP address.

The NameVirtualHost *Directive*

In order to implement name-based virtual hosts, you use the `NameVirtualHost` directive. When you specify an IP address for this directive, the specified IP address becomes available only as a name-based virtual host. In other words, after specifying the IP address in the `NameVirtualHost` directive, non-HTTP /1.1 clients cannot access the virtual host on the specified IP address.

As soon as Apache encounters a `NameVirtualHost` directive, it sets up a virtual host table and adds the entry for the virtual host. Any number of hostnames can be used with a single IP address.

When a request is sent to the Apache Web server that has been configured with several name-based virtual hosts, Apache scans the NameVirtualHost directive for the IP address. After it tracks the IP address, Apache tries to scan the virtual host table to determine the hostnames that are associated with the specified IP address.

Next, Apache tries to match the hostname specified by the client browser in the Host header with the hostnames specified in the ServerName directive. After Apache recognizes the virtual host, it sends a response to the client depending on the configuration directives specified in the <VirtualHost> container for that particular virtual host.

If the hostname is not matched, the directives specified for the primary server are used by default. It is important to understand that the primary server used in the context of name-based virtual hosts is not the main Apache server. The primary server is the first name-based virtual host specified in the httpd.conf file. Also, the _default_ option cannot be used in the case of name-based virtual hosts because name-based virtual hosts require an IP address to be specified for each configuration.

Figure 6.2 shows how communication takes place when multiple name-based virtual hosts are configured.

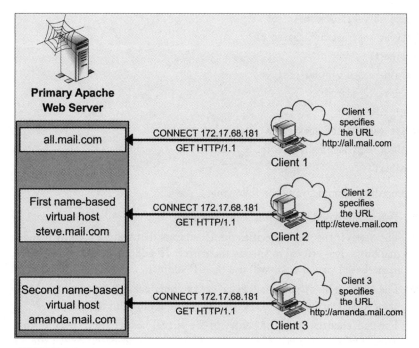

FIGURE 6.2 *An example of name-based virtual hosting*

NOTE

As far as possible, it is recommended that you specify only those directives in the main server configuration that should be common for all virtual hosts. In other words, don't flood the main server configuration section with all possible configuration directives that should not be applicable universally for all name-based virtual hosts. Always specify configuration directives that are specific to a virtual host in the <VirtualHost> container directive specific to that particular virtual host.

Consider the following example of name-based virtual hosts:

```
NameVirtualHost IP_address

#First name-based virtual host
<VirtualHost IP_address>
UseCanonicalName off
ServerName server1.somedomain.com
DocumentRoot /opt/web/html/somedir1
</VirtualHost>
#Second name-based virtual host
<VirtualHost IP_address>
UseCanonicalName off
ServerName server2.somedomain.com
DocumentRoot /opt/web/html/somedir2
</VirtualHost>
```

In the preceding example, note the following:

- ◆ Two name-based virtual hosts are specified.
- ◆ The NameVirtualHost specifies the IP address that will be used by name-based virtual hosts. It is critical to specify the correct IP address in this directive because name-based virtual hosts will use this IP address.
- ◆ The <VirtualHost> and </VirtualHost> container directives are used for each name-based virtual host to specify the configuration directives.
- ◆ The UseCanonicalName off entry in the virtual host column specifies that canonical names will not be used. When a user accesses a name-based virtual site, he doesn't know the IP address and recognizes the site by the hostname. Specifying off as a value for UseCononicalName indicates that the specified hostname will be specified as an alias in the DNS.

- The ServerName directive is assigned the hostnames server1.somedomain.com and server2.somedomain.com for the first and second virtual host, respectively.
- The DocumentRoot directive is used to specify the document root for the name-based virtual hosts. The document root for the first name-based virtual host is /opt/web/html/somedir1, and /opt/web/html/somedir2 is the document root for the second name-based virtual host.

 NOTE

When you use the preceding configuration, the client browsers that don't support HTTP /1.1 protocol cannot access the contents of either of the name-based virtual hosts. Browsers that are HTTP /1.1 compliant send the Host request header to the Web server, which helps recognize the hostname without specifying the IP address. This is not the case with browsers that use the HTTP /1.0 protocol.

Configuring Name-Based Virtual Hosts

I will now present an example and explain the step-by-step procedure for setting up name-based virtual hosts.

Edit the httpd.conf File

The first step for configuring name-based virtual hosts is to edit the httpd.conf file. I used a Linux server configured on the IP address 172.17.68.181 to configure the name-based virtual hosts. I made the changes described in the following subsections in the httpd.conf file.

Configure the NameVirtualHost *Directive*

To use name-based virtual hosts, the first thing that you need to edit in the httpd.conf file is the NameVirtualHost directive. The following extract from my httpd.conf file shows how I uncommented this directive and specified an IP address to be used:

```
# Use name-based virtual hosting.
#
NameVirtualHost 172.17.68.181
```

In the preceding extract, I specified the IP address 172.17.68.181 for the NameVirtualHost directive. This indicates that all name-based virtual hosts will point to this IP address.

CAUTION

You can specify multiple IP addresses using the `NameVirtualHost` directive to configure multiple name-based virtual hosts for each IP address. To use multiple IP addresses for name-based virtual hosts, you use a different `NameVirtualHost` directive for each IP address, in the httpd.conf file. In such cases, don't use the pre-allocated IP address of Linux server for name-based virtual hosts. A separate IP can be created on the same NIC by using interface aliasing/IP aliasing.

Add the <VirtualHost> and </VirtualHost> Directives for the Name-Based Virtual Hosts

The next step is to specify the configuration directives for the name-based virtual hosts that you want to configure. You do this using the `<VirtualHost>` and `</VirtualHost>` directives. All directives specified within these container directives will be applicable to the specific name-based virtual host. The following extract from the httpd.conf file shows the configuration for two name-based virtual hosts named `angela.developers.com` and `linda.developers.com`.

```
#Configuration for angela.developers.com
<VirtualHost 172.17.68.181>
    ServerAdmin root@angela.developers.com
    DocumentRoot /opt/web/html/angela.developers.com
    ServerName angela.developers.com
</VirtualHost>


#Configuration for linda.developers.com
<VirtualHost 172.17.68.181>
    ServerAdmin root@linda.developers.com
    DocumentRoot /opt/web/html/linda.developers.com
    ServerName linda.developers.com
</VirtualHost>
```

In the preceding extract, note the following:

◆ The IP address specified for both virtual hosts is `172.17.68.181`. This indicates that both are name-based virtual hosts.

◆ The `ServerAdmin` directive for `angela.developers.com` and `linda.developers.com` are `root@angela.com` and `root@linda.com`, respectively.

◆ The `DocumentRoot` directive for `angela.developers.com` is `/opt/web/html/angela.developers.com`.

◆ The DocumentRoot directive for linda.developers.com is
  /opt/web/html/angela.developers.com.

◆ The ServerName directive for both the servers is angela.developers.com and
  linda.developers.com, respectively.

Edit the */etc/hosts* File

Recall that I used the /etc/hosts file to configure the DNS while implementing IP-based virtual hosts. The same is applicable for name-based virtual hosts. In order to recognize the sites angela.developers.com and linda.developers.com, you will need to add the required entries in the /etc/hosts file. I made the following entries in the /etc/hosts file.

```
# Do not remove the following line, or various programs
# that require network functionality will fail.
127.0.0.1        localhost.localdomain   localhost
172.17.68.181    linux.server.com
172.17.68.181    angela.developers.com   angela
172.17.68.181    linda.developers.com    linda
```

As you can see, I added one entry for each of the virtual hosts. However, I assigned the same IP address to both hosts. This implies that both angela.developers.com and linda.developers.com will be resolved to the same IP address, which is 172.17.68.181. Instead of using the hosts file, you can configure DNS as discussed in the section, "Configure Linux as a DNS Server" while configuring IP-based virtual hosts.

 NOTE

Editing the /etc/hosts file on the Linux server on which the site is hosted will allow you to test the site from only that particular machine. If you want to access the Web page from other client computers, you will need to configure those clients as DNS clients. I discuss the steps for configuring Windows and Linux as DNS clients in the section "Configuring Windows and Linux as DNS Clients."

Creating the Document Root for the Virtual Hosts

When you edited the httpd.conf file to configure the name-based virtual hosts, you specified a document root for each of the sites. Now you need to ensure that the directories specified for the document root exist. You can create the document root directories for the virtual hosts using the following commands:

```
//Creating document root directory for angela
#mkdir /opt/web/html/angela.developers.com
```

```
//Creating document root directory for Linda
#mkdir /opt/web/html/linda.developers.com
```

After this, I placed two simple HTML files named index.html in each virtual host's document root.

Restarting the Essential Services

You edited the httpd.conf file and also the /etc/hosts file. So you need to restart the httpd service in order for your changes to take effect. Use the following command to start the httpd service:

```
//Starting httpd
#apachectl restart
/usr/local/bin/apachectl restart: httpd restarted
```

The output of the command indicates that the httpd service started successfully and that the changes have taken place.

Using *ping* to Check the Configuration

It is a healthy practice to ping to the newly added hosts so that you can be assured that hostnames are properly resolved. I always use the ping command to check whether the hosts are reachable.

```
//For angela.developers.com
[root@linux root]# ping angela.developers.com
PING angela.developers.com (172.17.68.181) from 172.17.68.181 : 56(84)
bytes of data.
Warning: time of day goes back, taking countermeasures.
64 bytes from linux.server.com (172.17.68.181): icmp_seq=0 ttl=255 time=169 usec
64 bytes from linux.server.com (172.17.68.181): icmp_seq=1 ttl=255 time=69 usec
64 bytes from linux.server.com (172.17.68.181): icmp_seq=2 ttl=255 time=76 usec
64 bytes from linux.server.com (172.17.68.181): icmp_seq=3 ttl=255 time=47 usec
64 bytes from linux.server.com (172.17.68.181): icmp_seq=4 ttl=255 time=85 usec

--- angela.developers.com ping statistics ---
5 packets transmitted, 5 packets received, 0% packet loss
round-trip min/avg/max/mdev = 0.047/0.089/0.169/0.042 ms
```

```
//For linda.developers.com
[root@linux root]# ping linda.developers.com
PING linda.developers.com (172.17.68.181) from 172.17.68.181 : 56(84)
bytes of data.
Warning: time of day goes back, taking countermeasures.
64 bytes from linux.server.com (172.17.68.181): icmp_seq=0 ttl=255 time=166 usec
64 bytes from linux.server.com (172.17.68.181): icmp_seq=1 ttl=255 time=75 usec
64 bytes from linux.server.com (172.17.68.181): icmp_seq=2 ttl=255 time=74 usec
64 bytes from linux.server.com (172.17.68.181): icmp_seq=3 ttl=255 time=72 usec
64 bytes from linux.server.com (172.17.68.181): icmp_seq=4 ttl=255 time=62 usec

--- linda.developers.com ping statistics ---
5 packets transmitted, 5 packets received, 0% packet loss
round-trip min/avg/max/mdev = 0.062/0.089/0.166/0.040 ms
```

As you can see from the preceding output, I was able to ping to both these hosts without any problem, and there was no packet loss while communicating. This ensures that both the hosts are working properly.

Testing in the Browser

After you confirm that the sites are reachable, it's time to check whether the index.html file that I placed in the document root of each of the sites is accessible from the browser. You can use any browser to check this. Figure 6.3 shows the default Web page when viewed using the Konquerer Web browser.

FIGURE 6.3 *The default Web page of* angela.developers.com

Configuring Windows and Linux as DNS Clients

The DNS configuration that I discussed in the previous sections is specific at the server end. Although you will be able to access the site from the Linux server, you will not be able to access it from other clients on the network. You will need to configure DNS at the client end so that clients on the same network can access your site.

Configuring Windows 2000 Server as a DNS Client

To configure Windows 2000 as a DNS client, you need to specify the IP address of the DNS server in the network settings of Windows 2000. To do so, follow these steps:

1. Click Start and choose Settings, Network and Dial-up Connections to open the Network and Dial-up Connections window (see Figure 6.4).

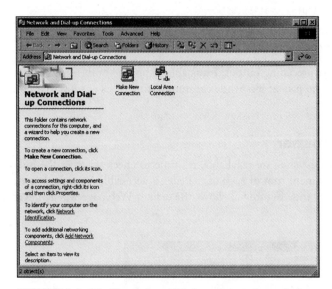

FIGURE 6.4 *The Network and Dial-up Connections window*

2. Double-click the Local Area Connection icon to open the Local Area Connection Status dialog box (see Figure 6.5).

3. Click the Properties button to open the Local Area Connection Properties dialog box (see Figure 6.6).

4. In the components list, double-click Internet Protocol (TCP/IP) to open the Internet Protocol (TCP/IP) Properties dialog box.

5. Select the option Use the following DNS server addresses.

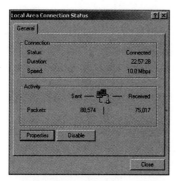

FIGURE 6.5 *The Local Area Connection Status dialog box*

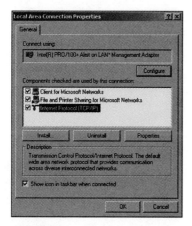

FIGURE 6.6 *The Local Area Connection Properties dialog box*

6. Specify the IP address of the Linux DNS server. Figure 6.7 shows the Internet Protocol (TCP/IP) Properties dialog box after the required settings are made.

7. Click OK to close the Internet Protocol (TCP/IP) Properties dialog box.

8. Click OK to close the Local Area Connection Properties dialog box.

9. Click Close to close the Local Area Connection Status dialog box.

In addition to the preceding steps, you need to check a few things in Microsoft Internet Explorer. Follow these steps to configure Internet Explorer so that you can access the site.

1. Open Internet Explorer.

2. Choose Tools, Internet Options to open the Internet Options dialog box (see Figure 6.8).

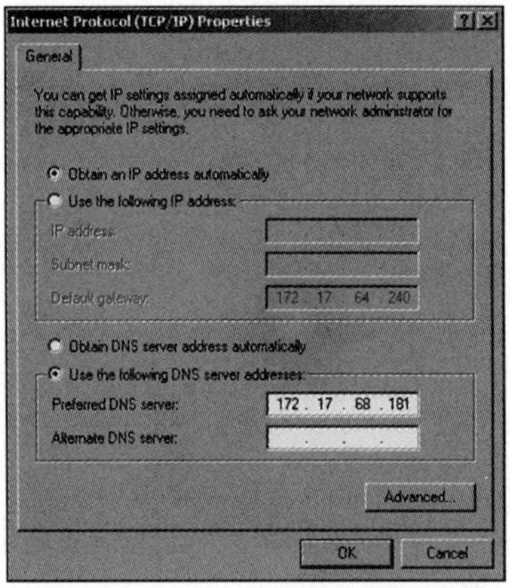

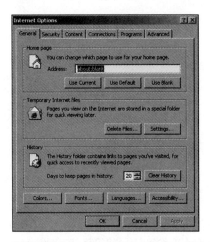

FIGURE 6.7 *The Internet Protocol (TCP/IP) Properties dialog box*

FIGURE 6.8 *The Internet Options dialog box*

3. Click the Connections tab.

4. Click LAN Settings to open the Local Area Network (LAN) Settings dialog box.

5. Verify that the Automatically detect settings option is checked. Figure 6.9 shows the Local Area Network (LAN) Settings dialog box after the required settings are made.

6. Click OK to close the Local Area Network (LAN) Settings dialog box.

7. Click OK to close the Internet Options dialog box.

After making the preceding settings, I was able to access the site angela.developers.com from a remote Windows 2000 machine by specifying the URL http://angela.developers.com in Internet Explorer. Figure 6.10 shows the site when accessed from Internet Explorer.

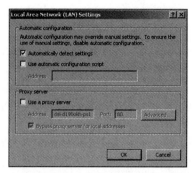

FIGURE 6.9 *The Local Area Network (LAN) Settings dialog box*

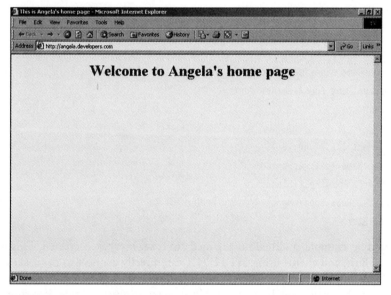

FIGURE 6.10 *The Web site when viewed from Internet Explorer*

Configuring Linux as a DNS Client

You can configure a Linux computer as a DNS client by adding an entry in the /etc/hosts file. You just need to add the IP address and the name of the site that you want to access on the Linux server, and you are ready to browse the site. A better option is to add the IP address of the server in the /etc/resolv.conf file on the client.

Support for HTTP /1.0 Clients

As discussed earlier, when the Apache Web server receives a request from a client that doesn't send a Host request header, the first virtual host configuration applies to the request. The problem with non-HTTP /1.1-compliant browsers is that the requests sent by them don't carry the Host request header with them. This results in all the requests sent by the legacy browsers being handled by the first named virtual host specified in the httpd.conf file.

Although name-based virtual hosts don't support HTTP /1.0 clients, it is totally wrong to conclude that building support for HTTP /1.0 clients while using name-based virtual hosts is impossible. Most browsers today support the HTTP /1.1 protocol. However, to eliminate the possibility of a non-HTTP /1.1 client being unable to access your Web site contents, it is a good idea to use the ServerPath directive.

The ServerPath directive enables you to specify a URL path name within the <VirtualHost> container tags in the httpd.conf file. In this case, Apache uses the virtual host in which the ServerPath is specified to handle requests sent by non-HTTP /1.1 clients. Consider the following example:

```
NameVirtualHost 172.17.68.181


    <VirtualHost 172.17.68.181>
        ServerName dummy.server.com
        DocumentRoot /opt/web/html/dummy/
    </VirtualHost>


    <VirtualHost 172.17.68.181>
        ServerName real.server.com
        ServerPath /accessibledomain
        DocumentRoot /opt/web/html/dummy/real
    </VirtualHost>
```

In the preceding example, a virtual host named real.server.com is created. This is a name-based virtual host, and clients using HTTP /1.1 can directly connect to real.server.com by using the URL http://real.server.com. However, when a non-HTTP /1.1-compliant browser sends a request, the request will be automatically directed to dummy.server.com simply because dummy.server.com is the first virtual host defined in the httpd.conf file.

This situation can be avoided by using the ServerPath directive as shown in the preceding example. This directive specifies the directory /accessibledomain. Therefore, clients that don't support the HTTP /1.1 protocol can access real.server.com by using the URL http://real.server.com/accessibledomain.

After using the ServerPath directive, you can rest assured that non-HTTP /1.1-compliant clients will also be able to access real.server.com. But there is more to it. All non-HTTP /1.1 clients will first access the first virtual host specified in the httpd.conf file. So you need to find a way in which the requests can be sent to real.server.com from dummy.server.com. Follow the next set of steps to accomplish this.

1. Use the first virtual host as a *fall through;* that is, use the first virtual host to just accept and redirect requests to the actual virtual host. The actual virtual host is the one whose URL the client has specified.

2. Choose a `ServerName` for the first virtual that can never be deduced by the client.

3. Use the `DocumentRoot` directive to specify a default Web page that redirects non-HTTP /1.1-compliant requests to the actual virtual host. The Web page might look something like this:

```
<HTML>
<HEAD>
<TITLE> This is a redirect for non-HTTP /1.1 compliant browsers</TITLE>
<BODY>
<H2><CENTER>Seems that you are using an old browser that is not HTTP /1.1
compliant.</CENTER></H2>
<BR>
<H2><CENTER>Please bookmark this page.</CENTER></H2>
<BR>
<CENTER><A HREF=/accessibledomain>http://real.server.com/accessibledomain</CENTER>
</A>
</BODY>
</HTML>
```

The preceding HTML code will help redirect non-HTTP /1.1 requests to `real.server.com`.

Dynamic Virtual Hosting

Dynamic virtual hosting is a mechanism used to host hundreds of virtual sites. Both IP-based and name-based virtual hosting have a drawback related to the limit on the number of virtual hosts that can be configured on a given computer. It is no more feasible to have one Web site on one server or to use a different IP for each virtual host.

The Internet is evolving every day, and the number of Web sites is growing by leaps and bounds. This situation makes it ideal to use dynamic virtual hosting. Most Web-hosting companies today use dynamic Web-hosting to host hundreds of sites on a single server. The need for dynamic virtual hosting emerged because it became difficult for administrators to continually add entries subject to each new virtual host in the httpd.conf file.

You can use the module `mod_vhost_aliases` to utilize dynamic virtual hosting in Linux. This module implements dynamically configured hosts by specifying templates for the `Document-Root` and the `ScriptAlias` directives. You then use the templates to create actual paths to these directories after examining the incoming URL. Both name-based and IP-based virtual hosting can be implemented in Apache.

Directives for Name-Based Virtual Hosting

Use the following directives for name-based virtual hosting:

◆ **VirtualDocumentRoot.** This directive specifies how the module will construct a path to the DocumentRoot for a dynamic virtual host using the URL of the request received from the client.

◆ **VirtualScriptAlias.** This directive is similar to the ScriptAlias directive. Its function is to construct a path to a directory on the Web server that contains the CGI (Common Gateway Interface) scripts (see Chapter 7, "Dynamic Content with CGI," for more on CGI scripts).

Directives for IP-Based Virtual Hosting

Use the following directives for IP-based virtual hosting:

◆ **VirtualDocumentRootIP.** This directive is similar to the VirtualDocumentRoot directive. The only difference is that this directive constructs a path to the virtual host's document root from the IP address on which the request was received.

◆ **VirtualScriptAliasIP.** This directive is similar to VirtualScriptAlias. The only difference is that this directive constructs a path to a directory on the Web server that contains the CGI scripts from the IP address on which the request was received.

Summary

In this chapter, I discussed all the concepts related to configuring virtual hosts in Apache. First, I discussed the Virtual Hosts section of the httpd.conf file to familiarize you with the directives used in relation to virtual hosts. Then I explained the concept of IP-based virtual hosts and how they are implemented. Next, I examined the steps for configuring name-based virtual hosts in Apache. Finally, I discussed the concept of dynamic virtual hosting and the directives that are used in conjunction with it.

Check Your Understanding

Multiple Choice Questions

1. Which of the following directives should be used only if you are implementing name-based virtual hosts?

   a. `NameVirtualHost`

   b. `DocumentRoot`

   c. `ServerRoot`

   d. `<VirtualHost>`

2. Which of the following directives should have the same value specified for all name-based virtual hosts configured for an Apache Web server?

   a. `DocumentRoot`

   b. `ServerName`

   c. `ErrorLog`

   d. `<VirtualHost IP_address>`

3. Which of the following are the features of IP-based virtual hosts? (Choose all that apply.)

   a. More than one virtual host can be configured on a single IP address.

   b. Are used for Web sites that use SSL connections.

   c. Every virtual host should have a unique IP address.

   d. Are not supported by HTTP /1.1-compliant browsers.

4. For what purpose is interface aliasing used? (Choose all that apply.)

   a. Assign multiple IP addresses to a single network interface card.

   b. Assign a single IP address to multiple network interface cards.

   c. Configure multiple IP-based virtual hosts on a single network interface card.

   d. Configure multiple name-based virtual hosts on a single network interface card.

5. Which of the following is true about name-based virtual hosts?

   a. Multiple virtual hosts can be configured using a single IP address.

   b. Don't support browsers that are HTTP /1.1 compliant.

   c. Every virtual host requires a unique IP address.

   d. Are ideal for Web sites that use SSL connections.

Answers

Multiple Choice Answers

1. a. The NameVirtualHost directive is used only if you want to implement name-based virtual hosts. All other directives specified can be used with both name-based and IP-based virtual hosts.

2. d. In the case of each name-based virtual host, the <VirtualHost> directive will contain the same IP address. This is because all name-based virtual hosts are configured using the same IP address.

3. b, c. Every site using SSL should be specified a unique IP address. IP-based virtual hosts are ideal for hosting Web sites that use SSL connections because each virtual host uses a separate IP address.

4. a, c. Interface aliasing is used to assign multiple IP address to the same network interface card. This helps you implement multiple IP-based virtual hosts using a single network interface card.

5. a. In the case of name-based virtual hosts, multiple virtual hosts can be configured using a single IP address.

Chapter 7

Dynamic Content with CGI

Gone are the days when all Web pages were created by using plain HTML. Web pages created using HTML were static and lacked interactivity. A Web server that is capable of displaying only static Web pages is not of much use in today's Internet scenario, which demands interactive, dynamic, and user-friendly Web pages. Times have changed, and the Internet has evolved to a point where even personal Web pages (for example, guest books, newsletters, user registrations, form mailers, and so on) require more than static outputs.

Thanks to *Common Gateway Interface (CGI)*, you can multiply the functionality of a Web server. You achieve this in Apache by executing external programs when required and receiving their output in a format that can reach your intended audience through a Web browser. Such a mechanism allows a Webmaster to write customized programs that work on the Internet. That is, a Webmaster can write a program in C or C++ that displays output in Internet Explorer or Netscape. In this chapter, I'll discuss how to use CGI with Apache to create dynamic programs.

Introducing the Common Gateway Interface

Common Gateway Interface (CGI) is a specification that determines how communications should take place between a HTTP server and resources located on the server's host computer. These resources could be programs or databases.

A program located on the HTTP server's host computer that follows the CGI specification for accepting and returning data is called a *CGI program*. A CGI program can be written in a variety of languages, including C, Java, Perl, and Visual Basic. The main advantage of using CGI programs is that they are executed in real-time. As a result, it is possible to produce dynamic output. When a HTTP request is sent to the Web server, the respective CGI program is executed at the server end and the output is rendered on the client browser.

How Does CGI Work?

The dynamic feature of CGI programs is the capacity to accept input from the browser and then return the output to the browser after processing user input at runtime. After a client submits information to the Web server, the information is handled in the following way:

1. The HTTP server accepts the information.
2. The HTTP server sends the input information to a program on the server via CGI.
3. The program is executed at the server end and the output is sent to the HTTP server via CGI.
4. The HTTP server responds to the HTTP request by sending the output to the client browser.

Types of CGI

You can broadly categorize CGI programs as two types, *CGI applications* and *CGI scripts*. In this section, I'll describe and explain how to use them.

CGI Applications

CGI applications are binary, executable programs that can be executed from the command line. These programs are written in languages such as C, Pascal, COBOL, Fortran, and others. You can divide CGI applications into two types, *static CGI* and *dynamic CGI*.

Static CGI

Static CGI files are compiled with options that instruct the compiler to embed all required libraries into the output and then to execute itself. Although this feature makes the script more independent and stable, it considerably increases the size of the executable file. Larger Cages perform slower and require many more resources than do Cages that use external libraries in order to run.

Imagine a scenario in which a user is trying to register his e-mail address to an e-mail newsletter. In such a case, a CGI file accepts the e-mail address, puts it in a database, and later displays the appropriate message depending on the success or failure of the request. Now, assume that the size of the CGI script is 2MB. When thousands of users press the Submit button simultaneously from various client computers, multiple copies of the CGI program will be executed in different memory locations in the server. This can cause a server with decent hardware configuration to crash miserably. Therefore, static CGI programs are less preferred on the Web.

Dynamic CGI

Dynamic CGI files contain the source code of the programs. These programs are compiled every time they are required. Such programs are much smaller than static CGI programs and generally contain links to external libraries. Dynamic CGI programs ensure better performance than do static CGI programs.

CGI Scripts

CGI scripts are the actual source code of the programs. These programs are compiled every time the server calls them. Because they are source code, they do not contain embedded libraries and depend on the compiler to provide them with library support. CGI scripts are much smaller than CGI applications and require less storage space than CGI applications.

Because they are the source code, CGI scripts do have a major security issue. The entire functionality and information stored in them could become visible to the world due to a slight mistake in the file permission settings. This means that if someone is able to download these scripts, they could gain access to critical information in the file. The critical information might be database passwords or structural information about the directories. A Web server administrator should always ensure that file permissions in the chi-bin/ directories of all Web sites are correctly set, and should never allow a visitor to download any unauthorized information. The administrator should also instruct the CGI programmers to include messages and notices at top of each script that prevent unauthorized use of information.

 CAUTION

Always keep all CGI scripts in the bin-bin/ directory or any other specified directory that contains only CGI scripts.

Accepting User Input in HTML Forms

Whether it is filling out an online application form or signing up for free e-mail on a Web site, HTML forms are used everywhere. HTML forms provide an interface for the user to enter information that is processed by CGI programs. You create these forms using the <FORM> and </FORM> tags in the HTML pages. These forms can accept data entered by a user on the client side using HTML input fields, such as text fields, multiple line text areas, radio buttons, check boxes, drop down menus, multiple selection boxes, and hidden fields. Each element on a form contains a NAME tag that is used to uniquely identify the element on the form and also to reference the information stored in the element. The information stored in each element is known as its value and is encoded with the rest of the form data when the information is sent to the calling CGI program. The information is passed in the form of pairs, each pair consisting of the element's name and its value. Each pair is separated from the other using the & character.

Before the CGI program on the Web server can process the information entered in a form, this information needs to be transmitted to the Web server. This is made possible by request methods that the browser uses, to submit the information. The two most common request methods used by the browser to submit information are the GET method and the POST method.

The *GET* Method

If you use the GET method for transmitting information from the browser to the Web server, all information is attached to the URL requested by the client machine. The information is stored in the QUERY_STRING environment variable maintained by the CGI program running on the Web server. Use of the GET method is recommended in situations where information must be added or removed from the database.

With the GET method, when information is submitted in the browser, it is transmitted along with the URL. This is a drawback to the GET method, because the URL can contain only a specific number of characters. Large URLs can cause Web browsers to stop responding to client requests due to the amount of information being passed to it. One possible solution is to use the POST method to reduce the load on the Web server.

The *POST* Method

If you use the POST method, the information is transmitted to the CGI program in the form of encoded information using *standard input (STDIN)*. As there is no provision for specifying the end of file, the environment variable CONTENT_LENGTH is used to determine the amount of information that should be read from STDIN.

Configuring Apache to Use CGI

Although configuring Apache to use CGI scripts requires little effort, you can do a lot to configure Apache to use CGI scripts *securely*. The following sections provide information that you need when using Apache with CGI. The sections explain the CGI related directives and how they can be used to configure Apache to use CGI.

The *ScriptAlias* Directive

You need to configure the ScriptAlias directive on Apache before you can execute CGI scripts on the server. The scripts are stored in a specific directory that is used exclusively by CGI. You then store all CGI programs in this directory, and searches for all client requests occur in this directory. All the ScriptAlias directives are stored in the httpd.conf configuration file. Consider the following example:

```
ScriptAlias /cgi-bin/ /usr/local/apache/cgi-bin/
```

If all the CGI files are stored in the directory specified by the DocumentRoot directive, they are easily accessible. However, if the files are stored in other directories, you will need to set links for those directories. The ScriptAlias directive, just like the Alias directive, is used to map a URL with its associated directory. The basic difference between the two directives is that ScriptAlias offers the added advantage of providing reference to CGI programs. The directive instructs Apache to search for all files or resources beginning with a certain name in a specific directory. You can create multiple entries to provide links to different kinds of files. For example, if a browser requests the URL http://www.mytestsite.com/cgi-bin/sources.pl, Apache will search for the file in its local directory at /usr/local/apache/cgi-bin/sources.pl. The file is searched for at the specified location, and, if it is found, the file is executed and its output is returned to the browser that requested the file. If the file doesn't exist or if the file is not executable, Apache returns an error to the client's browser.

Running Non-Script Alias CGI

As I explained in the previous section, you can assign a directory to store CGI files by using the ScriptAlias directive, because designating a specific directory restricts storage and use of CGI files to that directory. This also enhances administration because administrators can restrict access to the CGI programs based on the security requirements of the network. However, restricting the use of CGI programs to a single directory is not always necessary. If the administrator has implemented adequate security precautions on the Web server, the CGI programs can be stored and run from anywhere. These security measures can include authentication and assigning proper access rights. This facility is beneficial if the users need to access certain CGI programs that do not exist in the common directory and that require different levels of access rights.

Using the *Options* Directive

You use the Options directive to assign a specific directory for storing CGI files. You also need to inform the Web server which files are considered to be CGI files. You use the AddHandler directive for this purpose. The handler specifies that all files with the file extensions pl or cgi are considered as CGI programs. Following is the code you add to the server configuration file to assign a specific directory for CGI scripts and to assign extensions of CGI files:

```
<Directory /usr/local/apache/htdocs/CGIfiles>
            Options +ExecCGI
</Directory>
AddHandler cgi-script cgi pl
```

Learning to Script

This section discusses the important concepts related to CGI programming. Before I discuss the specifics of CGI programming and write a simple CGI program, though, it is imperative that you understand how a CGI script is different from other conventional Web-based programs. The following are the key features of CGI programs that differentiate CGI from other Web-based applications:

◆ **MIME-type header.** All CGI programs also send MIME header information along with the regular output returned by the program. This information generally informs the client browser about the type of information being returned and is stored along with the HTTP header information.

◆ **Output in HTML format.** All output that is returned by CGI scripts is sent to the client browser in HTML format. Although all the information is displayed in HTML, you can configure the programs to return the output in other formats that the browser supports. For example, in addition to displaying HTML information, browsers can display GIF files and other non-HTML information.

Following is a simple CGI script that prints the text "This is my first CGI program" when a client requests access to the program and the program is executed. The file is named msg-display.cgi and is stored in the cgi-bin directory.

```
#!/usr/bin/perl
print "Content-type: text/html\n\n";
print "This is my first CGI program"
```

The first line provides the path to the interpreter (a program used to understand and execute instructions written in a high-level language) that is used for executing the program. The second line contains the reference to the HTTP header that was mentioned previously. The line of code adds a carriage return after the Content-type declaration. A blank line is displayed to symbolize the end of the header information. The final line in the code displays the text "This is my first CGI program."

Troubleshooting

If the CGI script works correctly, it will display the correct output in the browser window. However, sometimes the browser does not display the correct output and, instead, displays an error. In such circumstances, you need to know how to troubleshoot the problem. The following problems commonly occur in CGI scripts:

- ◆ **Permission problem.** One of the most common problems is related to access permissions. If an administrator allows access to only certain users, other users will not be able to access the CGI programs stored on the Web server. In restricted access, a log on attempt made by a user is logged onto the Web server. If a user needs to be assigned access to the Web server, appropriate file permissions will need to be assigned (you will learn about file permission later in this chapter). Most error messages begin with the word Forbidden.

- ◆ **Errors on the server.** Sometimes access to CGI programs is refused or there is no output because of certain errors on the Web server. These errors will prevent the CGI programs from executing properly and will add an entry to the error log. The error message commonly contains the text "Premature end of script header." You need to study each entry in the error log and take appropriate action to solve these errors. Every logged entry contains a detailed description of why the error took place.

- ◆ **Code or POST not supported message.** In case of an error, the CGI programs might also display their code or a message stating that the POST method is not supported by the system. This error implies that Apache is not properly configured to service requests for CGI programs. Administrators need to configure Apache again to support the use of CGI scripts.

File Permissions

The Web server handles requests with a minimum level of rights and is assigned the permissions of nobody or www user accounts. These user accounts generally have read permissions for files and are not assigned execute permissions in most situations. In such situations, the server cannot run the files that are owned by other users. You can solve this problem by providing all users with the execute permission for all the files stored in the CGI directory. The command to set the right permission for specific files is as follows:

```
chmod a+x msgdisplay.cgi
```

You can similarly change access permissions for other CGI programs stored in the directory. If the CGI programs have certain dependency files to which they need to write to or read from, the administrator will need to assign the specific level of rights for those files or directories.

An exception to the preceding rule occurs if the server has permission to use the suexec command. The command provides CGI scripts the facility to run the programs under different levels of user rights. The type of access rights that needs to be assigned for a file depends on the directory in which it is stored. A critical level of authorization is implemented with the use of suexec. If a failure is encountered, an error is displayed on the server, and the program stops executing. You can check the log files that are generated to get an exact description of the problem and its cause.

Verifying Path Information

When certain CGI programs are executed from the command prompt, they also pass certain information to the shell. This information might contain the path to any dependency files required by the CGI command in order to execute. By default, when CGI programs are run on the Web server, they don't contain path information. However, any program that is executed or called from within the main CGI program requires its path to be clearly specified. A common example is the path for the interpreter that is specified in the beginning of the CGI program. If the path to the interpreter is not specified, the program will return an error and will not execute successfully.

Handling Syntax Errors

Many of the errors that cause CGI programs to stop executing or to display errors are a result of incorrect syntax. You have already learned about the three most common problems faced in executing CGI scripts. If these errors are taken care of, most of the CGI scripts will run without an error. A simple method to ensure that your script is running correctly is to execute it at the command line before testing it on a browser. You can diagnose and solve most of the errors at the command prompt.

Analyzing Error Logs

Apache maintains logs of all errors encountered on the Web server. The log files provide a rich source of information about the errors and their causes and provide assistance in identifying a solution. If you are not able to store log files on the Web server due to space or permission constraints, you should immediately shift the Web server to a computer that provides you with the disk space and permissions that you need.

CGI Environment Variables

An *environment variable* is a variable that is maintained by the operating system and Web servers. These variables exist in memory and are used by applications for obtaining specific information about the system. Environment variables are used primarily to store information about the current date, time, and log-in information. You can see a list of all environment variables configured on the operating system by using the env command.

Check out the following output of the env command:

```
[root@linux root]# env
PWD=/root
HOSTNAME=linux.server.com
PVM_RSH=/usr/bin/rsh
QTDIR=/usr/lib/qt-2.3.1
LESSOPEN=|/usr/bin/lesspipe.sh %s
XPVM_ROOT=/usr/share/pvm3/xpvm
KDEDIR=/usr
USER=root
LS_COLORS=no=00:fi=00:di=01;34:ln=01;36:pi=40;33:so=01;35:bd=40;33;01:cd=
40;33;01:or=01;05;37;41:mi=01;05;37;41:ex=01;32:*.cmd=01;32:*.exe=
01;32:*.com=01;32:*.btm=01;32:*.bat=01;32:*.sh=01;32:*.csh=01;32:*.tar=
01;31:*.tgz=01;31:*.arj=01;31:*.taz=01;31:*.lzh=01;31:*.zip=01;31:*.z=
01;31:*.Z=01;31:*.gz=01;31:*.bz2=01;31:*.bz=01;31:*.tz=01;31:*.rpm=
01;31:*.cpio=01;31:*.jpg=01;35:*.gif=01;35:*.bmp=01;35:*.xbm=01;35:*.xpm=
01;35:*.png=01;35:*.tif=01;35:
MACHTYPE=i386-redhat-linux-gnu
MAIL=/var/spool/mail/root
INPUTRC=/etc/inputrc
BASH_ENV=/root/.bashrc
LANG=en_US
LOGNAME=root
SHLVL=1
SHELL=/bin/bash
USERNAME=root
HOSTTYPE=i386
OSTYPE=linux-gnu
HISTSIZE=1000
LAMHELPFILE=/etc/lam/lam-helpfile
PVM_ROOT=/usr/share/pvm3
TERM=xterm
HOME=/root
SSH_ASKPASS=/usr/libexec/openssh/gnome-ssh-askpass
PATH=/usr/kerberos/sbin:/usr/kerberos/bin:/bin:/sbin:/usr/bin:/usr/sbin:
/usr/local/bin:/usr/local/sbin:/usr/bin/X11:/usr/X11R6/bin:/root/bin
_=/usr/bin/env
OLDPWD=/opt/web/cgi-bin
```

It is evident from the preceding output that environment variables are set on the server and contain information about the Web server. Some Web servers that run CGI scripts are the Apache and IIS servers. Some examples of browsers that interact with the Web servers are Microsoft Internet Explorer and Netscape Navigator.

Generally, all CGI programs receive data from Apache only through the environment variables present on the system, so understanding the relevance of environment variables with respect to CGI is important. Although it is not necessary that all the environment variables are always set, most of the environment variables are important. You can divide environment variables into the following basic categories:

◆ Non-request specific environment variables

◆ Request specific environment variables

◆ Non CGI-specific environment variables

◆ Environment variables related to `mod_rewrite`

Non-Request-Specific Environment Variables

These environment variables are not set for a single request but are applicable to all requests. The environment variables that are a part of this category are as follows:

◆ **SERVER_SOFTWARE.** Consists of the name of the Web server that is being used to answer HTTP requests. Also contains the version information about the server software.

◆ **SERVER_NAME.** Consists of either the hostname, the IP address, or the DNS alias of the server answering HTTP requests.

◆ **GATEWAY_INTERFACE.** Specifies the revision information of the CGI specification that the server complies with and is using.

Request-Specific Environment Variables

In addition to the environment variables that are non-request-specific, several environment variables are specific to requests fulfilled by the gateway program. The environment variables that fall in this category are as follows:

◆ **SEVER_PROTOCOL.** Specifies the information protocol used by the request received by the server.

◆ **SERVER_PORT.** Specifies the port on which the server received the request.

◆ **REQUEST_METHOD.** Specifies the request method used by the client to send the request. This could be GET, POST, PUT, HEAD, or any other request method.

◆ **PATH_INFO.** Refers to the extra information sent by the client along with the path name for the requested resource. The server decodes the additional information sent by the client before passing it to the CGI script.

◆ **PATH_TRANSLATED.** Specifies the translated version of the path information specified by the client. The server translates the path information for mapping purposes.

◆ **SCRIPT_NAME.** Refers to the virtual path used by the script being executed by the server. This information is primarily used for self-referencing URLs.

◆ **QUERY_STRING.** Specifies the information that follows the question mark in the URL. This URL is the one that was used by the client to reference a script.

◆ **REMOTE_HOST.** Specifies the hostname of the remote computer that sent the request.

◆ **REMOTE_ADDR.** Refers to the IP address of the remote computer that sent the request.

◆ **AUTH_TYPE.** Refers to the protocol-specific request method that is used by the server to validate the credentials of the user placing the request.

◆ **REMOTE_USER.** Set on the condition that the requested CGI script requires user authentication. It contains the username of the individual who was authenticated to access the script.

◆ **REMOTE_IDENT.** Set to the remote username retrieved from the server. This will be set only if the HTTP server supports RFC 931 identification.

◆ **CONTENT_TYPE.** Specifies the content type of the data for queries that have attached information, such as HTTP POST and PUT.

◆ **CONTENT_LENGTH.** Specifies the length of the content submitted by the client to the server.

Environment Variables that are not CGI-Specific

A few environment variables are not directly linked to the concept of CGI but are added by Apache. The following list covers these variables, which, after all, were built for your convenience.

◆ **DOCUMENT_PATH_INFO.** Refers to the path information passed to a document.

◆ **DOCUMENT_ROOT.** Refers to the directory path name specified in the DocumentRoot directive.

◆ **PATH.** Points to the PATH shell environment variable. The shell environment variable is set at the time Apache is started.

◆ **REMOTE_PORT.** Indicates the TCP port the client used to establish the connection.

◆ **SERVER_ADDR.** Specifies the IP address of the server that received the HTTP request.

◆ **SCRIPT_FILENAME.** Refers to the complete path, also known as the *absolute path* to the location of the CGI script.

◆ **SERVER_ADMIN.** Specifies the e-mail address of the server administrator. The value of this variable is the same as that specified in the ServerAdmin directive.

Environment Variables Related to *mod_rewrite*

The following environment variables are a significant part of the mod_rewrite module that provides a URL rewriting engine. These environment variables are widely used for URL mapping in Apache:

- ◆ SCRIPT_URI. Specifies the complete URL that includes information such as the protocol used for connection, the hostname, the port used, and the request.
- ◆ SCRIPT_URL. Specifies the URL path of the script. This is the script that was called.
- ◆ REQUEST_URI. Refers to the URL path sent by the client. This is the path that led the request to the script that was called.

STDIN and STDOUT

STDIN stands for *standard input*, and STDOUT stands for *standard output*. You may recall that Linux has three types of standard files: the standard input file, the standard output file, and the standard error file. In the context of the Linux operating system, a standard input file is a keyboard that can be used to enter data, and the standard output file is the screen where you see the output of the data entered. Although the logic for STDIN and STDOUT is the same with respect to using CGI scripts, the way in which you apply STDIN and STDOUT is different.

The following list describes what happens when a Web form is sent to a CGI program using the POST method:

1. The data present in the form is combined into a special format.
2. This format is delivered to the CGI program using STDIN.
3. The program processes this data as though it were entered from the keyboard and sends the output using STDOUT.

CGI Modules and Libraries

All system administrators should use CGI code modules and libraries when configuring Apache to use CGI programs. These modules and libraries help you develop efficient CGI code. The main benefits of using CGI modules and libraries are that they allow you to develop CGI programs with fewer errors and also lead to faster development.

If you are considering using Perl to write most of your CGI programs, you might want to use the modules available on Comprehensive Perl Archive Network (CPAN). CPAN is a wide network of resources related to Perl and the Perl community. It contains numerable resources related to Perl, such as utilities developed in Perl, books, documentation, and the entire Perl distribution. The most popular libraries available with Perl on CPAN are the following:

- ◆ **CGI Lite.** A library with a minimum set of functionality.
- ◆ **CGI.pm.** A popular and more comprehensive library.

Improving Performance of CGI Scripts

A variety of third-party tools are available that enable you to write CGI programs faster and more efficiently. Two of the important tools are FastCGI and CGI.pm. In this section, I'll discuss the benefits of using these tools and how they help developers write CGI scripts faster and more efficiently.

CGI.pm

CGI.pm is a Perl 5 CGI library that helps improve development speed of CGI scripts. This Perl library helps parse and interpret query strings before passing them to CGI scripts. When you use CGI.pm, almost every task is accomplished using a CGI object. You can use a CGI object for the following purposes:

◆ To examine the environment of a query string, to parse it, and to store its results.

◆ To return and modify query values.

◆ To handle POST and GET methods effectively.

FastCGI

FastCGI is an open source extension to CGI. The most important benefit of using FastCGI is that it facilitates high performance and it doesn't have limitations of server-specific APIs. You can include FastCGI with Apache by using the mod_fastcgi module. The benefits of using FastCGI are that it

◆ provides an easy to understand interface that is also easy to use.

◆ simplifies the migration of existing CGI applications. Applications that are built using the CGI library can also be run as CGI programs that are compatible with old Web servers.

◆ doesn't have language dependencies and can be used with many languages, such as Perl, Python, and Ruby.

◆ has processes that are isolated from each other run FastCGI applications. Therefore, an application that has bugs doesn't affect the performance of the Web server. This also applies to malicious applications. As a result of running applications in separate processes, the chances of inflicting harm on the server are substantially decreased.

◆ doesn't have a cost associated with procurement. It can be downloaded from its official Web site, http://www.fastcgi.com/, free of cost.

◆ is independent of the Web server architecture and can be used with different Web servers regardless of their threading architecture.

Securing CGI

Although CGI scripts are easy to use and serve many useful purposes, they are vulnerable to security attacks. As a result, CGI is sometimes considered too insecure to run on the server side. On the other hand, CGI has been on the Internet scene for quite some time, which is probably why its shortcomings are so globally evident. The truth is that if CGI scripts are written properly, they are as secure as any other application.

Security Tips

Following are a few tips for securing CGI applications:

◆ **Never run the Web server as a privileged user.** It is more than dangerous to run the Web server as a privileged user such as the root user. Only the root user should run the main Apache daemon. This is because the main Apache daemon doesn't handle client requests directly. All child processes directly handle client requests and should be run with the permissions of an unprivileged user.

◆ **Avoid passing input directly to the Linux shell.** Perl scripts can potentially pass data to the Linux shell for execution. This occurs when you enclose commands in the backtick (`) characters, which results in spawning a new shell for executing commands. Or the commands can be included as arguments with system( ) or exec( ) functions. Avoid both these methods while using Perl to pass user input directly to the Linux shell, because they make the system vulnerable to attacks.

◆ **Use Perl taint checking.** Perl has an optional mode of operation, called *taint checking*, that checks scripts run by privileged users for possible security problems. Opt to use Perl in this mode in order to be sure who is executing scripts on your server. This mechanism, in particular, detects scripts that are being run on behalf of unauthorized or unknown users.

◆ **Use the latest versions of CGI-supported modules.** If you are using CGI support modules, use the latest versions of the modules. For example, to use Perl, be sure to download the latest versions of cgi-lib.pl or CGI.pm.

◆ **Avoid using CGI if users are not trustworthy.** Avoid using CGI if you doubt the integrity of the users on your system. Internal users have comparatively more access rights than external users do. Even a small security hole might enable an internal user to exploit the vulnerability of a CGI script.

◆ **Use free CGI scripts with caution.** Several Web sites allow you to download free CGI scripts. Although you might want to access these sites and download CGI scripts, using downloaded CGI scripts in the production environment is very risky. The scripts could be a medium for gaining unauthorized access to your system or could even be created to inflict harm to your system. Unless you're sure of the source of a CGI script, you're better off not using it. Here a few guidelines to follow before using downloaded CGI scripts:

- Check the amount of code in scripts. The longer the code, the greater the chances that something hidden. It is always risky to download and use long CGI scripts.

- Check whether explicit path names are used to invoke external programs. Using the PATH environment variable to resolve incomplete path names can be a risky proposition.

- Check whether the script is running using suid privileges. Use scripts that run by utilizing *set-user-id* privileges with extreme care, and determine why the script is using suid.

- Check whether the CGI script is interacting with other programs in your system. If so, try to determine why and use it only if it doesn't disturb the settings of the other installed programs.

- Check whether the CGI program reads or writes to files on your file system. CGI programs that read or write to files on the file system could be designed to deliberately or inadvertently change access permissions or to modify and damage files.

◆ **Store CGI scripts in the right location.** Although it is possible to store CGI scripts anywhere on your file system, because of their vulnerabilities you should probably keep them in a selected single location where administrators can easily manage them. As far as possible, aim at storing the CGI scripts in a default location. On my custom system, I store them in the /opt/web/cgi-bin directory.

Security Tools for CGI

CGI applications are known for their vulnerability just as much as they are known for their benefits. Therefore, as a Web server administrator, you should do as much as possible to secure CGI applications. The good news is that some tools are available that you can use to ensure security for CGI scripts. Among these tools, my favorites are suEXEC and cgiwrap.

suEXEC

In the default installation of Apache, every CGI application runs under the same username that the parent process of Apache uses. This aspect alone can be a cause of concern for an Apache system administrator. If all the scripts created by different programmers run under the same username, then all the CGI programs have the same access permissions on the computer. In other words, one programmer who has direct access to only one cgi-bin/ directory can fiddle around with directories of other users. More importantly, if one of the cgi-bin/ directories is not well protected, the whole server is vulnerable to a security hole.

Apache has a solution for this problem. SuEXEC is a feature in Apache that enables administrators to allow CGI scripts of a particular virtual host to run under a special username. This means that, unlike the default installation of Apache in which every user can run the CGI under a single username, with similar permissions, each programmer has a separate access area and username. This protective measure enables distribution of access areas among different users.

suEXEC does not come enabled with the standard installation of Apache. This is primarily because an Apache server with a badly configured suEXEC can cause much more trouble than an Apache server without a suEXEC.

The cgiwrap Program

The cgiwrap program, in short, is a *CGI wrapper*. CGI wrappers are scripts that perform actions on the CGI scripts to help protect them from intrusion. Wrappers can perform various activities, such as regular security checks, using the chroot mechanism to place the script in a secure location on the file system, and changing the ownership of CGI processes.

The cgiwrap program has all the qualities of a good CGI wrapper. However, the main benefit of using cgiwrap is that it allows users to execute their scripts under their own user IDs. This greatly simplifies the job of the Web server administrator because it prevents users from tinkering with one another's scripts.

Summary

In this chapter, I introduced concepts related to the Common Gateway Interface. Then I discussed CGI in relation to the Apache Web server and how you can configure Apache to work with CGI. Next, I discussed how to create a basic CGI program and troubleshoot CGI related problems. I also discussed the environment variables. Finally, I described a few tools that you can use to improve the performance and security of CGI applications.

Check Your Understanding

Multiple Choice Questions

1. Which of the following directives is used to instruct the Web server regarding which files should be considered as CGI files?

    a. `Directory`

    b. `AddHandler`

    c. `Options`

    d. `ScriptAlias`

2. Which of the following statements is not true with respect to FastCGI?

    a. All tasks are accomplished using CGI objects.

    b. Simplifies the migration of existing CGI applications.

    c. Independent of the Web server architecture.

    d. Doesn't have language dependencies.

3. Which of the following environment variables is used to store the value of the IP address of a remote computer that sent a request?

    a. `REMOTE_HOST`

    b. `REMOTE_USER`

    c. `REMOTE_ADDR`

    d. `REMOTE_IDENT`

4. Which of the following environment variables is used to specify the complete URL that includes information such as the protocol used for connection, the hostname, the port used, and the request?

    a. `SCRIPT_URI`

    b. `SCRIPT_URL`

    c. `SCRIPT_FILENAME`

    d. `DOCUMENT_PATH_INFO`

5. Which of the following tools is primarily used to improve the security for CGI scripts? (Choose all that apply.)

    a. suEXEC

    b. CGI.pm

    c. FastCGI

    d. cgiwrap

Answers

Multiple Choice Answers

1. b. The AddHandler directive is used to instruct the Web server regarding which files should be considered as CGI files.

2. a. All tasks are accomplished using CGI objects in the case of CGI.pm and not FastCGI.

3. c. The REMOTE_ADDR environment variable is used to store the value of the IP address of a remote computer that sent a request.

4. a. The SCRIPT_URI environment variable is used to specify the complete URL that includes information such as the protocol used for connection, the hostname, the port used, and the request itself.

5. a, d. The suEXEC and cgiwrap utilities are used to improve the security for CGI scripts.

Chapter 8

Working With Apache Modules

The Apache Web server services clients' requests over the HTTP protocol. In the request-response mechanism, a client requests a service from the server, and the server sends a response back to the client. The response can be a static Web page or a dynamic Web page containing results of programs executed at the server. In addition to serving a client's requests, the Web server performs tasks such as authentication of the client, authorization of the clients for the services sought, and so on.

The Apache Web server is built on a modular concept, which ensures ongoing scalability of the server. This modular architecture means that you can easily enhance the Apache Web server by either expanding it or shrinking it to meet your needs. Here are some of the specific benefits you derive by using a modular architecture:

◆ You can easily add features to the server. Because of Apache's open source nature, programmers around the globe are able to develop and add features per their requirements. This enriches the Apache Web server's features. As a result, it has almost all the features that you might require in a Web server.

◆ You can add or remove functionality easily per your requirements. You don't need to recompile the entire source code when adding or removing functionality.

The Apache Web server consists of the Apache core and various other modules. As I stated in Chapter 2, "Introduction to Apache," the core provides the basic functionality for the Apache server, such as the use of directives and the capability to read configuration files, communicate with modules, provide access control, and so on.

The core receives requests from clients and delegates the request to modules. The modules process the requests and send responses back to the core. The core then forwards the response to the client.

Apache derives its modular architecture from modules. Before continuing, take a moment to check out these module benefits and features:

◆ You can extend the core Apache functionality.

◆ You can have modules embed themselves automatically into Apache functioning by using *hooks*, which enable Apache to pass control to the module at certain stages during request processing.

◆ You can add or remove modules without recompiling Apache.

◆ You load modules in a particular order as defined in the httpd.conf file.

Apache Standard Modules

As I said earlier, the Apache core provides the basic features of the Apache server, while a standard set of modules supplements the core's basic functionality. All of this combined functionality is required in order for the Apache server to work.

Modules are required to handle each stage in the request-response cycle that takes place between a Web server and Web browser. Various stages of the request-response cycle that are managed by modules are listed here:

◆ Determination of the physical file requested using the URI sent by the HTTP client

◆ Authentication

◆ Access control

- File permissions
- MIME type mapping of the object requested
- Response to the client
- Request logging

In the upcoming sections of this chapter, you'll discover that modules are available to control and manage each stage.

In the following sections, you'll learn about the standard set of Apache modules, which are categorized based on their functions.

Environment Creation Modules

Modules in this category are required in order to initialize the environment variables. The modules that fall in this category are as follows:

- **mod_env**. Controls the environment provided to CGI scripts and SSI pages. You can either use the shell that invoked the httpd process to pass the environment variable or set the environment variables during configuration.

- **mod_setenvif**. Sets the environment variables based on the requests received from the clients. The server uses environment variables to determine the actions to be taken while processing the client request.

- **mod_unique_id**. Sets the environment variable, UNIQUE_ID, which uniquely identifies each request.

Modules Used for Identifying the Content Type

Modules in this category are used to identify content type of different documents. The modules that fall in this category are described here:

- **mod_mime**. Interprets the types of files using the extension specified in the filename. For example, filenames with a .txt extension are interpreted to be text files. The mod_mime also associates handlers with files. The information regarding the file types is used for content-negotiation or is returned to the browser. The handlers determine how the document will be processed within the server.

- **mod_mime_magic**. Determines the type of content in the file requested (MIME type) by comparing certain parts of the contents to a file on the Linux system. This file is called the mime-magic file that is present in the /etc directory and stores information related to all supported MIME types.

- **mod_negotiation**. Handles content negotiation at the server end. Apache supports the content negotiation feature to meet HTTP/1.1 requirements. Content negotiation enables Apache to select the best representation of resources and efficiently handle the requests from the browsers.

Mapping Modules

You use the modules in this category for mapping URLs to files and directories in the file system. Some of the modules that fall in this category are as follows:

- ◆ `mod_alias`. Maps a URL with a file located in the file system.
- ◆ `mod_rewrite`. Provides a powerful URL rewriting engine. The module supports various rules to facilitate the rewriting mechanism.
- ◆ `mod_userdir`. Responsible for directory management in the user's home directory. This directory commonly uses the http://<hostname>/~username format and allows each user on a system to have a personal Web page.
- ◆ `mod_speling`. Corrects the typographical errors in the URLs that the users enter.
- ◆ `mod_vhost_alias`. Responsible for the virtual host support provided by the Apache server. It enables configuring of large number of virtual hosts with similar configuration.

Directory Handling Modules

Modules in this category support directory handling and listing. Some modules that belong in this category are listed here:

- ◆ `mod_dir`. Provides support for directory redirection and also helps serve directory index files.
- ◆ `mod_autoindex`. Provides support for automatic indexing of directories.

Authentication Modules

You use modules in this category to authenticate users and restrict their access based on authentication. Some modules that belong to this category are as follows:

- ◆ `mod_access`. Responsible for controlling access permissions granted to the client. The control can be based on host name, IP address, password, or any other criteria.
- ◆ `mod_auth`. Provides support for authenticating users based on the username and password entries in the password text files.
- ◆ `mod_auth_dbm`. Provides support for authenticating users based on the username and password entries in the DBM files.
- ◆ `mod_auth_db`. Provides support for authenticating users based on the username and password entries in the Berkley DB files.
- ◆ `mod_auth_anon`. Provides support for allowing access to the anonymous users.
- ◆ `mod_auth_digest`. Provides support for authenticating users based on the MD5 Digest authentication.
- ◆ `mod_ssl`. Provides support for establishing secure communication between the Web server and the client browser by using SSL.

HTTP Response Modules

The Apache Web server receives requests for services from the clients and then sends a response back to the clients. A large number of HTTP headers are exchanged in this request-response process. There are various modules available to manage the headers of the response. A few important modules are listed here:

◆ **mod_headers**. Controls the HTTP header that is sent with the response to client. The server sends the response after processing the client request. The module can be used to add, remove, or modify the existing headers of the HTTP response.

◆ **mod_expires**. Sets the expiration time of the HTTP response. The HTTP response becomes invalid after the specified expiration date and time.

◆ **mod_asis**. Sends HTTP response headers without any modification to the structure.

Dynamic Content Modules

Creating dynamic Web pages is one of the key tasks of a Web server. Dynamic pages are generated during runtime. This makes them flexible and capable of providing a wide range of functionality to a Web site. Some of the modules that control dynamic content generation in Apache are listed here:

◆ **mod_include**. Enables processing of documents at the server end before they are sent back to the client.

◆ **mod_cgi**. Responsible for executing CGI scripts on the server.

◆ **mod_actions**. Provides support for execution of CGI scripts based on media type or the request method used. This module uses two directives:

    • **Action** directive. Enables you to execute CGI scripts if a particular file type is requested.

    • **Script** directive. Enables you to execute CGI scripts if a particular method has been used for a request.

◆ **mod_isapi**. Provides support of Internet Server Extension API (ISAPI) only for Microsoft Windows platforms.

Internal Content Handlers Modules

System administrators need to be aware of their system's performance in order to avoid inconsistencies. This includes staying up-to-date on the system's status and on other information related to performance. The following modules provide Apache administrators with such information:

◆ **mod_status**. Used to obtain performance related information about the server that helps administrators perform meaningful analysis.

◆ **mod_info**. Used to obtain detailed configuration information about the server. You can obtain an exhaustive list of all modules and directives available in the configuration files.

Logging Modules

Modules in this category are responsible for maintaining different logs on the server. Modules that add logging capability to the server are as follows:

◆ `mod_log_config`. Provides support for logging information about the requests received from clients. Information can be logged to a file or a program in a customizable format.

◆ `mod_usertrack`. Enables the Web server to maintain logs related to user activities on a site. The module uses cookies to achieve this.

Miscellaneous Modules

In addition to the categorized modules listed in the previous sections, some other modules are available for performing miscellaneous tasks. They are:

◆ `mod_imap`. Enables imagemap processing on the Apache Web server.

◆ `mod_proxy`. Incorporates proxy capabilities into the Apache Web server.

◆ `mod_so`. Used to load executable programs and modules on the server during the start-up process. It can also be used to load modules at runtime.

◆ `mod_file_cache`. Adds caching capabilities to the Apache server.

Dynamic Shared Objects

You need to load a module to make it available to the Apache server. You can do so in two ways: *statically* or *dynamically*. After you statically compile a module to link it to the Apache core daemon file (httpd), the module can't be removed or added.

Apache supports dynamic loading by using the *Dynamic Shared Object (DSO)* mechanism. The DSO method was introduced in Apache 1.3. The support for DSO makes it possible for you to load modules into the Apache Web server without having to recompile the server. With this method, you load the DSO module into memory when needed and link it dynamically to the Apache core. This course of action uses the Shared Object mechanism in Linux and the DLL mechanism in Windows. Many third-party modules are available in the DSO compatible format.

Before you can dynamically load a module, you need to declare the module as dynamically loadable. The dynamically loadable modules are specified in the http.conf file. You declare all such modules using the `LoadModule` directive in the httpd.conf file. A sample of `LoadModule` directives in the httpd.conf file is given here:

```
LoadModule vhost_alias_module libexec/mod_vhost_alias.so
LoadModule env_module         libexec/mod_env.so
```

```
LoadModule config_log_module    libexec/mod_log_config.so
LoadModule mime_magic_module    libexec/mod_mime_magic.so
LoadModule mime_module          libexec/mod_mime.so
LoadModule negotiation_module   libexec/mod_negotiation.so
LoadModule status_module        libexec/mod_status.so
LoadModule info_module          libexec/mod_info.so
LoadModule includes_module      libexec/mod_include.so
LoadModule autoindex_module     libexec/mod_autoindex.so
LoadModule dir_module           libexec/mod_dir.so
LoadModule cgi_module           libexec/mod_cgi.so
LoadModule asis_module          libexec/mod_asis.so
```

The syntax of the LoadModule is as follows:

```
LoadModule <calling_name> <module_file>
```

In the syntax, <calling_name> is the name by which the module is referred. The module is stored in the <module_file>. This file is stored in a directory under the Apache ServerRoot. An example of the LoadModule directive is given here:

```
LoadModule vhost_alias_module modules/mod_vhost_alias.so
```

In the preceding example, vhost_alias_module is the calling name of the module. The file for the module is stored as mod_vhost_alias.so in the modules directory under the Apache ServerRoot.

The server reads the LoadModule during initialization. These modules are added to the list of available modules. However, you cannot use these modules until you specify them in the AddModule directive in the httpd.conf file. AddModule makes a module available to the server. Remember that AddModule is a core directive; it is not specific to the DSO modules. All other modules, even the ones that are linked to the Apache core, are made available through the AddModule directive. Unlike AddModule, the LoadModule directive is specific to the DSO modules. A sample entry of the AddModule directive is shown here:

```
ClearModuleList
AddModule mod_vhost_alias.c
AddModule mod_env.c
AddModule mod_log_config.c
AddModule mod_log_agent.c
AddModule mod_log_referer.c
#AddModule mod_mime_magic.c
AddModule mod_mime.c
```

```
AddModule mod_negotiation.c
AddModule mod_status.c
AddModule mod_info.c
AddModule mod_include.c
AddModule mod_autoindex.c
AddModule mod_dir.c
AddModule mod_cgi.c
```

Notice that the first line of the preceding sample, the ClearModuleList entry, erases the internal list of modules.

You can load all of the modules that are distributed with the Apache server at runtime except for the following two:

◆ The core module

◆ The mod_so module

The core module is linked to the Apache kernel. Therefore, it needs to be running before Apache can start functioning. The mod_so module provides the Apache server with the capability to dynamically load modules. Obviously, these two modules must be loaded before Apache can load dynamic modules.

To enable DSO support in the Apache server, add the following argument while configuring Apache or add it to the config.status file:

```
--enable-module=so
```

This argument enables DSO support on most platforms. However, on some platforms, you need to specify the following:

```
--enable-rule=SHARD_CORE
```

The preceding argument causes most of the code that comprises the Apache binary to be compiled into the DSO module libhttpd.so.

Next, to compile most of the standard Apache modules as DSO modules, you specify the following argument:

```
--enable-shared=max
```

The preceding statement uses DSO while compiling the modules with Apache.

You can also use a combination of the --enable-module and --enable-shared arguments to enable individual modules and to compile them as DSO modules.

The LoadModule and the AddModule directives can be located anywhere in the httpd.conf file. However, you need to ensure that the LoadModule directive is included before the AddModule directive. Whenever you add a LoadModule directive, a corresponding AddModule directive should be added. To disable a module, you can comment out the corresponding AddModule entry for the module. However, this is waste of resources because the module is loaded anyway, even though it is not used. On the other hand, if you specify a module in the AddModule directive for which the corresponding entry in the LoadModule directive is not present or is commented out, you might get a configuration error. This error occurs because you are trying to enable a module that is not available to the server.

The order in which the modules are specified in the LoadModule and AddModule directives is critical for the functioning of the server, because sometimes one module is dependent on another module. Specifying a module that is dependent on another module that is not loaded will produce an error. Also, modules affect the request object that is passed from module to module in the various stages of request processing. As a result, the effect of a change of a request object is passed on to all the subsequent modules. Apache, by default, has a well-planned sequence of modules that behaves correctly. If you change this order, changes in the request object might cause behavior that is really hard to debug—unless you fully understand how Apache works.

Advantages of DSO

Using DSO has several advantages. DSO is particularly useful because it allows you to easily add or remove functionality from Apache as the case may be. The following list discusses some of the advantages of using DSO:

◆ **Low memory usage.** You need to load only the required modules. The unnecessary modules can be left out. In this way, you free up the memory that would be consumed by unnecessary modules.

◆ **Flexibility.** The ability to load or unload a module makes the Web server flexible.

◆ **Extensibility.** The Web server can extend its functionality by using several third-party DSO compliant modules.

◆ **Easy-to-manage Web server.** You don't have to recompile the Web server every time you add or remove a module.

Disadvantages of DSO

Using the DSO feature can also have disadvantages. It is important to understand the disadvantages of DSO so that you can decide whether to use the DSO feature or not. The following list discusses the disadvantages of using the DSO feature:

◆ You can use the DSO feature only on the platforms that support dynamic loading of code into the address space of a program.

◆ There is some noticeable effect on the performance when the modules are dynamically loaded for the first time.

◆ For security reasons, many system administrators compile the whole server statically. Doing so prevents the addition of malicious modules or the alteration of the Apache modules.

Application and Language Support Modules

One important feature of Apache is that it is possible to add programming language support by simply installing the respective module. For example, to build support for PHP scripting language in Apache you can simply install the respective module and you are ready to use PHP.

You can broadly categorize some modules as those that support applications and languages. Some such commonly used modules are listed here:

- **mod_cgi**. Provides support for CGI.
- **mod_perl**. Provides the server API with the Perl language interpreters and the Perl interface.
- **mod_python**. Provides support for the Python language interpreter.
- **mod_php**. Provides support for the PHP server-side scripting language.
- **mod_javascript**. Incorporates support for JavaScript.
- **mod_serv**. Provides support for Java servlet programs.

According to a survey posted at https://secure1.securityspace.com/s_survey/data/man.200207/apachemods.html, the following are the five most popular modules:

- mod_php
- mod_perl
- OpenSSL
- mod_ssl
- FrontPage

In the section "Installing Modules," I discuss mod_php and mod_perl, which are the modules most often used with Apache. The mod_php module allows the use of server-side PHP scripts, while mod_perl allows the use of Perl scripting languages.

Installing Modules

You can install Apache modules several ways. First, you can install Apache modules either within the Apache source code tree or outside it. The modules installed within the source tree are basically a part of the Apache standard distribution. These modules are usually placed in the /src/modules directory. To install the module this way you must pass some configuration directives to the Apache AutoConf-style Interface (APACI). APACI compiles the modules with the Apache server, and the modules are linked during runtime. You need to make the required changes to the httpd.conf to enable the module.

Second, you can configure modules as dynamically linked modules (refer to the section "Dynamic Shared Objects" for the details on dynamically linked modules).

Third, you can install modules by using the Apache Extension, which is covered in the next section.

Using the Apache Extension (apxs)

The Apache Extension (apxs) is a Perl script that you can use to compile and install Apache modules. The benefit of using apxs is that it can handle modules containing many source files. You can compile nearly every module using apxs. However, there are exceptions, such as the modules that modify the Apache source.

Here is the syntax for using the apxs command:

```
apxs [options] <module_name>
```

The [options] can have the following values:

- **-a**. Adds the LoadModule and AddModule directives to the httpd.conf file to activate the module.
- **-n**. Specifies the module name.
- **-q**. Queries for default values for various variables hard-coded in apxs.
- **-s**. Specifies the apxs settings.
- **-g**. Generates a template of source code directory with the module name specified.
- **-c**. Compiles and links a DSO module.
- **-o**. Specifies the name of the resulting DSO file.
- **-D**. Specifies the directives to be used while module compilation.
- **-I**. Specifies the directories that will be searched for include files during compilation.
- **-l**. Specifies the libraries to be linked to the modules.
- **-Wc**. Passes additional flags during the compilation process.
- **-Wl**. Passes additional flags during the linking process.
- **-i**. Installs a module that has already been created.

The *mod_php* Module

The mod_php module provides support for the PHP language. PHP initially stood for *Personal Home Page* tools. More recently, PHP has been popularized as *HyperText PreProcessor*. PHP is a server-side scripting language that is used to create dynamic Web pages. You can use PHP to perform all programming tasks (tasks such as database connectivity, input-output to various devices, complex string and mathematical calculations, and so on). You can embed PHP in HTML pages or use it to generate an entire HTML page. PHP 4.0 supports object-oriented features. The mod_php module provides support for PHP.

NOTE

You can obtain information on the latest releases of PHP, changes from previous versions, as well as bug reports, at http://www.php.net.

Installing mod_php

Go to the PHP download site at http://www.php.net/downloads.php, then follow these steps to install mod_php:

1. At the PHP Web site, download the file php-4.2.1.tar.bz2 and save it on your hard drive.

2. Copy the downloaded file to the /usr/local/src/ directory using the following command:

   ```
   [root@linux root]# cp php-4.2.1.tar.bz2 /usr/local/src/
   ```

3. Go to the /usr/local/src directory by typing the following command:

   ```
   [root@linux root]# cd /usr/local/src/
   ```

4. Extract the contents of the file php-4.2.1.tar.bz2 in the /usr/local/src directory by using the following command:

   ```
   [root@linux src]# tar xvjf php-4.2.1.tar.bz2
   php-4.2.1/
   php-4.2.1/build/
   php-4.2.1/build/bsd_makefile
   php-4.2.1/build/build.mk
   php-4.2.1/build/build2.mk
   php-4.2.1/build/buildcheck.sh
   php-4.2.1/build/dynlib.mk
   php-4.2.1/build/fastgen.sh
   php-4.2.1/build/genif.sh
   php-4.2.1/build/library.mk
   php-4.2.1/build/ltlib.mk
   php-4.2.1/build/mkdep.awk
   php-4.2.1/build/print_include.awk
   php-4.2.1/build/program.mk
   php-4.2.1/build/rules.mk
   php-4.2.1/build/rules_common.mk
   php-4.2.1/build/rules_pear.mk
   php-4.2.1/build/shtool
   php-4.2.1/build/sysv_makefile
   ```

```
php-4.2.1/configure
php-4.2.1/CODING_STANDARDS
php-4.2.1/CREDITS
php-4.2.1/ltmain.sh
php-4.2.1/acconfig.h
php-4.2.1/config.guess
php-4.2.1/missing
php-4.2.1/EXTENSIONS
php-4.2.1/INSTALL
php-4.2.1/LICENSE
php-4.2.1/Makefile.in
php-4.2.1/NEWS
….numerous deleted lines
```

5. Use the **cd** command to go to the php-4.2.1 directory that is created automatically when you uncompress the file.

```
[root@linux src]# cd php-4.2.1
```

6. Check the options available with the configure script using the following command:

```
[root@linux php-4.2.1]# ./configure --help
Usage: configure [options] [host]
Options: [defaults in brackets after descriptions]
Configuration:
  --cache-file=FILE     cache test results in FILE
  --help                print this message
  --no-create           do not create output files
  --quiet, --silent     do not print `checking...' messages
  --version             print the version of autoconf that created
configure
Directory and file names:
  --prefix=PREFIX       install architecture-independent files in PREFIX
                        [/usr/local]
  --exec-prefix=EPREFIX install architecture-dependent files in EPREFIX
                        [same as prefix]
  --bindir=DIR          user executables in DIR [EPREFIX/bin]
  --sbindir=DIR         system admin executables in DIR [EPREFIX/sbin]
  --libexecdir=DIR      program executables in DIR [EPREFIX/libexec]
  --datadir=DIR         read-only architecture-independent data in DIR
                        [PREFIX/share]
```

```
    --sysconfdir=DIR        read-only single-machine data in DIR [PREFIX/etc]
    --sharedstatedir=DIR    modifiable architecture-independent data in DIR
                            [PREFIX/com]
    --localstatedir=DIR     modifiable single-machine data in DIR [
PREFIX/var]
    --libdir=DIR            object code libraries in DIR [EPREFIX/lib]
    --includedir=DIR        C header files in DIR [PREFIX/include]
    --oldincludedir=DIR     C header files for non-gcc in DIR [/usr/include]
    --infodir=DIR           info documentation in DIR [PREFIX/info]
    --mandir=DIR            man documentation in DIR [PREFIX/man]
    --srcdir=DIR            find the sources in DIR [configure dir or ..]
    --program-prefix=PREFIX prepend PREFIX to installed program names
    --program-suffix=SUFFIX append SUFFIX to installed program names
    --program-transform-name=PROGRAM
                            run sed PROGRAM on installed program names
...numerous deleted lines
```

TIP

When installing PHP as a DSO module, as I am, it's a good idea to view the configure options that can be used with the configure script in order to choose the best options.

7. MySQL is the preferred database to use with PHP, and you should add MySQL support before installing PHP. Be sure that the mysql and mysql-devel RPMs are installed. To check whether these RPMs are installed, type the following commands:

```
[root@linux php-4.2.1]# rpm -q mysql
mysql-3.23.41-1
[root@linux php-4.2.1]# rpm -q mysql-devel
mysql-devel-3.23.41-1
```

NOTE

I recommend that you download and install mysql and mysql-devel RPMs before you proceed with the installation, if you haven't done so already.

8. Run the `configure` script with the options specified in the following command:

```
[root@linux php-4.2.1]# ./configure --with-apxs=/usr/local/apache/bin/apxs
 --with-mysql=/usr
loading cache ./config.cache
checking for Cygwin environment... (cached) no
checking for mingw32 environment... (cached) no
checking host system type... i686-pc-linux-gnu
checking for a BSD compatible install... (cached) /usr/bin/install -c
checking whether build environment is sane... yes
checking for gawk... (cached) gawk
checking whether make sets ${MAKE}... (cached) yes
checking whether to enable maintainer-specific portions of Makefiles... no
checking how to run the C preprocessor... (cached) cc -E
checking for AIX... no
checking for gcc... (cached) gcc
checking whether the C compiler (gcc  ) works... yes
checking whether the C compiler (gcc  ) is a cross-compiler... no
checking whether we are using GNU C... (cached) yes
checking whether gcc accepts -g... (cached) yes
checking for style of include used by make... GNU
checking dependency style of gcc... (cached) none
checking whether gcc and cc understand -c and -o together... (cached) yes
checking for gcc option to accept ANSI C... (cached) none needed
checking how to run the C preprocessor... cc -E
checking whether compiler supports -R... (cached) no
checking whether compiler supports -Wl,-rpath,... (cached) yes
checking for ranlib... (cached) ranlib
checking whether ln -s works... (cached) yes
…numerous deleted lines
```

9. After the `configure` script runs successfully, you will see the following message:

```
Thank you for using PHP.
```

10. After running the configure script, use the `make` command to proceed with the installation. You will see output similar to the following:

```
[root@linux php-4.2.1]# make
Making all in Zend
make[1]: Entering directory `/usr/local/src/php-4.2.1/Zend'
```

```
/bin/sh ../libtool --silent --mode=compile gcc -DHAVE_CONFIG_H -I. -I. -I
../main   -DLINUX=22 -DUSE_HSREGEX -I../TSRM  -g -O2 -prefer-pic -c -o
zend_language_parser.lo `test -f zend_language_parser.c || echo './'`
zend_language_parser.c
/bin/sh ../libtool --silent --mode=compile gcc -DHAVE_CONFIG_H -I. -I. -I
../main   -DLINUX=22 -DUSE_HSREGEX -I../TSRM  -g -O2 -prefer-pic -c -o
zend_language_scanner.lo `test -f zend_language_scanner.c || echo './'
`zend_language_scanner.c
/bin/sh ../libtool --silent --mode=compile gcc -DHAVE_CONFIG_H -I. -I. -I
../main   -DLINUX=22 -DUSE_HSREGEX -I../TSRM  -g -O2 -prefer-pic -c -o
zend_ini_parser.lo `test -f zend_ini_parser.c || echo './'`zend_ini_parser.c
/bin/sh ../libtool --silent --mode=compile gcc -DHAVE_CONFIG_H -I. -I. -I
../main   -DLINUX=22 -DUSE_HSREGEX -I../TSRM  -g -O2 -prefer-pic -c -o
zend_ini_scanner.lo `test -f zend_ini_scanner.c || echo './'`zend_ini_scanner.c
/bin/sh ../libtool --silent --mode=compile gcc -DHAVE_CONFIG_H -I. -I. -I
../main   -DLINUX=22 -DUSE_HSREGEX -I../TSRM  -g -O2 -prefer-pic -c -o
zend_alloc.lo `test -f zend_alloc.c || echo './'`zend_alloc.c
...numerous deleted lines
```

11. Use the make install command to proceed with the installation:

```
[root@linux php-4.2.1]# make install
Making install in Zend
make[1]: Entering directory `/usr/local/src/php-4.2.1/Zend'
make[2]: Entering directory `/usr/local/src/php-4.2.1/Zend'
make[2]: Nothing to be done for `install-exec-am'.
make[2]: Nothing to be done for `install-data-am'.
make[2]: Leaving directory `/usr/local/src/php-4.2.1/Zend'
make[1]: Leaving directory `/usr/local/src/php-4.2.1/Zend'
Making install in main
make[1]: Entering directory `/usr/local/src/php-4.2.1/main'
make[2]: Entering directory `/usr/local/src/php-4.2.1/main'
make[2]: Nothing to be done for `install-p'.
make[2]: Leaving directory `/usr/local/src/php-4.2.1/main'
make[1]: Leaving directory `/usr/local/src/php-4.2.1/main'
...numerous deleted lines
```

If everything works correctly in the installation, you should find a module file named libphp4.so in the /usr/local/apache/libexec directory. To check whether the module file is in this directory, execute the following command:

```
[root@linux root]# ls -l /usr/local/apache/libexec/libphp4.so
-rwxr-xr-x   1 root     root      2783369 Jun 27 01:45
/usr/local/apache/libexec/libphp4.so
```

It is evident from the output that the file libphp4.so is present in the /usr/local/apache/libexec directory.

Configuring Apache to Use mod_php

After installing PHP, you modify the httpd.conf file for Apache with the AddModule and LoadModule directives for the PHP module that you installed. You need to check whether the following entries are in the httpd.conf file:

```
LoadModule php4_module        libexec/libphp4.so
AddModule mod_php4.c
```

Next, you need to ensure that the respective AddModule and LoadModule directives are in the httpd.conf file; you then need to check for the existence of a PHP mime-type handler directive for files with the .php extension. If you can't find one, add the following lines to the end of the httpd.conf file:

```
AddType application/x-httpd-php .php
AddType application/x-httpd-php-source .phps
```

After adding the required lines, check whether the Apache configuration file has any errors by using the following command:

```
[root@linux root]# apachectl configtest
Syntax OK
```

The preceding output means that the Apache configuration file is free of problems. You are now ready to test whether PHP is working.

 NOTE

Remember to restart Apache after you configure PHP.

Testing the Install

Testing whether PHP was installed properly is easy. You just create a simple PHP script using the phpinfo() function. The phpinfo() function is a built-in function in PHP that displays a Web page indicating the installation options used to install PHP on the system.

To test the installation, create a file named test.php and copy it in the document root directory. Put the following code in the file:

```
<?php
phpinfo();
?>
```

In the preceding code, note the following:

◆ <?php is the opening tag used in PHP code. This tag indicates to the parser that this is where the PHP code starts.

◆ phpinfo() is a built-in function that displays the installation options used while installing PHP.

◆ The ; (semicolon) signifies the end of a statement in PHP.

◆ ?> is the closing tag, which indicates the end of the PHP code.

After creating the file and copying it to the document root directory, you can try opening this file from the browser. Figure 8.1 shows the Web page that appears when you try to open the file test.php.

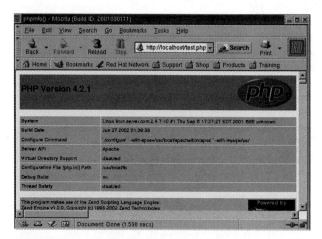

FIGURE 8.1 *The output of test.php in the browser*

The *mod_perl* Module

Perl is an *interpreted language* (language that allows you to write programs, which consist of instructions that are handled by a command interpreter present on the operating system) that was developed in 1987. Perl is known for its power and flexibility. The language was designed to facilitate the work of Unix system administrators who were familiar with sed, awk, or C language. Perl was revised throughout the 1990s to provide a high-level interface for networks, databases, system utilities, and Web applications. Perl 4 gained widespread acceptability among programmers. However, as it is an interpreted language, Perl is not suitable for high-traffic Web applications if used as a CGI because the program is executed every time a request arrives, causing high memory usage and delays in response. These problems don't exist in the case of mod_perl.

The mod_perl module provides support for the Perl language in Apache. The goal behind mod_perl is to allow Perl programmers to write modules for Apache Web server. mod_perl also provides improved performance and continued compatibility for CGI scripts written in Perl.

You can gain more flexibility and better performance by using mod_perl. When using mod_perl, you do not have to restart the Perl interpreter every time you execute a Perl program, so you can save on time and performance. You can also use mod_perl to create sophisticated Web applications.

Installing mod_perl *as a DSO*

Before beginning to install the mod_perl module as a DSO, go to the mod_perl Web site at http://perl.apache.org/download/index.html and follow these steps:

1. At the Perl Web site, download the mod_perl-1.27.tar.gz file (Version 1.27) and save it on any directory on the file system. I downloaded the file in the /root directory. However, you generally use the /usr/local/src directory to store source code.

2. Use the following command to extract the installation files from the compressed file:

```
[root@linux root]# tar xvzf mod_perl-1.27.tar.gz
mod_perl-1.27/
mod_perl-1.27/t/
mod_perl-1.27/t/docs/
mod_perl-1.27/t/docs/env.iphtml
mod_perl-1.27/t/docs/stacked.pl
mod_perl-1.27/t/docs/LoadClass.pm
mod_perl-1.27/t/docs/auth/
mod_perl-1.27/t/docs/auth/.htaccess
mod_perl-1.27/t/docs/content.html
mod_perl-1.27/t/docs/STAGE/
```

```
mod_perl-1.27/t/docs/STAGE/u1/
mod_perl-1.27/t/docs/STAGE/u1/nada.txt
...numerous deleted lines
```

3. Use the following command to go to the Perl installation directory:

```
[root@linux root]# cd mod_perl-1.27
```

4. Type the following command to specify that axps will be used to compile and install the module:

```
 [root@linux mod_perl-1.27]# perl Makefile.PL USE_APXS=1
WITH_APXS=/usr/local/apache/bin/apxs
Will configure via APXS (apxs=/usr/local/apache/bin/apxs)
PerlDispatchHandler.........disabled (enable with PERL_DISPATCH=1)
PerlChildInitHandler........enabled
PerlChildExitHandler........enabled
PerlPostReadRequestHandler..disabled (enable with PERL_POST_READ_
REQUEST=1)
PerlTransHandler............disabled (enable with PERL_TRANS=1)
PerlHeaderParserHandler.....disabled (enable with PERL_HEADER_PARSER=1)
PerlAccessHandler...........disabled (enable with PERL_ACCESS=1)
PerlAuthenHandler...........disabled (enable with PERL_AUTHEN=1)
PerlAuthzHandler............disabled (enable with PERL_AUTHZ=1)
PerlTypeHandler.............disabled (enable with PERL_TYPE=1)
PerlFixupHandler............disabled (enable with PERL_FIXUP=1)
PerlHandler.................enabled
...numerous deleted lines
```

5. Type the make command to proceed with the installation:

```
[root@linux root]# make
```

6. Next, type the make install command to complete the installation, as shown here:

```
[root@linux mod_perl-1.27]# make install
(cd ./apaci && PERL5LIB=/root/mod_perl-1.27/lib: make)
make[1]: Entering directory `/root/mod_perl-1.27/apaci'
make[1]: Nothing to be done for `all'.
make[1]: Leaving directory `/root/mod_perl-1.27/apaci'
make[1]: Entering directory `/root/mod_perl-1.27/Apache'
```

```
make[1]: Leaving directory `/root/mod_perl-1.27/Apache'
make[1]: Entering directory `/root/mod_perl-1.27/Connection'
make[1]: Leaving directory `/root/mod_perl-1.27/Connection'
make[1]: Entering directory `/root/mod_perl-1.27/Constants'
make[1]: Leaving directory `/root/mod_perl-1.27/Constants'
make[1]: Entering directory `/root/mod_perl-1.27/File'
make[1]: Leaving directory `/root/mod_perl-1.27/File'
make[1]: Entering directory `/root/mod_perl-1.27/Leak'
...numerous deleted lines
```

You have completed the installation of mod_perl. You are now ready to configure the httpd.conf file so that the Apache Web server can use mod_perl.

Configuring Apache to Use Perl Programs

After you've installed mod_perl, you must make a few modifications to the httpd.conf file in order to execute Perl programs. I describe those modifications in this section.

1. Stop the Apache Web server if it is running by executing the following command:

   ```
   [root@linux root]# apachectl stop
   ```

2. Open the httpd.conf file and check whether the associated AddModule and LoadModule directives are present.

3. Add the following code at the end of the httpd.conf file:

   ```
   <Files ~ "\.pl$">
   SetHandler perl-script
   PerlHandler Apache::Registry
   Options ExecCGI
   </Files>
   ```

   The addition of this code to httpd.conf ensures that all files ending with .pl are sent to the mod_perl handler, and the rest of the files in the cgi-bin directory are executed as regular CGIs.

4. Start the Apache Web server using the following command:

   ```
   [root@linux root]# apachectl start
   ```

Testing the Install

After you make the necessary changes in the httpd.conf file, check whether the installation and configuration of Perl was successful.

To check whether the installation was a success, follow these steps:

1. Create a file named test.pl using the following code:

```perl
#!/usr/bin/perl

print "Content-type: text/plain\n\n";
print  "Hi User!\n";

if(exists $ENV{MOD_PERL}) {
    print "We're running under mod_perl\n";
}  else {
  print "We're NOT running under mod_perl\n";
}
```

2. Copy the file into the /opt/web/cgi-bin directory.
3. Grant executable permissions for the test.pl file using the following command:

```
[root@linux root]# chmod a+x /opt/web/cgi-bin/test.pl
```

4. Start the Apache Web server.
5. Set the executable permission for the test.pl file using the chmod command.
6. Open the browser and specify the URL as http://localhost/cgi-bin/test.pl.

If you successfully configured Perl, you will see the output shown in Figure 8.2.

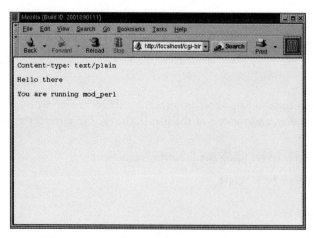

FIGURE 8.2 *The output of the test.pl file in the browser*

Summary

In this chapter, you learned about Apache modules. Modules are the core of the Apache server, and they provide added functionality that enables the server to function properly. I discussed the various standard modules that are shipped with the default Apache installation. A benefit of using Apache modules is that you can enable or disable the modules during runtime without having to recompile the Apache server. The LoadModule and AddModule directives in the httpd.conf file play an important role in determining which modules are available to the Apache server. You found detailed coverage of these directives in this chapter. Finally, you learned how to install two the most popular modules, mod_php and mod_perl.

Check Your Understanding

Questions

1. Which module uses the Action and the Script directives to execute CGI scripts based on media type or request method?

   a. mod_actions

   b. mod_include

   c. mod_cgi

   d. mod_negotiate

2. Select the advantages of using Apache modules. (Choose all that apply.)

   a. Low memory usage

   b. Flexibility

   c. Extensibility

   d. High performance during the first-time loading of modules

   e. Easy to manage

3. The _____ file helps you ensure that PHP is installed successfully.

4. Which of the following directives in the httpd.conf file do you use to specify the PHP extensions?

   a. AddType

   b. AddExtension

   c. AddPHPType

   d. AddPHPExtension

5. Which of the following modules do you use for URL mapping? (Choose all that apply).

   a. mod_rewrite

   b. mod_alias

   c. mod_access

   d. mod_negotiation

Answers

1. a. mod_actions module uses the Action and the Script directives to execute CGI scripts based on media type or request method.

2. a, b, c, e. The advantages of the Apache modules are low memory usage, flexibility, extensibility, easy to manage.

3. The libphp4.so file ensures that PHP is installed successfully.

4. a. You use the AddType directive in the httpd.conf file to specify the PHP extensions.

5. a, b. You use the mod_rewrite and mod_alias modules for mapping URLs.

PART III

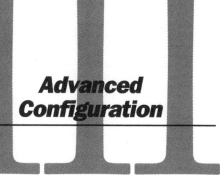

Advanced Configuration

Chapter 9

Improving Apache's Performance

Performance is always one of the major determining factors of the effectiveness of any software program. As a system administrator, you want to optimize performance as much as possible. In regard to Web servers, performance can be a cumulative measure of availability, time taken to retrieve resources from the server, or the number of requests handled in a given time. However, every setup is unique, and performance will be considered differently in different situations.

Apache is a full-feature Web server, and you can tweak it to a great extent. If you like experimenting with software, you might design your own plan for optimizing Apache's performance. However, years of research and testing have resulted in Apache's performing at the highest possible level.

In this chapter, I'll begin with a few directives that you can tweak to ensure maximum performance according to your needs. Then I'll discuss how you can use Apache as a proxy server and a cache server. Finally, I'll cover the concept of "logging" in the Apache Web server, which you can monitor using built-in and custom log files.

Performance-Related Directives

As discussed, you can configure a couple of directives to improve the performance of Apache. This will depend entirely on your setup and how you want to use Apache. In this section, I'll discuss how the main performance directives work and how to configure them for maximum performance in different situations.

Configuring Performance-Related Directives

One of the main elements of performance is speed. The higher the speed, the faster you are able to address client requests. In a production environment, thousands of clients might be concurrently connected to a Web server at a given point in time. Things are different when you are using Apache on a local area network, or LAN, where the client requests are minimal compared to the requests handled by a public Web server. Depending on the requirement and how you want to use Apache, you can configure the performance-related directives in Apache.

A method frequently used to improve Apache's speed and availability is to increase the number of process threads available to handle requests. By default, Apache is configured in the stand-alone mode. As a result, Apache starts at boot time with the main server process. This main process gives birth to a pool of child processes that handle incoming requests. The role of the main server process is simply to start the child processes; it is not responsible for answering client requests. The main Apache process starts 256 child processes by default. These child processes are responsible for handling client requests.

If there are less than 256 requests at a given time, the main server process maintains a pool of waiting processes. The number of processes in the pool keeps changing from time to time, depending on the requirement.

You can also change the default number of child processes invoked by the main server process according to your requirements. In order to understand the number of server processes that you can set, you need to be familiar with three server directives in the httpd.conf file that have server-wide scope. They are the following:

◆ The MinSpareServers directive
◆ The MaxSpareServers directive
◆ The StartServers directive

The MinSpareServers Directive

The MinSpareServers directive specifies the minimum number of idle servers that should be maintained in the process pool. These servers are waiting for requests. You specify the number of minimum spare servers to ensure that these servers are always ready to address client requests. The main server process ensures that a minimum number of servers specified in this directive are always kept idle. The default value set for this directive is 5, which means that the main server process will keep a minimum of five servers idle.

The default value was set for this directive after years of testing and observation. Therefore, you might not want to change the default value for the MinSpareServers directive unless required to do so. Consider the following situations in which you might want to change the value of this directive:

◆ **Using Apache as a production server.** If you are using Apache as a production server, chances are your Web server is required to answer thousands of requests at a given time. This means that the server requires more processes to address the high number of connections. You handle this by increasing the number of processes specified in the MinSpareServers directive. As a result, a higher number of idle processes are waiting to process incoming requests, thereby reducing the delay experienced by users (otherwise, extra time would be needed to create another process to address the request).

◆ **Using Apache on a local area network (LAN).** The situation is entirely different when you are using Apache on a LAN. In this case, the connections handled by the Web server will be significantly fewer than those handled by a production server. So, it is advisable to reduce the number of servers specified in the MinSpareServers directive for lightly loaded servers. The idle processes specified in MinSpareServers constantly hog system memory, so you are better off reducing the number of idle processes if you don't need them.

The MaxSpareServers *Directive*

The MaxSpareServers is exactly the opposite of the MinSpareServers directive. Whereas you use the MinSpareServers directive to specify the minimum number of spare servers to be maintained in the process pool, you use the MaxSpareServers directive to specify the maximum number of spare servers that need to be maintained in the process pool. The default value specified for this directive is 10. This directive specifies the upper limit for servers that can remain idle in the process pool. The fact that Apache is receiving fewer requests might result in many idle server processes in the process pool. More idle server processes hog the system memory without serving a purpose. So, the best approach is to specify a higher limit for idle server processes. The main Apache server "kills" the idle server processes above the specified limit.

The default value for this directive is seldom changed, and any changes there are depend on the load on the server. For production servers with very high traffic, you can increase the number of maximum spare servers. On the other hand, for servers on the local area network, keep the maximum limit as is or reduce it for servers handling light loads.

The StartServers *Directive*

As the name suggests, the StartServers directive specifies the number of spare server processes that should be created when Apache starts. The default value of 5 specified for this directive seldom needs to be changed, but you might need to change it if a situation arises in which the server will have to handle a significantly higher load.

Specifying the Optimum Listener Processes

By now, you know that three directives manage listener processes, and that you can configure these directives to specify the minimum spare servers, the maximum spare servers, and the start servers. You also know that you can alter the values of these directives depending on how you want to use Apache. The values for these directives might differ for production servers or servers that are being used on the local area network or as intranet servers that serve only selective clients. Determining the values for these directives is important, because an incorrect value might adversely affect performance.

If you are an inexperienced Web server administrator, you shouldn't make decisions based on gut feeling—chances are great that your decisions will be wrong. Better ways of determining the optimum values to set for these directives are available to you.

One good option is to use benchmarking tools such as ApacheBench and WebStone. You can use these tools to determine exactly when you need to increase or decrease the values specified for these directives.

You may be using a production server that does not allow you to make use of these benchmarking utilities. In that case, you might create a setup in which you make a non-production server imitate a production server. You can do so in the following ways:

- ◆ **Use a large number of test URLs.** This would help test Apache's performance by sending a large number of URLs and observing how Apache responds.

- ◆ **Vary the number of server processes.** This would help monitor the change in Apache's performance by varying the number of server processes. You could specify a range of high and low server processes to determine the conditions in which Apache performs the best.

- ◆ **Vary the number of client processes.** This would help monitor the performance of Apache by varying the number of client processes. This would help determine the optimum number of client processes that Apache can handle in a given situation.

- ◆ **Use software that emulates a production server environment by creating thousands of concurrent requests.** This would help send thousands of concurrent requests to the Apache server to determine how it functions under extreme loads.

 TIP

Configure software such as WebStone so that it automatically increases the number of concurrent requests submitted to the Web server. Doing so helps you analyze the degree to which performance decreases as a result of an increase in load.

After following the preceding suggestions to test the performance of your Web server, you can estimate the following:

♦ A baseline for the number of requests that your Web server can handle.

♦ The breakpoint after which the performance of your server begins to degrade.

♦ The percentage of decrease in server performance based on the number of concurrent requests.

After you determine the preceding estimates, you can more easily specify logical values for the MinSpareServers, MaxSpareServers, and StartServers directives.

 TIP

Be sure to check the connection time of the Web server at regular intervals. This involves sending a request to the Web server and recording the time it takes for the server to respond. If the time taken to respond is more than expected, it might be because the client processes are queued to be handled by the next listener process. In such cases, revisit your configuration and use benchmarking tools to determine how to configure the optimum listener processes.

Effectively Managing Client Connections

In the previous section, I discussed the directives that manage server processes. In this section, I'll discuss the important directives that you use to manage client connections.

 NOTE

I provide an overview to these directives in Chapter 4, "Configuring Apache Server." In this chapter, I'll discuss how to use these directives to enhance the performance of Apache Web server.

You use the following directives to manage client connections:

♦ The MaxClients directive

♦ The ListenBacklog directive

♦ The Timeout directive

♦ The SendBufferSize directive

- The KeepAlive directive
- The KeepAliveTimeout directive
- The MaxKeepAliveRequests directive
- The LimitRequestBody directive
- The LimitRequestFields directive
- The LimitRequestFieldSize directive
- The LimitRequestLine directive

The MaxClients *Directive*

As the name suggests, you use the MaxClients directive to specify the maximum number of client connections that will be allowed on the Apache Web server. The httpd listener processes handle client connections. Each listener process is allocated a client connection. The maximum number of listener processes that are set in Apache is 150. However, it is possible to increase the value of this figure depending on the Web traffic your Web server handles. However, increase the value of the MaxClients directive only after considering the following:

- Be sure that your computer's hardware configurations can handle the higher number of client requests. No matter how powerful Apache is, you are always dependent on your hardware limitations. Therefore, it is preferable to opt for a faster CPU, a fast disk I/O, and extra RAM.

- Make whatever value you decide to set for the MaxClients directive 25 percent more than the expected network traffic. This will reduce the chances of the system crashing because of increased server processes.

- If a Web site hosted on your server is very busy and the default of 150 server processes won't be enough for you, use another physical server on the network.

- Set the MaxClients directive to a lower number if you are running Apache on a server with limited hardware resources. For example, if you are running the Apache server on a computer with 32MB or 64MB of RAM, set a lower value for Max-Clients to prevent a server crash.

When you have sufficient experience with the Apache Web server you will be able to set the correct value for this directive. If you're new to Apache, you might want to indulge in some experimentation to reach the optimal figure for this directive.

CAUTION

If, after a lot of research and experimentation, you set the optimal value for the Max-Clients directive but your system still crashes, decrease the number specified in this directive. You don't want to lose data because of a system crash.

The ListenBacklog *Directive*

As discussed earlier, a maximum limit is specified for the number of httpd processes in the MaxClients directive. However, Apache doesn't immediately deny requests after this limit is reached. Instead, it maintains a queue that holds the requests until one of the processes is free to accept a request. There is a limit on the requests that can be kept in the queue; you specify this limit in the ListenBacklog directive. When the maximum limit of the requests specified in the ListenBacklog directive is reached, no more requests are accepted, and the 503 (Service Unavailable) response code is sent to the client. The default value set for the ListenBacklog directive is 511.

You will seldom need to change the default value specified in this directive. However, if the backlogs frequently reach the limit, reduce the number of requests specified in the directive; having a high number of requests in the backlog is not good for Apache's performance.

The Timeout *Directive*

Use this directive to specify the time at which the Apache Web server will no longer wait to accept a response from the client. When the time specified in the Timeout directive is exceeded, the connection with the client is closed. The time specified in the Timeout directive is applicable in the following situations:

◆ The time taken to receive a GET request from the client after a connection is established.

◆ Time taken to receive one TCP packet after another using POST and PUT HTTP requests, where the Web server is accepting a stream of data from the client after the connection is established.

◆ Time taken to receive acknowledgement for the TCP packets sent to the client after the Web server receives the request.

The time specified in the Timeout directive is applicable to all the preceding conditions. The default value specified for this directive is 300 seconds, which is more than enough time for the server to wait before closing the connection. The time specified in the Timeout directive can be safely reduced to 60 seconds. By specifying 60 seconds as the time-out period, you will avoid client connections that are particularly slow. However, 60 seconds is a long time to wait in today's Internet atmosphere!

The SendBufferSize *Directive*

You use the SendBufferSize directive to specify the size of the TCP output buffer size, in kilobytes. The default size that is specified for TCP output buffer size is specified in the Linux kernel. However, you can override this value if you need to maintain a queue for the data for high-latency links.

The KeepAlive *Directive*

HTTP /1.1 has a feature known as *persistent connections* that is supported by the Apache Web server. You use the KeepAlive directive to specify whether persistent connections should be allowed or not. This is a simple directive that can have a value of on or off. If you want Apache to use persistent connections, you need to specify the value on for this directive.

 NOTE

Persistent connections is a feature of the HTTP /1.1 protocol that is used by all HTTP /1.1-compliant browsers to send requests to the Web server. This highly useful feature enables the browser to send multiple requests over a single connection, which greatly increases the download speed. Imagine that you want to download a Web page that has several graphics, audio, and video files. With only a single connection from the client, you can request each of the inline documents separately.

The KeepAliveTimeout *Directive*

The client uses the HTTP Keep-Alive header to indicate to the Web server that it requires a persistent connection. After the Web server receives this header, it waits for a subsequent request from the same client. The time that the Web server waits before closing the connection is specified in the KeepAliveTimeout directive.

The default time specified for this directive in the httpd.conf file is 15 seconds. After a lapse of 15 seconds, the Apache Web server processes the request already received from the client and then closes the connection.

The default time specified in the httpd.conf file is considered to be the perfect value for this directive, so leave this directive unaltered.

The MaxKeepAliveRequests *Directive*

When a persistent connection is established, the client is able to place multiple requests on a single connection. You use the MaxKeepAliveRequests directive to specify the number of requests that should be allowed per connection. By default, the value specified for this directive is 100, which means that for each persistent connection, a client can send 100 requests to the Web server.

It is possible to set a value of 0 for the MaxKeepAliveRequests directive. However, doing so will mean that you are allowing an unlimited number of requests per connection. This is not advisable from performance and security points of view. An unlimited number of requests on a single connection can result in poor performance of the Web server. In addition, individuals with malicious intent could exploit it. So, it is best to keep the default value for this directive.

The LimitRequestBody *Directive*

Different clients request different resources from the Web server. The size of the HTTP request body submitted by the client can differ depending on the request. However, it is important to specify a limit for the size of incoming requests submitted by the client. Use the Limit-RequestBody directive for this purpose and set the size of the HTTP request body in bytes.

The LimitRequestFields *Directive*

Each request sent by the client contains several HTTP headers. Use the LimitRequestFields directive to specify the maximum number of headers that should be allowed for an incoming request. Typically, a client sends about 20 headers with an HTTP request. The default value set for this directive is 100, which is much higher. Setting a high value for this directive might cause malformed requests. Therefore, it is best to specify a value slightly more than 20 for this directive.

The LimitRequestFieldSize *Directive*

Use this directive to specify the maximum size (in bytes) for all HTTP requests. The default value specified for this directive is 8190. You can alter this value to receive HTTP requests that are bigger or smaller, but I advise keeping this directive unaltered unless altering it is required.

The LimitRequestLine *Directive*

Use the LimitRequestLine directive to specify the maximum allowed size of all HTTP request lines. The request line sent by any client consists of a HTTP method, URI, and the protocol version. Rarely will you need to alter the default value 8190 bytes already specified for this directive in the httpd.conf file.

Sample Configuration

The following is a sample configuration specified in the httpd.conf file for all the directives that control client connections on a production server that is heavily loaded:

```
MaxClients 300
ListenBacklog 1000
Timeout 60
KeepAlive On
KeepAliveTimeout 15
MaxKeepAliveRequests 200
LimitRequestBody 10000
LimitRequestFields 100
LimitRequestFieldSize 8190
LimitRequestLine 8190
```

In the preceding example, note the following:

◆ The MaxClients directive is set to 300. The default value for this directive is 150. However, due to the increased load, this directive is configured with a higher value.

◆ The ListenBacklog directive is set to 1000.

◆ The Timeout directive is reduced to 60.

◆ The KeepAlive directive is given the value On to allow persistent connections.

◆ The value for the KeepAliveTimeout is retained at 15.

◆ The MaxKeepAliveRequests is increased to 200 so that 200 requests are allowed per connection.

◆ The value for LimitRequestBody is set at 10000. This enables the Apache Web server to accept requests that are up to 10,000 bytes.

◆ The value for LimitRequestFields is set at 100. This indicates that a maximum of 100 request fields will be acceptable from a client per request.

◆ The LimitRequestFieldSize is set to 8190. This indicates that the maximum size allowed for a request field is 8190 bytes.

◆ The LimitRequestLine is set at 8190. This indicates that the maximum size allowed for a request line is 8190 bytes.

Proxying Using Apache

One of the many benefits that the Apache Web server can provide you is the ability to use it as a proxy server. A *proxy server* enables you to use one and only one network address to external sites and handles exchanges between the Internet and your LAN, essentially protecting your network's security and when used as a caching server, also enhancing its performance.

In order to configure Apache to act as a proxy server, use the mod_proxy module. In this section, I'll discuss the directives you use to configure Apache as a proxy server. I'll also discuss how to configure Apache to act as a proxy server.

Benefits of a Proxy Server

As I just mentioned, using a proxy server provides several benefits, particularly the following three:

◆ **Improves performance.** The first and foremost benefit of using a proxy server is increased performance. With proxies, you can cache frequently requested documents; then, as you need the data, you can download it directly from the proxy. For example, consider this scenario: A local area network has several users, and each user connects to the Internet using the proxy server. A user named "abc" accesses a site on the Internet for the first time. The proxy forwards the request to the Web server on the Internet and downloads the requested Web page for the user "abc." It also retains a copy of the Web page. So, when a user named "xyz" wants to access the same data, he does not need to go to the Web site. He can just quickly download it from the proxy.

◆ **Enhances security.** Using a proxy server, you can filter requests sent by clients as you see fit. You can also configure a proxy server to deny a client's request for unauthorized access to proprietary files.

◆ **Reduces bandwidth use.** When data is retrieved from the proxy, the need to contact the Web site again is eliminated.

Types of Proxy Server Configurations

In this section, I discuss the proxy server configurations that you can use. Depending on your particular setup, you can configure a proxy in one of the following two ways:

◆ A forwarding proxy server

◆ A reverse proxy server

Forwarding Proxy Server

As the name suggests, you use a forwarding proxy server to forward client requests from an internal network to a Web server on the Internet. This is perhaps the most common configuration for a proxy server. Figure 9.1 illustrates how a forwarding proxy server works. The setup in Figure 9.1 allows clients to request documents through a firewall to a proxy server, mainly because the clients on the LAN (internal network) don't have direct access to the Internet. This is very important from a security perspective because exposing a computer on the LAN directly to the Internet makes the computer *and* other computers on the internal network susceptible to intrusion. So, using a proxy adds a thick layer of security.

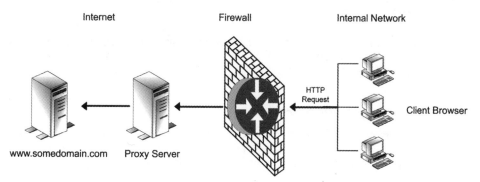

FIGURE 9.1 *An example of a forwarding proxy server*

The computers on the internal network are allocated IP addresses locally. On the other hand, the proxy server that has direct access to the Internet possesses a *registered IP address*, also known as a *real IP address*. The computers on the internal network specify the IP address of the proxy server in a browser. When the proxy server receives a request from a client browser, the IP header contains the local IP address of the computer on the internal network. The proxy server reissues the request and a new IP header is attached to the request before finally sending it to the Web server.

Going from right to left, here is the process shown in Figure 9.1:

1. The internal client browser, which is part of the corporate LAN, sends an HTTP request.
2. The request is passed to the proxy server via a router setup on the firewall.
3. The proxy server receives the request and examines the IP header.
4. The proxy server reissues the request.

The most common purpose for using a forwarding proxy server is caching. Once the proxy server receives the documents, they are retained until they expire. Other clients on the internal network can access this content without resubmitting a request to the Internet. The cache maintained on the proxy server is called *shared cache* because it is accessible to a number of clients on the LAN/internal network. In my opinion, maintaining cache on a proxy server (using shared cache) is always more efficient than maintaining it in client browsers. Cache stored in client browsers is called *private cache* and can be retrieved by the client whose browser stores the cache. Implementing shared cache on your proxy server helps everyone retrieve the document much faster. In other words, if the speed of your local area network is 100 Mbps, the documents from the cache are retrieved at a speed of 100 Mbps.

 NOTE

You can use a proxy server for communications that utilize protocols such as HTTP, HTTPS, and FTP.

Reverse Proxy Server

Unlike the forwarding proxy server, a reverse proxy server is located outside the local intranet. Its main purpose is to filter client requests from the Internet that are directed to a Web server located on the intranet. Figure 9.2 illustrates a reverse proxy server.

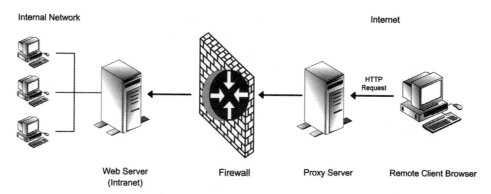

FIGURE 9.2 *An example of a reverse proxy server*

Going from right to left, here is the process shown in Figure 9.2:

1. A remote client browser sends an HTTP request.
2. The request is intercepted by the proxy server and forwarded to the Internet router setup on the firewall.
3. The router forwards the request to the internal Web server that processes the request.
4. The primary purpose of using a reverse proxy is to secure the internal network. Caching of resources is a secondary concern when a reverse proxy is configured.

TIP

You can use the same proxy server as both forwarding proxy server and reverse proxy server. In such cases, you use a single proxy server as a cache repository as well as a security layer that protects the internal network.

Configuring Apache as a Proxy Server

You can use several directives to configure Apache as a proxy server. All of these directives are implemented using the mod_proxy module that is shipped with the default Apache installation. The mod_proxy module is a flexible module, so you can integrate it with other proxy modules and other protocols that are not supported by default.

The features of the mod_proxy module are as follows:

◆ Supports proxying for protocols such as HTTP /0.9, HTTP /1.0, and FTP.
◆ Supports TCP port 443 (for SSL) by default.

In the sections that follow, you configure a forwarding proxy server and a reverse proxy server. In the process, you learn about the directives required to configure Apache as a proxy server.

Checking the mod_proxy *Installation*

Before proceeding with the steps to configure Apache as a proxy server, you need to check whether mod_proxy is installed. If you compiled Apache using source code and used the --enable-shared=most option while running the configure script, you will find mod_proxy in the httpd.conf file by the name libproxy.so. The following excerpt from the httpd.conf file shows the presence of this module:

```
LoadModule proxy_module        libexec/libproxy.so
AddModule mod_proxy.c
```

If the preceding values for AddModule and LoadModule directives are present in the httpd.conf file, you can use the mod_proxy module without any hassles.

The Proxy Server Section in the httpd.conf File

If mod_proxy is properly installed on your system, a whole section on configuring Apache as a proxy server will appear in the httpd.conf file. Check out the following extract from the httpd.conf file that deals with configuring Apache as a proxy server:

```
# Proxy Server directives. Uncomment the following lines to
# enable the proxy server:
#
#<IfModule mod_proxy.c>
#    ProxyRequests On

#    <Directory proxy:*>
#        Order deny,allow
#        Deny from all
#        Allow from .your-domain.com
#    </Directory>

   #
   # Enable/disable the handling of HTTP/1.1 "Via:" headers.
   # ("Full" adds the server version; "Block" removes all outgoing Via:
   #headers)
   # Set to one of: Off | On | Full | Block
   #
#    ProxyVia On
```

```
#
# To enable the cache as well, edit and uncomment the following lines:
# (no caching without CacheRoot)
#
#     CacheRoot "/usr/local/apache/proxy"
#     CacheSize 5
#     CacheGcInterval 4
#     CacheMaxExpire 24
#     CacheLastModifiedFactor 0.1
#     CacheDefaultExpire 1
#     NoCache a-domain.com another-domain.edu joes.garage-sale.com


#</IfModule>
# End of proxy directives.
```

As you can see, many directives are included in this section. I will discuss each of these directives in an upcoming section, when I take up the actual configuration of Apache as a proxy server. Also notice that the directives specified in this section are commented out by default. You will need to uncomment them in order to use Apache as a proxy server.

Configuring Apache as a Forward Proxy

This section presents general concepts for and information on using directives for configuring Apache as a forward proxy server.

Getting Started: The *ProxyRequests* Directive

The first directive that you need to uncomment is the ProxyRequests directive. This simple yet most important directive accepts two values, on and off. In order to use Apache as a forward proxy, you specify the value on for this directive as shown here:

```
ProxyRequests On
```

Uncommenting the ProxyRequests directive has the following effects:

♦ Apache will retain its original functionality of serving documents present in the document root.

♦ Apache will act as a proxy server for requests directed to other Web servers on the Internet. The clients will need to manually send requests to the Apache proxy server before reissuing the request to the appropriate Web server as specified in the request URL.

◆ After retrieving the document from the Web server, Apache will send the document to the computer from which the request originated and, at the same time, retain a copy of the document.

Although it is accurate to specify the `ProxyRequests` directive in the main server configuration, you might want to configure a virtual host as a proxy server. This is not a problem in Apache. All you do is specify the `ProxyRequests` directive in the virtual hosts section, as illustrated here:

```
<VirtualHost 172.17.68.181:8080>
ServerAdmin root@linda.com
DocumentRoot /opt/web/html/linda.developers.com
ServerName linda.developers.com
ProxyRequests On
</VirtualHost>
```

In the preceding example, note the following:

◆ The `ProxyRequests` directive is specified within the `VirtualHost` container tags. This indicates that the virtual host, `linda.developers.com`, will be used as a proxy server.

◆ The port has been specified as 8080. Proxy servers most often use this port for communications. Although proxy servers work equally efficiently on port 80, using the port 8080 is more of a convention than a rule. If you plan to use port 8080 as the standard port to which the proxy server will listen, you will also need to specify this port in the `Listen` directive located in the main server configuration section. If you don't, Apache will not accept the requests addressed to this port.

TIP

You can also assign the value `off` to the `ProxyRequests` directive. This value signifies that the proxy server should not be used. The only real advantage to using this value, however, is that it can be useful when you want to temporarily disable the proxy server without commenting out the rest of the directives in the section.

Creating a Mirror: The *ProxyPass* Directive

Another useful functionality when using Apache as a proxy server is its ability to map a resource on a remote site onto a local URL. (To *map* means to replicate a Web or FTP site on another server.) After you map the remote site, Apache can serve documents locally. As I explained previously, the first time a document is retrieved from a remote site, a copy is kept in the server on the internal network. For all consecutive requests, the document is retrieved locally.

You use the `ProxyPass` directive to map remote resources on a local URL in Apache. Consider the following example, in which requests addressed to the site http://www.linuxdocs.org are stored in a local directory named /documentation:

```
ProxyPass /documentation http://www.linuxdocs.org
```

When you specify the preceding directive, all requests to the remote site can be sent using a local URL. Although the URL points to a local directory, the contents will be retrieved from the remote site. As a result, you will be able to access the home page of www.linuxdocs.org by specifying the URL http://linda.developers.com/documentation.

 NOTE

In the preceding example, linda.developers.com is a virtual host configured on my Linux machine.

Once the documents on the remote site are cached on the local directory named "documentation," the contents appear to be served from the local directory. This, in turn, reduces the download time and bandwidth use.

Configuring Apache as a Reverse Proxy

In addition to configuring a forward proxy, you can use the `mod_proxy` module to configure a reverse proxy. As discussed earlier, the reverse proxy is set up primarily for the purpose of security and avoiding direct connections from remote clients. It is used to accept requests from remote clients and submit them to a Web server configured on an internal network. By using a reverse proxy and implementing a firewall, you can ensure some level of safety for the servers on the intranet.

Ensuring that *mod_proxy* Is Installed

As is the case when setting up a forwarding proxy server, you first need to ensure that the `mod_proxy` module is installed on your computer. After ensuring that this module is in the httpd.conf file, you can proceed with the configuration.

Enabling Proxy Services

The next step is to enable proxy services, which you do using the `ProxyRequests` directive. You need to specify the value on in order for this directive to start using proxy services.

Mapping URLs to the Internal Web Server

When a remote client requests a resource, the proxy server is the only server that is visible to remote client. In addition, the internal Web server that is delivering the content is completely invisible to the client. So, all documents requested by the client seem to be provided by the proxy server instead of the internal Web server. However, all this doesn't happen automatically. You need to use the `ProxyPass` directive to map URLs received by the proxy server to the actual server that will deliver the Web content. Consider the following example, in which the `Proxy-Pass` directive maps URLs received by the proxy server to a URL on the Web sever on the LAN/internal network:

```
ProxyPass /images http://linda.developers.com/images
ProxyPass /docs http://linda.developers.com/docs
ProxyPass /fun http://funngames.com/fun
```

In the preceding example, the `ProxyPass` directive maps the URLs addressed to the `/images` and `/docs` directory on the proxy server to the URLs on the Web server that will actually deliver the Web content. Also, notice the value specified for the third `ProxyPass` directive. In this case, the request is being directed to another Web server. This indicates that the `ProxyPass` directive can be used to map URLs to more than one Web server on the internal network.

Using the *ProxyReverse* Directive

When a remote client sends a request, the request is redirected to an internal Web server. In order for this to happen, a redirect request is sent to the client browser. The `Location` header of the redirect request consists of the hostname of the internal Web server that will process the request. The purpose of using the `ProxyReverse` directive is to replace the hostname specified in the `Location` header in the redirect request. By using the `ProxyReverse` directive, you can replace the hostname in the `Location` header with the hostname of the server configured as a reverse proxy.

Use of the `ProxyReverse` directive is similar to the use of the `ProxyPass` directive, although their purposes are completely different. Consider the following example of the `ProxyReverse` directive:

```
ProxyReverse /images http://linda.developers.com/images
ProxyReverse /docs http://linda.developers.com/docs
ProxyReverse /fun http://funngames.com/fun
```

In the preceding example, the `ProxyReverse` directive changes the value of `Location` headers. As a result, the value of the Location headers will contain the hostname of the proxy server instead of the internal servers from which the documents are actually being retrieved.

Configuring LAN Clients to Use the Proxy Server

When you configure Apache as a proxy server, a few settings at the client end need to be made before the clients can start using the proxy services. In this section, I discuss the steps to configure both Netscape Navigator and Microsoft Internet Explorer at the client end so that users on the internal network can benefit from the proxy services offered by the Apache Web server.

Configuring Netscape Navigator

The steps for configuring Netscape Navigator to use proxy services are as follows:

1. Open Netscape Navigator.
2. Choose Edit, Preferences to open the Preferences dialog box.
3. In the left pane, choose Proxies from the Advanced group to open the Proxy settings in the right pane.
4. Select the Manual proxy configuration option.

    Figure 9.3 shows the Netscape Preferences dialog box with the Manual proxy configuration option selected.

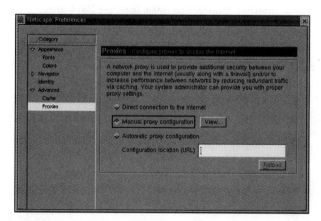

FIGURE 9-3 *The Manual proxy configuration option*

5. Click the View button to open the View Manual Proxy Configuration dialog box.
6. In the HTTP Proxy box, specify the IP address/hostname of the proxy.
7. In the corresponding Port box, specify the port number as **8080**.

    Figure 9.4 shows the View Manual Proxy Configuration dialog box after all the settings are made.

Now you are ready to utilize proxy services using Netscape Navigator.

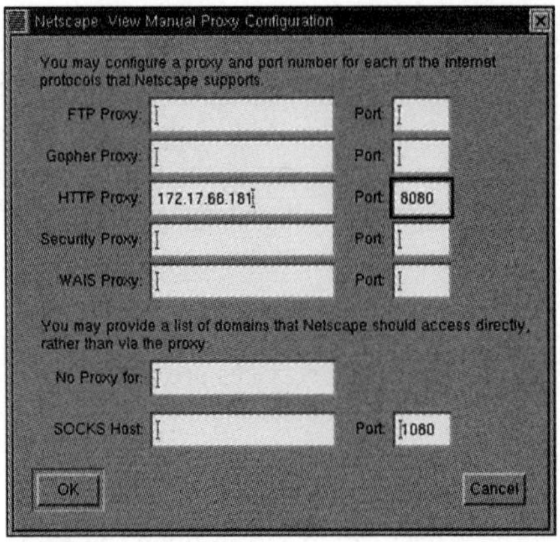

FIGURE 9-4 *The View Manual Proxy Configuration dialog box*

Configuring Internet Explorer

The steps for configuring Internet Explorer to use proxy services are as follows:

1. Choose Start, Programs, Internet Explorer to open Internet Explorer.

2. Choose Tools, Internet Options to open the Internet Options dialog box (see Figure 9.5).

3. Select the Connections tab in the Internet Options dialog box. Figure 9.6 shows the Connections tab in the Internet Options dialog box.

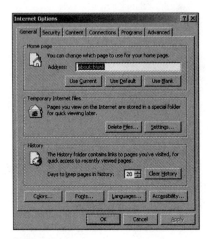

FIGURE 9.5 *The Internet Options dialog box*

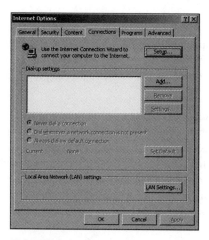

FIGURE 9.6 *The Connections tab in Internet Options dialog box*

4. Click the LAN Settings button to open the Local Area Network (LAN) Settings dialog box.

5. In the Local Area Network (LAN) Settings dialog box, check Use a proxy server.

6. In the Address box, specify the IP address/hostname of the proxy server.

7. In the Port box, specify the port used by the proxy server. If you have configured the proxy to use port 8080, you need to specify that port.

   Figure 9.7 shows the Local Area Network (LAN) Settings dialog box with required settings.

8. Click OK twice to apply the settings and close all open dialog boxes.

Now you are ready to use the proxy services provided by the Apache Web server with Internet Explorer.

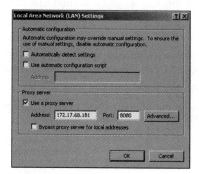

FIGURE 9.7 *The Local Area Network (LAN) Settings dialog box*

Handling Resource Expiration

When you use Apache as a proxy server, a copy of the downloaded resource is retained in the proxy server. This resource is retained until the time it is set to expire. Web sites are constantly updated, and you can't be sure at any point in time that the resource on the proxy server is up-to-date.

Ideally, you'd have a mechanism for maintaining resources for some time and then discarding them so that the client on the local intranet gets to view the latest version located on the remote server on the Internet. Is this what resource expiration is all about? The answer is *yes*. A proxy needs to act intelligently and determine whether it is safe to serve the resource available in the cache. It is quite possible that the resource present in the proxy is old. In such cases, the best option is to discard the old resource and download the new resource from the Web site of origin. The issue is how to do so, and that's the subject of this section.

The HTTP Expires *Header*

Before moving on to the directives that help you handle resource expiration in Apache, turn your attention to the HTTP Expires header. This is the most important HTTP header as far as controlling resource expiration is concerned. When a Web server sends a response to an HTTP request, the HTTP Expires header is attached to the response. This header helps determine the life of a resource. The expiration date and time in this header are expressed in Universal Coordinated Time (UCT). The following procedure explains how resource expiration is handled and what role the HTTP Expires header plays in this procedure:

1. The information in this header proves useful for proxies that maintain shared cache, as well as browsers that maintain private cache. Whenever a client requests a document, the proxy checks the original Web site to validate whether the document stored in the cache has changed in any respect.

2. The original server compares the resource present in it with the resource present in the shared cache of the proxy server. It checks the timestamp of the document present in the proxy server. Then the origin server checks the date and time that the document was last modified.

3. Next, the original server compares the timestamp of the document present in the shared cache of the proxy with the last modified time of the original document. If the last modified time of the document is later than the timestamp of the document present in the proxy, the document present on the proxy needs a replacement.

4. Finally, if the document present in the cache is old, the proxy deletes it and requests the latest document from the original Web server.

The mod_expires *Module*

In Apache, the mod_expires module is responsible for handling the HTTP Expires header. In order to use this module's directives and manage resource expiration, you need to be sure this module is enabled in the httpd.conf file. Check whether the following lines are present in the httpd.conf file:

```
LoadModule expires_module     libexec/mod_expires.so
AddModule mod_expires.c
```

If the preceding lines are present in the httpd.conf file, you are ready to use the directives associated with the mod_expires module.

 NOTE

If you compiled Apache using the --enable-shared=most option, you will find this module installed and enabled in the httpd.conf file.

The Associated Directives

Now I'll discuss the various directives that allow you to handle resource expiration and deliver the latest resources to a client on the local intranet. The mod_expires module is easy to use and consists of three associated directives that together handle resource expiration. The following sections cover these three directives.

The *ExpiresActive* Directive

The ExpiresActive directive is the basic directive used with the mod_expires module. This directive can be given two values, on and off. If set to on, this directive enables the pool of Expires headers for the documents in its scope. For example, if the ExpiresActive directive is specified in the .htaccess file, only the documents in the specified directory will be affected.

```
ExpiresActive On
```

The *ExpiresDefault* Directive

Use the ExpiresDefault directive to specify the algorithm on which the default expiration time for documents within a realm is calculated. You can specify this directive either within Directory container tags or in .htaccess files. The expiration time can be calculated in two ways:

◆ On the basis of the last modified time of the document.
◆ On the basis of the last time the client accessed the document.

The time for this directive can be specified in two ways:

◆ The first way is to specify the number of seconds for which the document will be valid, prefixed by either the letter A (which stands for *last access time*) or M (which stands for *last modified time*). The default value is one week, which is equivalent to 604800 seconds. Consider the following example:

```
ExpiresActive On
ExpiresDefault M604800
```

◆ The second way is to specify the time in years, months, weeks, days, hours, minutes, and seconds. In this method, the time specified is also relative either to the last access time or to the last modified time. Consider the following example:

```
ExpiresActive On
ExpiresDefault modification plus 1 week
```

The *ExpiresByType* Directive

Use the ExpiresByType directive to specify an Expires header for a document based on its content (MIME) type. This is another useful way for specifying the expiration time for documents. The format for specifying the time is similar to that of the ExpiresDefault directive. The time value specified for this directive can be expressed relative to either the last modified time or the last access time. Consider the following example:

```
ExpiresActive On
ExpiresByType application/x-tar A604800
ExpiresByType image/gif M604800
ExpiresByType text/html A2592000
```

In the preceding example, note the following:

◆ The ExpiresActive directive is used to specify that the Expires headers will be allowed.

◆ The ExpiresByType directive is used to specify the expiration time on the basis of the document type.

◆ In the first instance, the ExpiresByType directive specifies that the expiration time for MIME type application/x-tar will be 604800 seconds (1 week) after the last access time.

◆ In the second instance, the ExpiresByType directive specifies that the expiration time for MIME type image/gif will be 604800 seconds (1 week) after the last access time.

◆ Finally, in the last instance, the ExpiresByType directive specifies that the expiration time for MIME type text/html will be 2592000 seconds (1 week) after the last access time.

Controlling the Proxy Engine

You can tweak several directives to ensure that the proxy engine performs as you want it to. The directives in this section will enable the proxy engine to receive resources on behalf of the clients:

◆ The `ProxyReceiveBufferSize` directive

◆ The `ProxyDomain` directive

◆ The `ProxyRemote` directive

◆ The `NoProxy` directive

◆ The `ProxyBlock` directive

The ProxyReceiveBufferSize *Directive*

The `ProxyReceiveBufferSize` directive increases the request throughput. Although the mod_proxy module rarely requires any performance tuning, this directive allows you specify a buffer size for HTTP and FTP requests. You can specify the buffer size in bytes for this directive. However, whatever value you decide to specify should be greater that 512 bytes. Consider the following example:

```
ProxyReceiveBufferSize 4096
```

TIP

To use the operating system's default buffer size, specify the value for the `ProxyReceiveBufferSize` directive as 0. The default buffer size used by Linux is 64 KB, which is the maximum limit.

The ProxyDomain *Directive*

Use this directive to set up a default proxy domain for clients on the intranet. The domain name of the proxy server can be specified in this directive. As a result, the clients need not specify the domain name while requesting documents from the proxy server. The domain name specified in the `ProxyDomain` directive is automatically appended to the URL before the document is retrieved. Consider the following example, wherein the `ProxyDomain` directive is used to specify a default domain:

```
ProxyDomain developers.com
```

In the preceding example, I set the `ProxyDomain` as developers.com. Now, consider that the client computer specifies only the hostname of the proxy server in the URL, as shown here:

```
http://linda/images/mypic.gif
```

The URL, which consists of the hostname of the proxy (linda) will be appended by the domain name specified in the `ProxyDomain` directive. As a result, the Web server will try to retrieve the requested document from the following URL:

```
http://linda.developers.com/images/mypic.gif
```

As you can see, the domain name is appended to the URL. This is a very useful feature wherein the client on the local intranet doesn't require that the complete URL for requesting a resource be typed.

The ProxyRemote *Directive*

If you have a huge internal network comprised of hundreds of clients that are connected to the Internet most of the time, it is advisable to share the workload of the proxy with another physical computer. Doing so eases off the load from a single proxy server. The `ProxyRemote` directive helps you achieve this sharing of wokload. This directive can be used to share tasks such as document retrieval and caching among different proxy servers. After you set this directive, the proxy that listens to your request will be able to forward your request to other proxy servers. Consider the following example for a better understanding of this directive:

```
ProxyRemote http://www.somesite.org/ http://somehost.corporate.com
```

In the preceding example, the client requests directed to www.somesite.com are forwarded to a computer on the corporate LAN available at the URL http://somehost.corporate.com.

The `ProxyRemote` directive can also be configured such that all the requests sent by clients are forwarded to an alternate proxy server. The following configuration allows you to do so:

```
ProxyRemote * http://somehost.corporate.com
```

In the preceding example, the wildcard character * represents all the requests sent to the proxy server. As a result, all the requests are forwarded to the remote proxy available on the URL, http://somhost.corporate.com.

The NoProxy *Directive*

Use the `NoProxy` directive to negate the effect of the `ProxyRemote` directive. `NoProxy` allows you to specify the IP address, domain names, hostnames, or subnets for computers for which you want to turn off the `ProxyRemote` behavior. Consider the following example:

```
ProxyRemote * http://somehost.corporate.com
NoProxy www.somedomain.com 172.17.68 172.17.65.222
```

In the preceding example, I turned off the `ProxyRemote` feature for requests originating from the domain, `www.somedomain.com`, the subnet, `172.17.68`, and the individual IP, `172.17.65.222`.

The ProxyBlock *Directive*

The `ProxyBlock` directive is a pretty useful directive from a system administration point of view because it allows you to block access to certain sites. These sites could be pornographic or entertainment sites that you don't want the employees on the corporate LAN to access. In fact, using this directive, it is even possible to block sites based on keywords. Therefore, it is possible to block access to most mp3 sites by specifying mp3 as the keyword with the `ProxyBlock` directive. Consider the following example:

```
ProxyBlock unethical.com mp3
```

The preceding example shows the use of the `ProxyBlock` directive to block all requests directed to unethical.com as well as all mp3 sites that contain the text mp3 in the URL. If you are wondering whether it is possible to block requests that use IP addresses and not hostnames using the `ProxyBlock` directive, the answer is yes. Whenever a request is sent to the proxy, it tries to map the specified hostname to an IP address. After it resolves the IP address, it stores the IP address also in the cache. Therefore, if a request is sent using the IP address of the remote site, the user will be caught.

Although you can use the `ProxyBlock` directive to keep clients from accessing specific sites on the proxy server, with this directive, you can't allow or deny specific clients access to the proxy server. To control access to the proxy server, you use a different procedure. When a client browser is configured with the address of a proxy server, the URL that originates from the client browser begins with proxy://, not with http://. This process can be monitored using `Directory` container tags to allow clients to use the proxy server or block such use. Consider the following example, which shows how URLs that begin with the text `proxy:` are verified before giving access:

```
<Directory proxy:*>
    Order allow deny
    Allow from 172.17.68
    Deny from 172.17.68.222
</Directory>
```

In the preceding example, all URLs that begin with the text `proxy:` are checked. All requests from the subnet `172.17.68` are allowed to access the proxy server except the requests originating from the IP address `172.17.68.222`.

Managing Shared Cache

In addition to the directives that control the behavior of the proxy engine, the `mod_proxy` module provides a set of directives that maintain shared cache on the proxy server. These directives play a major role in managing the cache after it is retrieved and stored in the proxy server.

The important directives are as follows:

- ◆ The `CacheRoot` directive
- ◆ The `CacheSize` directive
- ◆ The `CacheGcInterval` directive
- ◆ The `CacheDefaultExpire` directive
- ◆ The `CacheMaxExpire` directive
- ◆ The `CacheLastModifiedFactor` directive
- ◆ The `CacheDirLevels` directive
- ◆ The `CacheDirLength` directive
- ◆ The `CacheForceCompletion` directive
- ◆ The `NoCache` directive

The CacheRoot *Directive*

You use the `CacheRoot` directive to specify the location of the directory that will store the cached files. Unless you specify the value for this directive, Apache will not store any cache. Consider the following extract from my httpd.conf file:

```
CacheRoot "/usr/local/apache/proxy"
```

The CacheSize *Directive*

As its name suggests, you use the `CacheSize` directive to specify the maximum limit for the cache that can be stored on the proxy server. The size of the cache is specified in Kilobytes. Although the cache size might sometimes exceed the value, it is reduced to the limit during a cleanup phase. The default value specified for this directive in the httpd.conf file is 5 kilobytes, which is negligible. Consider the following example, in which I set the value for `CacheSize` at 50 Megabytes:

```
CacheSize 51200
```

The CacheGcInterval *Directive*

Use the `CacheGcInterval` to specify the time interval in which the total size of the cached files is checked. If the current size of cached documents is more than the size specified in the `CacheSize` directive, the older documents in the cache are deleted in order to be within the allowed size limit. The default value specified for this directive is 4 hours. However, for an intranet that experiences high traffic, it is best to set it to 2 hours as shown below. because cache tends to accumulate quickly.

```
CacheGcInterval 2
```

The CacheDefaultExpire *Directive*

Sometimes a document cached by the proxy server doesn't have an expiration date or time associated with it. In such situations, a default expiration time is used. The default expiration time is specified in the CacheDefaultExpire directive. The default value specified for this directive is 1 hour, which is very low. I set this value at 168 hours (one week), as shown here:

```
CacheDefaultExpire 168
```

The CacheMaxExpire *Directive*

Use this directive to set a maximum time for which the cached resources are stored without validating them on the original server. The time specified in this directive overrides the expiration date of the resource. The default value for this directive is 24 hours. On my server, I increased this value to 72 hours, as shown here:

```
CacheMaxExpire 72
```

The CacheLastModifiedFactor *Directive*

Use the CacheLastModifiedFactor directive to store a formula. This formula calculates the expiration time for resources for which it is not specified. In addition, the formula used to calculate the expiration date is always related to the last modified date:

```
CacheLastModifiedFactor 0.1
```

As you can see, the value set for this directive is set to 0.1, the default value.

The CacheDirLevels *Directive*

This directive specifies the number of subdirectories you can use to store the cache. It is useful to specify a larger number of directories in this directive. Doing so makes searching for a particular cache easier. The default value for this directive is set to 3:

```
CacheDirLevels 3
```

The CacheDirLength *Directive*

Use the CacheDirLength directive to specify the number of characters in the proxy cache subdirectory names. As a result, subdirectories of the cache appear as shown:

```
/usr/local/apache/proxy/n/A/w
```

The CacheForceCompletion *Directive*

Use the `CacheForceCompletion` directive to specify a percentage value. This percentage value determines whether a particular resource should be downloaded and cached if the HTTP transfer is aborted midway. For example, if the value specified for this directive is 90 and the HTTP transfer is aborted after 80 percent of the document is downloaded, the downloaded portion will be discarded and won't be cached. However, if 92 percent of the document has already been downloaded, the document will be downloaded completely and then cached. The default value for this directive is 90. However, I set this value to 80 because I think 90 percent is too high:

```
CacheForceCompletion 80
```

The NoCache *Directive*

The `NoCache` directive is very useful for specifying a list of domain names, hostnames, and IP addresses from which documents are retrieved but not saved in the cache. These are, ideally, the sites that continually update their content.

Logging in Apache

Maintaining logs is an integral part of Apache server administration. An efficient administrator has the ability to analyze logs and maintain a healthy server. Logs are analyzed from time to time to ensure that the system is safe from intrusion. Logs are also examined whenever there is a problem. Log files help you determine what went wrong, frame a solution for the problem, and later troubleshoot it. The Apache Web server uses several built-in log files. During runtime, Apache appends the log files to statements that help determine how the Web server is functioning.

Apache uses two main types of log files. The first type records the network activity of the Web server, information about the client requests, and information that can be gathered about the client sending the request. These logs are called *request logs*.

Apache also uses error logs. *Error logs*, as the name suggests, record errors that take place while the Apache Web server is running. The error log records errors, warnings, and abnormal conditions encountered while it is running.

If you compiled Apache using the source code, you will find the log files in the /usr/local/apache/logs directory. Otherwise, you might want to track down the log file by looking for the logs directory in the directory specified as the `ServerRoot` in the httpd.conf file. Consider the following output of the `ls -l` command that I executed after moving to this directory:

```
[root@linux logs]# ls -l
total 7568
-rw-r--r--    1 root     root      7558617 Jun 19 22:17 access_log
-rw-r--r--    1 root     root       166446 Jun 19 22:17 error_log
```

In this section, I'll discuss the different types of log files that are used by the Apache Web server. I'll also cover particular log files in detail. Then I'll examine the procedure for creating custom log files in Apache.

Managing Error Logs

Error logs are logs that you can directly examine in order to determine what has gone wrong. Errors can occur for several reasons, including the following:

◆ Malformed HTTP requests

◆ Problems encountered by the server while performing regular activities

◆ Execution of scripts that contain bugs

◆ Broken links

◆ Links to files that the httpd daemon fails to interpret

The error logs in Apache are implemented using the mod_core module. All error logs are stored in the error_log file present in the /usr/local/apache/logs directory. This file contains hundreds of log statements. Therefore, you use the tail command to view the most recent error messages in the file. The tail command extracts the last 10 lines from the log file and displays them on the console. Consider the following:

```
[root@linux logs]# tail error_log
[Wed Jun 19 22:17:33 2002] [error] [client 172.17.68.181] File does not
exist: /opt/web/html/scripts/fpcount.exe
[Wed Jun 19 22:17:33 2002] [error] [client 172.17.68.181] File does not
exist: /opt/web/html/cfdocs/expelval/openfile.cfm
[Wed Jun 19 22:17:33 2002] [error] [client 172.17.68.181] File does not
exist: /opt/web/html/cfdocs/expelval/exprcalc.cfm
[Wed Jun 19 22:17:33 2002] [error] [client 172.17.68.181] File does not
exist: /opt/web/html/cfdocs/expelval/displayopenedfile.cfm
[Wed Jun 19 22:17:33 2002] [error] [client 172.17.68.181] File does not
exist: /opt/web/html/cfdocs/expelval/sendmail.cfm
[Wed Jun 19 22:17:33 2002] [error] [client 172.17.68.181] File does not
exist: /opt/web/html/iissamples/exair/howitworks/codebrws.asp
[Wed Jun 19 22:17:33 2002] [error] [client 172.17.68.181] File does not
exist: /opt/web/html/iissamples/sdk/asp/docs/codebrws.asp
[Wed Jun 19 22:17:33 2002] [error] [client 172.17.68.181] File does not
exist: /opt/web/html/msads/Samples/SELECTOR/showcode.asp
[Wed Jun 19 22:17:33 2002] [error] [client 172.17.68.181] File does not
exist: /opt/web/html/search97.vts
[Wed Jun 19 22:17:33 2002] [error] [client 172.17.68.181] File does not
exist: /opt/web/html/carbo.dll
```

If you're using a log file for the first time, you might find the preceding output confusing. I'll discuss the standard format used by the error_log file to store logs in the section "Standard Format for error_log," later in this chapter.

The ErrorLog *Directive*

The ErrorLog directive is the main directive for specifying the path to the error_log file in the Apache configuration file. The following is an extract from my httpd.conf file:

ErrorLog /usr/local/apache/logs/error_log

In the preceding example, the full path for the error log file is specified. You can also specify a path relative to the server root directory as shown here:

ErrorLog logs/error_log

In the preceding example, the specified path doesn't begin with a /. This indicates that the specified path is relative to the server root directory.

The LogLevel *Directive*

The second most important directive associated with error logs is the LogLevel directive. You use the LogLevel directive to specify verbosity levels for error messages. Consider the following example of a LogLevel directive:

LogLevel error

In the preceding example, the LogLevel directive is set to error, which reports error conditions. You can specify several values for the LogLevel directive. In the following list, you'll find a description of each of the values that you can set for the LogLevel directive, followed by an example of each log level:

◆ **alert**. This log level means that immediate action should be taken to rectify the reported problem.

   [Mon May 13 12:39:52 2002] [alert] [client 172.17.68.222]
   /opt/web/html/.htaccess: order not allowed here

◆ **crit**. This log level means that the condition is critical.

   [Tue May 21 21:12:37 2002] [crit] (98)Address already in use:
   make_sock: could not bind to port 80

◆ **debug**. This log level indicates debug level messages.

   [Wed May 21 21:12:37 2002] [debug] Loaded module mod_vhost.c

◆ **emerg**. This log level lists the emergency conditions that make the system unusable.

   [Wed May 21 21:12:37 2002] [emerg] Child cannot open lock file. Exiting

◆ **error.** This log level indicates the error conditions.

```
[Thu May 30 13:51:46 2002] [error] [client 172.17.68.222] Directory index
forbidden by rule: /opt/web/html/
```

◆ **info.** This log level is referred to as the *informational log level* and provides general information about the functioning of the server.

```
[Thu May 30 13:51:46 2002] [info] Shutdown event signaled. Shutting the
server down
```

◆ **notice.** This log level specifies advisory conditions. These conditions don't indicate abnormal activity.

```
[Mon May 13 11:16:59 2002] [notice] Apache/1.3.24 (Unix) configured --
resuming normal operations
```

◆ **warn.** This log level issues warning conditions.

```
[Mon May 13 11:16:58 2002] [warn] child process 6697 did not exit, sending
another SIGHUP
```

Standard Format for error_log

As you have noticed by now, the logs that are stored in the error_log file or any other log file follow the format in which data is written to them. To become familiar with the format in which logs are maintained, check out the following list, which describes the information in a single log entry:

◆ **Time.** Specifies the exact date and time when the error occurred.

◆ **Log level.** Specifies the type of log level associated with the log message, such as error, notice, warn, and so on.

◆ **Client address.** Specifies the IP address/fully qualified domain name of the client who made the request.

◆ **Error message.** Contains the reported error message.

◆ **Reason for the error.** Specifies the reason for which the error was caused.

◆ **Service name.** Specifies the name of the service for which the error was generated.

◆ **Apache response.** Specifies the action taken by the Web server to rectify the error.

Managing Access Logs

As stated earlier, access logs are maintained by the Apache Web server to keep track of the requests received by the server. You can use the data in the access logs to create statistical reports on use of the site. In addition, you can filter out information in the access log file in order to receive only the desired information. Access logs are stored in a file named access_log that is located in the /usr/local/apache/logs directory. Following is the output of the `tail` command when used to view the contents of the access_log file:

```
[root@linux root]# tail /usr/local/apache/logs/access_log
172.17.68.181 - - [19/Jun/2002:22:17:33 +0530] "GET /scripts/fpcount.exe
HTTP/1.0" 404 291
172.17.68.181 - - [19/Jun/2002:22:17:33 +0530] "GET /cfdocs/expelval/
openfile.cfm HTTP/1.0" 404 300
172.17.68.181 - - [19/Jun/2002:22:17:33 +0530] "GET /cfdocs/expelval/
exprcalc.cfm HTTP/1.0" 404 300
172.17.68.181 - - [19/Jun/2002:22:17:33 +0530] "GET /cfdocs/expelval/
displayopenedfile.cfm HTTP/1.0" 404 309
172.17.68.181 - - [19/Jun/2002:22:17:33 +0530] "GET /cfdocs/expelval/
sendmail.cfm HTTP/1.0" 404 300
172.17.68.181 - - [19/Jun/2002:22:17:33 +0530] "GET /iissamples/exair/
howitworks/codebrws.asp HTTP/1.0" 404 312
172.17.68.181 - - [19/Jun/2002:22:17:33 +0530] "GET /iissamples/sdk/asp/
docs/codebrws.asp HTTP/1.0" 404 308
172.17.68.181 - - [19/Jun/2002:22:17:33 +0530] "GET /msads/Samples/SELECTOR/showcode.asp
HTTP/1.0" 404 307
172.17.68.181 - - [19/Jun/2002:22:17:33 +0530] "GET /search97.vts
HTTP/1.0" 404 284
172.17.68.181 - - [19/Jun/2002:22:17:33 +0530] "GET /carbo.dll
HTTP/1.0" 404 281
```

Contents of the access_log File

The contents of the access_log file are maintained in a standard format called the *Common Log Format (CLF)*. Most log analyzing software assumes that the logs are maintained in the common log format. Here is a sample log entry, followed by a discussion of the various columns into which a log is divided:

```
172.17.68.181 - - [19/Jun/2002:22:17:33 +0530] "GET /scripts/fpcount.exe
HTTP/1.0" 404 291
```

In the preceding extract of the access_log file, the information is divided into the following columns:

◆ **Hostname.** Consists of the IP address or fully qualified domain name of the client computer from which the request originated. However, the fully qualified domain name will be logged only if `HostNameLookups` is set to `on`. In the preceding sample log entry, the IP address is 172.17.68.181.

◆ **Remote logname**. Specifies the identity information reported by the client. However, this information will be visible only when IdentityCheck is enabled and the identd service is running at the client end.

◆ **Remote user**. Specifies the username entered by a user on being prompted to do so. The value for this field will be visible only for authenticated portions of the Web site.

◆ **Time**. Specifies the time when a particular request was served. In the preceding example, the time specified is [19/Jun/2002:22:17:33 +0530].

◆ **Request**. Specifies the first line of a request that was originally sent to the server. The request could be HEAD, GET, or POST followed by the URL requested by the client. In the preceding example, the request is a GET request.

◆ **Response code**. Specifies the status of the request in question. That is, it indicates whether the request was successful. In the preceding example, the Web server generated a response code of 404, which means that the document was not found at the expected location.

◆ **Bytes transferred**. Specifies the total number of bytes transferred to the client while responding to the request.

Associated Directives

In Apache, access logs are maintained using the mod_log_config module. You can use the directives described in the following subsections with this module to maintain access logs.

The *TransferLog* Directive

Use the TransferLog directive to specify the location of the file that will be used for maintaining access logs. Consider the following extract from the httpd.conf file:

```
TransferLog /usr/local/apache/logs/access_log
```

Another way to denote the location for the access_log file is by specifying a path relative to the server root directory as shown here:

```
TransferLog logs/access_log
```

The *LogFormat* Directive

The LogFormat directive is an important directive used with the mod_log_config module. LogFormat allows you to customize the format in which logs should be added to the access log file. The syntax of using the LogFormat directive is as follows:

```
LogFormat format [nickname]
```

In the preceding syntax, note the following:

◆ `format` is a parameter that defines a set of fields that will be added to the log file.

◆ `nickname` is any name that can be assigned to the given format.

Consider the example of a `LogFormat` directive extracted from the httpd.conf file:

```
LogFormat "%h %l %u %t \"%r\" %>s %b" common
```

This example illustrates the common log format discussed earlier. The characters specified in the format are *log format variables*. Although these variables appear to be junk characters, they carry a great deal of meaning. The variables that you can use with the `LogFormat` directive are as follows:

◆ **%a**. IP address of the remote host.

◆ **%A**. IP address of the local host.

◆ **%b**. The number of bytes sent to the client, excluding the bytes used by HTTP headers. When no characters are sent, this variable sends a dash character instead of zero in order to be CLF compliant.

◆ **%B**. The number of bytes sent to the client, excluding the bytes used by HTTP headers.

◆ **%{ENV VAR}e**. Environment variables specified by `ENV VAR`.

◆ **%f**. The name of file used for log maintenance.

◆ **%h**. Information about the hostname of the remote computer. This will work only if `HostNameLookups` are enabled. However, if the hostname cannot be resolved, the IP address is used rather than the hostname.

◆ **%H**. The name and version information for the protocol.

◆ **%{header_line}i**. Contents of one or more than one header_line entries extracted from the request sent to the server.

◆ **%l**. Remote logname of the client machine. However, this will work only when `ListenLogName` directive is enabled and the client is running the identd service.

◆ **%m**. Name of the request method used for the transaction. The `GET` request method is used most often.

◆ **%{note}n**. Contents of one or more than one note entries taken from another module.

◆ **%{header_line}o**. Contents of one or more than one header_line entries extracted from the request sent to the client.

◆ **%p**. Canonical TCP port of the server. This port is used to serve requests of clients.

◆ **%P**. Process ID of the child process that was used to answer the request sent by the client.

◆ **%q**. Query string if it exists. If not, an empty string.

- ◆ **%r**. First line of the request sent by the client.
- ◆ **%s**. Status of internally redirected requests.
- ◆ **%t**. Time specified in common log format.
- ◆ **%{format}t**. Time specified in the format specified within the braces.
- ◆ **%T**. Time taken (in seconds) by the server to answer a client request.
- ◆ **%u**. Remote user who was unable to gain access due to incorrect credentials.
- ◆ **%U**. URL path that the client requested.
- ◆ **%v**. Canonical ServerName of the server that addressed the request.
- ◆ **%V**. Server name specified in the UseCanonicalName directive.

The *CustomLog* Directive

The CustomLog directive is one that you will need to use whether you plan to specify custom access logging using the LogFormat directive or use the default CLF. The fact is that unless you instruct Apache to use the format using the CustomLog directive, not one of the specified options is possible. You use the CustomLog directive for the following purposes:

- ◆ To create and enable a log file
- ◆ To specify the location and name for the log file
- ◆ To specify a name for the previously defined log format

The default httpd.conf file consists of the following pair of directives that are used to specify CLF logging:

```
LogFormat "%h %l %u %t \"%r\" %>s %b" common
CustomLog /usr/local/apache/logs/access_log common
```

The preceding directives allow the standard CLF logging into the access_log file. If you examine the httpd.conf file, you will find a few other LogFormat directives as shown here:

```
LogFormat "%h %l %u %t \"%r\" %>s %b \"%{Referer}i\" \"%{User-Agent}i\""
combined
LogFormat "%{Referer}i -> %U" referer
LogFormat "%{User-agent}i" agent
```

Although the preceding LogFormat directives are uncommented, the corresponding CustomLog directives are commented. This prevents the use of these LogFormat directives. The corresponding commented CustomLog directives in the httpd.conf file are as follows:

```
#CustomLog /usr/local/apache/logs/access_log combined
#CustomLog /usr/local/apache/logs/referer_log referer
#CustomLog /usr/local/apache/logs/agent_log agent
```

As you can see, the corresponding `CustomLog` directives are commented. The second and third `CustomLog` directives are different and don't store the logs in the conventional access_log file that uses the CLF log format.

The first `CustomLog` directive specified in the example refers to a combined log format. This directive should be uncommented only if you comment the CLF log. This is because the combined log format is used as a replacement for CLF log. If you decide to use both common and combined log formats, you will end up using two `CustomLog` directives that are writing to the same log file, access_log. Although this can be done, you will need to live with the fact that two different log entries with a different format will be appended to the log file every time a request is sent to the server.

The SetEnvIf *Directive*

You also use the `CustomLog` directive for implementing conditional logging in Apache. When I say that `CustomLog` is a *conditional directive,* I mean that this directive checks for the existence of environment variables before logging a particular request. The checking bit is handled by another directive called the `SetEnvIf` directive. This directive is not present in the default httpd.conf file. Therefore, you need to add it manually in order to use it.

Maintaining Logs for Virtual Hosts

If you configured virtual hosts on your system, it is advisable to maintain separate log files for virtual hosts. To do so, you can specify logging directives within `VirtualHost` container tags. As a result, all logs pertaining to virtual hosts will be maintained in isolation from the logs maintained for the primary server. However, there is a catch. The Linux kernel uses a resource known as a *system file handle,* which is used to open log files. If separate log files are used for different virtual hosts, a separate system file handle will be required. Since the release of kernel 2.4 in Linux, the limits imposed on the system file handles are lenient, and using separate log files for virtual hosts isn't much of a problem.

If you don't specify separate `TransferLog` and `CustomLog` directives for virtual hosts, the virtual hosts inherit the logs defined for the main server. This could result in the log file being flooded with too much information, making it difficult for you to extract the relevant information from the log file.

If you are using a large number of virtual hosts, you might want to tweak the log format a bit to accommodate logs pertinent to all virtual hosts in the same log file. Just specify the `%v` variable in the `LogFormat` directive; this will record the domain name of the virtual host at the end of a log entry, making it convenient to find out which log entry is meant for which virtual host. Consider the following example:

```
LogFormat "%h %l %u %t \"%r\" %>s %b Domain Name: %v" revised
CustomLog /usr/local/apache/logs/access_log revised
```

Notice that the %v variable is added to the LogFormat directive. As a result, the domain name of the virtual host is also displayed in the log file. Also notice that the name of the format is changed from common to revised. This is because as soon as you add the %v variable, the format ceases to be a common log format.

Tools for Monitoring Logs

One of the most important jobs of an administrator is to monitor and analyze logs effectively. This is important from both a security and a performance perspective. The log files store huge amounts of information, and it might be difficult for inexperienced administrators to extract the information pertinent to a given situation. Several system tools, as well as third-party tools, can not only help you analyze logs, but help you extract meaningful data from them as well. A few utilities also generate automated reports at regular intervals, so that you can keep a constant eye on the logs. In this section, I'll discuss a few third-party tools that prove highly useful for maintaining a sound and secure Web server.

The logrotate *Utility*

You use the logrotate utility to manage the log files on your Linux system. If you did a Custom-Everything install of the Linux operating system, you will find this utility already installed on your machine. You can do the following using the logrotate utility:

- ◆ **Rotate logs.** The logrotate utility uses a mechanism called *log rotation*. Log rotation causes system logs to be copied to an alternate location leaving blank files in the original location. As a result, several log files considerably smaller in size are saved on the file system.

- ◆ **Compress logs.** You can also use the logrotate utility to compress the log files, including the rotated log files. Compressing the saved log files saves considerable disk space.

- ◆ **Back up logs.** The logrotate utility also makes regular backups of the log files. All log files (including those created in the rotation phase) are put together in a sequential format. This makes it much simpler to review older log files.

- ◆ **Export system logs.** This process involves transferring the log files from the system to cheaper backup mediums. The backup medium can be a tape drive or another machine that is set aside for storing backups. Exporting system logs frees a significant amount of server disk space. Exporting system logs also helps secure the log files. So, in times of contingencies or situations such as server crashes, the stored log files are protected.

The primary benefit of logrotate is the ability to manage logs on servers that deal with very high network traffic—high network traffic can result in large log files that hog system resources. To become accustomed to using logrotate, I suggest that you read its man page before you start using it.

NOTE

Although the `logrotate` utility is used to maintain the system logs in general, as a system administrator, you should be familiar with this utility.

Webalizer

Webalizer is a free third-party software that is specifically used for analyzing Web server logs and generating reports.

This tool is probably the easiest one to install and use. Its primary purpose is to help you generate summaries of log data using a wide range of graphs. You can generate hourly, daily, monthly, and yearly reports using Webalizer. The only drawback to Webalizer is that you can use it only with log files that follow the format specified by CLF. In spite of this, you will no doubt enjoy working with this interesting tool.

Installing Webalizer

Follow these steps to install Webalizer:

1. Go to http://www.mrunix.net/webalizer/download.html, and from the Complete source distribution section download the file webalizer-2.01-10-src.tgz by clicking on the Tar/Gzip archive link.

2. Be sure that you are logged in as root and type the following command to extract the contents of the compressed file:

```
[root@linux root]# tar zxvf webalizer-2.01-10-src.tgz
webalizer-2.01-10/
webalizer-2.01-10/aclocal.m4
webalizer-2.01-10/CHANGES
webalizer-2.01-10/webalizer_lang.h
webalizer-2.01-10/configure
webalizer-2.01-10/configure.in
webalizer-2.01-10/COPYING
webalizer-2.01-10/Copyright
webalizer-2.01-10/country-codes.txt
webalizer-2.01-10/DNS.README
webalizer-2.01-10/dns_resolv.c
webalizer-2.01-10/dns_resolv.h
webalizer-2.01-10/graphs.c
webalizer-2.01-10/graphs.h
...Many delete lines
```

3. Go to the webalizer-2.01-10 directory and run the configure script by using the following command:

```
[root@linux webalizer-2.01-10]# ./configure
creating cache ./config.cache
checking for gcc... gcc
checking whether the C compiler (gcc  ) works... yes
checking whether the C compiler (gcc  ) is a cross-compiler... no
checking whether we are using GNU C... yes
checking whether gcc accepts -g... yes
checking whether ln -s works... yes
checking for a BSD compatible install... /usr/bin/install -c
checking how to run the C preprocessor... gcc -E
checking whether char is unsigned... no
checking for main in -l44bsd... no
checking for main in -lm... yes
checking for main in -lz... yes
checking for gzrewind in -lz... yes
checking for main in -lpng... yes
checking for gdImagePng in -lgd... yes
checking for gd.h... /usr/include
checking for getopt.h... yes
checking for math.h... yes
checking default config dir... /etc
checking for language file... yes - english
updating cache ./config.cache
creating ./config.status
creating Makefile
linking ./lang/webalizer_lang.english to webalizer_lang.h
```

4. After running the configure script, use the make command, as shown here:

```
 [root@linux webalizer-2.01-10]# make
gcc -Wall -O2 -DETCDIR=\"/etc\"  -DHAVE_GETOPT_H=1 -DHAVE_MATH_H=1   -c
webalizer.c
gcc -Wall -O2 -DETCDIR=\"/etc\"  -DHAVE_GETOPT_H=1 -DHAVE_MATH_H=1   -c
hashtab.c
gcc -Wall -O2 -DETCDIR=\"/etc\"  -DHAVE_GETOPT_H=1 -DHAVE_MATH_H=1   -c
linklist.c
```

```
gcc -Wall -O2 -DETCDIR=\"/etc\"  -DHAVE_GETOPT_H=1 -DHAVE_MATH_H=1  -c
preserve.c
gcc -Wall -O2 -DETCDIR=\"/etc\"  -DHAVE_GETOPT_H=1 -DHAVE_MATH_H=1  -c
dns_resolv.c
gcc -Wall -O2 -DETCDIR=\"/etc\"  -DHAVE_GETOPT_H=1 -DHAVE_MATH_H=1  -c
parser.c
gcc -Wall -O2 -DETCDIR=\"/etc\"  -DHAVE_GETOPT_H=1 -DHAVE_MATH_H=1  -c
output.c
gcc -Wall -O2 -DETCDIR=\"/etc\"  -DHAVE_GETOPT_H=1 -DHAVE_MATH_H=1  -I
/usr/include -c graphs.c
gcc  -o webalizer webalizer.o hashtab.o linklist.o preserve.o parser.o
 output.o dns_resolv.o graphs.o -lgd -lpng -lz -lm
rm -f webazolver
ln -s webalizer webazolver
```

5. Finally, use the `make install` command, as shown here:

```
[root@linux webalizer-2.01-10]# make install
/usr/bin/install -c webalizer /usr/local/bin/webalizer
/usr/bin/install -c -m 644 webalizer.1 /usr/local/man/man1/webalizer.1
/usr/bin/install -c -m 644 sample.conf /etc/webalizer.conf.sample
rm -f /usr/local/bin/webazolver
ln -s /usr/local/bin/webalizer /usr/local/bin/webazolver
```

Now that you have installed the package, you are nearly ready to use it—you just need to adjust a few settings first. After you install Webalizer, a file named webalizer.conf.sample is created in the /etc directory. Rename this file webalizer.conf. This is the configuration file for Webalizer. After renaming the file, edit it as described here:

1. Uncomment the `LogFile` option and specify the path of access_log file:

```
# LogFile defines the web server log file to use.  If not specified
# here or on the command line, input will default to STDIN.  If
# the log filename ends in '.gz' (ie: a gzip compressed file), it will
# be decompressed on the fly as it is being read.


LogFile        /usr/local/apache/logs/access_log
```

2. Uncomment the `LogType` option. This option should contain the value `clf`, as shown here:

```
# LogType defines the log type being processed.  Normally, the Webalizer
# expects a CLF or Combined web server log as input.  Using this option,
```

```
# you can process ftp logs as well (xferlog as produced by wu-ftp and
# others), or Squid native logs.  Values can be 'clf', 'ftp' or 'squid',
# with 'clf' the default.


LogType clf
```

3. Uncomment the OutputDir option and specify the path of the directory in which you want to store the output files. I used the /root directory for convenience, but I recommend using a separate directory for storing the output files.

```
# OutputDir is where you want to put the output files.  This should
# should be a full path name, however relative ones might work as well.
# If no output directory is specified, the current directory will be used.


OutputDir      /root
```

Using Webalizer

After installing Webalizer, you can invoke it from the command prompt by using the webalizer command. You can use a series of command line options with the webalizer command. To print a brief description of the available options, type the following command:

```
[root@linux root]# webalizer --help
Usage: webalizer [options] [log file]
-h         = print this help message
-v -V      = print version information
-d         = print additional debug info
-F type    = Log type.  type= (clf | ftp | squid)
-f         = Fold sequence errors
-i         = ignore history file
-p         = preserve state (incremental)
...many deleted lines
```

Although there are several options, you can use the webalizer command without specifying any options. The following shows what happened when I executed the webalizer command from the console:

```
[root@linux root]# webalizer
Webalizer V2.01-10 (Linux 2.4.7-10) English
Using logfile /usr/local/apache/logs/access_log (clf)
Creating output in /root
Hostname for reports is 'linux.server.com'
Reading history file... webalizer.hist
```

```
Generating report for April 2002
Generating report for May 2002
Generating report for June 2002
Generating summary report
Saving history information...
104650 records in 2.44 seconds, 42889/sec
```

The output of the command suggests that the log file was analyzed and certain reports were generated. These reports are the output files that were stored in my /root directory as a result of running Webalizer. Figure 9.8 shows one of the graphs generated by the Webalizer utility displaying statistics on the usage of linux.server.com.

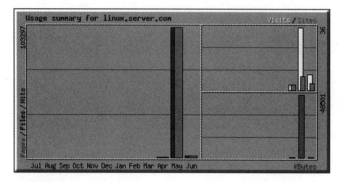

FIGURE 9.8 *The usage statistics report for linux.server.com*

Analog

Analog is another popular third-party tool used for monitoring Apache logs. Many Web server administrators rely on this tool for monitoring logs generated by the Apache Web server. The following features of Analog make it the choice of most Apache administrators:

◆ It's available free of cost from its official Web site

◆ It's easy to install and compile

◆ It's very fast

◆ It provides extensive configurable options

◆ It provides fully customizable output

Installing Analog

You can install Analog by following these steps:

1. Go to http://www.analog.cx/download.html and download the analog-5.24.tar.gz file to any directory in the filesystem.

2. Uncompress the contents of the file by typing the following command:

```
[root@linux root]# tar zxvf analog-5.24.tar.gz
analog-5.24/
analog-5.24/docs/
analog-5.24/docs/LicBSD.txt
analog-5.24/docs/Licapach.txt
analog-5.24/docs/Licgd.txt
analog-5.24/docs/Licpcre.txt
analog-5.24/docs/Licpng.txt
analog-5.24/docs/Liczlib.txt
analog-5.24/docs/Readme.html
analog-5.24/docs/acknow.html
...many deleted lines
```

3. Go to the analog-5.24 directory and type the following command to install Analog:

```
[root@linux analog-5.24]# make
cd src && make
make[1]: Entering directory `/usr/local/analog-5.24/src'
gcc          -02     -DUNIX        -c alias.c
gcc          -02     -DUNIX        -c analog.c
gcc          -02     -DUNIX        -c cache.c
gcc          -02     -DUNIX        -c dates.c
gcc          -02     -DUNIX        -c globals.c
gcc          -02     -DUNIX        -c hash.c
gcc          -02     -DUNIX        -c init.c
gcc          -02     -DUNIX        -c init2.c
gcc          -02     -DUNIX        -c input.c
gcc          -02     -DUNIX        -c macinput.c
...Many deleted lines
```

After you install Analog, you'll need to follow a series of configuration steps before you can actually start using it. The configuration file for Analog is the analog.cfg file, which is located in the installation directory of Analog. This file needs to be configured before you can start using Analog to generate reports. In the analog.cfg file, follow these steps to configure Analog:

1. Uncomment and specify a value for the HOSTNAME. The value does not have to be the hostname of the server. This value appears when the usage statistics are generated.

   ```
   HOSTNAME "Apache Zone"
   ```

2. Uncomment the LOGFILE option and specify the path for the file access_log for your Apache Web server, as shown here:

   ```
   LOGFILE "/usr/local/apache/logs/access_log"
   ```

3. Uncomment the OUTFILE option and specify a file that will be used as the OUTFILE.

   ```
   OUTFILE "/opt/web/html/analog.html"
   ```

Using Analog

If you installed and configured Analog properly, you will be able to generate a report on the usage of your Web server. You can invoke the analog utility by issuing the following command:

```
[root@linux bin]# /usr/local/analog-5.24/analog
```

After the command is executed, the analog utility generates an HTML report, and the file is created with the name analog.html. The report that is generated is huge and consists of the following:

◆ **General Summary**. Displays the information on overall statistics of the Web server.

◆ **Monthly Report**. Displays the activities undertaken in the current month, for all the months in the period for which the report is generated.

◆ **Daily Summary**. Displays the list of activities for each day of the week, for all the weeks in the period for which the report is generated.

◆ **Hourly Summary**. Displays the list of activities for each hour of the day, for all days in the period for which the report is generated.

◆ **Domain Report**. Lists the countries of the world that requested files from the Web server.

◆ **Organisation Report**. Lists the organization of computers that requested files from the Web server.

◆ **Search Word Report**. Lists the words specified by people in search engines to find the site.

◆ **Operating System Report**. Lists the operating system used by visitors who accessed the Web server.

◆ **Status Code Report**. Lists the HTTP status codes for all the requests received until date.

- ◆ **File Size Report**. Lists the sizes of files requested from the Web server.
- ◆ **File Type Report**. Lists the file extensions of the files requested by the client.
- ◆ **Directory Report**. Lists the names from which the visitors requested files.
- ◆ **Request Report**. Lists the files on the site that were requested.

This file resided in the /opt/web/html directory as specified in the analog.cfg file. Figure 9.9 shows part of the report that appears after you use the Analog utility.

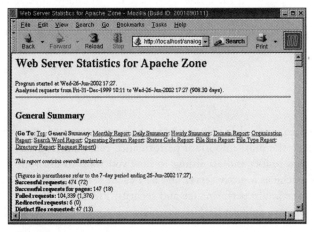

FIGURE 9.9 *The Web server statistics generated using Analog*

Miscellaneous Tips for Performance Tuning

I've discussed most, but not all, of the steps you can take to improve the performance of the Apache Web server. Following are a few more suggestions for improving performance:

- ◆ **Choose adequate RAM**. The most important hardware component that directly affects the performance of a Web server is the RAM. Be sure to select the appropriate amount of RAM for your server. Another option is to set the MaxClients directive in a way that is optimum for the RAM you are using. Inadequate RAM can force the server to respond to requests by using the SWAP memory. This is not recommended because it increases the time it takes the Web server to answer the request.

- ◆ **Use the AllowOverride directive**. Wherever possible, avoid specifying the value all for AllowOverride directive. When using .htaccess files, you need to set this directive as all. As a result, for every request, the .htaccess files are opened and checked by the Apache Web server.

◆ **Avoid content negotiation**. If performance is the only thing that you are looking for, consider not using content negotiation.

◆ **Use FollowSymLinks and FollowSymLinksIfOwnerMatch**. Use these options when they are required the most. When you use these options, Apache uses an additional system call to check the symbolic link increasing the load on the Web server.

◆ **Use Allow and Deny directives**. When specifying a value for the Allow and Deny directives, specify the IP address of hosts rather than the domain name for maximum performance. Specifying the domain name results in double reverse DNS lookups.

◆ **Use the HostNameLookUps directive**. Unless required, this directive should be set to off.

Summary

In this chapter, I discussed concepts that help you tune the performance of your Apache Web server. I began by discussing the most important performance-related directives and how you configure them for optimum results and according to how you want to use your Web server. Next, I discussed using Apache as a proxy server and as a cache server. Then I discussed how to manage logs to ensure maximum performance and security. Finally, I presented a few miscellaneous tips that will help you achieve peak performance.

Check Your Understanding

Multiple Choice Questions

1. Which of the following directives is used to specify the maximum number of headers that should be allowed for an incoming request?

    a. `LimitRequestBody`

    b. `LimitRequestFields`

    c. `LimitRequestFieldSize`

    d. `LimitRequestLine`

2. Which of the following statements will not hold true with respect to configuring Apache as a proxy server?

    a. Apache can be configured as a forward proxy.

    b. Apache can be configured as a reverse proxy.

    c. Apache can be configured to act as a forward proxy and at the same time also configured to act as a reverse proxy.

    d. Apache can be configured either as a forward proxy or as a reverse proxy at a given time.

3. Which of the following directives is used to share the workload of the proxy with another computer?

    a. The `ProxyReceiveBufferSize` directive

    b. The `ProxyDomain` directive

    c. The `ProxyRemote` directive

    d. The `ProxyBlock` directive

4. Which of the following directives is used to specify the maximum limit for the cache that can be stored on the proxy server?

    a. The `CacheRoot` directive

    b. The `CacheSize` directive

    c. The `CacheDirLength` directive

    d. The `CacheDefaultExpire` directive

5. Which of the following directives are associated with the `mod_log_config` module? (Choose all that apply.)

    a. The `TransferLog` directive

    b. The `LogLevel` directive

    c. The `ErrorLog` directive

    d. The `LogFormat` directive

Answers

Multiple Choice Answers

1. b. The `LimitRequestField` directive is used to specify the maximum number of headers that should be allowed for an incoming request.

2. d. Apache can be configured as a forward as well as a reverse proxy at the same time.

3. c. The `ProxyRemote` directive is used to share the workload of the proxy with another computer.

4. b. The `CacheSize` directive is used to specify the maximum limit for the cache that can be stored on the proxy server.

5. a, d. The `TransferLog` and the `LogFormat` directives are related to the `mod_log_config` module.

Chapter 10

Using Server-Side Includes (SSI)

Gone are the days when entire Web sites were created using HTML. Those sites were static and inflexible, making the content on the Web pages appear dull because there was no user interaction possible. Times have changed, and now you can use several client-side and server-side scripting languages to generate dynamic Web pages.

Apache supports a wide range of scripting languages such as Perl, PHP, and ASP. These scripting languages can be used to create full-fledged, feature-full, and dynamic Web sites. In addition to supporting popular scripting languages, Apache supports a mechanism called *server-side includes* (SSI). Server-side includes are used in Apache to generate dynamic content on HTML Web pages.

In this chapter, I focus on the meaning and use of server-side includes. I then discuss the important directives that are used in conjunction with server-side includes. Next, I discuss the tags that are used with SSI. Finally, I consider the various situations in which using server-side includes will be most useful.

Introduction to SSI

Server-side includes are nothing but simple tags used by the Apache Web server. These tags are placed within HTML code of a Web page as comment statements. When Apache encounters these statements at runtime, it interprets them and performs the specified action, thereby making HTML Web pages dynamic and flexible. In order to configure Apache to use SSI, you need to either edit the directives in the httpd.conf file or include the appropriate configuration directives in the .htaccess file.

A few directives must be configured in order to direct Apache to parse Web pages and to detect statements within the HTML code as server-side includes. Server-side includes are named as such because the tags that you specify within the HTML file are processed at the server-side before delivering the requested resource to the client.

Purposes of SSI

You can use SSI to perform a wide range of activities at the server-side. A few server-side activities that you can perform include the following:

◆ **Display content based on certain conditions.** SSI provides a simple if/else structure that can be used to define certain conditions within the source code of the Web page. The result of these conditions can be used to prompt the Web server to perform certain activities.

◆ **Call a CGI program.** By way of SSI you can include configuration directives that call CGI programs at runtime.

◆ **Include external files.** By appropriately specifying the required SSI tags, you can even use the data contained in external files. This data can then be processed, and the result can be combined to any other server-parsed document.

◆ **Access environment variables.** A few tags that are a part of SSI also allow you to access environment variables. The environment variables are powerful variables that allow you to perform complex operating system-related activities.

You will have a better understanding of how these things are handled using SSI after you complete this chapter.

CGI versus SSI

Both CGI and SSI can be used to generate dynamic content, and whether to use CGI or SSI should depend entirely on the degree of dynamism that you want to impart in your Web pages. If you want minimal dynamic content, SSI is the better proposition. However, if you want substantial dynamic content, CGI is the "blindfolded choice."

Configuring Apache for SSI

Configuring Apache to use SSI is an easy task. However, always remember that after you make the required settings, Apache will parse the defined files to look for SSI directives. As soon as it encounters a SSI directive, it will process the directive and generate the desired result.

As mentioned earlier, you can configure SSI for Apache by editing the httpd.conf file or by using .htaccess files. By default, the SSI-related configuration options in the httpd.conf file are commented for security reasons. For example, using SSI, it is possible to access external files. As a result, anybody on the Internet can use SSI to display the /etc/passwd file, which could leak out potentially sensitive information to unauthorized users.

You can configure Apache to use SSI in a variety of ways, including the following, which I discuss in this chapter:

◆ By using a file extension
◆ By using the XBitHack directive
◆ By enabling SSI using MIME types

Using a File Extension

The most common way to configure SSI is by specifying a file extension that directs the server to parse the document with the specified extension for SSI tags. Typically, the file extension used by SSI is .shtml. After you configure Apache to use SSI, the Web server searches for files with the .shtml extension and parses them before sending them to the client computer.

To configure the Apache Web server to use server-parsed HTML files, you need to find the following lines in the httpd.conf file and uncomment them:

```
# To use server-parsed HTML files
#
#AddType text/html .shtml
#AddHandler server-parsed .shtml
```

In the preceding extract, note the following:

◆ The lines are commented by default. You will need to uncomment these lines to use server-parsed HTML files.

◆ The AddType directive is used to specify that all files that end with a .shtml extension will be recognized and served by the Web server with a MIME type of text/html.

◆ The AddHandler directive is used to specify that the server-parsed handler will be used for .shtml files. The server-parsed handler is a built-in handler in Apache. This handler is used to tell the Apache Web server that the files with a .shtml extension need to be parsed for SSI.

After uncommenting the preceding lines, you need to check for the following:

◆ The `libexec` directory consists of a copy of `mod_include.so` that is loaded and enabled in httpd.conf.

◆ The `Options` directive is specified for the directory in which you will store .shtml files. If the `Options` directive is not specified, add the following line:

```
Options Includes
```

After making the preceding changes, restart Apache using the `apachectl` command to apply the changes that you made to the configuration file.

Although this is a simple and ideal approach to configuring Apache to use SSI, you will want to avoid using this approach in the following situations:

◆ **Adding SSI capability to an existing site.** It is advisable not to use this method for configuring SSI for existing Web sites. Doing so will require you to manually change the file extension for each Web page of the Web site to `.shtml`. Unless you do that, the Apache Web server will not parse the Web pages for SSI. In addition, you will need to update the links to these Web pages wherever they occur. This means a lot of wasted time and energy.

 NOTE

A few administrators have tried to add a handler for .html files in addition to .shtml files, so that all .html files are parsed for SSI. Although this helps to some extent, it is not recommended because doing so requires the server to parse each and every HTML file, thereby increasing server load.

◆ **User friendliness.** Although this is a non-technical reason, it is important. When you create a Web site, you must take into consideration the user friendliness of the site. A site should have URLs that can be understood by users. Using file extensions such as .shtml makes it difficult for users to comprehend the URL and to find specific information on the Web site.

Using the XBitHack Directive

Another way to enable SSI is by using the `XBitHack` directive. This directive doesn't appear in the httpd.conf file. Therefore, if you want to use it, you must specify it manually either in the httpd.conf file or in the .htaccess file. If set, this directive enables the Apache Web server to parse all HTML documents on which the user-execute bit is set.

The XBitHack directive can contain three values, On, Off, and Full. The implications of using each of these options with the XBitHack directive are as follows:

- **On**. All files of type text/html present on the Web server with the execute bit set are parsed for server-side includes irrespective of the file extensions.

- **Off**. The default option for the XBitHack directive is used to turn off the use of the XBitHack directive for the files located in the specified directory. By default, if the XBitHack is enabled for a directory, all the sub-directives within the specified directory are also affected. To avoid such a situation, you can use the Off option to turn off the use of the XBitHack directive for a specific sub-directory.

- **Full**. This option is an extension to the On option. The Full option checks all files for SSI that have user-execute bit and the group-execute bit.

Here are few advantages to using the XBitHack directive:

- Setting this directive has nothing to do with file extensions. Therefore, in order to enable server-side parsing for SSI, you don't have to rename files to possess a new file extension. This makes it a lot simpler to use the XBitHack directive.

- Because the file extensions of the files are retained as HTML, users who are accessing your Web pages have no idea whether you are using dynamic content in the pages.

Enabling SSI by MIME types

Using MIME types is another way to enable SSI. However, I don't recommend that you use this method; it exists only for the purpose of backward compatibility. When you enable SSI by specifying MIME types, documents with the MIME types text/x-server-parsed-html and text/x-server-parsed-html3 are parsed for SSI directives. After Apache parses such documents, it sends them with a text/html MIME type.

To use MIME types to enable SSI, you can use either of the following methods:

- Use the AddType directive to specify that a particular sort of file should have the specified MIME type.

- Add the particular file to the mime.types file.

Tags Used with SSI

The best part about SSI is that you implement it using SSI tags that are easy to use. SSI tags are embedded in HTML in the form of comments and have special meaning only for the SSI parser. The Web server deletes the SSI tags and their enclosing comments. Therefore, the SSI tags are not visible to the client browsers.

Syntax for Using SSI

The syntax for using SSI tags is as follows:

```
<!--#command_name attribute=value attribute=value…-->
```

In the preceding syntax, note the following:

◆ command_name is the command/tag that you specify.

◆ attribute is the option used with the command/tag.

◆ value is an element that is specified for each attribute.

Now that you are familiar with the syntax of using SSI, turn your attention to the tags that are used with SSI.

The *<config>* Tag

You use the config tag to specify how certain elements of SSI should be displayed or formatted. Three attributes can be used with this tag. They are as follows:

◆ **errmsg**. The value of this attribute is displayed if an error is encountered while processing/parsing the SSI directive present in the Web page. This attribute only indicates that something went wrong. However, because of the poor error-handling capabilities of SSI, not much can be done other than customizing the error message.

◆ **sizefmt**. Use this attribute to determine the file size returned by the fsize tag. The value of sizefmt can be expressed either as bytes or abbrev. When expressed as bytes, the size is displayed in bytes; when the size is expressed in abbrev, the file size is displayed in Kilobytes (KB) or Megabytes (MB). The main purpose for using this attribute is to affect the use of the fsize tag.

◆ **timefmt**. Use this attribute to format the strings that are used to display the date and time information in Linux. The customizable options are similar to the Linux date. Anybody who is familiar with the date utility will find this attribute useful. The format of this attribute is the same as the format used by the strftime() function in Linux.

The list of strings that can be used with the config tag for formatting the output is as follows:

◆ **%%**. Escapes a % character.

◆ **%a**. Depicts a weekday in abbreviated form. For example, Thu represents the day Thursday.

◆ **%A**. Depicts a weekday in full form. For example, Thursday represents the day Thursday.

◆ **%w**. Displays a number that signifies a day of the week. The count starts with the number 0, which represents Sunday.

◆ **%b**. Displays a month of the year in abbreviated form. For example, Sep represents the month September.

◆ **%B**. Displays a month of the year in full form. For example, September represents the month September.

◆ **%d**. Displays a number that depicts a day of the month. The number is from the range 01–31.

◆ **%e**. Displays a number that depicts a day of the month. The number is from the range 1–31.

◆ **%H**. Displays a number that depicts the hour of the day. The number is from the range 00–23.

◆ **%I**. Displays a number that depicts an hour from a 12-hour day. The number is from the range 01–12.

◆ **%j**. Displays a number that depicts a day in the year. The number is from the range 001–366.

◆ **%M**. Displays a number that depicts minutes. The number is from the range 00–59.

◆ **%p**. Depicts the state of the day in AM or PM.

◆ **%S**. Displays a number that depicts seconds. The number is from the range 00–59.

◆ **%y**. Displays the last two digits of a year. For example, the number 77 depicts the year 1977.

◆ **%Y**. Displays a year as a four-digit number, such as 1977.

◆ **%Z**. Depicts the time zone in CST.

Consider the following example, which uses the config tag to display the current day and date:

```
<HTML>
<HEAD>
<TITLE>Using the config tag</TITLE>
</HEAD>
<BODY>
<H1><CENTER>Using the config tag</CENTER></H1>
<!--#config timefmt="%A"-->
<CENTER>Today is a <!--#echo var="DATE_LOCAL"-->
<!--#config timefmt="%B %d, %Y"-->!</CENTER><BR>
<CENTER>The date today is <!--#echo var="DATE_LOCAL"--></CENTER>
</BODY>
</HTML>
```

In the preceding example, note the following:

◆ The config tag is used with the timefmt argument.

◆ The value specified for the timefmt argument is %A. This indicates that the full name of the day of the week will be displayed.

◆ The echo tag is used to print the values of the environment variable DATE_LOCAL.

 NOTE

I discuss the echo tag and the associated environment variables in the next section.

◆ The variable var consists of the value of the environment variable named DATE_LOCAL. This variable contains the system date in local time. The config tag is used to extract only the name of the current day of the week from this environment variable.

◆ The config tag is used again. This time the timefmt argument is specified the values %B, %d, and %Y.

◆ %B is used to display the full name of the current month.

◆ %d is used to display the numeric day of the month.

◆ %Y is used to display the year in numeric format.

◆ The echo tag is used again, and the variable named var stores the environment variable DATE_LOCAL. The options specified with the config tag are used to extract the required information from the DATE_LOCAL environment variable.

Figure 10.1 shows the Web page that appears when you use the config tag as shown in the preceding example.

FIGURE 10.1 *Using the config tag to display the current day and date*

The *<echo>* Tag

You use the echo tag to print the values of SSI variables. This tag requires that at least one attribute of the variable, the name of the variable, is printed. If you specify a variable in the attribute and don't set it, no errors occur. Instead, the variable is displayed as (none).

Numerous variables are available with the CGI environment. In addition, there are a few SSI-specific variables. These variables are as follows:

- ◆ **DATE_GMT**. Represents the date in GMT (Greenwich Mean Time).
- ◆ **DATE_LOCAL**. Represents the system date in local time.
- ◆ **DOCUMENT_NAME**. Represents the filename of the requested SSI document.
- ◆ **DOCUMENT_URI**. Represents the URL path of the SSI document requested.
- ◆ **LAST_MODIFIED**. Represents the last modified date of the requested SSI document.

Consider the following example, which uses the echo tag:

```
<HTML>
<HEAD>
<TITLE>Using the echo tag</TITLE>
</HEAD>
<BODY>
<H1><CENTER>Using the echo tag</CENTER></H1> <BR>

<B>The value of DATE_GMT environment variable is:
<!--#echo var="DATE_GMT"--></B> <BR>

<B>The value of DATE_LOCAL environment variable is:
<!--#echo var="DATE_LOCAL"--></B> <BR>

<B>The value of the DOCUMENT_NAME environment variable is:
<!--#echo var="DOCUMENT_NAME"--> </B><BR>

<B>The value of DOCUMENT_URI environment variable is:
<!--#echo var="DOCUMENT_URI"--> </B><BR>

<B>The value of LAST_MODIFIED environment variable is:
<!--#echo var="LAST_MODIFIED"--> </B>

</BODY>
</HTML>
```

In the preceding example, the echo tag is used to display values of the SSI-specific environment variables. Figure 10.2 shows the Web page that displays the environment variables and their values.

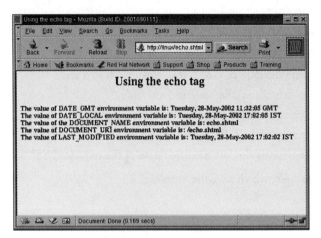

FIGURE 10.2 *Using the echo tag to display the values of environment variables*

The *<exec>* Tag

The exec tag is a useful tag that you can use to execute an external command and display the output of the command. The command can be either a Linux shell command or a CGI script.

A Linux Shell Command

To use a Linux shell command, employ the following syntax:

```
<!--#exec cmd="shell_command arg1 arg2 …"-->
```

In the preceding syntax, note the following:

- ◆ The exec tag is used to specify a command.
- ◆ The keyword cmd is used to signify that a shell command will be used.
- ◆ arg1 and arg2 are arguments that are used with the specified shell command.

A CGI Script

To use a CGI script, employ the following syntax:

```
<!--#exec cgi="/path/of/cgifile"-->
```

In the preceding syntax, note the following:

◆ The exec tag is used to specify that a CGI script will be executed.

◆ The keyword cgi should be specified to signify that a CGI file will be executed.

◆ The value of the cgi attribute represents the path of the CGI file that needs to be executed.

Using the <exec> Tag

Now that you have the basic knowledge for using the exec tag, take a look at this simple example of using the exec tag:

```
<HTML>
<HEAD>
<TITLE>Using the exec tag</TITLE>
</HEAD>
<BODY>
<H1><CENTER>Using the exec tag</CENTER></H1><BR>
<H4>The uptime information about the server is as follows:</H4>
<pre>
<!--#exec cmd="/usr/bin/uptime" -->
</pre>
</BODY>
</HTML>
```

In the preceding example, note the following:

◆ The exec tag is used to execute a command at the server-end.

◆ The cmd argument signifies that a Linux shell command will be specified.

◆ The path /usr/bin/uptime is the location of the uptime command.

When the server encounters the exec tag, a command or a CGI script can be executed. Figure 10.3 shows the Web page that displays the uptime information of the Web server.

The *<fsize>* Tag

You use the fsize tag to insert the file size of a specified file into a server-parsed HTML file. Two options can be used with this tag. Each option has its own way of locating the file and then displaying the size of the file. The options that can be used are as follows:

◆ **file.** This option is used to locate a filename and path specified is relative to the default location of the directory containing the SSI document.

◆ **virtual.** This option is used to locate a filename and path specified as relative to the DocumentRoot directive of Apache. Use this option when you want to specify partial URLs.

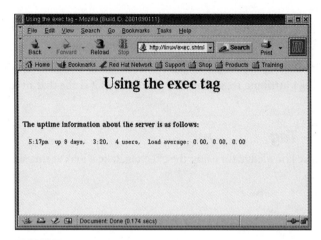

FIGURE 10.3 *Using the* exec *tag to display server uptime*

Consider the following example:

```
<HTML>
<HEAD>
<TITLE>Using the fsize tag</TITLE>
</HEAD>
<BODY>
<H1><CENTER>Using the fsize Tag</CENTER></H1>
<!--#config sizefmt="bytes"-->
<H4><CENTER>The size of the file config.shtml (in bytes) is:</CENTER></H4>
<H4><CENTER><!--#fsize file="config.shtml"--></CENTER></H4>
</BODY>
</HTML>
```

In the preceding example, note the following:

◆ The config tag is used with the sizefmt argument to specify that the size of the file will be expressed in bytes.

◆ The fsize tag is used with the file argument to specify that the size of the file will be displayed.

◆ The value specified for the file argument is config.shtml. This is the file whose size will be displayed on the Web page.

Figure 10.4 shows the result of using the fsize tag.

FIGURE 10.4 *Using the* `fsize` *tag to display the file size of* `config.shtml`

The *<flastmod>* Tag

You use the `flastmod` tag to display the last modified date and time of a specified file. The last modified date is inserted into the SSI document when it is parsed. The `flastmod` tag uses two arguments:

◆ **file.** This option is used to locate a file with respect to the filename and the relative path to the directory, which is the default location for the SSI documents.

◆ **virtual.** This option is used to locate a filename and path that is relative to the DocumentRoot of the Apache Web server.

Consider the following example in which the last modified date of a specified file is displayed using the `flastmod` tag:

```
<HTML>
<HEAD>
<TITLE>Using the flastmod tag</TITLE>
</HEAD>
<BODY>
<H1><CENTER>Using the flastmod tag</CENTER></H1>
<!--#config timefmt="%A, %B %d %Y"-->
<H4><CENTER>You last modified the file on:</CENTER></H4>
<H4><CENTER><!--#flastmod file="config.shtml"--></CENTER></H4>
<!--#config timefmt="%H:%M %S %p"-->
<H4><CENTER>The time when you last modified the file was:</CENTER></H4>
<H4><CENTER><!--#flastmod file="config.shtml"--></CENTER></H4>
</BODY>
</HTML>
```

In the preceding example, note the following:

◆ The config tag is used with the timefmt argument to display the day of the week and the date on which the file was last modified. The %A, %B, %d, and %Y values are used to display the name of the day, month, date, and year, respectively.

◆ The flastmod tag is used to specify the name of the file for which the last modification details need to be displayed. The filename specified is config.shtml.

◆ The config tag is used again with the timefmt argument to specify the exact time the file was modified.

◆ The flastmod tag is used again to specify the name of the file for which the time of last modification needs to be displayed. The filename specified is config.shtml.

Figure 10.5 shows the Web page that displays the last modification details of the file config.shtml.

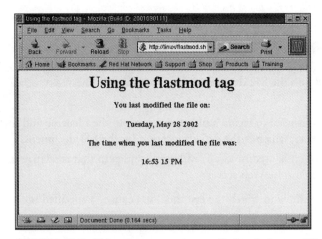

FIGURE 10.5 *Using the* flastmod *tag to display the last modification details of* config.shtml

The *<include>* Tag

You use the include tag to locate an external file, execute it, and return the output to the SSI document being parsed. Two arguments can be specified with this tag:

◆ **include file.** This argument is typically used to include HTML files whose contents need to be included in multiple Web site files. Examples of such files are footers, headers, and sidebars. When you intend to display a footer with the Web page, you specify the path to the HTML file that you want to use as footer. The path specified should be relative to the directory of the calling document. An absolute path should not be specified in this case because it might generate errors.

◆ **include virtual**. This argument is preferred when using the include tag. In this case, a relative rather than a relative path identifies the resource on the Web server. This is particularly useful because the location of the resource is made independent of the system path. When you use include virtual, mod_include creates a URL and then includes the document referenced by the URL in the calling document.

You can also use both of these methods to include CGI scripts. However, the include virtual argument is preferred over the include file argument for embedding the output generated by CGI scripts into server-parsed documents.

TIP

It is recommended that you use include virtual to include CGI scripts rather than exec cgi. Moreover, if your task requires passing the information present in an SSI document to an existing CGI script, the exec cgi method doesn't work. For this purpose, you will need to use the include virtual method.

Consider the following example, which illustrates how the include tag works. In the following example, I created the file include.shtml, which contains the following code:

```
<HTML>
<HEAD>
<TITLE>Using the include tag</TITLE>
</HEAD>
<BODY>
<H1><CENTER>Using the include tag</CENTER></H1>
<!--#config timefmt="%A"-->
<CENTER>Today is <!--#echo var="DATE_LOCAL"-->
<!--#config timefmt="%B %d, %Y"-->
and the date is <!--#echo var="DATE_LOCAL"--></CENTER>
<!--#include file="footer.shtml"-->
</BODY>
</HTML>
```

The preceding example indicates that an include file method is used to call a file named footer.shtml to be included in the document. The footer.shtml file contains the following text:

```
<HR>
</H1><CENTER>In case of a problem contact <A
HREF="admin@somedomain.com">admin@somedomain.com</A></CENTER></H1>
```

This file contains the e-mail ID of the person who should be contacted in case there is a problem with the site. It would be tedious and time consuming to add these lines of code for every page on the Web site. Luckily, the `include file` method is ideal for including footer information with every file. By using it, you ensure that the footer is displayed at the end of every file. Figure 10.6 shows the Web page with the footer below the contents of the page.

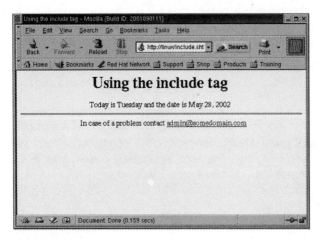

FIGURE 10-6 *Using the* `include` *tag to add a footer to a Web page*

The *<printenv>* Tag

This tag is the simplest SSI tag because, unlike other tags, it doesn't require arguments. As its name suggests, you can use the `printenv` tag to display all system environment variables in a single unformatted list. Because the `printenv` tag doesn't generate a formatted list of environment variables, you should use the `<pre>` and `<code>` HTML tags with it. The `<pre>` and `<code>` HTML tags enclose unformatted text in HTML pages in a comparatively readable format.

```
<HTML>
<HEAD>
<TITLE>Using the printenv tag</TITLE>
<BODY>
<H1><CENTER>Using the printenv tag</CENTER></H1>
<pre>
<!--#printenv -->
</pre>
</BODY>
</HTML>
```

In the preceding example, the `printenv` tag is used to display a list of all the environment variables. The `printenv` tag has been deliberately enclosed within the `<pre>` and `</pre>` HTML tags so that a formatted list appears. Figure 10.7 shows the Web page that appears when the `printenv` tag is used.

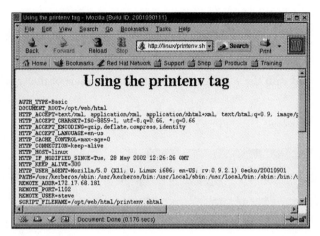

FIGURE 10.7 *Using the* `printenv` *tag to display a list of environment variables and their values*

The *<set>* Tag

You use the `set` tag to set a value for a variable. If the variable doesn't exist, it is created automatically when you use the `set` tag. These are the two attributes that are used with the `set` tag:

◆ `var`. The name of the variable to be set.

◆ `value`. The value attribute assigned to the variable set.

While using the `set` tag, you need to specify both the `var` and `value` attributes individually, as shown in the following example:

```
<!--#set var="somename" value="somevalue" -->
```

In the preceding syntax, a variable named `somename` is set with a value named `somevalue`. Consider this example, in which the `set` tag is used to set a variable and to assign a value to it:

```
<HTML>
<HEAD>
<TITLE>Using the set tag</TITLE>
</HEAD>
<BODY>
<H1><CENTER>Using the set tag</CENTER></H1>
```

```
<!--#set var="steve" value="Steve is a system administrator!"-->
<H2><CENTER><!--#echo var="steve"--></CENTER></H2>
</BODY>
</HTML>
```

In the preceding example, note the following:

◆ The set tag is used with the var argument to set a variable with the name steve.

◆ The value argument is used to set a value for the variable named steve.

◆ The echo tag is used with the var argument to display the value of the variable named steve.

Figure 10.8 displays the Web page that appears when the set tag is used.

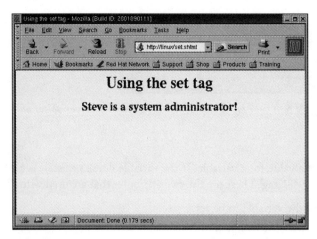

FIGURE 10.8 *Using the set tag to specify a name and a value for a variable*

Using Flow Control Elements in SSI

SSI is not a powerful programming language. It is a simple mechanism to generate dynamic Web pages. Therefore, all of the control structures that are available with a full-fledged programming language are not available with SSI. However, basic level of flow control can be implemented in SSI. SSI supports simple statements such as if and else. But these statements/operators don't support the function of nesting that is available with other programming languages. The syntax for using these operators is as follows:

```
<!--#if expr="any_condition"-->
    HTML code
<!--#elif expr="any_condition"-->
    HTML code
```

```
<!--#else -->
   HTML code
<!--#endif-->
```

In the preceding syntax, note the following:

- ◆ The if and else operators are used.
- ◆ The expr keyword is specified. This keyword should always be specified when you use these operators.
- ◆ The if expr element performs the same task as any other if statement in any programming language. You use it to check whether the specified condition is true. If the condition returns a true value, the HTML code that follows the if operator is executed. If the condition is false, the next elif statement is evaluated.
- ◆ The endif statement is specified to mark the end of the if statement.

You can specify several conditions while using flow control elements in SSI. Table 10.1 lists a few conditions and also explains when the condition will be true.

Another way to compare a string is to compare it with a regular expression. Say there are two strings, string1 and string2. If you want to express string2 as a regular expression, you will need to specify it as /string2/. Examine the following example:

```
<!--if expr=string1=/string2/-->
```

Table 10.1 Possible Conditions to Use with Flow Control Elements

Conditions	Explanation
somestring	Is true only when somestring contains a value. Is false when empty.
string1=string2	Is true only when the value of string1 is identical to value of string2.
string1>string2	Is true only when string1 is greater than string2.
string1<string2	Is true only when string1 is less than string2.
string1!=string2	Is true only when string1 is not equal to string2.
string1<=string2	Is true only when string1 is less than or equal to string2.
string1>=string2	Is true only when string1 is less than equal to string2
condition1&&condition2	Is true only when both condition1 and condition2 are true.
condition1||condiiton2	Is true if either of the specified conditions is true.

In the preceding example, you check whether the values of string1 and string2 match. But in this case, string2 is a regular expression.

Now consider this example, which demonstrates the use of flow control elements:

```
<HTML>
<HEAD>
<TITLE>This is a test for flow control</TITLE>
</HEAD>
<BODY>
<H1><CENTER>This is a test for flow control</CENTER></H1>

<!--#if expr="$REMOTE_ADDR=/^172.17.68./"-->
<H4><CENTER>Your IP address is <!--#echo var="REMOTE_ADDR"--></CENTER>
</H4>
<H4><CENTER>Your computer belongs to a subnet which is allowed access to
this site!</CENTER></H4>

<!--#elif expr="$REMOTE_ADDR=/^172.17.69.68/"-->
<H4><CENTER>Your IP address is <!--#echo var="REMOTE_ADDR"--></CENTER>
</H4>
<H4><CENTER>Your computer belongs to a subnet that is denied access to
this site!</CENTER></H4>

<!--#else-->
<H4><CENTER>You are connecting from a remote network!</CENTER></H4>

<!--#endif-->
</BODY>
</HTML>
```

In the preceding code, note the following:

◆ The if statement is used to check the value of the variable, REMOTE_ADDR. If the value of this variable, which is an IP address, begins with 172.17.68., a message indicating that the client is allowed access is displayed.

◆ The elif statement is used to check another condition. In this condition, the client whose IP address begins with 172.17.69. is displayed a message indicating that access is denied.

◆ The else statement is used to specify another message for all remote clients whose IP addresses don't match any of the aforementioned criteria.

Figure 10.9 shows the Web page that appears when I connect from a Windows client whose IP address is 172.17.68.222.

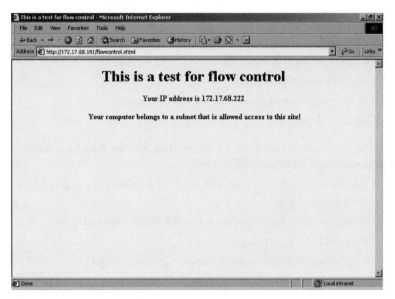

FIGURE 10-9 *The Web page that appears when you connect from a Windows client on the local intranet*

Summary

In this chapter, I discussed server-side includes. I started with a brief introduction to server-side includes and how they are used. Next, I discussed the SSI tags and how they are embedded in HTML to generate dynamic Web pages. Finally, I discussed the concept of flow control in SSI where I explained how conditionals, such as `if` and `else`, are used with SSI.

Check Your Understanding

Multiple Choice Questions

1. Which of the following is not possible with respect to SSI?

   a. Access environment variables

   b. Create dynamic Web pages

   c. Create complex programs using nested operators

   d. Call a CGI program

2. Which of the following methods for configuring SSI for Apache is not recommended if you already have an existing Web site?

   a. Uncommenting the AddType and AddHandler directives in httpd.conf to allow server-side parsing

   b. Adding the XBitHack directive manually in the httpd.conf file

   c. Using MIME type configuration

   d. Using .htaccess files to specify the configuration directives

3. Which of the following strings is used with the config timefmt option to display a weekday in abbreviated form?

   a. %a

   b. %A

   c. %b

   d. %B

4. Which of the following SSI tags are used to display the last modified information about a file?

   a. U

   b. printenv

   c. set

   d. flastmod

5. Which of the following SSI tags is used to assign a name and value to a variable?

   a. exec

   b. set

   c. include

   d. config

Answers

Multiple Choice Answers

1. c. It is not possible to create complex programs in SSI using nested operators because SSI doesn't support nested operators.

2. a. For existing Web sites it is not recommended that you configure the Web server for SSI by uncommenting the AddType and AddHandler directives in httpd.conf. This would involve changing the file extensions for all the existing Web pages to .shtml, which is a tedious and time-consuming task.

3. a. The %a string is used to display the weekday in abbreviated form.

4. d. The flastmod tag is used to display information about when a particular file was last modified.

5. b. The set tag is used to assign a name and value to a variable. The var argument is used with the set tag to assign a name to the variable, and the value argument is used to assign a value to the variable.

Chapter 11

Security is an integral part of life. Anything important in your life needs to be secured in some way. This could be your house, which you keep locked when you're away, or money that you keep safe in a bank. In simple language, *security* is a basic activity that you need to perform in order to safeguard your resources. The same holds true for a Web server. In today's Internet age, growing awareness and technical expertise have allowed malicious people to find and exploit system vulnerabilities. Security stays a step ahead by performing a systematic check to discover vulnerabilities and loopholes and then taking appropriate corrective actions.

An essential part of Web server administration is ensuring that the resources on the server are not tampered with. Remember the adage, "An ounce of prevention is worth a pound of cure"—that's what security is all about. Security involves protecting the resources of a Web server by preventing unauthorized access to it.

These days, you can't be sure of the security of your Web server, and there is no 100 percent foolproof mechanism for ensuring security. However, this doesn't mean that you can't do anything. Security is an on-going activity that you should take seriously. Many companies hire their own security experts to maintain the security of their Web servers, but every Web server administrator should be familiar with the basic tasks required to ensure security. Although security is an expense that doesn't generate revenue, it ensures that there are minimal contingencies.

One way to keep a Web server secure is to configure such that Internet users are unable to access resources on it. However, this would negate the purpose of having a Web server in the first place. The real challenge is giving legitimate Internet users access to your Web server and, at the same time, restricting access to users with malicious intentions.

Security also involves estimating the costs involved and ensuring that the investment doesn't exceed the benefits. In other words, it would be highly illogical to buy a $1,000 safe to secure a $10 watch.

In this chapter, I first discuss the important issues concerning security of the Apache Web server. Then I discuss basic security needs that Web server administrators should meet when using Apache and operating system and network security that will help you create a sound security plan.

Securing Web Server Files

A Web server is a repository of numerous resources. These resources need to be protected from unauthorized access at all times. Implementing a strong security policy is the only logical solution to this state of affairs. The issue is how to protect resources.

All Web server files are essentially disk files, which, if accessed by an unauthorized user, could provide important information to an unintended participant. The root cause for several security problems is poorly managed files. You can address this problem by taking the following measures:

◆ Setting appropriate access rights
◆ Setting appropriate symbolic links
◆ Using the Indexes option with care

Setting Appropriate Access Rights

The way the Apache Web server operates and the access rights allowed to the server depend on the access rights of the user ID running the Apache service. In Linux systems, the root user starts the Apache Web server. However, when the client requests need to be answered, a non-root user runs Apache. By default, in Red Hat Linux 7.2, the user that runs the Apache service is apache. However, when you compile Apache using the source code, you can designate the name of an alternate user. In Chapter 3, "Installing Apache," I specified the user www for running Apache instead of apache.

All tasks that Apache performs are dependent on the access rights of the user who is running Apache. So, take extra care in assigning access rights or privileges to the user running the Apache service.

Most files that assist in Apache functioning are under the server root directory. However, there are a few exceptions, such as .htaccess files or database authentication files. In regards to Apache administration, the server that is run by the non-root user has considerably fewer privileges than the root user. Therefore, the server doesn't have the ability to alter the configuration files that are used to control Apache. The only Apache-related files that can be controlled by the server are the log files that are appended by the server from time to time. This is the default setting and should not be altered. In simpler language, the server should not be allowed to write to main configuration files that control the functioning of the Apache Web server. The administrator (the root user) should be the only user who has the privilege of writing to the main configuration files.

Allowing the server to write to main configuration files can result in server vulnerablity. In such a situation, a poorly configured option could help an unauthorized user access the resources on the server and cause potential damage.

In addition to the server root directory, the document root directory should have restricted access. As much as possible, the document root directory should be read-only for the user ID used by the Web server. This is not a mandatory rule; a few situations might require that the user ID be given access rights that allow writing to or executing the files in the document root. In such situations, you should move these files to a sub-directory in the document root so that security is not compromised.

The bottom line is that Apache-related files and Web site files should be read-only unless you want to allow all users to alter the files. So, grant modify permissions with care.

Setting Appropriate Symbolic Links

Symbolic links are a powerful concept and are used only with UNIX-based operating systems. Symbolic links, also known as *soft links*, are utilized to point to a file that a user can work on from an alternate location. If saved, modifications are applied to all links that point to the file and to the original file.

Administrators often create symbolic links for convenience. However, this could also lead to a security threat. If the administrator ends up creating a lot of symbolic links, it might eventually become difficult to keep track of them. So, the symbolic links on a Linux system should be tracked at regular intervals to ensure that an important file cannot be accessed from an alternate location.

You need to check the symbolic links that point to your document root directory and determine whether these links are actually required. Disable unnecessary links. You can use the following command to list the symbolic links in a particular directory:

```
#find /opt/web/html -type 1 -print
```

In the preceding example, note the following:

◆ The `find` command is used to locate the symbolic links for the document root directory `/opt/web/html`.

◆ The `-type` command option is used to specify that the `find` command should locate only the symbolic links.

◆ The `1` is the type of file to be located. The letter `1` is used to specify that only symbolic links should be listed.

◆ The `-print` option is used to display the search results on the screen.

While using Apache Web server, you can utilize different directives to allow or disallow the use of symbolic links. Use the `Options` directive to specify whether symbolic links should be used. Setting the `FollowSymLinks` value for the `Options` directive can help you use symbolic links while serving documents via Web. The `FollowSymLinks` option indicates that the Apache Web server will follow the symbolic links to locate the file to which they point. In other words, if this option is not used, Apache will not be able to use symbolic links. Don't use this option if you are not using symbolic links. If you do decide to use symbolic links, use them carefully and check the links at regular intervals so that unauthorized users don't gain access to files that should, under normal circumstances, be inaccessible to them.

In Apache, another directive, the `FollowSymLinksIfOwnerMatch` directive, is also used to allow symbolic links. However, by reading the name of this directive carefully, you'll notice that a condition is attached. This directive allows a user to access a file using the symbolic link if, and only if, the user is the owner of both the original file and the symbolic link. Apache determines the authenticity of the user accessing the file by examining the user ID prior to granting access to the file.

If you want to follow a stringent security model, use the `FollowSymLinksIfOwnerMatch` directive in most cases. Doing so ensures that the user accessing the file is the file owner.

Using the *Indexes* Option with Care

Whenever a request is sent to the Apache Web server, the request transforms to a disk file, which is then downloaded by the client browser. Sometimes, the URL specified by the client transforms into a directory rather than a file. In such a situation, Apache can respond in several ways.

◆ It can look for a special file in the directory, process it, and then return it to the client. The best example is the index.html file, which is returned automatically without requiring the client to explicitly specify it in the request URL.

◆ It can display the complete list of files in the directory in question.

◆ It can display an error message indicating that the client is not allowed to access the requested resource.

Each of these approaches work hand-in-hand. When Apache first receives a request, it checks the DirectoryIndex directive. If files are listed in the DirectoryIndex directive, the Apache Web server extracts the first of the listed files, processes it, and returns it to the client.

If no files are specified in the DirectoryIndex directive, Apache checks the status of the Indexes option. If this option is not enabled, Apache returns an error message indicating that the requested resource cannot be made available. In this situation, Apache returns the 403 status code, which means that access to the requested resource is denied.

Another possibility is that you have enabled the Indexes option in the httpd.conf file. This will result in Apache displaying a complete list of files in the directory in question. You can customize the display of the files using the FancyIndexes option.

In terms of security, you should ensure that the directories accessible through your Web server are carefully checked. Negligence on your part could inadvertently reveal sensitive information. If not properly configured, the Indexes option can prove to be a source of information such as filenames that shouldn't be displayed to the users. Adding lines such as Options - Indexes in the <Directory> container in httpd.conf or .htaccess files can ensure a higher level of security. The leading - in the configuration means that the option will be turned off for the specific directory without affecting the other directories.

Safeguarding URLs

In addition to securing Web server files, another important aspect of security is to safeguard URLs. This is essential because merely setting access rights for a file doesn't necessarily mean that the filename is hidden from the user. A user might not have access to a file, but may be allowed to read the name of the file. In some situations, even revealing the name of the file can cause potential harm to system resources, because the name of the file might indicate the information's degree of sensitivity. Protecting URLs helps to prevent the divulging of even small pieces of information and ensures that this information is restricted to specific users only. Ensuring security at this level is mandated when you undertake Web hosting on a large scale, when potentially millions of users have access to your site at any point in time.

Mandatory and Discretionary Access

To ensure that you maintain a high level of security for your Web site, you must be familiar with the concepts *mandatory access control (MAC)* and *discretionary access control (DAC)*.

Mandatory access control is based on certain characteristics possessed by the requester. The requestor has absolutely no control over these characteristics. On the other hand, discretionary access control requires a user to specify certain details that, if genuine, will help the requestor access a particular resource.

Access control is based on the following factors:

◆ What you have

◆ What you know

◆ Who you are

The first factor, "what you have," allows access depending on the possession of a user. Consider the example of a bank locker: Only a single key opens the locker. In such a case, your ability to access the valuables in the locker depends solely on having possession of that key.

The second factor, "what you know," allows access depending on specific credentials that should be valid. Consider the example of a user checking his e-mail: The user will be able to check e-mail only after supplying a valid password. Only if the user remembers the password will he be able to access mail.

The third attribute, "what you are," allows access depending on certain characteristics possessed by the user. Unlike other factors, the user has no control over this one. Consider the example of access by use of a fingerprint: An individual's fingerprint is distinct from everyone else's fingerprint, and cannot be altered. As a result, a user cannot gain access if his fingerprint is rejected.

 NOTE

These three attributes have special relevance to security and can be used in a combination to allow or deny access. Consider the example of an ATM machine: In order to withdraw money, you first need to insert your ATM card and then specify the PIN number to gain access to your savings account.

These three factors affect the discretionary and mandatory access control mechanisms. Discretionary access control, as the name suggests, is based on the discretion of the user. This means that the user should be involved in specifying the credentials that will help him access the resources on the server. You can say that discretionary access control mechanisms operate on the "what you know" attribute. If you know the password, you can access a resource; if you don't know the password, you can't access a resource.

On the other hand, mandatory access control mechanisms work on the "what you are" factor. A common way of restricting access is to deny access to specific IP addresses. An IP address is something that cannot be changed randomly. Therefore, the user doesn't have control of the IP address that he is using to connect to the server.

The most common way to implement discretionary access control is to allow access on the basis of a username and a password. For mandatory access control, a good example is restricting access based on the IP address of the client placing the request.

Another way of distinguishing between discretionary and mandatory access control is by comparing the way failures are handled. In the case of discretionary access control, when you specify an incorrect password, you get another opportunity to restate the password. In the case of mandatory access control, when you are restricted on the basis of your IP address, you simply receive a "forbidden" error.

Access Control, Authentication, and Authorization

Apache uses three basic mechanisms to secure resources on the Web server. These mechanisms are *access control, authentication,* and *authorization.* All three mechanisms are closely linked to one another.

◆ **Access control**. Access control is a powerful mechanism that you can use to allow or restrict access to resources on the Apache Web server. With access control, the HTTP request is rejected or accepted depending on the information contained in the HTTP request headers or the encapsulating IP packet.

◆ **Authentication**. Authentication is a mechanism used to validate the identity of a user. In order to prove his authenticity, the user specifies a unique combination of username and password to gain access to the resources on the Web server. The credentials supplied by the user can also be digital certificates, which are considered to be a more elaborate method of authentication.

◆ **Authorization**. Authorization refers to the permissions that a user possesses for a resource on the Web server. Authorization is different than authentication because authentication merely validates the credentials of the user, whereas the access rights possessed by the user determine whether a user is authorized to access a resource.

In Apache, you can easily implement the modules that are responsible for controlling these mechanisms. Regardless of the complexity of the concepts of access control, authentication, and authorization, all HTTP transactions result in one of two outcomes: the transaction is accepted or it is rejected.

 NOTE

I discuss access control, authentication, and authorization in detail in Chapter 5, "Implementing Access Control in Apache."

Often-Neglected Security Concerns

In this section, I introduce the most common security concerns that you'll face as a system administrator. The concepts discussed are simple but useful guidelines that, in my experience, have proven useful. No threat is as harmful as a system administrator's negligence; however, the following information can help you avoid making mistakes that might damage your system.

Always Back Up the Configuration File

No matter how experienced a Web server administrator you are, it is wise to always make a back up of the original configuration file before making any changes to it. You might make a mistake while configuring the server and then be unable to track it down later.

Consider a situation in which you start making changes to the configuration file without making a backup. After making the required changes, you restart Apache but the changes you made aren't taking effect. Instead, the Web pages are displaying improperly, and you are encountering error messages. You had made changes with the intention of adding more functionality to your Apache server, but you ended up messing up your configuration file! Such situations can cause server downtime, and if your site is frequented by millions of users, you cannot take your sweet time rectifying the error.

What you should have done, of course, was to make a backup before you started editing the configuration file. You do so as follows:

```
#cp /usr/local/apache/conf/httpd.conf //usr/local/apache/conf/httpd.conf.bak
```

In the preceding command, I copied the `httpd.conf` file with a different name. I can always revert to the original configuration file if I make a mistake in editing the configuration file.

Never Disclose Sensitive Information

As an administrator, you must keep some information an absolute secret. Information shared with even a single individual ceases to remain confidential. Following are some things you should never do if you're serious about maintaining security:

◆ **Share system passwords.** Ensure that passwords are kept secret. In case of dire circumstances, the passwords should be given only to a trusted individual.

◆ **Grant server access.** Never grant server access to unknown or unreliable people. A server is certainly the most important entity, and it contains a great deal of sensitive information. A user with malicious intentions could misuse this information.

◆ **Publicly declare what you do to secure your Web server.** You might implement countless procedures to ensure the security for your Web server. However, these efforts are zilch if you publicly share what you have done for security. People who have a fair idea about how to intrude into a server could work on the hints you provide to break through the security barrier.

TIP

In certain cases it might be essential to disclose your security setup. For example, Web-hosting companies publicize their setup to potential clients so that the clients know what all has been done to secure the server. In such cases you should use discretion when disclosing sensitive information.

Keep Updated

You need to keep abreast of the changes in the world of Apache. A sensible proposition is to sign up with sites that send security updates and security-related information. This helps you decide what extra steps you need to take for additional security. The official Apache site is a good reference point for digging up information related to security. You will also find several links to useful sites that give pointers on maintaining a secure Web server. Another healthy practice is to apply bug fixes and patches as they are released. Doing so helps make your server less vulnerable to security threats.

TIP

Keep abreast of other (not Apache specific) security information that could affect your server. This would involve updating your server with kernel patches and glibc vulnerabilities.

Check Logs at Regular Intervals

The Apache Web server uses a powerful mechanism to keep track of activities. It does so by using log files. Log files store information related to failures of the software to perform a specific action. They also store generic information related to the operation of the Apache Web server. To be an efficient administrator, check the log files at regular intervals. The log files not only give you insight into the functioning of the Web server, but also help you determine whether intruders are trying to access your Web server. Keeping an eye on the log files warns you about problems that might crop up at a later stage. For example, by examining the logs, you can keep a track of unsuccessful logon attempts made by an unauthorized user. Also, you can become aware of other warning messages generated by the Apache Web server. One way to keep a constant check on log files is to use log watcher software that extracts suspicious records from the log files and mails them regularly.

CAUTION

In addition to keeping an eye on the logs generated by the Apache Web server, it is important to keep a regular check on the Linux log files. Don't forget that the Apache Web server is installed on your Linux system, and the security of your Linux system is equally important. No matter how many pains you take to secure Apache, unless your requirement of basic platform security is met, your efforts will be futile.

Double-Check Downloaded Scripts

If you download scripts for use on your Apache Web server, be sure to change the filenames so that intruders can't easily determine the name of the script. You should also carefully read the contents of a downloaded script before putting it to use; if the script is not downloaded from an authentic site, the script might contain commands that can harm your server. In addition, you should change the default names of log files and use package signatures while downloading. Package signatures ensure the authenticity of the package being downloaded.

Password Management

Passwords are the most commonly used means of securing resources on an operating system and a Web server. As long as the intruder does not know the passwords, a system cannot be easily harmed. However, some individuals can figure out a poorly chosen password with ease. Take special care in choosing a root password, because the root password is the most important password in a Linux system. Passwords should be long and difficult to figure out. Preferably, they should not be based on a word in the dictionary and should be a combination of letters and numbers.

Make Regular Backups

An absolutely essential part of system administration is making regular backups. Backups ensure that data is not lost if an unforeseen event occurs. If your setup doesn't include a daily backup, then do weekly backups. One way of making backups is to use tapes, which can accommodate a large amount of data.

If you find that tapes are a burden, Linux provides you with an ideal utility for making backups, the tar utility. tar stands for *tape archive*. Just execute a command, and the data you're backing up is wrapped into a *tarball* (a tar file). Later, you can use FTP to transfer this tarball to a different machine, preferably a computer used solely for backups. (Transferring thousands of small files using FTP would take up too much of your time, resources, and effort.)

If you are one of the "smarter administrators," go ahead and write a script and set it as a *cron* (a daemon that helps schedule the execution of commands) job to ensure that backups are automated. Then all you need to do is transfer the tar file to the backup server by using FTP.

To use the tar utility, type the following command:

```
#tar cvf dailybackup.tar /usr/local/apache/somedir
```

In the preceding command, the tar utility is used to make backups of the contents in the somedir directory. After using the tar utility, you also have the option of compressing the tar file so that it occupies minimal space on the backup server. To do so, use the following command:

```
#gzip dailybackup.tar
```

In the preceding command, the gzip (GNU Zip) utility is used to compress the tar file that you created. Remember that after you use the gzip utility the backup file will possess a .tar.gz extension. Files compressed using the gzip utility can also be uncompressed using WinZip on Windows platforms.

Never Run Server as Root

The word *root* is the most powerful four-letter word in the world of the Linux operating system. You should, therefore, reserve the root user ID for the most important services or processes. This rule also applies to the Web server. As a result, you should never run the Apache Web server with the root user ID—or, for that matter, any user ID that has root privileges on your Linux machine. Typically, users that have administrative privileges are lp, daemon, and bin. In addition, you should ensure that the user is in a group of its own. For example, if Apache is being run as a user named www, the group to which this user belongs should also be www. The group to which the Apache user ID belongs should not have special permissions.

If you don't follow this guideline, you risk some serious problems. For example, say that a script or application is being run as a root user on a Linux machine. In such a scenario, it is possible for a user to exploit a loophole in the Linux script and gain access to your system.

Another situation might require the Apache Web server to write to files in a Linux system. In this situation, if Apache is being run with root privileges, it is quite possible that Apache gains access to configuration files. When such vulnerability exists, an intruder can easily access important files and damage them.

Vulnerabilities in Server Side Includes

I discussed server side includes in Chapter 10, "Using Server Side Includes." Although using server side includes is a good idea for generating dynamic content on the Web site, you must, as a system administrator, ensure that using server side includes doesn't leave any security loopholes. There are many reasons for using server side includes. However, doing so poses potential security risks, including the following:

◆ Increased load on the server. When you enable server side includes, the Apache Web server tries to parse each of the Web pages to look for SSI tags. This results in a load increase on the server. The load could be very heavy if you are running Apache Web server in a shared server environment.

◆ Using the "exec cmd" element in SSI-enabled files. This element allows the execution of CGI scripts or other programs under the permissions of the user specified in the User directive and the group specified in the Group directive. The user and group specified in these directives are the ones that Apache uses. You need to closely monitor whether the CGI scripts or programs being executed by the Web server pose any risk to the setup.

Every problem has a solution. You can take certain measures to address problems while using SSI. Consider the following guidelines before using server side includes for user-generated pages:

◆ Avoid using the .shtml extension for files that require a user to append them or even create them.

◆ Create a script that ensures the HTML code added by the user doesn't contain comments. Server side includes are used within comments. Therefore, if the comments are removed from the HTML contributed by user input, there will be less possibility for a user executing a system command using server side includes.

◆ Disable the feature for automatically executing server side includes. You can do so by using the following directive in the .htaccess file:

```
Options IIncludesNoExec
```

◆ Another alternative is to place all user-generated files in the same directory. Then create an .htaccess file for the same directory and set the value of the Options directive as none. If the Options directive is specified the value none, it will not be possible to use server side includes for the files in the directory.

```
Options None
```

◆ Avoid using server side includes for user-generated pages; that is, if you are using an application that allows users to enter HTML scripts, avoid using server side includes. This is because it is possible to execute system commands using server side includes.

◆ Never enable SSI for .html and .htm files. This causes the Web server to parse each and every Web page whether or not the Web page contains SSI tags. The best way to counter this problem is to use a separate extension, .shtml, for Web pages in which you use SSI tags.

◆ You can run scripts and programs using SSI tags within the Web pages. If you really don't want to run executables using SSI tags, you should disable the ability to run scripts and programs from SSI pages. But, if you think that you need the ability to run executable files using SSI, another solution is to use suEXEC. SuExec was introduced with Apache 1.2. This feature helps you run CGI and SSI programs. The only difference is that suEXEC doesn't use the user ID of the calling Web server. If used properly, this feature can help reduce a lot of risks associated with the execution of CGI and SSI pages.

NOTE

I discussed suEXEC in more detail in Chapter 7, "Dynamic Content With CGI."

CGI-Related Security Issues

This section covers a few CGI-related issues that can help you ensure maximum security for your Web server. CGI scripts are perhaps the most vulnerable feature in the Apache Web server. A poor configuration or even fragile (poorly written) CGI code can result in users gaining unauthorized access and, as a result, damaging the setup. Your best approach is to take precautions that make the Web server less vulnerable to attacks. The following topics discuss a few guidelines that you should always keep in mind.

Script Aliased CGI

Script Aliased CGI requires all the CGI scripts to be stored in a single directory. This option is considered to be more secure than the non-script aliased CGI option. Only the root user (administrator) and a few trusted users are given write access to the directory containing all the CGI scripts. However, using script aliased CGI would be more beneficial if the administrator could afford to check each and every script added to the directory for vulnerabilities. This option is most popular for sites that use CGI.

Non-Script Aliased CGI

As just discussed, the non-script aliased CGI option is the less-preferred option because it allows users to execute CGI scripts in any directory—in other words, no directory is used exclusively for storing CGI scripts. However, you should consider using this option under the following circumstances:

◆ When all users accessing your system are trusted. This means that none of the users will accidentally or deliberately write scripts that expose your system to a security attack.

◆ When you are using Apache as an intranet Web server, and you choose not to worry much about security.

◆ If your site has no users.

◆ If users seldom visit your site.

CGI in General

As an administrator, you should not trust the developers to write CGI scripts and programs that don't pose a threat to security either deliberately or accidentally. You should be aware of the fact that all CGI scripts will run as the same user in Apache. The possibility exists that the scripts written by one developer might clash with the scripts written by another developer.

One way to ensure that CGI scripts written by different developers don't collide and have a negative impact on security is to check the scripts before uploading them. However, a better alternative is to use the suEXEC feature in Apache. This feature allows you to run CGI scripts as other users. As a result, each developer can run his scripts as a different user.

In addition to the suEXEC feature, you also have the option of using the CGIWrap utility. CGIWrap is a gateway program that you can use to execute CGI scripts on the server side without compromising security.

Offsite Execution of CGI Scripts

If not used properly, CGI scripts can create numerous opportunities for vulnerability. When using CGI scripts, you need to take steps to disallow offsite execution of these scripts. The Webmaster should always pay attention to the location from which a CGI script is called. The location of the CGI script should not allow the user to access and modify the script. If allowed, the user could modify the variable names and could also interfere with the orderly execution of scripts.

To avoid such a situation, always use the CGI environment variable named HTTP_REFERER. This environment variable tries to prevent programs outside your site from linking to your scripts.

Passing Unchecked CGI Input to the Linux Console

If you are using CGI scripts that call for executing Linux commands, you should be extra careful. The situation is more sensitive if you are allowing users to execute CGI scripts (that allow execution of commands) without checking the presence of Linux shell meta characters.

Consider the following example of a worst-case scenario in which you prompt the user to enter the e-mail ID on the command prompt. The user enters the following e-mail ID:

```
nobody@somedomain.com; /bin/rm -r /[a-z]*
```

In the preceding example, assuming that the server is running as a root user, note the following:

◆ The use of the shell meta character ; (the semicolon) indicates the end of the line to the operating system.

◆ The command that follows the semicolon is interpreted as a valid command by the operating system and is executed as a result, deleting the contents of the /bin directory.

◆ The /bin directory contains all the binary files, which if deleted will make the system unstable. As a consequence, you will need to reinstall the entire operating system.

The preceding example examined how allowing execution of CGI scripts from the console without checking for the presence of shell meta characters could prove harmful. Be sure to avoid such situations. If you really want to allow execution of CGI scripts with user input from the Linux console, write a script that checks for illegal characters that are specified by a user with malicious intentions.

Security for .htaccess Files

To always be on the safe side, you should ensure that users are not allowed to set up .htaccess files that could override the original settings in the Apache configuration file. This could have a negative impact on the security of the site. You need to prevent the use of .htaccess files in all directories other than those specifically enabled. You can do so by setting the AllowOverride directive within the Directory directive, as shown here:

```
<Directory /somedir>
AllowOverride None
</Directory>
```

Setting the None value to the AllowOverride directive can prevent the use of .htaccess files in all directives other than those specifically enabled.

Disabling Unnecessary Services

As a Web server administrator, you can disable or eliminate the services that you don't really use. These services will differ based on your requirements. To make your system safer, also close open ports that are not used. In this section, I focus on the services that can be disabled based on how you want to use the Apache Web server. In short, you can use the Apache Web server for the following purposes:

◆ **Public Web host**. This type of Web host provides Internet connections and is available 24 hours a day. Anybody connected to the Internet can access the resources on a public Web host.

◆ **Private and extranet Web host**. The hosts that provide Internet connectivity to limited people fall in the category of private and extranet Web hosts.

◆ **Intranet Web host**. Set up an intranet Web host to allow access to the resources on the Web server only to users on the local intranet. This type of host doesn't have Internet connectivity.

Depending on the type of host you are using, you can decide which services to keep and which to discard. For example, if you are using an intranet host, you can provide additional network services such as Telnet and FTP. However, this is not possible if you are using a public Web host. Web hosts are more vulnerable to security attacks, and it is more difficult to manage thousands of users connected at the same time.

The default Linux installation includes many services that you can do without. Here is a list of the services that you can eliminate if you are using Apache as a public Web host:

◆ Telnet

◆ File Transfer Protocol (FTP)

◆ The `finger` utility

◆ Network File System (NFS)

◆ Samba server

◆ Remote services

◆ Other RPC services

Telnet

You use the `telnet` command to log in to a server from a remote client. With this useful command, you can configure and administer Apache from a remote location. However, you need to consider certain things before allowing Telnet to your Web server:

◆ **Disable Telnet**. I strongly recommend that you disable Telnet for non-root users. Although `telnet` is a useful utility, passwords specified during a connection are transmitted as clear text. It is quite possible for an individual to intercept the connection and determine the password, so you should opt for disabling Telnet unless it is really required.

◆ **Use Secure Shell (SSH)**. SSH allows secure remote login. A SSH connection is more secure than a Telnet connection because the passwords are encrypted before transmission. As a result, it is very difficult to crack a password specified at the time of connection.

 TIP

Because of its security features, I strongly recommend SSH as the only preferred method for remote administration.

FTP

File Transfer Protocol (FTP) is a standard mechanism used on a Linux system to exchange files among different systems. FTP is a convenient way for clients to download and upload files. You can use this protocol as an alternative to HTTP connections. However, consider the following information before deciding whether to use FTP.

FTP connections are preferred for use with intranet or private Web hosts because the threat of security attacks is not too high with these types of hosts. However, avoid enabling FTP service if your Web server is a publicly accessible host. For public Web servers, allowing anonymous FTP can pose a considerable threat, as indicated in the following examples:

- ◆ FTP can be used by externally by a user with the malicious intent of skipping your firewall.
- ◆ The directories in an FTP server can be accessed and modified by users if write permission is granted. This vulnerability could be exploited to put junk data in the directories.
- ◆ A poorly managed FTP server could allow users to gain privileged access to the resources and damage them.

If, after reading the preceding information, you still think that FTP is essential, be sure to use it on a dedicated server that operates in isolation. Here are a few precautions that you can take to secure an FTP server:

- ◆ Use log files to constantly monitor user activity on the FTP server.
- ◆ Deny non-root users the right to use specific commands such as `chmod` and `rm`.
- ◆ Place the FTP files in a separate file system. This way, even if the system is hacked, damage will be inflicted to only that particular file system.

The *finger* Utility

You use the `finger` utility to look up user-specific information. You just provide the username, and all the necessary details pertaining to that user are displayed. You can use this utility to display the following important information about a user:

- ◆ **Username.** The username created on the system.
- ◆ **Real name.** The real name of the user.
- ◆ **Shell.** The default shell used by a specific user after logging in.
- ◆ **Directory.** The default home directory of the user.
- ◆ **Telephone number.** The user's telephone number, if specified.

Consider the following example, which shows the use of the `finger` utility:

```
[root@linux root]# finger -l
Login: steve                          Name: (null)
Directory: /home/steve                Shell: /bin/bash
```

```
On since Mon Jun 17 14:00 (IST) on pts/1 from 172.17.68.222
   57 seconds idle
No mail.
No Plan.


Login: linda                        Name: (null)
Directory: /home/linda              Shell: /bin/bash
On since Mon Jun 17 14:02 (IST) on pts/2 from 172.17.68.181
   9 seconds idle
No mail.
No Plan.
```

As you can see in the preceding output, using the -l option with the finger command can disclose a great deal of information about a user who is logged in (and intruders could use this information to track users). Your safest approach is to disable the finger utility.

Network File System (NFS)

The *Network File System (NFS)* is a handy mechanism that lets users access file systems present on a remote computer. Mounting the remote file system from afar allows users to access the files and directories from a network file system as though it were a local file system. Using NFS has benefits as well as security threats. I will first discuss the benefits of using NFS and then discuss the precautions to take when doing so.

By using NFS, you can

◆ **share a central directory that can be accessed by each user.** This directory can contain important tools accessible to all workstations of a particular class.

◆ **share default home directories of users.** This enables users to access their files even if they log on to another computer.

◆ **install an operating system.** You can install an operating system on different computers by exporting the file system of a NFS server.

Although using NFS can prove highly useful for internal Web servers, be sure to take these precautions if you use it:

◆ Always create a separate file system if you intend to export it to other computers on the network.

◆ If possible, export the file systems with read-only permissions.

◆ Keep the default NFS server setting that disallows access to remote users even if they are logged in as root.

◆ Avoid exporting the root file system.

◆ Allow portmapper (a software that allows remote hosts to determine the status of ports on a computer) access for only trusted hosts. One way to do this is to add portmapper and the allowed hosts list to the hosts.allow file that is located in the /etc directory. Then add portmapper to the hosts.deny file and specify the value ALL. These steps allow only the hosts specified in the hosts.allow file to use portmapper.

 CAUTION

Don't use NFS if you are using Apache as a public Web server. In this case, the benefits of using NFS are greatly overshadowed by the possible risks of using it.

Samba Server

Samba server is configured on a Linux server to achieve interoperability between the Linux and Windows computers on the intranet. The main configuration file of Samba is smb.conf, which is located in the /etc/samba directory in Linux. Although this is a useful utility that can enable file sharing among computers running Windows and Linux, use it only when you use Apache as an intranet Web server. It is best to disable this service if you plan to use Apache as a public Web server.

Remote Services

The remote services include different commands that you can use to perform several tasks from the command prompt. You can use most of these commands for interactivity with different hosts on a network. These services are best used in closed environments where only a limited number of clients will be using them. Don't use them when you are using Apache as a public Web server. The services or utilities that I categorize as remote services include the following:

◆ rshd
◆ rlogin
◆ rexec
◆ rwhod

rshd

The Remote Shell Server (rshd) allows a user to execute commands from a remote system. Users can connect to the server using a client program called rsh to log in and then execute commands. It is strongly recommended that you disable rshd for Apache if it is being used as a public Web server, in order to decrease the threat of a security attack.

rlogin

The rlogin utility is similar to the telnet utility. After you log in to a system using rlogin, you will notice that commands execute in exactly the same way they would if you were using telnet. The only difference between rlogin and telnet is that the former allows you to log in to trusted hosts without specifying any credentials. Disable this utility if you plan to use Apache as a public Web server.

rexec

Remote Execution Services (rexec) are somewhat outdated. However, they are still used in some Linux systems. This utility allows users to execute commands on a remote host. This utility is quite similar to the rsh utility with which a user can log on to a remote shell on a remote computer. The only difference between the rsh utility and the rexec utility is that the former requires the user to specify a password for successful connection. Disable this utility if you are using Apache as a public Web server.

rwho

Use the Remote who (rwho) to display the information about the users currently logged on. This utility is similar to the who utility used in Linux to determine the currently logged on users. The only difference is that when using the rwho utility, you can display the information of users who are logged on a remote system. Disable this utility if you are using Apache as a public Web server. This utility can leak out sensitive information related to the currently logged on users to a hacker who can then build user lists and usage timetables based on the information.

Other RPC Services

You should disable certain Remote Procedure Calls (RPC) services to ensure maximum security for your Web server and your operating system. A few of these RPC services are as follows:

- The rpc.ruserd service
- The rwalld service
- The rstatd service

The rpc.ruserd Service

This service can expose sensitive information to potential intruders. The results of this service are similar to those of the finger utility. The ruser command that is associated with this service is used to display a list of users logged in to machines on local network.

The rwalld Service

Use this service to send messages to users logged on to a host. The command `rwall` that is associated with this service is of no use and should be disabled; doing so could prevent troublesome users from sending gibberish messages on a network.

The rstatd Service

Use this service to return performance statistics. The performance statistics displayed are related to the kernel. You can use the `rup` command to display these statistics. The `rstatd` daemon is invoked by `inted`. Disable the `rstatd` service for maximum security.

OS Level Security

All software is installed on operating systems, and Apache is no exception. Regardless of what you do to secure Apache, you cannot rest until you're sure that the operating system on which you installed Apache is also secure. This section provides a few concepts related to Linux security.

Physical Security

Although this might sound a little offbeat while discussing technical content, the fact is that physical security is an absolute essential. Exercise care when deciding on the location of the server, and keep it locked so that only the administrator has access to it. The following list describes precautions to take in order to ensure that the server is not vulnerable to physical threats:

◆ Lock up the CPU of your server and retain personal responsibility for the keys. This would help secure the hardware present in the CPU.

◆ If it is not possible to lock all hardware connected to the server, set up a surveillance camera that continuously monitors people's activity near the server.

◆ Attach security devices, such as alarms, that will notify you if somebody tries to tamper with the server.

◆ After you make backups, store the backup media in a safe place.

◆ Use surge protectors for power cords and modem cables. Another option could be to use a Ground Fault Circuit Interrupter (GFCI) protected circuit. GFCI is an electrical device that is used to detect electrical faults. Using GFCI could prevent fatal electrical fires.

◆ If you plan to use a firewall, configure it on a separate computer. By configuring the firewall on another computer, you add an additional layer of security.

◆ If you have very critical data on your server, consider using security devices that authenticate users based fingerprints and voice.

Data Security

Storing huge amounts of data on the server is not always feasible. In such situations it is critical to make backups and store the data at a secure place. Making backups also ensures that there is no data loss in the event of a hard disk crash or theft. So, before you start operations, have a data recovery plan in place that boldly faces any contingencies. Following are some ways to ensure the security of data:

◆ **Secure data deletion.** When you delete a file in Linux, it becomes inaccessible. However, the file that you deleted is not permanently removed from the file system. Instead, it is marked as bad and the block (space) occupied by the file on the file system is available as free space. When data is copied to the block where the file is located, the file is overwritten. Therefore, it is possible to recover deleted files until the space occupied by the file is overwritten. This can pose serious problems if the deleted file contained sensitive information and is recovered by an individual who should not be reading its content. To avoid such a situation, consider using security tools that rewrite the file system several times with dummy data so that the originally deleted file becomes irrecoverable.

◆ **Data encryption.** Encryption is possibly the best way to secure data. Encryption enables you to apply an algorithm to convert readable data to unreadable data. After the data is encrypted, only someone who knows the decryption key can decrypt it back to a readable format. You can use several programs to encrypt stored data as well as data that is in transit. Pretty Good Privacy (PGP) is one such program. PGP is available as a free download at http://www.pgpi.org/download/.

TIP

Another program for data encryption is GNU Privacy Guard (GPG). GNU Privacy Guard is free software and doesn't use the patented IDEA algorithm. Therefore, it can be used without any restrictions. You can find more information about GPG from http://www.gnupg.org/.

◆ **The /etc/shutdown.allow file.** The shutdown.allow file allows the administrator to specify the usernames of those individuals who are allowed to shut down the server. This file is not present in the Linux system by default. However, using this file could help you prevent loss of any unsaved data because of improper shutdown. After you specify the names of users in this file, other users will not be able to use the Ctrl+Alt+Del key combination to reboot the system. However, to use this file you need to add the -a option to the following line in the /etc/inittab file:

```
ca::ctrlaltdel:/sbin/shutdown -a -t3 -r now
```

NOTE

The shutdown.allow file is not included in the Red Hat Linux system by default. Therefore, you need to create this file manually after editing the /etc/inittab file.

Password Security

The basic way of implementing password security is to use shadow passwords on a Linux system. By default, the passwords of all users are stored in a file named passwd, which is located in the /etc directory. Although the passwd file is read-only, it is accessible to all users on a Linux system, including the non-root users. Regardless of whether the passwords are stored in encrypted form in the passwd file, it is not secure to use this file for storing passwords.

A better proposition is to enable the shadow password system and store the files in the shadow file. The shadow file is also located in the /etc directory. The security benefit of using the shadow file is that it is accessible only to the root user of the Linux system. This ensures maximum security for the system passwords in Linux. Consider these sample contents of the shadow file:

```
root:$1$Al_èÏÑQN$dL4jWxi/GMNSQvcWMqhYu0:11796:0:99999:7:::
angela:$1$vNbLjhDy$BXsS2yTg2INI1AS/9rb3v.:11827:0:99999:7:::
steve:$1$1F3afnwt$iBi9IZv9Mz7B9JuDEAdON.:11855:0:99999:7:::
linda:$1$DqyOP3Ho$2vAnB1iF5YnbnDrtN.6VI.:11855:0:99999:7:::
```

The preceding file excerpt displays the passwords of the root user and the non-root users on a Linux system. As you can see, the passwords are encrypted. Remember that only a root user can open this file.

 TIP

It is recommended that you also enable MD5 passwords along with shadow passwords on your Linux server. MD5 is a cryptographic function that uses a unique algorithm to convert text to a hash value (fixed string of digits). This hash value is impossible to reverse engineer and ensures maximum security for passwords.

In addition to storing passwords in the shadow file, you need to follow a few more password-related guidelines when choosing a password for the system. The following guidelines apply not only to the root user but also to non-privileged users of a Linux system:

◆ The password that you set should be difficult to interpret. For example, never set the password as "password" or "qwerty" (the first six alphabets on the keyboard). Also, never use the name of your spouse, children, or pets as a password.

- Never base the password on a word in a dictionary because someone can easily crack it using tools that perform dictionary attacks.
- The password should be long, if possible.
- The password should be a combination of upper- and lower-case characters.
- Use a combination of letters and numbers for the password.
- Change the password at regular intervals.

User Accounts Security

As an administrator, you might add and delete user accounts whenever the need arises. Here are some security helpful guidelines with respect to user accounts:

- Ensure that the user has minimal privileges at the time you create user accounts.
- Remove or terminate user accounts as soon as an employee leaves the organization.
- Provide a restricted shell to users that don't belong to a trusted group.
- Never assign 0 as the UID/GID for any user. This UID/GID is reserved for the root user. Assigning the UID/GID of 0 would mean giving root access to a user.
- Always monitor logs at regular intervals to keep track of login attempts made by users. This could help track a user who is trying to break into your system.
- Always assign permissions with care.
- Check the bandwidth on a regular basis. Abnormal bandwidth could be a result of a user trying to send multiple network packets with the idea of clogging the network.

File System Security

A file system is the mechanism used by the operating system to manage files. By default, Linux uses the ext2 file system, though various other file systems can be used with Red Hat Linux 7.2. You can use do several things to help secure a file system:

- Unmount the file system that is not in use. This is a healthy practice because an unmounted system is much safer from security threats than a mounted system.
- While configuring NFS, ensure that you set restricted access in the /etc/exports file. Do not allow wild cards. In addition, disallow write access for the root user.
- The SUID/SGID programs are never run from the home directory of the user. It is recommended that you provide the nosuid option in the /etc/fstab file for the file systems that have write permissions for a user. For added security, you could also prohibit users from executing programs by specifying the noexec option in the user's home partition in the /etc/fstab file.
- Set the umask value in such a way that the newly created files have restricted permissions.

◆ Closely monitor the /var/log/wtmp and /var/log/utmp log files to keep a check on the login records. Use the wtmp file to record information about logins and logouts on a Linux system. On the other hand, the utmp file contains information about the currently logged in users.

◆ Set the immutable bit for files that are not supposed to change. This will prevent the files from being deleted accidentally or being overwritten.

◆ The SUID and SGID files allow special privileges to users who execute them. Closely monitor these files to avoid security risks. One way to avoid problems is to ensure that programs that are insecure are not installed. Use the `chmod` command to change the access permissions for SUID and SGID files.

◆ Locate all the files (especially system files) on your system that can be modified by all the users in your system. Analyze whether these files should possess the write permission. Remove the write permissions for files that could cause vulnerability because a user can modify them. Use the following command to find the files:

```
# find / -perm -2 ! -type l -ls
```

◆ A file without an owner should raise a suspicion. An unauthorized user who has already gained access to your system could have created this file. Therefore, locate all such files using the file command and try to track the owner. Use the following command to do so:

```
#find / -nouser -o -nogroup -print
```

◆ Always think twice before changing a default permission for a file. Don't change permissions simply for the sake of convenience, because intruders are waiting for just one chance.

◆ Use the `fsck` utility to check for file system errors and rectify them.

Intrusion Detection

Would-be intruders try to detect vulnerabilities that will help them get unauthorized access to a system. A mechanism that can track down these vulnerabilities is an absolute must. This is where *intrusion detection* comes into the picture. Intrusion detection involves creating a plan that helps detect attempts by intruders to gain access to your system. It also involves deciding in advance what should be done if an intruder is caught.

System administrators usually use a combination of tools that help them detect intrusions. We refer to such tools as *intrusion detection systems (IDS)*. The security of your server depends on the effectiveness and efficiency of your intrusion detection system. Intrusion detection can be placed in the following categories:

◆ **Host-based intrusion detection.** Checks the events that occur in an operating system. If used, this mechanism checks each and every system event.

◆ **Network-based intrusion detection.** Keeps track of network activity. This mechanism keeps tracks network traffic and detects patterns that indicate intrusion.

◆ **File integrity checks.** Checks for system integrity. These are ideal for detecting files that have been modified by an intruder.

◆ **Log file checks.** You can use various tools that quickly scan log files to detect any intrusion-type activity, such as failed login attempts.

Considerable experience and knowledge are needed to diagnose problems based on signs of intrusion detection. However, be careful when you detect the symptoms. The following list includes some possible results of intrusion detection:

◆ System crash or repeated system reboots

◆ Modified system files and disturbed software settings

◆ Login attempts at atypical hours

◆ Degraded system performance

◆ Incomplete log files

◆ Log files containing strange timestamps

◆ Unfamiliar processes running in the background

◆ Change in file permissions, filenames and file sizes

◆ Unusual error messages

Intruders often leave behind evidence of their intrusion. Here are some things that you can do to detect that evidence:

◆ **Use log files.** The log files are the most convenient way to detect intrusion. Examining the log files using the `tail` command from time to time can prove useful.

◆ **Useful commands.** Use commands such as `last`, `lastcomm`, and `netstat` to detect intrusion. Consider using these commands at regular intervals.

 NOTE

You can find more information about the `tail`, `last`, `lastcomm`, and `netstat` commands in their respective man (manual/help) pages by typing the man command followed by the command name.

◆ **Physical intrusion.** Look for clues that indicate physical intrusion, such as signs of tampering and trespassing.

◆ **Unauthorized hardware and software.** Look for unauthorized hardware and software installed on your server. This could be a deliberate attempt to intrude on the server.

Network Security

The final phase of ensuring security is to secure your network. No matter how safe your computer is, if the network is down, you can't use network resources. Consider the following list when setting up your network's security:

◆ Using secure protocols

◆ Securing a network using firewalls

◆ Securing FTP

◆ Securing DNS

◆ Securing NIS

◆ Securing network configuration files

◆ Network monitoring

◆ Securing a network using TCP wrappers

Using Secure Protocols

Protocols are set of rules that are used by two computers on a network to interact with each other. To ensure maximum network security, use a secure means of communication on the network. This section focuses on the secure protocols that you can use to ensure security of data while in transit. Two of the most popular secure protocols are Secure Shell (SSH) and Secure Sockets Layer (SSL).

SSH

The SSH protocol is ideal for establishing secure connections over a network. The SSH protocol allows a user to access a server remotely. The strength of this protocol is its ability to encrypt the information exchanged between computers on the network. I recommend that you use `ssh` utility rather than utilities such as `telnet`, `rlogin`, or `rsh` for managing remote connections on a network.

SSL

This is perhaps the most important protocol with respect to Apache. The SSL was developed by Netscape and is used to ensure that the Internet connections that are established with the Web servers are secure.

The SSL protocol is divided into two layers, the *SSL Handshake Protocol* and the *SSL Record Protocol*. The purpose of the SSL Handshake Protocol is to ensure that the connections established between the client and the server are secure. The SSL Record Protocol is used to encapsulate information from higher-level protocols such as telnet, FTP, and HTTP. You reap the following benefits when using SSL:

- ◆ Encryption
- ◆ Flexibility
- ◆ Extensibility
- ◆ Interoperability

Securing Networks Using Firewalls

A firewall is one of the most useful mechanisms for securing networks. It is implemented in the network layer. A firewall filters information and keeps the unwanted information at bay. You can either configure a network router as a firewall or use dedicated firewall hardware. The latter has advanced features and is preferred for securing highly sensitive data. Here is a broad categorization of firewalls:

- ◆ **Internet facing firewalls**. For maximum security, use these firewalls to deny intranet users access to restricted sites. These types of firewalls disallow access to FTP, Lightweight Directory Access Protocol (LDAP), Simple Mail Transfer Protocol (SMTP), and HTTP.

- ◆ **Internal firewalls**. The primary purpose of using internal firewalls is to secure the data transmitted within an intranet. This type of firewall protects the corporate network from intrusion.

 NOTE

Another entity that is related to firewalls and used for security is a Demilitarized Zone (DMZ). It is a combination of firewalls, front-end, and back-end servers. A DMZ is a dual-purpose model that not only secures data transmitted between the Internet and front-end servers but also secures data transmission between intranet and back-end servers.

Securing FTP

I recommend keeping the FTP service disabled unless you can't do without it. If your setup requires you to use the FTP service, take precautions for its security. The following precautions are a must if you use FTP:

- ◆ Enable logging so that you can keep track of logs to determine any change in behavior.

- ◆ Review the /etc/ftpusers file. This file contains the users who are not allowed to use FTP on the server. Ensure that this file contains only those users who should not be allowed to use FTP.

- ◆ Never share directories on the server with the write permission unless required to do so.

◆ Grant FTP users the least possible amount of access permissions.

◆ Review the /etc/ftpaccess file to ensure that anonymous users are not allowed to modify writable directories.

Securing DNS

As an administrator, it is your responsibility to keep abreast of the DNS information of your server. This will keep you informed about all the hosts that are a part of your server, and will also help you identify an unauthorized host on the basis of its missing DNS entry. When adding hosts to a DNS server, exercise care in assigning host names to computers. Base the names on a common pattern to avoid confusion.

Securing NIS

NIS stands for *Network Information Services*. NIS can be implemented on a client/server network. To implement NIS, you need a NIS client and a NIS master (server). All NIS clients log on to the network after being authenticated from the NIS server. Use a dedicated Linux server for configuring NIS to ensure maximum security.

The NIS server shares account information of a user that is stored in the /etc/passwd file or /etc/shadow file depending on whether shadow passwords are enabled. This feature of centralized password maintenance eases administration to a great extent. However, you should avoid using NIS if not required; it is not recommended that you use it where security is the primary concern.

Securing Network Configuration Files

As an administrator, you are responsible for overseeing the location and use of network configuration files. Linux is a powerful operating system only when you know how to use the configuration files properly. A poorly configured network configuration file could lead to several security threats to your system. Be sure to consult an experienced administrator before trying to configure something new. It is always easy to make things work somehow, but system administration is all about making things work in the best possible way. The ideal situation is to configure the network configuration files in such a way that they also ensure security.

Network Monitoring

As you know, a network is a collection of numerous computers all connected to one another. If one user indulges in an illegal activity on a network, other users on the network can be affected. Closely monitor network activities so that you can detect anything close to an intrusion. Following are some activities to watch for:

◆ Abnormal system activities

◆ Increased disk usage

♦ Slower network connection

♦ Error messages

♦ Unfamiliar processes running in the background

Several tools are available for monitoring network activity and security. A few of the tools were developed for other operating systems before being ported for use in Linux. A few popular security tools are SATAN, portmap, and logdaemon.

 NOTE

In the sections "Using Security Tools" and "Other Third-Party Tools Used for Security" later in this chapter, I briefly discuss a few of the available network monitoring and security tools that you can use to monitor network activity and ensure maximum security.

Securing a Network Using TCP Wrappers

TCP wrappers are among the most useful security mechanisms for tracking intruder activity that can be configured on the Linux operating system. Since their inception, many new features have been added to ensure security. The main features of TCP wrappers are as follows:

♦ They provide a cross-platform mechanism to maintain logs for various applications. syslog is a standard utility that is used for maintaining logs.

♦ They provide a non-interactive method of authenticating hosts (and sometimes users).

 NOTE

You'll find more about TCP wrappers in the section "Other Third-Party Tools Used for Security," later in this chapter.

Using Security Tools

Available with Linux are a wide range of security tools that you can use to ensure Web server, operating system, and network security. In this section, I discuss a few tools that can help you maintain a secure server.

Using Nmap

The Nmap is a very useful, open source, command-line tool that you can use to scan large networks and determine which hosts are available on the network and what services they are running. You can also use Nmap to determine operating system identification. The open ports detected by this utility determine the services the remote host is running.

The following use of nmap command detects the open ports on a Linux system:

```
[root@linux home]# nmap -sT 172.17.68.181


Starting nmap V. 2.54BETA22 ( www.insecure.org/nmap/ )
Interesting ports on linux.server.com (172.17.68.181):
(The 1533 ports scanned but not shown below are in state: closed)
Port        State       Service
21/tcp      open        ftp
22/tcp      open        ssh
23/tcp      open        telnet
80/tcp      open        http
111/tcp     open        sunrpc
113/tcp     open        auth
514/tcp     open        shell
1024/tcp    open        kdm
6000/tcp    open        X11


Nmap run completed -- 1 IP address (1 host up) scanned in 1 second
```

The preceding output displays all the open ports of my server. According to the output, the ftp, ssh, telnet, http, sunrpc, auth, shell, kdm, and X11 services are running, and their respective ports are open. In the preceding output, only port 80 is required for the Apache Web server to function. If the rest of the ports were left open, there would be a threat to the server.

 NOTE

If you use SSL on your Web server, you need to keep port 443 open because all SSL connections are made on port number 443.

In the preceding example, I show how `nmap` command is used to scan TCP ports. In addition, you can use `nmap` command to scan UDP ports. To scan the server for open UDP ports, use the following command:

```
[root@linux home]# nmap -sU 172.17.68.181


Starting nmap V. 2.54BETA22 ( www.insecure.org/nmap/ )
Interesting ports on linux.server.com (172.17.68.181):
(The 1449 ports scanned but not shown below are in state: closed)
Port       State      Service
111/udp    open       sunrpc
517/udp    open       talk
852/udp    open       unknown
1024/udp   open       unknown


Nmap run completed -- 1 IP address (1 host up) scanned in 5 seconds
```

As evident from the example, you use the `-U` option with the `nmap` command to detect the open UDP ports on your server.

The Netcat (nc) Utility

Netcat is used on the Linux system to determine the name and version of the Web server that the specified host is running. You can use this tool to establish a raw connection to port 80. Consider the following example, in which I send a simple HTML HEAD request to the Web server to determine its version.

```
 [root@linux root]# nc 172.17.68.181 80 <press enter>
GET HEAD/HTTP1.1 <press enter>
<!DOCTYPE HTML PUBLIC "-//IETF//DTD HTML 2.0//EN">
<HTML><HEAD>
<TITLE>400 Bad Request</TITLE>
</HEAD><BODY>
<H1>Bad Request</H1>
Your browser sent a request that this server could not understand.<P>
Invalid URI in request GET HEAD/HTTP1.1<P>
<HR>
<ADDRESS>Apache/1.3.24 Server at localhost.localdomain Port 80</ADDRESS>
</BODY></HTML>
```

In the preceding output, the version of Apache that my server is running (1.3.24) is displayed within the `<ADDRESS>` and `</ADDRESS>` tags.

Whisker

Whisker is a handy tool that scans the Apache Web server. It is a third-party tool that does-n't come bundled with the standard Red Hat Linux software. However, the uses of this soft-ware are so many that you should consider downloading and using it to scan Apache at regular intervals to detect possible security loopholes. You can download Whisker for free at http://www.wiretrip.net/rfp/p/doc.asp/i5/d21.htm.

Follow these steps to install and use Whisker on a Linux server:

1. Go to http://www.wiretrip.net/rfp/p/doc.asp/i5/d21.htm and download the file whisker.tar.gz.

2. Copy the file to the /root directory.

 NOTE

Be sure that you are logged in as the root user before you proceed with the installation.

---

3. Uncompress the contents of the .tar.gz file as shown here:

```
[root@linux root]# tar zxvf whisker.tar.gz
v1.4/BUGS
v1.4/CHANGELOG
v1.4/brute.db
v1.4/dumb.db
v1.4/install.txt
v1.4/listgen.pl
v1.4/lists/
v1.4/lists/lnames.txt
v1.4/lists/fnames.txt
v1.4/lists/cfnames.txt
v1.4/lists/clnames.txt
v1.4/lists/CREDIT
v1.4/lists/tech.txt
v1.4/lists/pr0n.txt
v1.4/lists/pass.txt
v1.4/multi.pl
v1.4/scan.db
v1.4/server.db
```

```
v1.4/whisker.pl
v1.4/whisker.txt
```

After you complete the preceding command, the contents of the compressed file are uncompressed in the v1.4 directory.

4. Move to the v1.4 directory by typing the following command:

```
[root@linux root]#cd v1.4
```

Now that you are in the v1.4 directory, you can execute the executable file that will allow you to scan your Apache Web server.

5. Type the following command to begin the scan:

```
[root@linux root]# ./whisker.pl -h 172.17.68.181 -i -v
-- whisker / v1.4.0 / rain forest puppy / www.wiretrip.net --
- Loaded script database of 1968 lines


= - = - = - = - = - =
= Host: 172.17.68.181


= Server: Apache/1.3.24 (Unix)^M


-  www.apache.org
+ 404 Not Found: GET /cfdocs/
+ 404 Not Found: GET /scripts/
+ 404 Not Found: GET /cfcache.map
+ 404 Not Found: GET /cfide/Administrator/startstop.html
+ 404 Not Found: GET /cfappman/index.cfm
+ 403 Forbidden: GET /cgi-bin/
+ 404 Not Found: GET /cgi-bin/dbmlparser.exe
+ 404 Not Found: HEAD /_vti_inf.html
+ 404 Not Found: HEAD /_vti_pvt/
+ 404 Not Found: HEAD /cgi-bin/webdist.cgi
+ 404 Not Found: HEAD /cgi-bin/handler
+ 404 Not Found: HEAD /cgi-bin/wrap
+ 404 Not Found: HEAD /cgi-bin/pfdisplay.cgi
+ 404 Not Found: HEAD /cgi-bin/MachineInfo
+ 404 Not Found: HEAD /mall_log_files/order.log
+ 404 Not Found: HEAD /PDG_Cart/
```

```
...many deleted lines


+ 200 OK: HEAD /manual/
+ 404 Not Found: HEAD /marketing/
+ 404 Not Found: HEAD /msql/


+ 200 OK: HEAD /new/
+ 404 Not Found: HEAD /odbc/
+ 404 Not Found: HEAD /old/
+ 404 Not Found: HEAD /oracle/
+ 404 Not Found: HEAD /order/
+ 404 Not Found: HEAD /outgoing/
+ 404 Not Found: HEAD /pages/
+ 404 Not Found: HEAD /passwords/
+ 404 Not Found: HEAD /perl/
+ 404 Not Found: HEAD /private/
+ 404 Not Found: HEAD /pub/
+ 404 Not Found: HEAD /public/
+ 404 Not Found: HEAD /purchase/


    many deleted lines


+ 404 Not Found: HEAD /password
+ 404 Not Found: HEAD /cgi-bin/password
+ 404 Not Found: HEAD /password.txt
+ 404 Not Found: HEAD /cgi-bin/password.txt
+ 404 Not Found: HEAD /status/
```

The output of the whisker executable file might look confusing if you are using it for the first time. If you closely observe the output, you will see that three different results are in the output: 200 OK, 403 Forbidden, and 404 Not Found.

- ◆ **200 OK.** This result indicates that the exploit check successfully detected a potential vulnerability in the specified file or directory in the document root directory.

- ◆ **403 Forbidden.** This result indicates that the file was found but that the exploit could not be attempted on the file because of inadequate access.

- ◆ **404 Not Found.** This result indicates that the scanner failed to discover the exploitable file, which is a good sign. Getting the 404 Not Found result indicates that either the file has been removed from the system or it cannot be attacked.

The *cgichk.pl* Script

In addition to the security tools just discussed, you can use the cgichk.pl tool to check CGI vulnerabilities on your Apache Web server. CGI scripts are perhaps the most prominent security threat to an Apache Web server. The cgichk.pl tool that is written in Perl is a freely downloadable utility that can do wonders by reporting the CGI vulnerabilities on an Apache server. You can download this script at http://packetstormsecurity.nl/9905-exploits/indexsize.shtml.

 NOTE

In Windows, the downloaded file will have a .txt extension (cgichk.pl.txt). Before using the file, you must rename it as cgichk.pl.

Follow these steps to use the cgichk.pl tool:

1. Go to http://packetstormsecurity.nl/9905-exploits/indexsize.shtml and download the file cgichk.pl.

2. Execute the Perl script by using the following command:

   ```
   [root@linux root]# ./cgichk.pl
   ```

   As soon as you perform the preceding command, the CGI scanner is invoked and you are prompted to enter the host name or IP address of the Linux server running Apache.

3. Specify the IP address of the host that you want to scan for vulnerabilities, as shown:

   ```
   CGI scanner [in Perl] v1.0


   Host:172.17.68.181
   ```

4. After you specify the IP address, you are prompted for the port number. Assign the port number as shown here:

   ```
   HTTP Port [80]: 80
   ```

5. After you assign the port number, you are asked whether you want to log the session. Type **y** to log the session, as shown here:

   ```
   Log Session?(y/n)y
   ```

6. You are then asked to specify the name of the log file, which you do as follows:

   ```
   Log File [172.17.68.181.scan]: newlog
   ```

7. When prompted, press Enter to proceed and check the `httpd` version. You will see the following output:

```
Press [enter] to check the httpd version...


HTTP/1.1 200 OK
Date: Wed, 19 Jun 2002 16:45:46 GMT
Server: Apache/1.3.24 (Unix)
Last-Modified: Thu, 30 May 2002 08:24:25 GMT
ETag: "a9a21-cf-3cf5e1b9"
Accept-Ranges: bytes
Content-Length: 207
Connection: close
Content-Type: text/html
```

8. When prompted, again press Enter, this time to check CGI vulnerabilities. You will see the following output:

```
Press [enter] to check for CGI vulnerabilities...


Searching for THC - backdoor    : Not Found
Searching for phf               : Not Found
Searching for Count.cgi         : Not Found
Searching for test-cgi          : Not Found
Searching for nph-test-cgi      : Not Found
Searching for nph-publish       : Not Found
Searching for php.cgi           : Not Found
Searching for handler           : Not Found
Searching for webgais           : Not Found
Searching for websendmail       : Not Found
Searching for webdist.cgi       : Not Found
Searching for faxsurvey         : Not Found
Searching for htmlscript        : Not Found
Searching for pfdisplay         : Not Found
Searching for perl.exe          : Not Found
Searching for wwwboard.pl       : Not Found
Searching for www-sql           : Not Found
Searching for view-source       : Not Found
Searching for campas            : Not Found
Searching for aglimpse          : Not Found
```

```
Searching for glimpse          : Not Found
Searching for man.sh           : Not Found
Searching for AT-admin.cgi      : Not Found
Searching for filemail.pl       : Not Found
Searching for maillist.pl       : Not Found
Searching for jj                : Not Found
Searching for info2www          : Not Found
Searching for files.pl          : Not Found
Searching for finger            : Not Found
Searching for bnbform.cgi        : Not Found
Searching for survey.cgi         : Not Found
Searching for AnyForm2           : Not Found
Searching for textcounter.pl     : Not Found
Searching for classifields.cgi   : Not Found
Searching for environ.cgi        : Not Found
Searching for wrap               : Not Found
Searching for cgiwrap            : Not Found
Searching for guestbook.cgi       : Not Found
Searching for edit.pl            : Not Found
Searching for perlshop.cgi       : Not Found
Searching for _vti_inf.html      : Not Found
Searching for service.pwd        : Not Found
Searching for users.pwd          : Not Found
Searching for authors.pwd        : Not Found
Searching for administrators     : Not Found
Searching for shtml.dll          : Not Found
Searching for shtml.exe          : Not Found
Searching for args.bat           : Not Found
Searching for uploader.exe       : Not Found
Searching for rguest.exe         : Not Found
Searching for wguest.exe         : Not Found
Searching for bdir - samples     : Not Found
Searching for CGImail.exe        : Not Found
Searching for newdsn.exe         : Not Found
Searching for fpcount.exe        : Not Found
Searching for openfile.cfm       : Not Found
Searching for exprcalc.cfm       : Not Found
Searching for dispopenedfile     : Not Found
```

```
Searching for sendmail.cfm      : Not Found
Searching for codebrws.asp      : Not Found
Searching for codebrws.asp 2    : Not Found
Searching for showcode.asp      : Not Found
Searching for search97.vts      : Not Found
Searching for carbo.dll         : Not Found
No known CGI vulnerabilities found.
```

It is evident from the output that no CGI vulnerabilities were found. The result might be totally different in the case of your server. Therefore, it is worth using this simple but highly useful tool to keep an eye on CGI vulnerabilities.

The Md-webscan Tool

Another useful free tool is Md-webscan. This tool performs a generic check rather than a specific check; in other words, you don't use it to check for a specific vulnerability. Download this tool from http://www.linuxsecurity.com/resources/host_security-7.html. The Md-webscan tool is available as a .tar.gz file, so you will need to extract it before using it.

Other Third-Party Tools Used for Security

If you are curious enough to search the Internet for newly released security tools, you will find dozens of them. However, the tools you choose will depend on your exact requirements. However, only after learning about the various tools can you make the right choices. In this section, I discuss a few third-party tools that are used for securing the network, the operating system, and the Apache Web server.

SATAN

System Administrator Tool for Analyzing Networks (SATAN) is specifically designed for system administrators who must keep an eye on their networks. SATAN is a powerful tool developed by Dan Farmer and Wietse Venema. It scans a system connected to the network to detect often-exploited vulnerabilities. SATAN offers a tutorial for each of the vulnerabilities that it detects. System administrators can refer to this tutorial for in-depth information about a vulnerability and the corrective actions that can be taken to get rid of it. You can download SATAN free of cost at ftp://ciac.llnl.gov/pub/ciac/sectools/unix/satan/.

TCP Wrappers

TCP wrappers, formerly called log_tcp, is a tcp_wrapper package developed by Wietse Venema. You use this tool to monitor logon activity at a host site. You can monitor the following services on a Linux server using TCP Wrappers:

◆ telnet

◆ ftp

◆ tftp

◆ rsh

◆ finger

◆ systat

◆ exec

◆ rlogin

Another advantage of using TCP Wrappers is that it includes a library that can be controlled and used as other services. You can download TCP Wrappers for free at ftp://ftp.cerias. purdue.edu/pub/tools/unix/netutils/tcp_wrappers/tcp_wrappers_7.6.tar.gz.

Portmap

The Portmap software is a replacement for the portmap utility in Linux. This tool was developed for the purpose of closing all known holes in a port map. A few uses for this tool are as follows:

◆ Preventing theft of NIS password files

◆ Protecting the system from unauthorized ypset commands

◆ Protecting the system from NIS file handle theft

You can download portmap for free at ftp://ftp.cerias.purdue.edu/pub/tools/unix/netutils/ portmap/.

Logdaemon

As the name suggests, logdaemon is a useful tool that maintains log files more efficiently than the standard logging features available with the operating system. This helps diagnose an existing problem more effectively. The logging versions of logdaemon are available for the following services:

◆ login

◆ telnet

◆ ftpd

◆ rexecd

◆ rlogind

◆ rshd

You can download logdaemon for free from ftp://ftp.porcupine.org/pub/security/ logdaemon-5.8.tar.gz.

Screend

You can use the screend package, developed by Jeff Mogul, to implement daemon and kernel modifications to allow packet filtering. Packet filtering ensures an added level of security. The packets can be filtered based on the following information:

- ◆ Source address
- ◆ Destination address
- ◆ Byte or set of bytes in the packet

SARA

Security Auditor's Research Assistant (SARA) is a security tool for UNIX platforms that is based on SATAN. With it, you can perform most of the security activities that you can when using SATAN.

Summary

In this chapter, I discussed security-related issues and how they are addressed in Apache. I began by discussing the steps used for securing files and URLs. Then I discussed the common mistakes made by administrators with respect to security and how they can be rectified. Next, I discussed SSI and CGI vulnerabilities followed by securing .htaccess files. I also discussed the services that should be disabled if you are using the Apache Web server. Then I discussed certain concepts on OS level security and network security. Finally, I discussed the security tools that can be used with Apache to constantly monitor whether there is any possibility of intrusion.

Check Your Understanding

Multiple Choice Questions

1. Which of the following options will ensure maximum security for CGI scripts? (Choose all that apply).

    a. Use script-aliased CGI.

    b. Use non-script-aliased CGI.

    c. Allow offsite execution of CGI scripts.

    d. Pass CGI input to the command line.

2. Which of the following activities can lead to a security threat? (Choose all that apply).

    a. Making a backup of your configuration file

    b. Running the Apache Web server as the root user

    c. Never checking log files

    d. Running the Apache Web server as a non-root user

3. Which of the following remote services is used to establish a secure connection over a network and at the same time allow the user to use a separate shell after logging in?

    a. rsh

    b. rlogin

    c. ssh

    d. rwho

4. Which of the following utilities comes bundled with Red Hat Linux and is used to scan large networks and determine which hosts are available on the network and the services they are running?

    a. Whisker

    b. Md-webscan

    c. Nmap

    d. Netcat

5. Which of the following third-party tools was developed by Jeff Mogul and can be used to implement daemon and kernel modifications to allow packet filtering?

    a. SATAN

    b. SARA

    c. Portmap

    d. screend

Answers

Multiple Choice Answers

1. a. Using script-aliased CGI will ensure maximum security for CGI scripts on your Web server. This is because using script-aliased CGI requires you to store all CGI scripts in the same directory.

2. b, c. Running the Apache Web server as the root user could help an intruder to execute or access files to which only the root user has access. If you don't check log files, it will be difficult for you to detect intrusion.

3. c. Use the ssh utility to establish a secure connection over a network and at the same time allows the user to use a separate shell after logging in.

4. c. Nmap comes bundled with Red Hat Linux and is used to scan large networks to determine which hosts are available on the network and the services they are running.

5. d. The screend security tool was developed by Jeff Mogul and is used to implement daemon and kernel modifications to allow packet filtering.

Chapter 12

URL Mapping

By now, you know that the files served by Apache are stored in the document root directory. Generally, when a client specifies the URL of a site, the site's index page is retrieved from the document root and displayed on the client browser. However, sometimes the documents that clients need to access are not in the document root directory. This is where URL mapping comes in; it helps locate resources that are not necessarily located in the document root directory.

In this chapter, I discuss URL mapping and how a request can be redirected to a directory in the file system other than the document root directory. I also discuss the various modules and directives that you use to achieve URL mapping.

Aliasing and Redirection

Before I discuss how URL mapping can be implemented in Apache, it is essential that you understand the methods that make URL mapping possible. In this section, I discuss aliasing and redirection, the most basic methods used for URL mapping.

In Apache, you can map a URL to a destination resource in two ways:

◆ **Aliasing.** In Apache, *aliasing* is a mechanism used to map a URL specified by a client to a location other than the document root. The location could be any directory on the file system.

◆ **Redirection.** *Redirection* is similar to aliasing. Like aliasing, redirection allows a client to retrieve a resource from any directory located on the file system of a Web server. However, with redirection, the Web server analyzes the requested URL and determines where it is located in the file system. Then the Web server sends an indication to the client saying that the requested resource is not accessible at the specified URL but is available at another URL. The Web server sends this URL to the client. The client browser then sends another request to the Web server with the new URL and the resource is retrieved. All this usually happens in a matter of seconds. The browser makes the second request automatically, and the user is not required to type the URL when sending the second request.

 NOTE

Redirection is most commonly used for redirecting requests that specify a URL without a trailing slash (/). Consider an example in which a user requests the URL http://www.somesite.com/somedir. As you can see, the trailing slash is missing. This doesn't mean that the Web server will immediately display an index of the contents located in the directory. Instead, the Apache Web server will first send a redirect response to the browser. The new URL will be specified in the Location header of the redirect response with the trailing slash (http://www.domesite.com/somedir/). The browser will then accept this redirect response and send a request with the new URL (with the trailing slash) specified by the Apache Web server. The time taken to receive the redirect response and respond by reissuing the request is minimal.

The main differences between aliasing and redirection are as follows:

◆ Aliasing occurs at the server-end. In other words, a browser doesn't play a role in retrieving the resource. In redirection, the browser is also involved and sends a new request to the Web server for the same resource that was earlier requested.

◆ In aliasing, when the Web server retrieves the document from an alternate location, the client doesn't know about it because the URL used is the same, even though the resource is being retrieved from an alternate location. However, in redirection, the client is aware that the resource is being retrieved from an alternate location. This is because the client sends a new request to the Web server using a different URL, which, of course, is specified by the Web server.

Modules Used for URL Mapping

Apache supports several modules for URL mapping. Each module consists of directives that can be configured in the httpd.conf file or in .htaccess files. In this section, I will discuss the modules that can be used with Apache for URL mapping. The modules are:

- ◆ `mod_alias`. The directives that use this module manipulate and control URLs whenever a request is sent to the Apache Web server.
- ◆ `mod_rewrite`. This module provides a mechanism for rewriting URLs. It uses a rule-based rewriting engine to accomplish this task.
- ◆ `mod_userdir`. This module is used for providing user-specific directories.
- ◆ `mod_speling`. This module is used to check the spellings of URLs and correct them as needed. Mistakes related to capitalization are also checked.
- ◆ `mod_vhost_alias`. This module is used when you implement dynamically configured mass virtual hosting.

Among the preceding modules, the most important ones for URL mapping are `mod_alias` and `mod_rewrite`. I explain these modules in detail in the sections "The `mod_alias` Module" and "The `mod_rewrite` Module," later in this chapter. Of the two, the `mod_alias` module is most commonly used. The `mod_rewrite` module is only for performing complex tasks. So, I suggest that you use the `mod_alias` module unless you need to perform a complex task that is possible only by using the `mod_rewrite` module.

The mod_alias Module

This `mod_alias` module is an important module in URL mapping. Both aliasing and URL rewriting are possible using this module. The `mod_alias` module is a standard module, which means that it is compiled in the Apache Web server by default. This module can handle most of the tasks related to URL redirection and aliasing and is easy to use from an administrator's point of view.

Using *mod_alias* for Aliasing

Using the `mod_alias` module for aliasing is similar to creating symbolic links in Linux. This is the module that you will use most often for aliasing URLs in Apache. When you create a symbolic link, you can point to a file using the name of the file (which might be different from the original file) that you have created as a symbolic link. Similarly, in Apache, URL aliasing helps you point to a resource present in a directory other than the document root directory.

Before learning how to implement URL aliasing using the mod_alias directive, you need to know about the following directives, which are associated with mod_alias and make URL aliasing possible:

◆ The Alias directive

◆ The AliasMatch directive

◆ The ScriptAlias directive

◆ The ScriptAliasMatch directive

The Alias *Directive*

You use the Alias directive to map a URL to a location other than the document root. As a result, a resource does not have to exist in the document root directory in order for the client to access it. To use the Alias directive, just provide the pathname of directory or file as a replacement for the address specified in the URL, as illustrated here:

```
Alias /images "/usr/local/apache/images"
```

In the preceding example, the Alias directive is used to map the URL that points to the /images directory to the /usr/local/apache/images directory.

 NOTE

When you use the Alias directive, be sure to use the exact pathname. Even a missing trailing slash can cause the Web server to decline a request. For example, if you were to specify the pathname /usr/local/apache/images/ in the Alias directive, a request using the URL /usr/local/apache/images would be declined by the server because of the missing trailing slash.

The AliasMatch *Directive*

The AliasMatch directive is similar to the Alias directive. The only difference is that it extends the functionality of the Alias directive to use standard regular expressions (a method with which you can describe a pattern, and later perform actions after the specified pattern is matched). In other words, the AliasMatch directive is used to specify regular expressions to match the requested URL. Consider the following example, which illustrates the use of the AliasMatch directive:

```
AliasMatch ^/images/(.*) "*/usr/local/apache/images/$1"
```

In the preceding example, note the following:

- ◆ Regular expressions are used with the `AliasMatch` directive to match URLs specified by the client.
- ◆ The ^ symbol indicates that the beginning of the string will be matched.
- ◆ The . symbol is used to match any character except newline.
- ◆ The * symbol is used to match zero or more occurrences of the preceding character.
- ◆ The () symbols are used for grouping.
- ◆ The $ symbol stands for the variable recovered from the first grouping.

The ScriptAlias *Directive*

The `ScriptAlias` directive works like the `Alias` directive, with only one difference. Unlike the `Alias` directive, the `ScriptAlias` directive targets a particular directory as the one that contains CGI scripts. In other words, it sets the MIME type for all the files present in the directory to `application/x-httpd-cgi`. Consider the following example:

```
ScriptAlias /cgi-bin/ "*/usr/local/apache/cgi-bin/"
```

Use of this directive results in all the files requested from the specified directory being treated as CGI scripts. When you request a file named `sometxt.txt` by specifying the URL http://www.somdomain.com/cgi-bin/sometext.txt, the file is retrieved from the /usr/local/ apache/cgi-bin directory. Although the file is a text file, the Web server attempts to execute the file `sometext.txt` as though it were a CGI script.

The ScriptAliasMatch *Directive*

The `ScriptAliasMatch` directive is similar to the `ScriptAlias` directive. However, using this directive, you achieve the additional functionality of permitting the use of standard regular expression for the URL match. Consider the following example, which uses a `ScriptAlias-Match` directive:

```
ScriptAliasMatch ^/cgi-bin/(.*) "/usr/local/apache/cgi-bin/$1"
```

In the preceding example, note the following:

- ◆ The `ScriptAliasMatch` directive is used to map the directory /cgi-bin to the directory /usr/local/apache/cgi-bin/.
- ◆ The ^ symbol is used to match the beginning of the line.
- ◆ The . symbol is used to match any character except newline.
- ◆ The * symbol is used to match zero or more occurrences of the preceding character.
- ◆ The () symbols are used for grouping.
- ◆ The $ symbol stands for the variable recovered from the first grouping.

Using *mod_alias* for Redirection

In addition to aliasing, the mod_alias module can be used for redirection. You can use the mod_alias module for basic redirection, which involves implementing a one-to-one match between the request URL and the destination to where you want to redirect the request. Here are a few directives that help implement redirection when using the mod_alias module:

◆ The Redirect directive

◆ The RedirectMatch directive

◆ The RedirectTemp directive

◆ The RedirectPermanent directive

The Redirect *Directive*

The Redirect directive is undoubtedly the easiest directive that you can use for URL redirection. You just specify the old URL and the destination to where you want to redirect the URL. The following is the syntax of the Redirect directive:

```
Redirect [status] oldURL newURL
```

In the preceding syntax, note the following:

◆ status signifies the HTTP response code sent to the client. If no status code is specified, the default status code of 302 is used. I discuss status codes in detail later in this section.

◆ oldURL is the prefix for the old URL. This identifies the URLs that need to be redirected.

◆ newURL is the URL for the new destination.

◆ After Apache indicates the browser that the requested resource is now available in an alternate location, it is up to the browser to send another request for the URL specified by Apache.

Status Codes Used by the *Redirect* Directive

The status codes for specifying the HTTP response that will be sent to the client can be specified as a valid numeric value or any of the following:

◆ **permanent.** Indicates that the resource has been moved permanently. The numeric status code used for permanent is 301.

◆ **temp.** Indicates that the resource has been found but is temporarily unavailable. The numeric status code used for temp is 302.

◆ **gone.** Indicates that the resource no longer exists. The numeric status code used for gone is 410.

◆ **seeother.** Indicates that the resource has been replaced with another resource. The numeric status code used is 303.

Numeric Codes

In addition to the preceding options, you can specify several other numeric status codes as follows:

♦ **300.** Indicates that multiple variations of the requested resource are present in alternate locations. When the browser is sent this status code, it selects the most appropriate variation and sends another request for its preference.

♦ **301.** Indicates that the resource has been moved permanently to a new location. The browser of the client is informed that the resource will be available on the new location for all future requests.

♦ **302.** Indicates that the resource has been found but is temporarily unavailable. Although the client is redirected to a new location, the browser is informed that the URL is still valid and can be used at a later time.

♦ **303.** Indicates that the request will be redirected temporarily.

♦ **304.** Indicates that the requested document has not been modified and the client can continue using it. This status code is not used to indicate a redirection, but is used only when the Apache Web server receives conditional requests. For example, if the client request consists of an If-Modified-Since header, this status code informs the client that the resource is not modified.

♦ **305.** Indicates that the requested resource should be obtained via a proxy server. In this case, the Location response header contains the URL of the proxy through which the resource should be accessed.

♦ **306.** This is a deprecated status code and should not be used.

♦ **307.** Indicates that the requested resource is temporarily unavailable but the URL is still valid. This status code is similar to the 302 status code but is used with browsers that are HTTP /1.1-compliant.

The RedirectMatch *Directive*

The RedirectMatch directive is similar to the Redirect directive, the only difference being that it is used to match regular expressions. Consider the following example:

```
RedirectMatch (.*)\.jpeg$ http://new.somedomain.com$1.gif
```

In the preceding example, note the following:

♦ The portion of the URL that contains the host name is checked to see whether it contains the characters .jpeg.

♦ The $ character is used to match the end of the line only in the regular expression.

♦ The backslash is used as an escape character to negate the existence of the . character.

♦ $1 is used to specify the new URL portion of the directive.

◆ As a result, all requests ending with the string `.jpeg` that are made to the Web server will be redirected to an alternate location. For example, a request to http://www.somedomain.com/images/someimage.jpeg will be redirected to the URL http://new.somedomain.com/images/someinmage.gif.

The RedirectTemp *Directive*

The `RedirectTemp` directive is used to redirect a URL to a temporary location. When you use the `RedirectTemp` directive, the 302 status code is used. As a result, the client browser communicates that the URL is valid but that the resource is temporarily available only on an alternate location. Consider the following example:

```
RedirectTemp /somedir /home/someuser
```

In the preceding example, the `RedirectTemp` directive indicates that the contents available in the `/somedir` directory are temporarily available only in the `/home/someuser` directory. The functionality of the `RedirectTemp` directive is no different from the functionality of the `Redirect` directive, except that it indicates a temporary redirect.

The RedirectPermanent *Directive*

As the name suggests, you use the `RedirectPermanent` directive to permanently redirect a URL to new location. This means that the older location is no longer valid. When you use this directive, an HTTP status code of 301 is sent to the browser indicating that the location of the resource has changed permanently. Consider the following example:

```
RedirectPermanent /somedir /home/someuser
```

In the preceding example, the `RedirectPermanent` directive specifies that the URLs pointing to the `/somedir` directory are permanently redirected to the directory `/home/someuser`.

The mod_rewrite *Module*

Another module that you can use for URL mapping is the `mod_rewrite` module. As I discussed earlier, most of the tasks related to URL redirection can be handled by the `mod_alias` module, except a few tasks that are more complicated and are best handled using the `mod_rewrite` module. The powerful `mod_rewrite` module can be used in the following situations:

◆ When URLs need to be rewritten on the basis of certain conditions
◆ When URLs need to be rewritten on the basis of information contained outside the URL
◆ When database lookups are involved
◆ When file lookups are involved

The mod_rewrite module is defined as a rule-based rewriting engine. It is called so because it operates on the basis of certain predefined rules. When a request is received, these rules are applied, and the request is redirected to a newly rewritten URL. The ability to use rules takes URL redirection to a new dimension of complexity and dynamism. The mod_rewrite module enables a system administrator to be creative and design customized URL redirection schemes for the Apache Web server.

The mod_rewrite module is so complex and the customizable solutions offered by it are so many that I could go on explaining them for pages. Instead, I want to focus on the basic utility of this module. I also will discuss the associated directives and how to put the mod_rewrite module to its best use. With this strong base, you will be able to come up with your own creative ideas and implement optimized URL redirection solutions for your Apache Web server. A thorough knowledge of this directive will help find solutions to a few bottlenecks that the mod_alias module cannot help you address.

How *mod_rewrite* Handles URL Redirection

In Apache, most of the modules can register internal functions as *callbacks*. Callbacks are programming functions that are executed based on the occurrence of specific types of events. This means that during the document request cycle, the Web server can, at one or more instances, call the internal functions.

The mod_rewrite module is no exception. This module uses two callbacks for two different phases:

- ◆ **URL translation phase**. In this phase, the URL is translated to a file located on the server.
- ◆ **Fixup phase**. In this phase, all final processing is handled at the server end before delivering the resource to the client.

Now, turn your attention to how the Apache Web server handles requests when you use the mod_rewrite module.

When Apache receives a request, the first phase of the request cycle is initiated. This phase is called the *Post-Read-Request* phase. In this phase, the server hands over the request to the host that is supposed to handle the request. For example, in this phase, the Apache Web server determines which virtual host should answer the request. The next phase is the *URL translation* phase. In this phase, the mod_rewrite module redirects the request. In some cases, the mod_rewrite module needs to be used in the final phase, called the *Fixup request* phase, for redirection.

You might find a situation in which you don't want to use the mod_rewrite module for the main server configuration. In other words, you might want to use the mod_rewrite module only for the virtual hosts that are set up on your Web server. In such a situation, you can use the .htaccess file to configure the mod_rewrite module so that you set different rewriting rules for different directories.

Apache processes the directives in the .htaccess files much later in the request cycle. This means that by the time Apache processes the directives in the .htaccess files, the URL has already been translated into a filename. However, the mod_rewrite module uses a callback to the server for the Fixup request phase, which performs perfunctory duties before the resource is delivered to the client. During this phase, the Apache Web server tries to process the rewriting rules set for different directories. As a result, the already-translated URL no longer remains valid, and a new URL is created. This new URL is resubmitted to the Apache server, and the request cycle starts all over again.

 CAUTION

Use.htaccess files to specify URL rewriting rules intelligently, and only when it is absolutely required. Extensive use of .htaccess files can slow the Apache Web server's performance.

Configuring Apache to Use *mod_rewrite*

Mod_rewrite is a standard module included with regular Apache distribution. However, in order to use the mod_rewrite module, you need to make certain settings in the Apache configuration file. To ensure that everything is set up properly for the mod_rewrite module, first check for the following lines in the httpd.conf file:

```
LoadModule rewrite_module libexec/mod_rewrite.so
AddModule mod_rewrite.c
```

In the preceding example, the LoadModule directive loads the mod_rewrite module, and the AddModule directive adds the mod_rewrite module to the list of usable modules.

Rulesets

As discussed earlier, the mod_rewrite module operates on the basis of certain predefined rules. Together, these rules are referred as a *ruleset*. A ruleset contains rewriting rules that can be based on predefined conditions.

The use of a rewriting rule is similar to that of a Redirect directive that is used in relation to the mod_alias directive. A rewrite rule contains a pattern that is used to match a requested URL. If the match is successful, a substitution is applied to the requested URL, guiding it to a new location. Consider this example of a redirect using the RewriteRule directive:

```
RewriteRule /somedir /home/someuser
```

The preceding example accomplishes a task that can also be handled using the mod_alias module. For simple redirection, the mod_rewrite can offer little more than the mod_alias module. The importance of using mod_rewrite comes when multiple rules need to be applied based on predefined conditions. Consider the next example.

```
RewriteCond %{REMOTE_ADDR} ^172\192\.168\.1\.*
RewriteRule .* /localweb/ [R]
```

In the preceding example, a ruleset is used to redirect requests received from clients in the local area network. These requests are redirected to a different set of Web pages. I used the RewriteCond and the RewriteRule directives to achieve this. The purpose and use of these directives become clear in the section "Directives Associated with mod_rewrite," later in this chapter.

Directives Associated with *mod_rewrite*

You can use a number of directives with the mod_rewrite module. All of these directives have different uses depending on the situation. You will find these directives categorized and defined in the following subsections.

The Mandatory Directives

Two directives are required when using the mod_rewrite module: the RewriteEngine directive and the RewriteRule directive. I describe these two directives and their use in the following subsections.

The *RewriteEngine* Directive

You use the RewriteEngine directive to enable or disable the rewriting engine. If this directive is not used to enable the rewriting engine, none of your specified rulesets will work. The two values that you can specify for this directive are on and off. By default, the value specified for this directive is off. You need to change it to on when using the mod_rewrite module.

You have the choice of specifying this directive in the httpd.conf file or in the .htaccess file. Consider the following example, in which the RewriteEngine directive is used to enable the rewriting engine:

```
RewriteEngine on
```

 NOTE

One thing worth mentioning about the mod_rewrite module is that the virtual hosts configured in the httpd.conf file do not inherit the configuration directives specified in the main server configuration. Any directive that you specify in the main server configuration will have no effect on the virtual hosts. This applies to the RewriteEngine directive also. As a result, the RewriteEngine directive specified in the main server configuration will have no effect on the virtual hosts setup on your server. Therefore, you will need to specify a separate RewriteEngine directive and enable it for the virtual host for which you want to implement URL rewriting.

The *RewriteRule* Directive

The RewriteRule directive is required when employing the directives associated with the mod_rewrite module. The syntax of the RewriteRule directive is as follows:

```
RewriteRule pattern substitution
```

The preceding syntax indicates how the RewriteRule directive works. For every rule that you define using this directive, you should have a pattern followed by a substitution. A pattern is a regular expression on the basis of which URLs sent by clients are checked. When a URL specified by a client matches the regular expression specified at the server end, the substitution is applied to the URL.

Note that the pattern specified will always match the current URL. The current URL does not have to be the URL requested originally. This is because the originally requested URL might have been altered earlier by a RewriteRule directive or an Alias directive. Therefore, the mod_rewrite module expands the regular expression pattern in the following ways:

◆ You can negate a regular expression by using the ! character. The ! character is referred to as the logical NOT character.

◆ Back references can be used with the regular expressions specified in the RewriteRule directive. Back references can be of the form $N, where N is an integer in the numeric range of 0 to 9. The value N is filled with the nth set of parentheses in the pattern of the rule. The following example illustrates this point:

```
RewriteRule ^/~(.*)/(.*) /home/$1/$2
```

In the preceding example, two sets of parentheses are used in the pattern portion of the RewriteRule directive. $1 corresponds to the first set of parentheses, and $2 corresponds to the second set of parentheses.

◆ You can use back references with the regular expressions specified in the RewriteCond directive. They can be in the form %N, where N is an integer in the numeric range of 0 to 9. The back references are filled with the contents of the nth parentheses in the last matched RewriteCond directive, which I explain in the section "Conditional Rewriting: The RewriteCond Directive," later in this chapter.

◆ Server environment variables can be specified in the format, %{env_variable}. When specified in this format, the value of the specified environment variable can be extracted at a given time.

◆ You can call previously defined mappings by using mapping function calls. You define mappings by using the RewriteMap directive, which I will discuss later in the section "Mapped Rewriting Using the RewriteMap Directive."

You must specify all rewriting rules by using a separate RewriteRule directive. Because the RewriteRule directives are applied one after the other at runtime depending on the order specified, you need to be careful as you craft the order in which you specify the RewriteRule directives.

You can set several flags for substitution. You can specify flags in the [flag] format immediately after the substitution, and you can specify multiple flags by using commas as separators. Here are the flags that you can utilize:

- ◆ **R|redirect [=code]**. This flag treats the rewritten URL as a redirect.
- ◆ **F|forbidden**. This flag sends the client a response code of 403, which indicates that the client is forbidden to access the resource.
- ◆ **G|gone**. This flag sends the client a response code of 410 (Gone).
- ◆ **P|proxy**. This flag indicates that the rewritten URL can be accessed only via a proxy server.
- ◆ **L||last**. This flag indicates that the mod_rewrite module should not process any more rulesets after the one for which this flag is specified.
- ◆ **N|next**. This flag starts rewriting the URL applying the first RewriteRule directive in the current ruleset. The rewriting process is applied to the URL rewritten by the last RewriteRule directive.
- ◆ **C|chain**. This flag chains the specified rule with the next rule.
- ◆ **T|type=MIME-type**. This flag forces the requested resource to be of a specified MIME type.
- ◆ **NS|nosubreq**. This flag skips the current rule if an internal client has placed the current request.
- ◆ **NC|nocase**. This flag makes the pattern match case-sensitive, which means that the case used for the filename specified in the URL will determine whether the desired resource can be extracted.
- ◆ **QSA|qsappend**. Use this flag when the URL being rewritten is a query string and the resultant URL is also a query string. This flag helps replace only the query string part of the original URL, rather than the URL as a whole.
- ◆ **S|skip=num**. This flag specifies the num number of rules. This is applicable only when the pattern matches the URL in the current rule.
- ◆ **E|env=var:value**. This flag sets an environment variable. However, this flag will work only if the pattern matches the URL in the current rule.
- ◆ **PT|passthrough**. This flag instructs the rewriting engine to set the URI field of the internal request_rec structure. The URI field is set to the value of the filename field.

Conditional Rewriting: The RewriteCond *Directive*

The RewriteCond directive is a powerful tool that you can use to implement conditional rewriting. You can use multiple RewriteCond directives with a single RewriteRule directive. The RewriteCond directive specifies a condition that determines whether the rule should be applied. The rule is applied only if the result of the condition is True. So, if several RewriteCond directives precede a RewriteRule directive, each of the RewriteCond directives must be True in order for the rule to be applied. However, in order to check multiple conditions you must use the [or] flag. This is important because a rewrite rule will be ignored if the condition specified in the first RewriteCond directive is not True. The syntax for the Rewrite-Cond directive is as follows:

```
RewriteCond MatchString Pattern
```

In the preceding syntax, note the following:

◆ MatchString is a plain text string. This string can contain several constructs, such as RewriteRule back-references, RewriteCond back-references, server variables, environment variables, HTTP headers, and look-aheads (variable expansions performed by the subsequent Apache modules while handling the same request).

◆ Pattern is a regular expression. The regular expression specified is compared with the MatchString argument. If the match is successful, the entire RewriteCond directive equates to True. When the regular expression doesn't match the MatchString argument, the value of the RewriteCond directive equates to False.

PER-DIRECTORY REWRITING USING MOD_REWRITE

You might not want to use the mod_rewrite module with respect to the entire server. For example, a situation may exist in which you want to use the mod_rewrite module only for a particular directory. Enabling the mod_rewrite module for the entire Web server when you need to apply it only to a specific directory is not a good idea in terms of security and performance.

The better option in such situations is to use per-directory rewriting, which, in turn, means enabling the mod_rewrite module only for a particular directive. Although this is a sensible configuration, you need to be careful when using per-directory rewriting. Consider these guidelines:

◆ The FollowSymLinks option is a must when you are using per-directory rewriting. This means that the directory for which you want to enable the mod_rewrite module should contain the following line:

```
Options FollowSymLinks
```

If you are using .htaccess files, you need to ensure that the FollowSymLinks option is enabled in the .htaccess file, too.

◆ If you are using .htaccess files for specifying per-directory rewriting rules, be sure that MatchString does not contain the directory path. The mod_rewrite module behaves differently in per-directory and per-server contexts. In the per-directory context, the mod_rewrite module removes the per-directory prefix. Therefore, a server rule, ^/dir/ .*$, will not match because it will be interpreted as ^.*$.

The RewriteOptions *Directive*

As discussed earlier, the virtual hosts do not inherit the settings related to the mod_rewrite module even if specified for the main server configuration. So, it's wise to use the mod_rewrite module separately for the virtual host for which you want to implement URL rewriting. If you find that you have to retain the mod_rewrite module for the main server configuration as well as have it for a few virtual hosts defined in the configuration file, the best proposition is to enable the mod_rewrite module for the main server configuration and then inherit it for a specific virtual host. This approach saves you the time and effort required to explicitly enable the mod_rewrite module for a specific virtual host.

For such situations, you can use the RewriteOptions directive to specify that the virtual hosts should inherit the mod_rewrite module from the main server configuration. Consider the following example:

```
RewriteOptions inherit
```

It is evident from the preceding example that the RewriteOptions directive has been specified the inherit option. This option allows virtual hosts to inherit the mod_rewrite module from the main server configuration.

TIP

You can use the RewriteOptions directive's inherit option in the context of virtual hosts as well as directories. In the virtual host context, the settings are inherited from the primary server. In the directory context, the settings are inherited from the .htaccess file of the parent directory.

Maintaining Logs

A couple of directives available with the mod_rewrite module allow you to maintain logs related to URL rewriting. Logs are an essential part of any software because they help the system administrator identify and troubleshoot existing problems. The logging facility provided by the mod_rewrite module is highly efficient. I recommend that you enable logging while using the mod_rewrite module. I describe the directives used in the context of logging in the following subsections.

The *RewriteLog* Directive

You use the RewriteLog directive to specify the location of the file in which the server will store the logs related to URL rewriting, as illustrated here:

```
RewriteLog "/usr/local/apache/logs/mod_rewrite.log"
```

In the preceding example, a log file named mod_rewrite.log is specified for the mod_rewrite module. This file is located in the /usr/local/apache directory.

 NOTE

Many system administrators make the mistake of trying to disable logging by specifying the value /dev/null for the RewriteLog directive. This causes the log information to be written into the /dev/null directory, which is equivalent to discarding the logs. This doesn't disable the logging. Instead, it just discards the logs. However, the point to be noted is that at the same time, the server resources are being used to generate logs. To disable logging, it's smart to either remove the RewriteLog directive from the server configuration or specify a value of 0 for the RewriteLogLevel directive.

The *RewriteLogLevel* Directive

The RewriteLogLevel directive is used to specify the verbosity level of the log file maintained for URL rewriting. The default value for this directive is 0, which indicates that no logging will be performed. If the value is 9 or more, the implication is that almost all the actions related to rewriting URLs will be logged. Consider the following example:

```
RewriteLogLevel 9
```

In the preceding example, the log level is set to 9. But be careful when specifying the log level; as I said, a log level higher than 9 will cause the server to log almost all actions, resulting in adverse effects. Although is it is fine to set a higher log level for testing purposes, I recommend that you never use a higher log level on a production server.

Setting a Base URL Using the RewriteBase *Directive*

Use the RewriteBase directive to write the base URL. Because you employ this directive only within the context of directories, you can specify it in the .htaccess file in the <Directory> directive.

Whenever a rewriting rule is applied, the location is modified on a per-directory basis. As a result, the rewriting takes place late in the request cycle. This is because the rewriting takes place after all other related actions have occurred.

The per-directory rewriting occurs after the mod_rewrite and mod_alias modules are processed. The URLs resulting from these rewrites that occur late in the cycle are internally resubmitted to the server. After the URL is submitted, a new request cycle is initiated. When the rewrite rule is applied in the per-directory context, the RewriteBase (which is, by default, the local directory prefix) is removed from the URL, and the rule is applied to the remaining part of the URL. Next, the RewriteBase directive is pre-pended. The incoming URL need not necessarily map to the local file system. In such a case, you change the RewriteBase so that it matches the incoming URL prefix, not the local directory prefix. This is why you specify the RewriteBase directive.

For a clearer understanding, check out the following example:

```
#This is a per-directory configuration that illustrates the usage of the RewriteBase
#directive.
#The Alias directive is used to map the contents of a directory to /htdocs.
#
Alias /docs/ "/usr/local/apache/htdocs/"
#
RewriteEngine on
#
RewriteBase /docs
#
RewriteRule ^doc\.html$ documents.html
```

In the preceding example, note the following:

◆ The RewriteEngine directive enables the rewrite engine.

◆ The RewriteBase directive is specified as /docs.

◆ The RewriteRule directive tries to match the URL with the regular expression specified.

◆ When a client sends a request for /docs/doc.html, the Alias directive maps the request to /usr/local/apache/htdocs/doc.html.

◆ Next, the .htaccess file is examined for the presence of RewriteRule directive.

◆ The RewriteRule directive removes a part of the URL and tries to map the file doc.html to documents.html.

◆ Then the mod_rewrite module prepends the value RewriteBase to the URL before reinserting the URL. The URL is processed as /docs/documents.html.

If the RewriteBase directive is not specified in the .htaccess file, the mod_rewrite module will prepend the local directory prefix, which is also the default value for RewriteBase. In this case, the directory prefix will be /usr/local/apache/htdocs/. As a result, the new URL submitted to the server will be /usr/local/apache/htdocs/documents.html. Consequently, this request will be rejected.

Mapped Rewriting Using the RewriteMap *Directive*

Use the RewriteMap directive to specify a *rewriting map*. A rewriting map is nothing more than a lookup table that consists of numerous variable and value pairs. The purpose of specifying this directive is to be able to use the rewriting map specified in it at a later stage using the RewriteRule directive. This directive also specifies the rewriting source that can be used to search for specific information. This information can then be inserted into the `RewriteRule` substitution string. Consider the following syntax of the `RewriteMap` directive:

```
RewriteMap mapname maptype:mapsource
```

In the preceding syntax, note the following:

◆ mapname is the name assigned to the rewriting map.

◆ maptype is the type of rewriting map. For example, the `maptype standard plain` will signify plain text.

◆ mapsource is the depiction of the maptype. For example, for the `maptype standard plain` you will use the mapsource `maptype: txt`, which is the file extension used for text files.

Summary

In this chapter, I discussed the importance of URL mapping within the context of the Apache Web server. I discussed the concept of aliasing and redirection and later explained the `mod_alias` and `mod_rewrite` modules that are used for URL aliasing and redirection. I also discussed the directives that are associated with these modules and how they are used to implement URL aliasing and redirection.

Check Your Understanding

Multiple Choice Questions

1. Which of the following modules uses a rule-based rewriting engine to provide a mechanism for rewriting URLs?

    a. mod_alias

    b. mod_rewrite

    c. mod_speling

    d. mod_userdir

2. Which of the following directives is associated with the mod_alias module and is used to map a URL to a location other than the document root using regular expressions?

    a. The Alias directive

    b. The ScriptAlias directive

    c. The AliasMatch directive

    d. The ScriptAliasMatch directive

3. Which of the following directives associated with the mod_alias module is used to redirect a URL to a temporary location?

    a. The Redirect directive

    b. The RedirectTemp directive

    c. The RedirectPermanent directive

    d. The RedirectMatch directive

4. Which of the following directives are mandatory directives that need to be used with the mod_rewrite module? (Choose all that apply.)

    a. The RewriteOptions directive

    b. The RewriteEngine directive

    c. The RewriteLog directive

    d. The RewriteRule directive

5. Which of the following are true with respect to aliasing? (Choose all that apply.)

    a. Is used for URL mapping.

    b. Maps a URL specified by the client to a location other than the document root.

    c. Requires the client to submit the request twice to access the desired resource.

    d. Hides the actual location of the resource from the client.

Answers

Multiple Choice Answers

1. b. The mod_rewrite module uses a rule-based rewriting engine to provide a mechanism for rewriting URLs.

2. c. The AliasMatch directive is used with the mod_alias module to map a URL to a location other than the document root using regular expressions.

3. b. The RedirectTemp directive is used with the mod_rewrite module to redirect a URL to a temporary location.

4. b, d. The RewriteEngine and the RewriteRule directives are mandatory directives that need to be used with the mod_rewrite module.

5. a, b, d. Aliasing is a mechanism used for URL mapping, and the client is able to access the document from a location other than the default location. Aliasing is not transparent to the user because the user retrieves the document from the same URL, although it is being retrieved from an alternate location at the server end.

Chapter 13

A Web server is a repository of thousands of resources. To closely knit the world, it is important to make a resource available in representations. For example, a user in France would probably prefer a Web page to appear in French, whereas a user in Japan might want it to appear in Japanese.

One way to ensure that a resource is delivered as preferred by a user is to display an index page with all the possible options so that the user can choose the one he wants. However, this approach doesn't look professional, and it requires the user to read through and choose the preferred option.

Allowing the user to use his discretion is the way to go, but the difficulty lies in knowing what a particular user prefers. That's where HTTP /1.1 can help. HTTP /1.1 introduced request headers that allow users to send their preferences with their requests. Then the Web server interprets the requests and "negotiates" with the browser to display the preferred representations. This process is known as *content negotiation*. If the requested representation is not available, the Web server automatically switches to the next best alternative, which is also be specified by browser.

In this chapter, you'll learn how to accomplish content negotiation by using something called *metainformation.* The prefix *meta* means "about" and metainformation is commonly referred to as *information about other information.* The role of metainformation is to help the Web server analyze and process the information. It also instructs the browser to handle the data or determine the application that can handle the data in case the browser is not capable of handling it. Content negotiation is all about determining what kind of content is acceptable and what is not. Therefore, metainformation is useful for content negotiation.

As you know, although content delivered by Web servers is usually comprised of documents formatted in HyperText MarkUp language (HTML), other content exists on the Internet (for example, binary data files, streaming media types, and embedded images). In this chapter, you'll learn how download resources created in languages other than HTML by using metainformation. You also learn how to use metainformation to instruct the browser, set handlers, and implement content negotiation.

Understanding the Role of Metainformation

Because metainformation helps servers process data and transfer particular kinds of data to an alternate application as needed, it is essential to Web servers and browsers. It is important that you understand the different types of metainformation before I discuss the use of metainformation in detail. Metainformation can be categorized as:

◆ The type of content of the resource

◆ The language in which the text will appear

◆ The character set used for the text

◆ The encoding or the compression scheme used for the text

You know that metainformation assists in the interaction between a Web server and a Web browser. The following list discusses the uses of metainformation, which fall into three broad categories:

◆ **Instruct the browser.** Later, in the section "Related HTTP /1.1 Headers," I discuss a series of HTTP headers that you use to instruct browsers and help them handle content sent by the Web server. The primary role of these headers is to convey important information to the Web browser. The information that a Web server can send to a client includes the type of resource, the type of language used, and the character set that is required to display the information properly.

◆ **Determine the appropriate Apache handler** for a particular document. You use an Apache handler to perform certain predetermined functions on Web content prior to its delivery to the client. The best example is a server-parsed HTML, in which an Apache module examines a document for tags and processes the code within the tags before sending the document to the client.

◆ **Content negotiation.** This is probably the most important use of metainformation, and I discuss it in detail in the section "Content Negotiation" later in this chapter. Content negotiation is a mechanism by which a server and a browser negotiate which version of a document should be sent in response to a client request. The decision depends on whether the preference of the client computer is available on the server.

What Are the Types of Metainformation?

Before moving on to more technical information, turn your attention to the most important types of metainformation that Apache uses:

◆ MIME types
◆ MIME language
◆ MIME character set
◆ MIME encoding

MIME Types

MIME types are arguably the most important content types, and without them the functionality of Apache is next to useless. MIME, which stands for *Multipurpose Internet Mail Extensions*, was introduced to send non-text files that need to be encoded before being sent as attachments in e-mails. In other words, MIME types facilitate the transit of non-plain text files via e-mails. All MIME-encoded attachments also use headers that contain information about the attachments. These are called *MIME headers*. Consider the following example:

```
Content-Type: image/jpeg; name="someimage.jpg"
Content-Transfer-Encoding: base64
```

In the preceding example, two MIME headers that help the e-mail application to decode the information and interpret the results are used. The Content-Type header is not only used to instruct the email application on how to interpret the mail attachment, but also to invoke an application if required to handle the specified MIME type.

In order to help Apache understand a content type, you associate the document's filename extension to a MIME type that is supported by Apache. You can obtain a list of MIME types that are supported by Apache in the conf/mime.types file. The following is a sample of the contents of this file:

```
# This is a comment. I love comments.
# This file controls what Internet media types are sent to the client for
# given file extension(s).  Sending the correct media type to the client
# is important so they know how to handle the content of the file.
# Extra types can either be added here or by using an AddType directive
```

```
# in your config files. For more information about Internet media types,
# please read RFC 2045, 2046, 2047, 2048, and 2077.  The Internet media
#type
# registry is at <ftp://ftp.iana.org/in-notes/iana/assignments/media-
#types/>.


# MIME type                  Extension


...Many deleted lines


audio/x-pn-realaudio-plugin   rpm
audio/x-realaudio             ra
audio/x-wav                   wav
chemical/x-pdb                pdb
chemical/x-xyz                xyz
image/bmp                     bmp
image/cgm
image/g3fax
image/gif                     gif
image/ief                     ief
image/jpeg                    jpeg jpg jpe
image/naplps
image/png                     png
image/prs.btif
image/prs.pti
image/tiff                    tiff tif
```

As you can see, this file maintains a list of supported MIME types for the Apache Web server. The format of the entries is as follows:

```
MIME type/subtype filename_extension
```

Whenever Apache receives a request, the extension of the file is examined. Then the line in the mime.types file instructs Apache to use the Content-Type HTTP header to identify the requested resource. Imagine that you request a wave (music) file from the Web server. In this case, using the Content-Type header, the Apache Web server will determine that the requested resource is of MIME type audio, subtype x-wave, and file extension .wav.

You can edit or append the contents of the mime.types file to disallow or allow the use of specific MIME types. However, this is a self-sufficient file, and you will seldom need to edit it in order to add support for MIME types.

MIME Language

MIME language refers to the languages that you can use to represent a particular resource on the Web server. A tremendous amount of information that is on the Internet needs to be accessible and understood by as many people as possible. MIME language comes to the rescue and tackles this problem.

MIME language allows a particular Web page to be displayed in several languages so that a maximum number of people can interpret it, regardless of language differences. With the help of MIME language, clients can request a resource on the Web server according to their language preference.

A filename extension is provided to help Apache associate a resource with a language. You use the AddLanguage directive to specify the languages with the associated extensions in the httpd.conf file.

MIME Character Set

You can also refer to a document by using a *character set*. A character set is a collection of characters that can be interpreted by specific hardware and software. One example of a character set is the ASCII character set. A number is used to depict a character in the character set.

In order to successfully identify documents using character sets, the client browsers also need to support the specified character sets. Also, the Apache Web server needs to pass the information about these character sets to the browsers. Apache uses the AddCharset directive that can be specified in the httpd.conf file to map a given character set to one or more filename extensions.

MIME Encoding

You can also encode a document delivered by the Web server. For Apache, the encoding is limited to a compression scheme such as compress or gzip. The AddEncoding directive, which can be specified in the httpd.conf file, is used to map an encoding type to one or more filename extensions. You can manually add entries in the httpd.conf file to support compression schemes over and above the default compression schemes that are available with Apache.

Using Metainformation

As discussed earlier, metainformation has three main uses with respect to Apache. In this section, you find a detailed discussion of those uses. You'll examine how Apache uses metainformation to communicate with the browser, assigns a handler for any server-side processing that is required, and negotiates content by analyzing the client preferences before sending the requested document to the browser.

Instructing the Browser

HTTP is a binary transfer protocol that transfers data without requiring specific encoding. Each HTTP transaction uses certain headers that help identify the type of data and how it should be handled at the client and server sides. One important and mandatory header is the Content-Type header. You need to include this header with every HTTP transaction. Like most Web servers, Apache also supports a wide range of standard MIME types; so do various browsers.

However, at the browser end, you can make appropriate settings to associate a particular MIME type with an alternate application. You can view a list of supported MIME types in Netscape and their associated applications in the Preferences dialog box. To access the Preferences dialog box in Netscape Navigator click Edit, Preferences.

Figure 13.1 shows the Preferences dialog box. Notice that when Applications is selected in the left pane, a list of supported file types appears in the right pane.

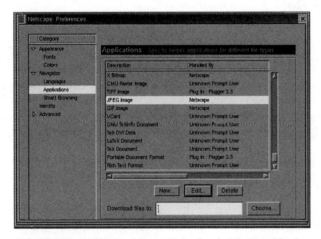

FIGURE 13.1 *The Preferences dialog box in Netscape Navigator*

You can edit the settings for a particular file type by clicking the Edit button. The Application dialog box that appears allows you to edit settings for a given file type by altering the MIME type and the file extensions associated with a particular MIME type. Figure 13.2 shows the Application dialog box in which you edit the settings for JPEG image files.

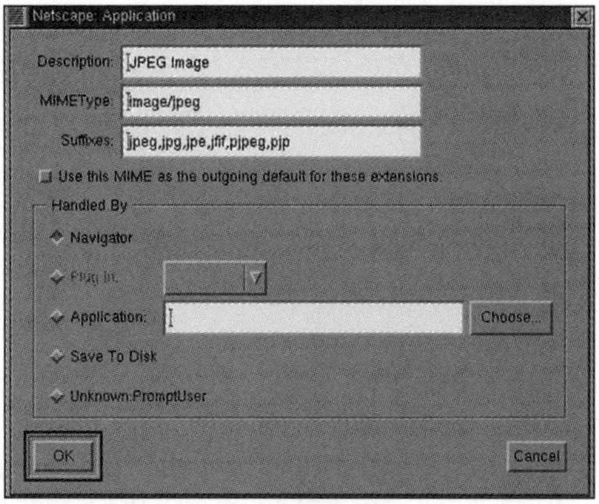

FIGURE 13.2 *The Application dialog box*

Setting a Handler

The second advantage of identifying the content type is the ability to access content handlers for a specified file depending on the file type and extension. A handler is a routine that is used to manage an operation, condition, or event. Setting a handler proves useful for processing documents at the server side and returning the resultant output to the client computer.

Apache uses a default handler known as just that, `default-handler`, for serving documents to a browser. All HTML-formatted documents pass through this handler before being delivered to the client. However, special handlers are needed for server-side processing that doesn't specifically require HTML. These special handlers manage server-parsed documents that result from using server side includes, PHP, Perl, CGI scripts, or any other server-side scripting language for that matter.

Associating a handler with a particular type of file is easy in Apache. You can specify the `AddHandler` directive in the httpd.conf file to accomplish this task. In order to specify a handler for a file type, you should associate a filename extension with a handler instead of associating a filename extension with a MIME type using the `AddType` directive. This is recommended because after you associate a filename extension directly to a handler, you don't need to specify a handler for the MIME type. Consider the following example in which the `AddHandler` directive is used:

```
AddHandler cgi-script .cgi
AddHandler server-parsed .shtml
```

You will find the preceding entries in the httpd.conf file. These entries are in the Apache configuration file by default. These entries identify two handlers, `cgi-script` and `server-parsed`. You use these handlers to manage files ending with the extensions .cgi and .shtml, respectively.

Another directive used in conjunction with handlers is the `SetHandler` directive. You use it to associate a named handler with a specific directory or request URI. Consider the following example:

```
<Location /opt/web/cgi>
SetHandler cgi-script
Order deny, allow
Deny from all
Allow from 172.17.68., 172.17.69.
</Location>
```

In the preceding example, the `SetHandler` directive is designated for the URL specified in the `Location` directive. The `SetHandler` directive will be applied to all URLs that begin with /opt/web/cgi. As a result, all requests that begin with the specified pattern will be passed to the `cgi-script` handler for processing.

Content Negotiation

As I mentioned earlier in this chapter, content negotiation is a mechanism used by the Apache Web server to determine the preference of the client requesting the resource and to display the content appropriately. Apache interprets the preference of the client by analyzing the request headers sent by the client browser. In other words, content negotiation enables the Web server to intelligently and automatically decide what representations the clients will prefer. For example, say a user located in Italy wants to view the contents of a Web site in Italian. To stipulate that the content is displayed in Italian, the request header that the browser sends to Apache should be something similar to the following:

```
Accept-Language: it
```

In the preceding example, the `Accept-Language` header depicts that the client wants to view the contents only in Italian. However, you can specify multiple preferences using the `Accept-Language` header. If it is not possible for the Web server to deliver the content in the first preferred language, the Web server considers the next preference specified by the client and tries to deliver the content accordingly.

Of course, a request can be more complex and can include several preferences from the client-side. But before considering a more complex example, turn your attention to the various HTTP /1.1 headers that the client browser uses to request a resource.

Related HTTP /1.1 Headers

In addition to the request header `Accept-Language`, clients can use several other headers to implement server-driven content negotiation, if the Web server supports them. Apache is a perfect example of a Web server that supports server-driven content negotiation.

The associated HTTP request headers that enable clients to specify preferences are as follows:

- ◆ Accept
- ◆ Accept-Language
- ◆ Accept-Charset
- ◆ Accept-Encoding

The *Accept* Header

The Accept request header consists of a list of representation schemes. Using these request schemes, you can tell the Web server which representation schemes the browser accepts and, therefore, in which schemes the content can be delivered. A semicolon separates each representation scheme specified in the Accept header. However, the Accept header might be different for different requests placed by the same user.

To be more specific, the client uses the Accept header to specify the content type metainformation values. Remember the ContentType directive in the Apache configuration file that is used to specify the content type of a specific request? The browser sends its content type preference using the Accept header. If a particular value is not specified for the Accept header, the default values, text/plain and text/html, are assumed. Consider the following example of an Accept header:

```
Accept: text/plain, text/html
Accept: text/x-dvi; q=.8; mxb=100000; mxt=5.0, text/x-c
```

In the preceding example, the Accept request header has the values text/plain and text/html, which are the default values.

The *Accept-Language* Header

You use the Accept-Language header to specify the language in which the client wants the content to be sent. This header might also contain multiple language preferences. In this case, the Web server will respond with appropriate content depending on the order of language preferences specified by the user. Consider the following example, in which the Accept-Language header specifies three languages.

```
Accept-Language: fr, it, en
```

In the preceding example, the Accept-Language request header indicates that the first language preferred by the client is French and the second preferred language is Italian. If the Web server is unable to provide content in either of these two languages, it will deliver the content in English.

The *Accept-Charset* Header

As the name suggests, the Accept-Charset header is used to specify the character sets that will be acceptable by the client browsers. You use this header to specify the ability of a client to understand and use more comprehensive and special-purpose character sets. When a Web server that supports special character sets comes across this header, it recognizes the client browser as one that supports special character sets. As a result, the Web server sends the requested documents to the client browser in the specified character sets. Consider the following example:

```
Accept-Charset: iso-8859-5
```

In the preceding example, the Accept-Charset request header is given the value iso-8859-5. If the Accept-Charset request header is not specified, all character sets are acceptable by default.

The *Accept-Encoding* Header

This request header is similar to the Accept request header. The only difference is that the Accept-Encoding request header restricts the content-coding that is acceptable in responses generated by the Web server. Whenever a Web server comes across an Accept-Encoding header, it checks the acceptability of content-coding according to the following standards:

- ◆ The Web server accepts only the content-coding specified in the Accept-Encoding header. However, the content-coding is unacceptable if it is accompanied by a q value of 0. A q value of 0 indicates that the content-coding is not acceptable.

- ◆ The * (asterisk) symbol is a wildcard indicating that the Accept-Encoding header will match all available content-coding, even if not explicitly specified in the Content-Encoding header.

- ◆ If multiple content-coding is specified in the Accept-Encoding header, the Web server checks the q value for each content-coding. The content-coding that possesses the highest nonzero q value is preferred over other content-coding that is specified.

- ◆ The *"identity" content-coding* (basic encoding supported by all Web servers) is generally acceptable by the client. If you want to explicitly refuse the identity content-coding you will need to explicitly refuse it by specifying a q value of 0 for it.

- ◆ If the Web server is unable to send a response that the specified Accept-Encoding header accepts, the server returns a 406 (Not Acceptable) status code.

- ◆ If Accept-Encoding header is not specified, the Web server assumes that the client will accept any content coding. However, if the "identity" content coding is one of the available content-coding, it is preferred over other content-coding, unless additional information regarding the use of some other content-coding is specified.

Here are a few ways to specify the Accept-Encoding header:

```
Accept-Encoding: compress, gzip
#Specifies that the content-coding used is gzip and compress.
Accept-Encoding: *
#Specifies that all content-coding types will be used.
Accept-Encoding: compress;q=0.5, gzip;q=1.0
```

```
#Specifies that the compress and gzip content-coding will be used. The
#qvalue of 1.0 specified for gzip
#indicates that gzip content-coding will take precedence over compress content-coding.
```

Directives Related to Content Negotiation

Before focusing on content negotiation in more detail, check out the directives related to content negotiation. You can find these directives in the httpd.conf file. In this section, I discuss the part of the httpd.conf file that deals with content negotiation, including the following directives:

- The AddEncoding directive
- The AddLanguage directive
- The AddCharset directive
- The AddLanguagePriority directive

The *AddEncoding* Directive

The function of the AddEncoding directive is to map filename extensions to an encoding type. For example, you can specify that the filename extension .Z be mapped to compress encoding type and that the filename extension .gz be mapped to the gzip encoding type. Consider the following example:

```
AddEncoding x-compress Z
AddEncoding x-gzip gz tgz
```

In the preceding example, the AddEncoding directive maps the filename extension .Z to compress encoding type and the filename extensions .gz and .tgz to map to gzip encoding type.

The *AddLanguage* Directive

The AddLanguage directive is very important in regard to content negotiation. This directive allows you to specify different languages in which the Web site can be rendered to a client, depending on the language preferred by the client. For each language that you choose, you need to specify an AddLanguage directive. Consider the following example:

```
AddLanguage da .dk
AddLanguage nl .nl
AddLanguage en .en
AddLanguage et .ee
AddLanguage fr .fr
....Many more AddLanguage Directives
```

In the preceding example, an AddLanguage directive is included for each language.

The *AddCharset* Directive

The main function of this directive is to map filename extensions to content character sets. The MIME type specified in the AddCharset directive overrides any mappings that already exist for the same file extension. You can use the AddCharset directive for the following purposes:

◆ To inform the client about the character encoding of the document that is sent as a response to a client request.

◆ To implement content negotiation in which the Web server returns one of several documents depending on the charset preferred by the client.

Consider the following example:

```
AddCharset ISO-8859-8 .iso8859-8

AddCharset Big5         .Big5    .big5

AddCharset WINDOWS-1251 .cp-1251

AddCharset CP866        .cp866

AddCharset ISO-8859-5   .iso-ru

AddCharset KOI8-R       .koi8-r

AddCharset UCS-2        .ucs2

AddCharset UCS-4        .ucs4

AddCharset UTF-8        .utf8
```

The *LanguagePriority* Directive

As the name indicates, you use this directive to set a priority for supported languages. The choices specified in this directive are used when the client doesn't specify a preference for a particular language. The list of languages specified in this directive is in the order of decreasing preference. In other words, the most preferred language is the first one specified in this directive. Consider the following example:

```
<IfModule mod_negotiation.c>
        LanguagePriority en da nl et fr de el it ja kr no pl pt pt-br ru
        ltz ca es sv
</IfModule>
```

In the preceding example, note the following:

◆ The IfModule directive checks whether the mod_negotiation.c is installed. Install this module if you want to use content negotiation.

◆ The LanguagePriority directive specifies the language preferences that will be used by Apache to display the Web page if the client doesn't specify a language preference. The most preferred language specified is English (en), and the least preferred language is Swedish (sv).

Terms Associated with Content Negotiation

A few terms are constantly used in relation to content negotiation, and you will find that I use them often as well. Following are brief definitions of these terms:

- ◆ **Resource.** An entity on the Web server that is requested by client computers. A resource is typically a Web page that is hosted on a Web server.

- ◆ **Representation.** A sequence of bytes with a defined media type, character set, and encoding. A single resource on a Web server can be displayed in several ways. For example, a Web page can be displayed in Spanish, English, or Japanese. Each of these is called a *representation*.

- ◆ **Negotiable resource.** A resource might have no representations at all, or it might have one or more representations. When a resource has more than one representation, it is considered to be a negotiable resource.

- ◆ **Variant.** Each of the multiple representations of a resource is called a variant.

- ◆ **Dimensions of negotiation.** Each variant of a resource is distinct from its counterparts. The ways in which each of these variants differs are called the dimensions of negotiation.

How Apache Uses Content Negotiation

In order for Apache to negotiate a resource, it must have adequate information about each of the variants of the resource. You can ensure that Apache has adequate information about each resource by using a type-map file and using MultiViews.

Using a Type-Map File

A type-map file is associated with a handler named type-map. You can use this feature only if you have set a handler in the configuration that defines a file suffix as type-map. You do this using the following configuration option:

```
AddHandler type-map .var
```

In the preceding example, an AddHandler directive is used to specify a type-map for files with a .var extension.

Features of Type-Map Files

You need to be aware of a few features of type-map files:

- ◆ Type-map files consist of entries for each variant that is available for a resource.
- ◆ The entries in the type-map files consist of HTTP-format header lines.
- ◆ Each entry in the type-map file signifies a variant.
- ◆ All entries in the type-map file are separated by using blank lines.

◆ By convention, type-map files should always begin with an entry that signifies the combined entity as a whole. However, it is not mandatory to include this entry, because it is ignored.

◆ You can express different source qualities with the help of the qs parameter.

 NOTE

I discuss the qs parameter in greater detail in the next section.

Consider a simple example of a type-map file:

```
URI: helo

URI: helo.en.html
Content-type: text/html
Content-language: en

URI: helo.ja.fr.html
Content-type: text/html;charset=iso-8859-2
Content-language: ja, fr
```

In the preceding example, note the following:

◆ The first line represents all the entries as a whole. In other words, the value helo is assigned to the file as a whole because all variants are based on this resource.

◆ In the first entry, the name of the variant is specified as helo.en.html.

◆ For the first entry, the Content-type is specified as text/html and the Content-language is specified as en (English).

◆ In the second entry, the name of the variant is specified as helo.ja.fr.html.

◆ For the second entry the Content-type specified is text/html and the charset specified is iso-8859-2. Finally, the Content-language specified for the second entry is ja (Japanese) and fr (French).

The qs Parameter

You use the qs parameter (also known as the *source quality parameter*) to specify the source quality for a resource. This parameter is useful when different variants have different source qualities. A resource might be available in different formats. For example, an image might be available in formats such as jpeg, gif, or ASCII-art. The purpose of the qs parameter is to indicate which of the formats is more preferred. The value of qs can be in the range of 0.000 to 1.000. If the qs is 0.000 for any element, the variant will never be chosen.

The qs parameter is a way of measuring the relative quality of a variant with respect to other variants. You should always remember that a qs value is specific to a variant and is dependent on the resource that it represents.

For a clearer idea of what the qs parameter means, imagine that you want to display a photograph on the Web. A photograph on the Web is best displayed in jpeg format. However, if the original file format of the photograph (resource) was ASCII, then ASCII will have higher source quality than jpeg.

Consider an example of a type-map file in which the qs parameter is specified:

```
URI: helo


URI: helo.gif
Content-type: image/gif; qs=0.8


URI: helo.jpeg
Content-type: image/jpeg; qs=0.5


URI: helo.txt
Content-type: text/html; qs=0.01
```

In the preceding example, note the following:

- ◆ The variants of the file named helo.gif are specified.
- ◆ Three variants for this file are present in different formats.
- ◆ The Content-type for the first entry is similar to the original file format of the file. Therefore, the qs value for this entry is the highest at 0.8.
- ◆ The Content-type specified for the second entry is image/jpeg. The qs value assigned for this variant is 0.5.
- ◆ The Content-type specified for the third entry is text/html. This Content-type is entirely different from the actual file format. As a result, the qs value for this variant is 0.01, which is minimum.

Using MultiViews

You use the MultiViews option with the Options directive. This option can be set for a specified directory using the <Directory>, <Location>, or <Files> directive in the httpd.conf file or the .htaccess file. However, if you want to specify this option in the .htaccess file, you must set the AllowOverride directive appropriately in the httpd.conf file.

Imagine that you have enabled MultiViews for the /sample/dir/dummy directory. However, the directory named "dummy" doesn't exist. In such a situation, the Apache Web server will start checking the /sample/dir directory for all files that begin with the string dummy.*. After it finds the files, it creates a type-map that names all those files, assigning them the same media types and content-encoding that they would have if the client were to directly request the file. Finally, the Web server chooses the best match per the client's requirement.

The MultiViews option might also apply for the searches made for a file specified by the DirectoryIndex directive. However, this is applicable only when a server is trying to index a directory. Consider the following example:

```
DirectoryIndex index
```

In the preceding example, the DirectoryIndex is assigned the value index. In such a situation, the Apache Web server will search for the files named index.html and index.html3 and finally decide which one to send to the client. If both files are not present and a file named index.cgi is present, the server will return the output of index.cgi.

Types of Content Negotiation

Whenever Apache receives a request for a document, it obtains a list of variants. The list of variants is either retrieved from the type-map file or from the filenames in the directory. After retrieving the information about the variants, the Apache Web server decides which among the list of variants is the best choice to send to the client. To do so, the Apache Web server uses one of the following types of content negotiation:

- ◆ Server-side negotiation
- ◆ Transparent Negotiation

Server-Side Negotiation

Server-side negotiation is the conventional way in which content negotiation takes place. To undertake server-side content negotiation, the Apache Web server uses an algorithm. When server-side negotiation is used, the Apache Web server can play with the quality factor of a particular dimension, thereby achieving better results.

Transparent Negotiation

Transparent content negotiation is not used by default. To use transparent content negotiation, the browser needs to specify that transparent content negotiation is to be used. The Web server doesn't play an important role in this type of content negotiation because the browser has full control over deciding which of the available variants is best suited.

The algorithm used by the browser determines the result of transparent negotiation. RFC 2296 defines an algorithm named "remote variant selection algorithm," which can be used for transparent negotiation.

The Apache Negotiation Process

Conventionally, Apache follows a process to implement content negotiation and return the most appropriate variant for a requested resource to the client. Though the process can be simple, it is sometimes very confusing. The module mod_negotiation is responsible for ensuring that the most appropriate variant is selected and sent to the client.

You can divide this process into a series of steps, which I'll discuss in the next subsections.

Putting the Information in Place

When a resource in the Apache Web server doesn't have variants, Apache sends the existing document to the client automatically. The problem arises when a resource has several variants to select from and send to the client. The following steps illustrate how Apache gathers the information related to the variants of a resource:

1. Apache collects all the available variants for a particular resource. The information regarding the variants is collected from a type-map file or is collected by using the MultiViews option.

2. If the variants are extracted from the type-map file, the variants are prioritized according to the source quality (qs) values assigned to them. The variant that possesses the highest qs value is given the highest priority. If the MultiViews option is used, all the variants have equal priority.

Processing the Accept Header

The second step involves analyzing the Accept header of the request sent by the client. This enables the Web server to understand which variants will be accepted by the client.

1. A list of acceptable variants is created.

2. The variants are then prioritized depending on the qs value assigned to them. If qs values are not specified, the default values are assigned.

3. This list is then compared to the list of variants created earlier. All variants that are not present in the list of acceptable variants are eliminated. After eliminating the variants that are not acceptable by the client, the Web server is left with the list of those variants that *are* acceptable by the client.

    At this point, processing of the Accept header is complete.

    In this step, it is quite possible that none of the variants located on the server are acceptable by the client. In such a situation, a 406 (No acceptable representation) HTTP error is returned to the client. The error message also contains a list of all variants that are available on the server. After going through this list, the client can resubmit the request depending upon the available variants.

Calculating the Quality Score

The next step involves calculating the quality score for all the variants that are present on the server as well as those acceptable by the client. The *quality score* is the product of the q value (quality factor) for the variants specified in the Accept header and the qs value specified in the type-map file or the MultiViews option (the qs value for each variant is always 1.0 for MultiViews).

The variant with the highest qs value is selected from among the lot and sent to the client browser. However, there might be a situation in which two or more variants have the same qs value. In this case, the selected elements are further processed, after eliminating all other variants, of course.

Examining the Language Quality Value

By now, the Apache Web server is left with only those variants that have matching scores. Therefore, it is important to choose the best option among the available variants. To do so, Apache uses the language quality value, which can be extracted from the Accept-Language header of the HTTP request.

If the client does not specify the Accept-Language header, the LanguagePriority directive in the httpd.conf file is considered. After examining the language quality, the variant with the highest language quality is selected and sent to the client.

However, it might be possible for more than one variant to possess an equal language quality value. In such situations, these variants are put through another test, which I discuss in the next subsection.

Selecting a Variant Depending on the Content Type

Another way to choose one of the remaining variants is to compare the values of their content type. After comparing the content type values, the variant with the highest content-type value is selected and sent to the client. If more than one variant is sharing the same content type value, more tests are performed.

Selecting a Variant Depending on the Character Set

The next set of remaining variants is put through another test that compares the character set values. This time, the variant with the highest character set value is selected and sent to the client. The choice of the variant is made on the basis of the Accept-Charset header specified by the client. Variants that are not using the ISO-8859-1 character set are eliminated (unless the browser has specifically requested for a character set other than ISO-8859-1), leaving behind only those that are using this character set. If only one variant is left, that variant is sent to the client. If more than one variant remains, another test is performed.

Selecting a Variant Depending on the Content-Encoding

If after checking and comparing the character set value, you are still left with more than one variant, examine the content-encoding of the variants. To do so, the Accept-Encoding header of the request is checked. Only the variants specified in the Accept-Encoding header are retained. If the Accept-Encoding header is not specified, variants that are not encoded are included. As a result, the new list is comprised of variants that are encoded or variants that are not encoded.

TIP

After examining the Accept-Encoding header, you may find that the list derived is comprised of variants that use encoding as well as variants that don't use encoding. In such cases, the variants that use encoding should be eliminated.

Eliminating on the Basis of Content Length

After going through the preceding steps, if you still have more than one variant, you need to select the smallest variant (the variant with the least content). Occasionally, you will be left with more than one variant with the same amount of content. Read the next subsection to see what to do in such cases.

Last Resort

If, after so many rounds of elimination, you are still left with more than one variant, as a last resort you must select one of the variants. In this case, you select the first variant in the list. If the type-map file is used, select the variant that is specified prior to all other remaining variants. If you are using MultiView, use the alphabet to select the first variant (that is, use an A to Z order).

Summary

In this chapter, I discussed metainformation and its importance. I also discussed the types of metainformation and the associated HTTP headers and directives that facilitate the use of metainformation. Finally, I explained how Apache uses metainformation to instruct Web browsers and set a handler. Finally, I discussed content negotiation and how it is implemented in Apache to deliver content based on the preferences specified by the client.

Check Your Understanding

Multiple Choice Questions

1. Which of the following metainformation is stored in the mime.types file that is located in the conf directory?

   a. MIME types

   b. MIME encoding

   c. MIME charset

   d. MIME Language

2. Which of the following request headers is sent by the client browser to specify the language in which the Apache Web server should deliver the content?

   a. The Accept request header

   b. The Accept-Language request header

   c. The Accept-Charset request header

   d. The Accept-Encoding request header

3. Which of the following directives is used to associate a handler with a particular type of file?

   a. AddHandler

   b. SetHandler

   c. AddEncoding

   d. AddCharset

4. Which of the following terms is used to define each of the multiple representations of a resource?

   a. Representation

   b. Resource

   c. Negotiable resource

   d. Variant

5. Which of the following statements are not true with respect to the source quality (qs) of a variant? (Choose all that apply.)

   a. The qs is a number in the range of 0.000 to 1.000.

   b. A qs of more than 1 indicates that the particular variant has high source quality

   c. A higher qs value depicts a higher priority for a particular variant.

   d. A lower qs value depicts a higher priority for a particular variant.

Answers

Multiple Choice Answers

1.   a. The MIME types supported by the Apache Web server are stored in the `mime.types` file.

2.   b. The `Accept-Language` header is sent by the client browser to specify the language in which the Apache Web server should deliver the content.

3.   a. The `AddHandler` directive is used to associate a handler with a particular type of file.

4.   d. A variant is used to define each of the multiple representations of a resource.

5.   b, d. The qs value for a variant cannot exceed 1.000, and a lower qs value signifies that the particular variant is lower in the priority ranking.

PART IV

Appendixes

Appendix A

If you have read this book, you now have a fairly good idea of the various security threats to your network. Apache provides you with a number of mechanisms and tools for safeguarding your Web server against the havoc caused by these threats. However, despite the best security mechanisms, at times your networks will be vulnerable to attack. This appendix describes the best practices you can take to secure Apache.

Network Filtering

Place your Web server in a Demilitarized Zone (DMZ). Set your firewall to drop connections to your Web server on all ports but HTTP (port 80) and HTTPS (port 443), if you are using SSL.

Denial of Service (DoS) Features

DoS attacks are typically targeted toward disrupting the network or the underlying operating system. Some attackers use techniques that can force application servers to start a large number of HTTP daemons. You should set appropriate limits on the HTTP daemon. To detect the occurrence of a DoS attack, evaluate server response under extreme load conditions.

In addition, modify the appropriate settings in the httpd.conf file based on your server configuration and risk assessment. Consider setting options such as the available bandwidth, the upper limit of "normal" requests that your Web site normally handles, and the processor capability of the system that hosts the application server. Then you can set the appropriate process limits for the HTTP daemon to handle requests. By using the following settings, you can minimize the risk of a Web server running out of memory or processor capability if a DoS attack does occur:

◆ The Apache configuration file uses the MinSpareServers, MaxSpareServers, and StartServers directives to determine the maximum number of clients that the server can handle at once. The MaxRequestsPerChild directive should always be set to zero (0) on Windows-based machines to stop the server from re-spawning the single thread and, therefore, reading the configuration file again.

◆ The MinSpareServers, MaxSpareServers, and StartServers directives have no effect on Windows NT operating systems. Windows starts a single httpd service, from which all requests are handled.

◆ The MaxClients directive determines the number of simultaneous connections that the Apache server can handle. This should be configured to the number of connections that the installed hardware and operating system can support without using SWAP memory.

◆ Configure the preceding settings based on the anticipated load. For systems with high possibility of attack, do intense load testing and evaluate the system response.

◆ Leave the ListenBacklog directive with the default values, but modify it when under direct attack.

Running CGI Programs as Other Users

CGI programs always run as the same user that owns the Apache server process. The user is set with the User directive in the configuration file. This user has minimal privileges. In most cases this is fine, because CGI scripts should run with few privileges to prevent potential malicious damage to the system. However, in some cases, it is desirable to run CGI programs as other users—for example:

◆ On a virtual host system with multiple customers, CGIs can run as the customer's user for each customer in order to read and write to the customer's files.

◆ On systems with multiple users, CGIs can be run as users in whose home directory they reside.

The ability to run CGI programs as other users is referred to as running setuid, in reference to the UNIX filesystem's capability to run a program as another user. Take care to ensure that the program running setuid cannot be invoked to inflict malicious damage to the system. Having setuid programs on a system can be dangerous if you do not trust all the other users on the system (which would be the case in both preceding examples). Other users could run the setuid program manually (from the command line) and give it environment or command arguments that make it perform malicious activities.

The suEXEC program used with Apache provides a method of running CGI programs as other users.

Host-Based Security

In order to ensure maximum host-based security it is imperative that you secure the platform in which you are running the Apache Web server. The following guidelines will help you implement host-based security:

◆ Never install R Services in the Web server. It provides insufficient levels of authentication. Never install services with plain text data (for example, ftp, Telnet, and so on). Always use services with encryption (for example, SSH, SSLftp, and so on). Remove all unnecessary services from your Web server.

◆ Limit the number of individuals having administrator or root-level access.

◆ Apply relevant security patches as soon as they are announced and tested on a pre-production system.

◆ Disallow all remote administration unless it is done using a one-time password or an encrypted link.

◆ If the machine must be administered remotely, the connection must require that a secure capability, such as secure shell, be used. Also consider limiting Telnet or ftp connections only to a minimum number of secure machines and have those machines reside within your intranet.

Configuring the Web Service/Application

As an administrator, it is your duty to prevent the system files from being tampered with. The following list provides guidelines for configuring the Web service/Application in the best possible way to ensure security:

◆ Run the Web server in a chroot-ed part of the directory tree. This will prevent the Web server from accessing the real system files and limit the functionality of your Web server.

◆ Run the anonymous ftp server (if you need it) in a chroot-ed part of the directory tree that is different from the Web server's tree.

Auditing and Logging

It is essential that you constantly track user activity. Conducting regular security audits and keeping a track of log files is critical to ensure security for your Web server at all times. The following are guidelines related to auditing and logging:

◆ To monitor user activity, log all user activity and maintain those logs in an encrypted form on the Web server. If it is not feasible to maintain logs on the local machine, consider storing them on a separate machine on your intranet. Another option would be to use a "write-once-read-many" media for backups.

◆ Monitor system logs regularly for any suspicious activity.

◆ Create macros that run every hour or so to check the integrity of the passwd file and other critical files.

◆ If the macros detect a change, they should be programmed to send an e-mail to the system manager or to write a message to logs.

For httpd server logging, W3C logging format is preferred, with the agent and referrer extensions in separate files. To enable logging, set the CustomLog fields in the httpd.conf files as follows:

```
LogFormat "%h %l %u %t \"%r\" %s %b" common
LogFormat "%{Referer}i-> %U" referer
LogFormat "%{User-agent}i" agent
CustomLog /path/to/audit/logs/access_log common
CustomLog /path/to/audit/logs/referer_log referer
CustomLog /path/to/audit/logs/agent_log agent
```

Content Management

Your Web server stores a large amount of content that needs to be managed and secured in an efficient way. The following guidelines help you manage and secure content on your Web site effectively:

◆ Perform all updates on the Web server from your intranet. Maintain your Web page originals on a server on your intranet to make all changes and updates. You can then transfer these updates to the public server through an SSH or SSL connection. If you do this on an hourly basis you can avoid having a corrupted server exposed for a long period of time.

◆ Write a script to download HTML pages and check these pages against a template to detect changes. If changes are noted, upload the correct version.

User Identification and Authentication

Apache supports several forms of user identification and authentication of varying security strength. The following are the authentication schemes supported by Apache:

◆ **Anonymous**. No authentication is requested from the user. This is the default setting for normal Web pages.

◆ **IP-level**. Some servers within an organization might benefit from basic IP Address and DNS Address authentication. A risk assessment analysis based on customer requirements will decide the extent of this type of authentication. You can specify the IP-level or DNS-based access controls by setting the `Allow From` and `Deny From` directives provided by the `mod_access` module within the scope of the `<Directory>` section. DNS lookups allow additional flexibility in the case of IP Address changes, but they can potentially slow the performance of the Web server. Also, the `mod_access` module overrides the `HostNameLookups` directive when DNS names are encountered within the configuration file.

◆ **Basic**. User ID and password are requested from the user and verified against a user ID and password file stored on the host server. The password file can be plain text or MD5 hashed. Enable basic authentication by using the `Require` directive in combination with the `AuthName` and `AuthType` directives, the `AuthUserFile` and `Auth-GroupFile` directives under `mod_auth`, or the database authorization configurations associated with `mod_auth_db` or `mod_auth_dbm`. However, if both IP-level and Basic authentication are used, the `Satisfy` directive should specify which has priority, as well as whether one or both should be used.

◆ **Client certificates (PKI)**. The addition of the client certificates requirement for authentication increases the complexity of both installation and ongoing management. Certificate generation, the maintenance of directory entries, the preparation of certificate revocation lists, and many other factors add to the complexity of this approach. However, significant value can be derived from a functional, well-managed implementation—particularly in distributed or heterogeneous environments. Certificate functionality is provided by mod_ssl in combination with a certificate generation tool such as Openssl.

Identity Checks

The IdentityCheck directive requests that the Web server attempt to establish a connection with the identd server on the client's machine (if it exists). This attempt is meant to verify or establish the requesting user's user ID.

Only a small number of sites actually run the identd service. The information returned by the server is completely under the control of the remote administrator. In general, the results returned from the identd lookup should not be trusted to provide identification or authentication information.

Server Certificates/SSL

You use SSL to establish an encrypted tunnel between the user and the Web server. SSL provides user-level authentication only by the addition of client-level certificates. Keep in mind that SSL slows the transaction process, particularly when you are initially setting it up.

The mod_ssl module facilitates Apache SSL encryption. Note that running Apache with mod_ssl in debug ssl mode will cause the server to use a default server certificate. Use this debug server certificate *only* for testing. A universally approved certificate provider should be able to provide an appropriate server certificate for use within the organization.

Client Certificates

As with server certificates, client certificates may be procured from an outside agency or generated within the organization. In general, you base encryption requirements on a risk assessment produced as part of the system security plan.

Intrusion Detection

Despite everything you have done to secure your Web server, there might still be vulnerabilities that you failed to detect. The possibility of your server falling prey to intrusion will always exist. As an administrator you should take precautions to detect intrusions on your server. The following guidelines will prove helpful for intrusion detection:

◆ Scan your Web server periodically with tools like ISS, nmap, or Satan to look for vulnerabilities.

◆ Monitor the connections to the server with intrusion detection software. Set the detector to send you an alarm when exploits and suspicious activities occur and to capture these sessions for review. This information can help you recover from an intrusion and strengthen your defenses.

Limitation of Information

By default, the Apache server includes a significant amount of information in the reply header of each HTTP request. This reply information is not used by the client's browser, but can be used by automated attack tools to exploit server-specific vulnerabilities. Although a competent end user can use other means to get this information, a minor configuration change of the ServerTokens option to Prod will reduce the server's exposure to automated attacks.

The Options directive, which is used within the <Directory> hierarchy, can enable the server to provide the client with a set of additional features in unusual circumstances. If, for example, a directory does not contain an index.htm or index.html file and the client requests a directory listing (that is a URL terminating in a forward slash), the Web server can be instructed to provide the requesting user with a full list of files contained in the specified directory. Although this may not be a security issue for the organization's servers, values of other options, such as FollowSymLinks, ExecCGI, or Includes, certainly can be security issues. This is what you can do to limit the information sent out by the Web server:

◆ In general, you should set the Options flag to None for the root directory and then specific options enabled from that point on, based on server requirements and the system security plan as follows:

```
<Directory />
Options None
</Directory>
```

◆ Set the ServerTokens option Prod (product information only).
◆ Set the Options flag to None for the root directory. Specific options should be enabled for subdirectories if required, subject to the your security plan.

Appendix B

Question: What is Apache?

Answer: Apache is an httpd server that:

- Is a powerful, flexible, and full-featured Web server.
- Implements the latest protocols, including HTTP /1.1 (RFC2616).
- Is easy to configure, and its functionality can be extended using third-party modules.
- Provides full source code and comes with an unrestrictive license.
- Allows you to customize its design by writing modules using the Apache module API.
- Runs on Windows NT/9x, Netware 5.x and higher, OS/2, and most versions of UNIX-based operating systems.
- Is actively being developed by members who voluntarily contribute to the source code.
- Encourages user participation for new ideas, bug reports, and patches.

Apache also implements many frequently requested features, including the following:

- **DBM databases for authentication.** The DBM databases allow you to easily set up password protection in your Web pages with enormous numbers of authorized users, without putting extensive load on the server.
- **Customized responses to errors and problems.** Apache allows you to set up files and even CGI scripts that are returned by the server in response to errors and problems; for example, you can set up a script to intercept 500 Server Errors and perform on-the-fly diagnostics for users.
- **Multiple DirectoryIndex directives**. Apache allows you to use the setting `DirectoryIndex index.html index.cgi`, which instructs the server to send back index.html or run index.cgi when a user requests a directory URL, whichever it finds in the directory.
- **Unlimited flexible URL rewriting and aliasing.** Apache has no fixed limit on the numbers of aliases and redirects that can be declared in the configuration files. In addition, you can use a powerful rewriting engine to solve most URL manipulation problems.
- **Content negotiation.** Content negotiation is the ability to automatically serve clients of varying sophistication. It also means HTML-level compliance, with documents that offer the best representation of information the client is capable of accepting.
- **Virtual hosts.** Also known as *multi-homed servers,* virtual hosts allow the server to distinguish among requests made to different IP addresses or names (mapped to the same machine). Apache also offers dynamically configurable mass-virtual hosting.

◆ **Configurable reliable piped logs.** You can configure Apache to generate logs in the format that you want. In addition, on most UNIX architectures, Apache can send log files to a pipe, allowing log rotation, hit filtering, real-time splitting of multiple vhosts into separate logs, and asynchronous DNS resolving on-the-fly.

Question: How is Apache better than other Web servers?

Answer: Apache is substantially faster, more stable, and contains more features than many other Web servers. Although certain commercial servers claim to exceed Apache's speed, it is better to have a considerably fast and free server than to have an extremely fast server that costs thousands of dollars. The speed of Apache allows you to run it on sites that get millions of hits per day, without performance difficulties.

Question: How thoroughly tested is Apache?

Answer: According to a survey conducted by Netcraft, in July 2002 Apache constitutes more than 57 percent of the Web server market share. It has been tested thoroughly by both developers and users. The Apache Group maintains rigorous standards before releasing new versions of its server, and the server runs without a hitch on more than half of all the World Wide Web servers available on the Internet. When bugs do show up, the company releases patches and new versions as soon as they are available.

Question: Whom do I contact for support?

Answer: Apache doesn't provide "official" support. You can send bug reports and suggestions via the bug report page at http://httpd.apache.org/bug_report.html. Direct other questions to the Apache HTTP Server Users List at http://httpd.apache.org/userslist.html. You will be able to find the Apache team along with many other httpd gurus who should be able to help. Commercial support for Apache is available from a number of third parties.

Question: Is there any more information available on Apache?

Answer: For more information on Apache, you can refer to the main Apache Web site (http://www.apache.org/httpd). A regular electronic publication called *Apache Week* (http://www.apacheweek.com/) is also available. Also, some Apache-specific books (http://httpd.apache.org/info/apache_books.html) are available.

Question: How do I add browsers and referrers to my logs?

Answer: Apache provides a couple of different ways of doing this. The recommended method is to compile the `mod_log_config` module into your configuration and use the `CustomLog` directive.

You can either log the additional information in files other than your normal transfer log, or you can add them to the records already being written—for example:

```
CustomLog logs/access_log "%h %l %u %t \"%r\" %s %b \"%{Referer}i\" \"%{User-Agent}i\""
```

This will add the values of the User-Agent and Referer headers, which indicate the client and the referring page, respectively, to the end of each line in the access log.

Question: How can I prevent DoS attacks on Apache?

Answer: The httpd.conf directives to control resource use are as follows:

◆ RLimitCPU. Limits server CPU time.

◆ RLimitMEM. Limits server memory usage.

◆ RLimitNPROC. Limits number of processes the server can spawn.

◆ LimitRequestBody. Limits size of the request body.

◆ LimitRequestFields. Limits the number of HTTP fields in header.

◆ LimitRequestFieldSize. Limits the size of the largest field in header.

◆ LimitRequestLine. Limits the largest request line that can be sent

Question: How can I allow selective access to pages to authorized individuals and organizations?

Answer: Host-based access control is used to allow access to selected hosts or subnets. In this type of access control mechanism, you control access by using

◆ restriction by DNS name, or

◆ restriction by IP address/subnet.

User authentication is used to allow access based on a user's credentials. You can utilize the following methods to provide user-based authentication:

◆ Basic authentication (passwords)

◆ Digest authentication (better passwords)

◆ Certificate-based authentication (cryptographic signatures)

Question: If the user supplies a password and username, how do I set up Apache to allow access to only local sites or to only external sites?

Answer: You can use the value any with the Satisfy directive to specify that the user can access certain documents on the site only if it is a local/external site or if the user supplies a username and password. This Satisfy directive takes any of the specified keywords:

◆ All. In order to gain access to documents within the scope of a Satisfy directive, a client must pass all applicable non-discretionary controls (such as Allow or Deny directives) *and* any discretionary ones (like Require directives).

◆ Any. Documents within the scope of a Satisfy directive are accessible to any client that either passes a non-discretionary check (which occurs first) or the discretionary ones

For example, adding the following configuration to an .htaccess or server configuration file will restrict access to people who are either accessing the site from a host under mydomain.com or who can supply a valid username and password:

```
Deny from all
Allow from .mydomain.com
AuthType Basic
AuthUserFile /usr/local/apache/conf/htpasswd.users
AuthName "special directory"
Require valid-user
Satisfy any
```

Question: Is it possible to prevent people from "stealing" the images from my Web site?

Answer: Preventing people from inlining the images directly from their Web site can do this. Users should be allowed to access the images only if they appear inline in your pages. You can allow for this by using a combination of `SetEnvIf` and the `Deny` and `Allow` directives. However, it is important to understand that any access restriction based on the `REFERER` header can cause problems, as browsers can send an incorrect `REFERER`, either because they want to avoid your restriction or simply because they didn't send the right header or any header at all.

The following configuration will produce the desired effect if the browser passes correct `REFERER` headers.

```
SetEnvIf REFERER "www\.mydomain\.com" linked_from_here
SetEnvIf REFERER "^$" linked_from_here


<Directory /www/images>
    Order deny,allow
    Deny from all
    Allow from env=linked_from_here
</Directory>
```

Question: Why is it recommended that I never run my Apache server as root?

Answer: If a user exploits a flaw in a script running with root's permissions that allows them to write to files, he can very quickly gain access to your system. If the Web server can write only to the files that it needs to, the damage can be limited to only those files. So, to emphasize the point: You should not run your Web server as root, and don't let your Web server run as a user with administrative privileges, such as lp, bin, and daemon. Also, make certain that your Web server is in a group of its own and not a member of a user or administrative group.

Question: Why should I never use server side includes with user-generated pages?

Answer: If you are using a guestbook or virtual card script that allows users to enter HTML, it is important that you do not allow these pages to be parsed by the server. I have tried to execute system commands by using includes and have been successful at doing so. Here are some tips:

◆ Do not use the .shtml extension for files that are created by a user or appended by user input.

◆ Make certain that your script removes the HTML comment tags from user input.

◆ Place all such files in a directory that has an .htaccess file forbidding server side includes. You can do so by using the Options directive as shown:

```
Options None
```

◆ Disable SSI direct program execution. Instead of using an exec option, use the virtual one. In the .htaccess file, use the following:

```
Options Includes IncludesNOEXEC
```

Question: How does Apache authenticate a user across a network?

Answer: You do this using two methods for passing credentials, *basic authentication* and *digest authentication*. Digest authentication is considerably more secure, but less widely deployed. Most authentication-based Web servers on the Web use basic authentication.

In basic authentication, the username and password are encoded using base64 scheme, which is then transmitted to the server. This means that if the username and password are valid and are authenticated successfully, anyone who can intercept the transmission can determine the username and password. In digest authentication, user credentials are encrypted and transmitted in a manner that cannot be so easily decoded.

Because basic authentication does not have a great protection mechanism for user credentials, the same authentication database can be used to store user information for multiple realms. On the other hand, the digest authentication includes an encoding of the realm for which the credentials are valid. This requires that you have a separate credentials database for each realm.

Question: Why doesn't Apache include SSL in the base package?

Answer: SSL (Secure Socket Layer) data transport requires encryption, and many governments have restrictions on the import, export, and use of encryption technology. If Apache included SSL in the base package, its distribution would involve all sorts of legal and bureaucratic issues, and it would no longer be freely available.

Appendix C

For nearly three years, the Apache Software Foundation worked on Apache 2.0. The latest version, Apache 2.0.40, was released on August 9, 2002. Apache Software Foundation Director, Greg Stein, released Apache 2.0.35 as the first general version of 2.0, and now recommends it over the earlier 1.3 versions.

The free availability of Apache and its numerous other features make it a universal product. By looking at auditing services sites, such as Security Space, or poll reporting sites, such as Netcraft, you can get a fair idea of Apache's popularity. Since 1996, regardless of the domain—.com, .org, .gov, and .net—more than half of all Web sites use Apache to serve their Web pages. Some of the Apache fanatics wondered, considering its dominance in the market share, what new features could be added to Apache.

The problems in version 1.3 are largely side effects of its evolution. Apache has been ported to virtually every existing platform. However, this was done a platform or two at a time. In addition to this, hacks were inserted wherever required for better adjustment with each platform. This modular architecture gives administrators a great deal of flexibility, but modules aren't really able to work together. Apache 1.3 uses a separate process to handle each connection, which allows it to be highly reliable but not highly scalable.

What Apache 2.0 Provides

Apache 2.0 runs faster; is highly scalable; has integrated support for secure, encrypted communications, and supports very sophisticated publishing systems that create Web pages easily. One of the major shortcomings of Apache 1.3 is the lack of support for Microsoft Windows. A number of assumptions about UNIX and forked-server behavior were removed in Apache 2.0 in order to support more platforms. Other important features are highlighted in the following sections.

Multi-Processing Modules

Multi-Processing Modules (MPMs) are a new feature in Apache 2.0. MPMs extend the functionality of the modular design in Apache 2.0 and are responsible for binding to network ports on the server, accepting requests, and dispatching children to handle the requests.

Scalability was the original reason for creating Apache 2.0. Scalability was addressed by creating a Web server that has both processes and threads. However, there is no perfect way to map requests to either a thread or a process. On platforms such as Linux, you want to have multiple processes, each with multiple threads that handle the requests. In this way, if a single thread dies, the rest of the server will continue to handle more requests. Other platforms, such as Windows, do not handle multiple processes well, so one process with multiple threads is required. Older platforms that do not have threads also had to be taken into account. For these platforms, you must continue with the 1.3 method of pre-forking processes to handle requests.

You can handle the mapping issue in a number of ways, but the most efficient way is to enhance the module features of Apache. The MPM feature in Apache determines how requests are mapped to threads and processes. By using MPMs in Apache 2.0, you can ensure that processes and threads are handled more efficiently. Each server uses a single MPM, and the correct one for a given platform is determined at compile time.

Apache Portable RunTime

Apache Portable Runtime (APR) is also a significant achievement in version 2.0. APR is a library of blocks for portability issues that will help smooth the transition among platforms on Windows, UNIX, and Mac.

APR was originally designed as a way to combine features across platforms. The APR library is built on the theory that some features should be different for different platforms and, conversely, some features can be common to all platforms.

Any program that interacts with the operating system will require communication across a network, performing process and thread management, memory management, and synchronization. The function of an APR is to take all of these features of the underlying operating system and wrap them up in a uniform interface, making all operating systems look the same as far as the program is concerned.

Apache has never been well-defined for porting purposes because the source code was originally designed for use on UNIX; this made porting to non-POSIX platforms difficult. With the addition of APR, all a developer needs to do is port the APR layer to another platform. An APR layer allows all platforms to use common code within Apache, making Apache equally reliable on all platforms and generally improving the readability of the code. Because APR is a separate library, any project can now take advantage of Apache's portability. A project can also be added to Apache without disturbing its portability. APR was designed with Windows, UNIX, OS/2, and BeOS in mind, and is more flexible.

APR acts as the abstraction layer in Apache 2.0. To allow the use of native types for best performance, APR has unified functions, such as sockets into a single type, which Apache will then use independent of the platform. The underlying type is invisible to the Apache developer, who is free to write code without worrying about how it will work on multiple platforms.

The success of this approach is evident in the diverse set of platforms to which APR has already been ported. The list includes UNIX, most versions of Windows, OS/2, and BeOS. Netware support is also under way.

Portability of this type often leads to compromises in performance. However, APR can easily address this issue by making itself transparent to the program using it and by providing only those features that are common to a large number of platforms. Using the native API and data structures of operating systems tends to be significantly faster than using the "compatibility" libraries those operating systems provide. Because each implementation of APR uses interfaces and data structures pertaining to the APR platform, the platform does not have to make changes to itself.

Filters

The final major difference between Apache 1.3 and 2.0 is the addition of filters. For programmers, filters are a powerful way to modify data that another module creates. For administrators, filters act on the stream of content as it is delivered to or from the server. This allows, for example, the output of CGI scripts to be parsed for server side includes directives using the INCLUDES filter in mod_include. In Apache 1.3, if you want all .shtml files to be parsed for server-side includes, you use the following line:

```
AddHandler server-parsed .shtml
```

Unlike Apache 1.3, Apache 2.0 does not have a server-parsed handler. Therefore, in order to get the same effect, you will need to add the INCLUDES filter with the SetOutputFilter directive as shown:

```
SetOutputFilter INCLUDES
```

You specify this directive in Files, Directory, or Location containers to make sure that data being sent to the client can be parsed for server-side includes. However, your configuration file will grow and be hard to read. It also means that mime-types and handlers are no longer very important. Most modules that generate data will just use the default-handler to read a file from the disk and use a filter to modify that data.

Will Apache 1.3 Modules Work?

Modules written for 1.3 will not work with 2.0 without modification. In Apache 1.3, each module uses a table of callback routines and data structures. In Apache 2.0, however, this table of callback routines is not used. Instead, a new function to register all required callbacks is used.

In the past, new features were added to each new version of Apache, requiring the callback table to be expanded, which caused existing modules to break. In Apache 2.0, each module can define how many callbacks it wants to use, instead of using a statically defined table with a set number of callbacks. If the Apache Group decides to add callbacks in the future, the changes are less likely to affect existing modules.

Index

A

Accept-Charset header, content negotiation, 377–378

Accept-Encoding header, content negotiation, 378–379

Accept header, content negotiation, 377

Accept-Language header, content negotiation, 377

access, Web server files, 306–307

access control, 119
  authentication-based, 123
    basic authentication, 124–126
    configuration, 140–147
    database-driven authentication, 127–135
    digest authentication, 126–127
  host-based, 120
    configuration, 139–140
    domain names, 121
    IP addresses, 121–122
  .htaccess files, 136–139
  overview, 120
  password files, 135–136
  Web servers and, 12

access logs, 263–269
  virtual hosts, 268–269

AccessConfig directive, 77–78

AccessFileName directive, 95–96

access_log file, 264–265

Action directive, 109

AddCharset directive, 380

AddEncoding directive, 379

AddLanguage directive, 379

AddModule directive, 86

agent-driven negotiation, HTTP 1.1, 14

Alias directive, 102–104

aliasing, URLs and, 350–351

Analog, log monitoring tool, 274–277

Apache 2.0, 408–410

Apache Web server, 9
  architecture, 32–36
  distribution, 29
  features, 28–32
  history, 28

Apacheconf, 114–116

apachectl command, 59–60

APACI (Autoconf-style Interface), 41

application support modules, 214

APR (Apache Portable Runtime), 408–409

apxs (Apache Extension), module installation, 215

architecture, 32–36

auditing, best practices, 396

authentication
  best practices, 397–398
  configuration, directives, 128–135
  DB files, configuration, 145–146
  URLs, 311

authentication-based access control, 123
  basic authentication, 124–126
  configuration, 140–147
  database-driven authentication, 127–135
  digest authentication, 126–127

authentication modules, 208

authorization, URLs, 311

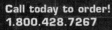